'To Meet and Satisfy
a Very Hungry People'

The Origins and Fortunes of English Pentecostalism
1907-1925

STUDIES IN EVANGELICAL HISTORY AND THOUGHT

A full listing of titles in this series
appears at the end of this book

'To Meet and Satisfy a Very Hungry People'

The Origins and Fortunes of English Pentecostalism
1907-1925

Timothy Bernard Walsh

Foreword by Ian M. Randall

British Library Cataloguing in Publication Data
A catalogue record for this book is available from the British Library

ISBN 978–1–84227–576–4

Typeset by T. B. Walsh
Printed and bound in Great Britain
by Lightning Source, Milton Keynes

Series Preface

The Evangelical movement has been marked by its union of four emphases: on the Bible, on the cross of Christ, on conversion as the entry to the Christian life and on the responsibility of the believer to be active. The present series is designed to publish scholarly studies of any aspect of this movement in Britain or overseas. Its volumes include social analysis as well as exploration of Evangelical ideas. The books in the series consider aspects of the movement shaped by the Evangelical Revival of the eighteenth century, when the impetus to mission began to turn the popular Protestantism of the British Isles and North America into a global phenomenon. The series aims to reap some of the rich harvest of academic research about those who, over the centuries, have believed that they had a gospel to tell to the nations.

Series Editors

David Bebbington, Professor of History, University of Stirling, Stirling, Scotland, UK

John H.Y. Briggs, Senior Research Fellow in Ecclesiastical History and Director of the Centre for Baptist History and Heritage, Regent's Park College, Oxford, UK

Timothy Larsen, McManis Professor Christian Thought, Wheaton College, Illinois, USA

Mark A. Noll, McAnaney Professor of History, University of Notre Dame, Notre Dame, Indiana, USA

Ian M. Randall, Director of Research, Spurgeon's College, London, UK, and Senior Research Fellow, International Baptist Theological Seminary, Prague, Czech Republic

*"We can't all let ourselves be washed away by the tide of history...
Some of us must tarry in order to gather up what has been left along the
river banks."*

Alberto Knox,
Sophie's World: A Novel about the History of Philosophy, p. 163

Contents

Foreword

This book is a significant addition to the growing body of literature on the history and identity of Pentecostalism. Timothy Walsh has undertaken a thorough and illuminating study of the origins, emergence, and development of the Pentecostal Movement in England in its crucial formative years. Although Pentecostalism world-wide is attracting a great deal of scholarly attention, the story of the Pentecostal movement in Britain has not received the coverage that it warrants. This work is a notable contribution to that field and one that should be read by all those who have an interest in the way the religious terrain in Britain has changed during the course of the last one hundred years.

Many generalized and often poorly substantiated statements have been made about Pentecostalism and a particular merit of this study is that it looks in detail at the stories of the movement as it took shape in specific locations. Although the role of the Sunderland Conventions and the magazine *Confidence*, both of which had an enormous influence in the early period, is reasonably well known, what we have here is an in-depth analysis not only of their impact but of the ways in which they related to broader evangelical spirituality. The study of Bradford's Bowland Street Mission is similarly illuminating. The idiosyncratic leader of the Mission, Smith Wigglesworth, has been portrayed in some popular evangelical literature as a heroic Pentecostal figure. What we have here is a much richer exploration, using personal letters and early records, which aims to understand Wigglesworth in a new way and which also deals with the demise of his leadership and the ultimate disintegration of the mission, aspects that have not hitherto been properly researched.

The other two centres investigated here were led by figures who are not as well known as Boddy or Wigglesworth. In the case of Bournemouth's Emmanuel Mission Hall, with its leader William Oliver Hutchinson, what seemed to take place (at least until recent years) was that Hutchinson's work was to a large extent written out of the larger Pentecostal story because of the bizarre nature of his later theological views. Yet Emmanuel was the first place of worship constructed for explicitly Pentecostal purposes in the British Isles. Also, Hutchinson's early evangelical experience was in a Baptist context – he was decisively affected through a sermon by C. H. Spurgeon in 1888 at the Metropolitan Tabernacle when Spurgeon singled him out with the words: "Awake, thou that sleepest - You! Sitting behind that pillar." His trajectory, not least his role in advocating *apostles*, is a complex and fascinating one, and full justice is done to it here. Croydon's Holiness Mission Hall is also worthy of examination since it was one of the surprisingly few Pentecostal centres to emerge in London in this period.

This study places Pentecostal developments in the framework of wider work being done on the history of spirituality, which yields very fruitful results as a way of understanding Pentecostal *ideology*. The probing that Tim Walsh undertakes of the relationship between the Wesleyan holiness spirituality of the League of Prayer and early Pentecostalism is particularly welcome, since often there has been a lack of connection between Wesleyan and Pentecostal scholarship. Many new insights are also offered here into Pentecostal apocalypticism. The study demonstrates, too, how the development of the Pentecostal movement's ideology was embodied in structural forms, and this method can serve as a model for those writing similar local histories of churches or movements of renewal. Often the focus is either on *spirit* or *structure*, and it is only rarely recognized that these are best examined together to give a full-orbed picture.

What we have in this substantial piece of research challenges received Pentecostal historiography at a number of points. On occasions Tim Walsh is provocative in the interpretative proposals he makes. However, the approach he takes is always fair and indeed sympathetic, and his work consistently draws from an impressive range of crucial primary sources to sustain the arguments that are made. I am delighted to be able to commend this outstanding addition to Pentecostal and wider evangelical studies.

Ian M. Randall
Director of Post-Graduate Research, Spurgeon's College, London,
Senior Research Fellow, IBTS, Prague

Preface

The six week mission conducted by T. B. Barratt in Sunderland during the latter half of 1907 proved the occasion of the introduction and propagation of the phenomenon commonly termed 'speaking in tongues' in Britain. The subsequent dissemination of this practice and its associated teaching was undertaken by the Rev. Alexander A. Boddy, vicar of All Saints', Monkwearmouth, by means of pamphlet, periodical, and conference platform. This study seeks to explore the resultant movement which crystallized around the central rubric of the baptism in the Holy Spirit. While its body of adherents proved small in numerical terms and disparate with respect of denominational affiliation, or the absence thereof, evidence of a distinctive form of association or *collegia pietatis* is advanced from an early juncture. The main concentration of this study is on the developments, *ideological* and *structural*, which occurred within this fledgling movement prior to, and in certain respects influencing, later denominational Pentecostalism.

While England's first Pentecostals may not have been noted for their theological innovation or sophistication, they espoused and embodied a dynamic form of religious primitivism which merits consideration on its own terms. Pertinent aspects of its thought and practice are examined here with particular attention being given to the seminal role of key leaders in the development and promotion of distinctive orthodoxies. A pervasive ethos of *reasonable enthusiasm* engendered and indeed enforced in the face of perceived extremist and deviant tendencies, is revealed to have characterized much of emerging Pentecostal lived religion. Something of the inevitability of the process of bureaucratization is made apparent, both in the manner in which particular difficulties, and the exigencies of the post-war period, were encountered. The disaffection of a second generation of leaders from original ecclesiological conceptions is underscored, while the challenges associated with such a paradigm shift are highlighted. The influence of transatlantic developments is noted, and insights are afforded into the uneven and, in certain respects, uneasy drift toward denominationalism in the English context.

The overall picture emerges of a movement characterized by pronounced and profound spiritual pre-occupations which from its earliest years was cohesive while diverse, radical while conservative, innovative and experimental, yet consistently adhering to a received evangelical and identifiably Holiness ethic. Other studies have examined various national and ethnic strains within what has become a global religious phenomenon - the present undertaking offers original insights into a distinctly English experience of the pioneering phase of the Pentecostal phenomenon.

Acknowledgements

It is appropriate that I begin by acknowledging the Rev. Dr. Keith Warrington as without his influence it is unlikely that I would have returned to the United Kingdom to undertake postgraduate research. I have very much appreciated his time, attention, and support throughout the process. His positive demeanour and capacity to encourage have inspired me as I am sure they will many other research students. I must also thank the Rev. Dr. Neil Hudson who introduced me to Britain's early Pentecostals on a sweltering August afternoon. In spite of my initial uncertainty, this proved to be an inspired suggestion as it encompassed both my own interests and his expertise. I am thankful to have had the opportunity to be among the first to investigate this neglected field of scholarship. The benefits of this became further apparent when I came to teach on Regents Theological College's Studies in Pentecostal Issues course in 2006. I would like to thank those students who since then have listened attentively, engaged with Pentecostal heritage, and offered positive encouragement and feedback afterwards. You were among the first to be exposed to this material and you made the countless hours of toil begin to seem worthwhile.

Beyond the immediate surroundings of Regents Theological College I have also benefitted significantly from involvement in the Department of Religions and Theology in the School of Arts, Histories and Cultures at the University of Manchester. In particular I must thank Dr. Jeremy Gregory, whose supervision has been exemplary. His attention to detail and breadth of historical appreciation have considerably enhanced this study. It is also to him that I owe my initial introduction to, and involvement in, the wider world of the religious historical research community. I would like to thank Professors George Brooke and Philip Alexander, both of whom offered expert advice and provided vital encouragement, particularly in the earlier, less certain, stages of the undertaking. It is imperative that I mention Dr. Ian Jones who took a very real interest in my progress both academic and otherwise.

I would like to thank the staff of Mattersey Hall, Nottinghamshire, who ensured that my time at the Donald Gee Centre for Pentecostal and Charismatic Research was more fruitful than I could have hoped for. I must particularly mention Dr. David Garrard and Dr. Anne Dyer who helped me to maximise my exposure to the wealth of material held at the Centre. I would also like to express my gratitude to Dr. David Allen who made time to see me and to offer encouragement to a fledgling scholar engaged in his beloved field of church history. I am grateful to Mr. Donald Maciver, Librarian at the Nazarene Theological College, Didsbury, for his helpfulness and efficiency. I am indebted to Dr. Hugh Rae, without doubt one of the warmest and most hospitable people I encountered during the course of my research. He opened not only his archive, but indeed his home to me, and I have fond recollections of a conversation which, after long hours of immersion in Holiness periodicals, significantly clarified my thinking on interrelations between erstwhile colleagues in Holiness and Pentecostal groupings.

It is imperative that I acknowledge the role of librarians and staff alike at Cheshire Libraries Nantwich branch. I should especially mention Janet Judge and Andrea Holmes who managed to acquire an astonishing range of resources for me which included unpublished dissertations, copies of frequently obscure journal articles, rare books, and historical monographs. Their exertions on my behalf were conducted with efficiency and good humour, and they proved indefatigable in the pursuit of my out-of-the-way requests.

I would particularly like to thank the Very Reverend Peter Francis, Warden of St. Deiniol's Library, Hawarden, Flintshire for his generous consideration in awarding me residential scholarships during 2005 and 2006. This enabled me to spend invaluable time in inspiring and more-than-agreeable surroundings. It also afforded the opportunity of meeting others involved in fascinating areas of research in the domains of history, theology, and religious studies, as well as clergy from various backgrounds. I consider myself honoured to have been among those who have engaged in 'the pursuit of divine learning' in such a very special setting.

Participation in events organised by the Ecclesiastical History Society and the Christianity and History Forum has afforded some of the most stimulating and rewarding highlights of my period of doctoral research. These forums have allowed me to meet not only peers and contemporaries, but also established and eminent scholars in the world of religious history. Having met with considerable generosity and approbation, I must single out three individuals who took an interest in the plight of a junior scholar of whom they had no prior knowledge or connection. Foremost among these is Prof. David Bebbington who, to my surprise, was one of the first people I encountered on arrival at Exeter University for the 2003 Summer Conference of the Ecclesiastical History Society. His graciousness and helpfulness made a very real difference as I undertook to read my first paper in such a setting. Since then he has kindly responded to queries and offered help and advice which has been very much appreciated. It was in a similarly auspicious manner that I met with Prof. Grant Wacker, the foremost authority on the early years of North American Pentecostalism, at the aptly named 'Signs, Wonders, Miracles: Representations of Divine Power in the Life and History of the Church' Conference in Exeter. It would be difficult to overstate the impact of his open and affirming demeanour at a significant juncture. Prof. John Wolffe of the Open University completes the triumvirate of church historians who have combined personal warmth and humanity with expert advice and insight in a manner which has markedly enhanced my doctoral experience.

I would also like to mention a number of individuals with whom I have made contact and who have offered assistance in a variety of guises. These include the Rev. Desmond Cartwright, Geoffrey Milburn, the Rev. Gordon Weeks, John W. West of the Croydon Citadel Corps. of the Salvation Army, Dr. Linda Wilson, Dr. Robert Pope, Dr. Alexandra Walsham, and Prof. Geoffrey Wainwright. Those associated with the monograph series at Paternoster Press have more recently helped smooth the way toward publication. In this respect I particularly need to thank Dr. Robin Parry, the Rev. Dr. Anthony R. Cross, and latterly Dr. Mike Parsons. The staff at Alpha Graphics have also provided valuable assistance during the type-setting process.

It is appropriate that I conclude by acknowledging the role in this undertaking of influences and relationships of a more immediate and personal nature. The Rev. Sean Byrne, Pastor of Dublin's Southside Vineyard, helped me find my way at the turn of the millennium and his impact is still being felt. I have had occasion to reflect on the formative influence of a friend of long-standing - Eugene Flanagan, known in Drogheda-parlance as 'Flan.' An inveterate bibliophile and autodidact, his passion for the past, and in particular Christian history and heritage, were a source of inspiration to me many years ago. Our annual 're-union' and the interest he has shown have provided encouragement more vital than he might appreciate.

Both my immediate family and in-laws have supported us in a variety of ways over the past several years. I have been drawn from my desk more than once by Greg's outrageous and inventive telephone messages. Not only were these hysterically amusing scenarios subjected to repeated listening, but they made us feel that we weren't so far away. My parents have borne the absence of their grandchildren with grace and fortitude. It is both remarkable, and a measure of their personal qualities, that they have managed to maintain their prominence and involvement despite the distance and physical separation.

It is natural that I should come to the most immediate fellow-pilgrims who have in the memorable words of John Milton, walked with me *hand in hand with wandering steps and slow*. It seems customary at this juncture to apologise to spouses and children who have endured neglect and absence during the completion of studies of this nature. Happily this has not been my experience. On the contrary, it is difficult to imagine another pursuit which would have granted me the involvement I have had in Aoife and Irvine's early years. This has been both a privilege and a delight and it is my fervent hope that we will continue to reap the benefits of our shared experiences for many years to come.

There is a definite absurdity about so brief an acknowledgement of the role of my most intimate companion on this adventure. But it must be said that throughout what has been an odyssey of several years, my wife Luchelle has been priceless – matchless in her support and encouragement, and all the more so when these were in short supply elsewhere. This undertaking would never have started, let alone been finished, had you not believed in its rightness, its worth, and in my ability to achieve it. You took me seriously when I needed it most. You, more than anyone, have seen and shared *the world in my eyes*.

Tim Walsh
The Gladstone Library at St. Deiniol's, Hawarden

INTRODUCTORY SECTION

Rationale

Pentecostalism began as a religious movement in the early years of the twentieth-century, its seminal manifestations were to be found on America's west coast, but it rapidly spread across continents, particularly in the wake of Anglo-Saxon missionary endeavours. It became apparent that this was a surprisingly fissiparous movement and a wide range of churches and denominations were formed during its second and third decades. From the 1960s onwards Pentecostalism began to both attract and generate its own scholarly pursuits. One of the pioneers in this field was Walter J. Hollenweger whose doctoral work, a ten-volume encyclopaedic treatment of international Pentecostal movements,[1] was significant in that it was one of the early academic works that sought to investigate this phenomenon. Since then there has been considerable advance in what might broadly be deemed Pentecostal studies, with attendant features such as the establishment of scholarly journals which include *Pneuma: The Journal of the Society for Pentecostal Studies* and the *Journal of Pentecostal Theology*, both of which emanate from North America, the *Asian Journal of Pentecostal Studies,* and the *Journal of the European Pentecostal Theological Association*. Hollenweger, as something of a founding father of this region of the *Republic of Letters*, commented more than a decade ago on what he termed a growing and commendable "critical tradition of Pentecostalism."[2]

It is interesting to note, however, that in comparative terms British Pentecostalism has not been well represented in this burgeoning arena. One indicator of this is the fact that of the more than twenty volumes which have appeared in the *Journal of Pentecostal Theology Supplement Series* published by the Sheffield Academic Press, British contributions have been notably few. That there is not, as yet, anything which could approach being described as an established body of specifically British Pentecostal studies is instanced by the fact that a compilation comparable to the survey titled "A Decade of Dissertations in Wesley Studies: 1991-2000"[3] would prove sparse if limited to

---

[1] The English edition of this appeared as Walter Hollenweger, *The Pentecostals* (London: SCM, 1972). His patriarchal status is confirmed by the publication of Lynne Davis, *Theology Out of Place: A Theological Biography of Walter J. Hollenweger* Journal of Pentecostal Theology Supplement Series, 23 (Sheffield: Sheffield Academic Press, 2002).

[2] Hollenweger, "The Critical Tradition of Pentecostalism," *Journal of Pentecostal Theology* 1 (1992): 7-17.

[3] Randy L. Maddox, "A Decade of Dissertations in Wesley Studies: 1991-2000,"

academic endeavours undertaken by or investigating Pentecostals/ism in Britain. It is in this relatively uncluttered context that a work devoted to the origins and early development of Pentecostalism in England seems requisite.

General Pentecostal studies has exhibited a significant trend toward the investigation and assertion of ethnic and national characteristics within what has become a diffuse movement of global proportions.[4] In his recent study of the Pentecostal phenomenon in its international context Anderson has commented on an Americo-centric approach which has characterised much of the twentieth-century perspective and has issued a call to aspiring historians, in particular, to seek to address this deficiency. A Pentecostalism that is "made in the USA is only one part of the total picture of many forms of 'Pentecostalisms,'" and he avers that "the hidden treasures of these local histories need to be discovered."[5] Ronald Bueno, a Pentecostal scholar from El Salvador, has brought his anthropological background to bear on the theoretical guidelines he advances for future studies of Pentecostalism. This present undertaking aims to fulfil some of the central aspirations he articulates:

> Studies of Pentecostalism should focus on how global worship 'styles,' liturgical practices and moral codes are integrated, rejected or adapted by localities; how mobile evangelists, pastors and lay-persons assimilate or transform new and old localities; how ethnicity, gender, class and other historically constructed social forms shape Pentecostal experiences and their institutionalization at specific moments in time and space.[6]

Objectives

This study has five primary objectives which can be stated succinctly:

Wesleyan Theological Journal 37.2 (Fall, 2002): 103-113.

[4] Examples of this include R. Andrew Chestnut, *Born Again in Brazil: The Pentecostal Boom and the Pathogens of Poverty* (New Brunswick, N. J.: Rutgers University Press, 1997); Frans H. Kamsteeg, *Prophetic Pentecostalism in Chile: A Case Study on Religion and Development Policy* Studies in Evangelicalism, 15 (London: Scarecrow Press, 1998); David Martin, *Pentecostalism: The World Their Parish* (Oxford: Blackwell, 2002); Cheryl J. Sanders, *Saints in Exile: The Holiness-Pentecostal Experience in African American Religion and Culture* (Oxford: Oxford University Press, 1996).

[5] Allan Anderson, *An Introduction to Pentecostalism: Global Charismatic Christianity* (Cambridge: Cambridge University Press, 2004), 166, 170.

[6] Ronald N. Bueno, "Listening to the Margins: Re-historicizing Pentecostal Experiences and Identities," in Murray W. Dempster, Byron D. Klaus, Douglas Petersen, eds., *The Globalization of Pentecostalism: A Religion Made to Travel* (Oxford: Regnum, 1999), 270.

-   To fill a noticeable gap in British Pentecostal scholarship, particularly in the area of credible historical investigation;
-   To explore the nature of the movement which came into existence in England post-1907, examining its aspirations, its vital functioning, and pertinent difficulties encountered in the implementation of its trans-denominational ethos;
-   To examine issues of churchmanship and historical relatedness and indebtedness exploring the contention that Pentecostal spirituality, as it developed in England, is best understood as part of the wider evangelical search for spiritual experience;
-   To challenge denominational perspectives where necessary and to redress denominational oversights where appropriate;
-   To challenge persistent and problematic features of Pentecostal historiography.

Origins and Emergence

An examination of the origins and emergence of a distinctively English version of the Pentecostal phenomenon is the primary aim of this study. Global worship styles, liturgical practice, and moral codes were indeed encountered and imbibed by those who would prove to be pioneers and key leaders by virtue of the internationalism of the Edwardian period. Significant means of diffusion were deployed when, as has been observed, the movement "raced across the planet" with something approaching "electrifying speed" and it displayed a propensity to "root itself in almost any culture."[7] This study aims to elucidate the origins of how the Pentecostal message came to England, highlighting reasons for its appeal to an initially small constituency, while tracing its emergence in specific religious localities which ranged from Anglican vestry, to mission hall platform, to domestic drawing room.

It is argued that an adequate understanding of the attraction and amenability of the Pentecostal message in 1907 and thereafter can only be approached in the context of an understanding of the old localities it encountered. Many of the early participants and virtually all leaders of note had had significant exposure to, and involvement in, England's Holiness fraternity, and the story of their emergence into a separate and identifiable movement is appreciably enhanced by this consideration. The rapid emergence of a distinctive Pentecostalism represented in vital respects the conjunction of a resurgent "primal piety"[8] with the received ethos and practice of English Holiness advocates. Essential questions such as, who emerged, what emerged, and how these emerged will receive primary attention in the pages that follow.

---

[7] Harvey Cox, *Fire From Heaven: The Rise of Pentecostal Spirituality and the Reshaping of Religion in the Twenty-first Century* (London: Cassell, 1996), 101.

[8] Cox, *The Rise of Pentecostal Spirituality*, 99.

Developments: Ideological and Structural

While multifarious developments were witnessed within English Pentecostalism during the seminal period between 1907 and 1925, these will be considered along two primary dimensions stated in their most elemental form as *ideological* and *structural*. Firstly, the development of an orthodoxy encompassing both theory and practice will be demonstrated to have occurred at an early stage of the movement's evolution. Spirituality will be adopted as the principal category for the study of early Pentecostal lived religion. Influential leaders and charismatic personalities proved adept at the orchestration and implementation of the, at times, complex and problematic process of establishing acceptable norms, mores, and parameters for Pentecostal praxis. It is contested that this approach will uncover much that was unique to the inner logic of developing Pentecostal spirituality, but it will also become apparent that early protagonists continued to betray on-going motivations and pre-occupations characteristic of the conservative evangelical constituencies in which they had been immersed. Inherited and ingrained dispositions will be shown to have fused with pneumatic dynamism to forge an identifiably English manifestation of enthusiastic Pentecostal religion.

Secondly, structural developments will be explored in terms of such identifiable power bases and organisational machinery as emerged during the years under consideration. A notable shift from *charismatic* to *bureaucratic* strains of leadership, along with resultant tensions, will be highlighted and in vital respects these could be broadly identified with pre- and post-war phases of development. Controversies, divergences, even crises and/or disaffection will be demonstrated to have proven integral to such structural developments as occurred, propelling the movement from its incipient phase toward a period of organisation. The original conception of a voluntary form of co-operative association for the purposes of mutual spiritual edification will be shown to have been embraced, implemented, overturned, and ultimately abandoned during the period under consideration.

Methodology

It is proposed for the purposes of undertaking an analysis of the emergence and early years of the movement in England, that four varied localities or Pentecostal *Centres* be examined.[9] The intention is that this framework will facilitate an examination of a diverse and otherwise potentially diffuse phenomenon. Wacker has highlighted the preponderance of figures who

---

[9] *Centre* was a term employed by early practitioners to denote a concentration of Pentecostal activity. It encompassed churches, mission halls as well as other less formal places of worship. The term was not original to Pentecostals, but as will become apparent, had been employed by Holiness leaders from the late nineteenth-century onwards.

walked across the early North American Pentecostal stage, making but fleeting appearances in rare periodicals, and then disappearing from view.[10]   His response to this particular challenge to the Pentecostal historian has been to present a topical study of the movement's first generation in his magisterial *Heaven Below: Early Pentecostals and American Culture*.[11] While a work of considerable scope which offers penetrating insights, the reader is, at times, presented with a bewildering array of characters, quotations, and geographical locations.

The intention of the present writer is to concentrate in Section 1 on historical localities which, in varying ways, received and were affected by the Pentecostal message.   It is hoped that in channelling investigations into "specific infrastructures"[12] an unwieldy or overly generalised treatment can be avoided.   Sections 2 and 3 will proceed to a more analytical consideration of salient issues associated with the emergence and development of the movement in general and relevant Centres and their associated figures in particular. An historico-thematic approach will be employed in the examination of some of the most pertinent features of emerging Pentecostal ideology and considerations relating to churchmanship, theological-world-view, and historiography will be particularly highlighted.   Structural developments will be outlined and analysed in terms of ecumenical perspectives and original conceptions of the movement, controversies and other factors which contributed toward bureaucratization, influence in this direction from developments in North America, and the reaction of the four Centres to an encroaching denominationalism.

Early Pentecostal Centres

Sunderland was not only the scene of the advent of Pentecostalism on English soil, but functioned as its undeniable nucleus in the period up to the First World War.   The status of Rev. Alexander A. Boddy, vicar of All Saints', Monkwearwouth, as Pentecostal grandee was attained by virtue of the three-fold influence which he exerted in the form of the annual Whitsuntide Convention which he convened between 1908 and 1914, his role in the oversight of the Pentecostal Missionary Union, and his founding and editorship of the singularly influential *Confidence* magazine.   As has latterly been observed: "What he taught, and the way he taught it, was to become

---

[10] Grant Wacker, "Travail of a Broken Family: Evangelical Responses to Pentecostalism in America, 1906-1916," *Journal of Ecclesiastical History* 47.3 (July 1996): 520.

[11] Wacker, *Heaven Below: Early Pentecostals and American Culture* (Cambridge, Mass.: Harvard University Press, 2001).

[12] Peter L. Berger, *The Social Reality of Religion* (London: Penguin University Books, 1973), 185.

normative..."[13]

Bradford's Bowland Street Mission quickly emerged as a Centre of significance within the emerging Pentecostal fraternity. This occurred, not least, because of the prominence attained by its flamboyant and popular leader, Smith Wigglesworth. Factors which include his eclectic spiritual background, founding of the mission while plying his trade as a plumber, its apparently uneasy transition toward Pentecostal participation, and the subsequent demise of his leadership and ultimate disintegration of the mission, render it an illuminating case study. Central to these developments, as will become apparent, were the fraught encounters and incompatibilities between an increasingly emphatic charismatic tendency and the mundane requirements of bureaucratic organisation and stability.

Bournemouth's Emmanuel Mission Hall, the first place of worship constructed for explicitly Pentecostal purposes in the British Isles, would be worthy of attention on the basis of this singular consideration alone. However the innovative, idiosyncratic, and ultimately aberrant tendencies of its leader William Oliver Hutchinson precipitated the marginalisation of a respected figure perceived to have transgressed the boundaries of consolidating ideological parameters. This departure, considered in the light of the issues involved as well as subsequent structural implications, renders this a fascinating Centre for investigation.

Croydon's Holiness Mission Hall was one of the surprisingly few Pentecostal Centres to emerge in the metropolis in the years prior to the First World War. Founded by a solicitor and lay-man more than two decades previously, this mission was exposed to, and adopted, the Pentecostal message soon after its initial propagation in England during the autumn of 1907. Although Pastor Inchcombe did not become a figure of note or influence across the wider movement, his leadership qualities are attested by the fact that he oversaw this mission and its development for more than forty years. Steady growth and stability engendered by means of uncontroversial, undramatic, yet highly effective inculcation of Pentecostal teaching, render the Holiness Mission Hall a closer approximation to the average and unexceptional Pentecostal Centre during this period.

England in the Context of the British Isles

It may be helpful, for the purpose of clarification, to point out that while Section 1 will deal with the emergence of Pentecostal Centres in England, Sections 2 and 3 will include representations, where appropriate, from the other quarters of the United Kingdom. While *England* remains the primary focus throughout, what occurred there both owed much to and, in turn, impinged

---

[13] William K. Kay, *Inside Story: A History of the British Assemblies of God* (Nottingham: Assemblies of God Publishing, 1990), 25.

upon developments across the British Isles. This perspective is justified on a number of grounds. Firstly three of the four Centres chosen for particular scrutiny were associated with leaders who came to exert an influence far beyond their immediate locality, and pertinent ramifications and outworkings of their various influences will be made apparent throughout this study. Secondly a recent doctoral dissertation, published as a volume in the Paternoster Press *Studies in Evangelical History and Thought* series in 2005, has expressly addressed the emergence of Pentecostalism and the process of denominational formation in Northern Ireland. It is not the intention of the present writer to replicate or presume to surpass the level of local detail amassed in this "synoptic regional study."[14] Its author has himself acknowledged that his work represents the first undertaking of its kind in connection with the history of Pentecostalism in the British Isles and has highlighted the need for others to embark on similar ventures for other regions. It is furthermore the case that the scholarly investigation of primary sources relating to the early years of Pentecostalism in Scotland and Wales is at an embryonic stage, awaiting more specific attention than has hitherto been attracted. The present study seeks to utilise available primary sources to uncover and develop a picture of the pre-denominational Pentecostal movement in England, while giving due consideration to the fact that this phenomenon emerged in the broader context of a United Kingdom of Great Britain and Ireland. Indeed it is respectfully suggested that, allowing for significant symbiotic exchange, the emergence and development of Pentecostalism across these regions is only comprehensible in the light of pivotal developments that occurred on English soil.

Review of Associated Literature

Sunderland/Alexander Boddy

Rev. Alexander A. Boddy (1854-1930), vicar of All Saints, Monkwearmouth, Sunderland, from 1886 to 1922, received scant attention for decades after his death. Despite his instrumental role in both the advent and propagation of the Pentecostal experience in England during the first two decades of the twentieth century, the memory of this had waned among, if not been deliberately marginalised by, much of later British Pentecostalism. His conviction that the phenomenon should be dispersed across denominations, rather than confined within new structures, and his consequent resistance of institutionalising tendencies, contributed to an increasingly marginal status. His seminal role was acknowledged by Donald Gee in his *The Pentecostal Movement: A Short*

---

[14] James Robinson, *Pentecostal Origins: Early Pentecostalism in Ireland in the Context of the British Isles* (Carlisle: Paternoster Press, 2005), xxvi. For further comment see my review of this volume in *Pneuma: The Journal of the Society for Pentecostal Studies* 29.1 (2007): 171-172.

History and an Interpretation for British Readers.[15] Gee was a figure of some stature within the Assemblies of God, a Pentecostal denomination founded in Britain in 1925. He has been described as the "most penetrating thinker and most prodigious writer" of the Pentecostalism of his era.[16] As a denominational leader, his *Short History* is a valuable chronicle and commentary, although it could by no means be regarded as a paragon of strict historical rigour, particularly on account of a conspicuous absence of documentation. His subsequent *Personal Memoirs of Pentecostal Pioneers* includes a further, if brief, positive assessment of Boddy's role in the early years of the movement.[17] While these works constitute something of an antidote to institutional neglect and oversight of pioneering figures, as will become apparent, they are replete with denominational perspectives.

The sympathies of the Charismatic Renewal of the 1960s and later, proved more appreciative of Boddy's disposition, and it was in this milieu that Martin Robinson sought to emphasise his continuing relevance in *The Charismatic Anglican: Historical and Contemporary.*[18] This M. Litt. thesis represented the first attempt at an academic appreciation of Alexander Boddy or the origins of British Pentecostalism generally, and contains much detail of historical value. Its limitation is that it is primarily an exploration and analysis of two "charismatic personalities,"[19] Alexander Boddy and Michael Harper, "historical and contemporary." The significance of this thesis has endured principally on account of the ongoing paucity of scholarly attention to Boddy or the early phase of the movement over which he presided.

A decade later the Wearside Historic Churches Group, at the instigation of Rev. Michael Barber, then Vicar of All Saints', commissioned the publication of a biography to mark the centenary of Boddy's installation in 1886. Peter Lavin's work is essentially a tribute to Boddy as "Pastor," "Prophet" and "doyen of the Pentecostalists," which reaches effusive conclusions regarding his role in the spread of what has since become a global religious phenomenon.[20] Awareness and interest within the developing Pentecostal scholarly fraternity was heightened at this time by an article which appeared in *Pneuma: The Journal of the Society for Pentecostal Studies.* This body had

---

[15] Donald Gee, *The Pentecostal Movement: A Short History and an Interpretation for British Readers* (London: Victory Press, 1941), 23-26, 40-46.

[16] Ian M. Randall *Evangelical Experiences: A Study in the Spirituality of English Evangelicalism 1918-1939* (Carlisle: Paternoster Press, 1999), 210.

[17] Gee, *These Men I Knew: Personal Memoirs of Pentecostal Pioneers* (Nottingham: Assemblies of God Publishing, 1980), 20-22.

[18] Martin Robinson, "The Charismatic Anglican - Historical and Contemporary. A Comparison of Alexander Boddy and Michael C. Harper," (Unpublished M. Litt. Dissertation: University of Birmingham, 1976).

[19] Robinson, "The Charismatic Anglican," 222.

[20] Peter Lavin, *Alexander Boddy: Pastor and Prophet* (Sunderland: Wearside Historic Churches Group, 1986), 4, 87-89.

been established in 1970 as a forum for scholars working within the charismatic tradition, and Edith Blumhofer's "Alexander Boddy and the Rise of Pentecostalism in Great Britain" represented a reintroduction of his role and significance in this context. Blumhofer principally examines the influence of Keswick and Holiness thinking, the phenomenon of the Welsh Revival of 1904-05, and comparisons with the emergence of the movement in North America.[21]

It could not be claimed that this short article precipitated an avalanche of scholarly outpourings, but Boddy's pioneering role has been more difficult to overlook than heretofore. He received the briefest inclusion in Malcolm Hathaway's overview of the origins of the Elim Pentecostal Church,[22] while William Kay has given fuller acknowledgement of the indebtedness of Pentecostal denominations to Boddy's foundational influence. His history of the Assemblies of God, *Inside Story*, and his subsequent and more expansive *Pentecostals in Britain*, both dealt with Boddy in their introductory sections.[23] Andrew Walker has described this latter work as "the most important study of British Pentecostals since Donald Gee's classic," mentioned above.[24] Yet neither of these works deal with Pentecostal origins at any length, or as their primary subject matter.

Neil Hudson's article "The Earliest Days of British Pentecostalism"[25] has underscored Boddy's role, while highlighting salient features of the nascent movement. In the context of a separate examination of Pentecostal worship, he has also identified the formative nature and enduring legacy of the annual Sunderland Conventions for the tenor of subsequent Pentecostalism.[26] Gavin Wakefield's short biography, which appears as one of the Grove Renewal Series booklets, seeks to present an outline of Boddy's life and ministry with a brief assessment of his significance for a primarily charismatic Anglican

---

[21] Edith Blumhofer, "Alexander Boddy and the Rise of Pentecostalism in Great Britain," *Pneuma: The Journal of the Society for Pentecostal Studies* 8:1 (Spring 1986): 31-40.

[22] Malcolm R. Hathaway, "The Elim Pentecostal Church: Origins, Development and Distinctives," in Keith Warrington, ed., *Pentecostal Perspectives* (Carlisle: Paternoster Press, 1998), 3.

[23] Kay, *Inside Story*, 17-40; and more recently *Pentecostals in Britain* (Carlisle: Paternoster Press, 2000), 11-15. This latter work is not primarily a work of history, but reflecting its author's research interests, seeks to advance theological, psychological and sociological perspectives on Britain's Pentecostals (p. xiii-xiv). Its main focus is on an empirical study of the contemporary situation and a survey of Pentecostal ministers has formed the basis of extensive statistical analysis.

[24] Andrew Walker, "Foreword," to Kay, *Pentecostals in Britain*, vii.

[25] Neil Hudson, "The Earliest Days of British Pentecostalism," *Journal of the European Pentecostal Theological Association* XXI (2001): 49-67.

[26] Hudson, "Worship: Singing a New Song in a Strange Land," in Warrington, ed., *Pentecostal Perspectives*, 179.

constituency.[27]   Wakefield has since then offered a more substantial study which is, to date, the sole rigorous modern biography of any British Pentecostal pioneer.   Written from the perspective of an Anglican scholar, this volume adopts a holistic approach to the extent that it concerns itself with the life and ministry of an active clergyman of that communion before, during, and after his Pentecostal involvement.   What emerges is a more rounded appreciation of this uniquely influential figure than may have been achieved by a writer solely concerned with the overtly sensational aspects of a decade of intensive involvement in, and leadership of, the fledgling Pentecostal movement.   This volume represents a significant step forward in scholarship relating to British Pentecostal origins and is destined to be required reading for any student or researcher of the history of the movement for the foreseeable future.[28]

Boddy founded the seminally influential *Confidence* magazine, which he styled as a "Pentecostal Paper for Great Britain," in 1908.   Although its principal influence was during the pre-war years, Boddy continued to preside as editor until its demise in 1926.   This periodical has been the subject of doctoral research, which has examined it as a unique instance of Pentecostal publishing.[29]   In addition to providing an examination of the vicissitudes of the eighteen year life of this particular magazine, Malcolm Taylor's dissertation explores factors which mitigated toward the advent of the Pentecostal phenomenon in a manner which encompasses North America and Britain. Wider issues relating to the utilization of the print medium for the promulgation of this particular religious message are also explored, although surprisingly little attention is given to the historical context in which religious periodicals were prolifically employed in Victorian and Edwardian Britain.   The main body of the work examines, under various headings, aspects of the teaching and doctrine that suffused the pages of *Confidence*.   These include the relation of *Spirit Baptism* to the *New Birth*, and the intricacies that surrounded the question of "Tongues as a Seal of Pentecost."[30]   All of the above is undertaken in terms of what might be deemed a Sunderland- or Boddy-centric perspective on early British Pentecostalism, as Taylor does not seek to address regional considerations or to examine the functioning or dynamics of a collective spiritual association or *collegia pietatis*.[31]

---

[27] Gavin Wakefield, *The First Pentecostal Anglican: The Life and Legacy of Alexander Boddy* (Cambridge: Grove Books, 2001).

[28] Wakefield, *Alexander Boddy: Pentecostal Anglican Pioneer* (Milton Keynes: Authentic Media, 2007).   For further comment see my review of this biography in *Pneuma: The Journal of the Society for Pentecostal Studies* 30.1 (2008): 180-181.

[29] Malcolm John Taylor, "Publish and Be Blessed: A Case Study in Early Pentecostal Publishing History, 1908-1926," (Unpublished Ph. D. Dissertation, University of Birmingham, 1994).

[30] Taylor, "Publish and Be Blessed," 175-207, 208-244.

[31] Joachim Wach, *Sociology of Religion* (London: Kegan Paul, 1947), 178. This term was first used for gatherings whose aim was the deepening of piety and devotion among

Bradford/Smith Wigglesworth

Stanley Howard Frodsham (1882-1969) was among those who underwent a Pentecostal initiation at All Saints' Vicarage in 1908. He moved to the United States before the First World War, and there his literary aspirations were fulfilled in his editorship of the *Pentecostal Evangel*, a weekly publication of the Assemblies of God. It is, however, for his book *Smith Wigglesworth: Apostle of Faith* which appeared in 1949, that he is most remembered.[32] It was not only the first but proved to be the most enduring biography of this celebrated preacher from Bradford. Frodsham acknowledged that he based his work on a combination of oral accounts provided by Wigglesworth, whom he had known in a personal capacity since 1909, and on material which had been received from the preacher's daughter and son-in-law. Alice and James Salter had been sometime travelling companions and ministerial colleagues to Wigglesworth and offered such insights as they had in view of Frodsham's editorial propensities.[33] Acknowledging some of the difficulties inherent in such an undertaking, Frodsham summarized his historiographical aims in the following statement:

> We have read some biographies, the writers of which have embalmed their heroes very deeply in honey. We read in Prov. 25:16, 'Hast thou found honey? Eat so much as is sufficient for thee, lest thou be filled therewith, and vomit it.' We have been so nauseated by this kind of biography that after reading a few chapters we have had no inclination to finish the book. We will endeavour not to serve up too much honey in this book, for the one of whom we write was just as human as the rest of us.[34]

These commendable aspirations are interesting, and not a little ironic, in the light of the fact that a high proportion of the works that have made up the minor publishing industry that has surrounded the personage of Smith Wigglesworth in the more than half century since this initial biography, have engaged in blatant and unashamed acts of embalmment. Myth and fable have wrestled with the factual and the historical in accounts presented of one of the most colourful and idiosyncratic of English Pentecostalism's early figureheads. Inspiration, edification and tendentious concerns have largely taken precedence over detached objectivity and rigorous documentation, the works for which

---

16th and 17th century Protestants. It was initially associated with figures such as Martin Bucer, John Calvin and Philipp Jakob Spener.

[32] W. E. Warner, "Stanley Howard Frodsham," in Stanley M. Burgess, ed., *The New International Dictionary of Pentecostal and Charismatic Movements* (Grand Rapids: Zondervan, 2002), 647-648.

[33] Stanley Howard Frodsham, *Smith Wigglesworth: Apostle of Faith* (London: Elim Publishing Co., 1949), v, 1.

[34] Frodsham, *Smith Wigglesworth*, 10-11.

Wigglesworth forms the principal subject matter, being almost uniformly of a popular and devotional nature.[35] Typical of this genre of writing is the intention to uncover, with a view to harnessing, "the secret of his power," which has been construed by later Pentecostal propagandists as nothing less than the "standard for God's end-time army."[36] The general tenor of these writings is reminiscent of a "major difficulty" which has been observed to beset "almost all" that has been written of the Welsh Revival: that of being based on "well intentioned piety which weakens or ignores the principles of historical criticism."[37] England's Pentecostals perceived themselves to be in spiritual continuity with this phenomenon which was heralded as a providential precursor or "preparation" for their own movement.[38] It transpired that they would, in turn, generate their own strain of "wistful evangelical"[39] writings which retained continuity with the "straight from heaven"[40] perspective.

A problematic feature of the body of what might be termed 'Wigglesworth literature' is the persistently episodic and anecdotal nature of these works. Many consist largely of a conglomeration of narratives, rarely documented, and often stretching credulity toward, if not beyond, the outer limits of its boundaries. It is not fanciful to suggest that these writings display notable characteristics of the "pious legend," the canonization *vitae,* and other literary devotional foci more readily associated with earlier patterns of Christian expression.[41]   A   pronounced   tendency   toward   "a   certain   uncritical

---

[35] Desmond Cartwright's *The Real Smith Wigglesworth* elicited considerable praise from a Pentecostal minister in a review for the popular *Direction* magazine. One of the more creditable works on Wigglesworth is tellingly described by its reviewer as a "treasure chest of authentic stories that draw me closer to God." It was also said to contain "a wealth of encouragement and information." Ray Jones, Review of Desmond Cartwright, *The Real Smith Wigglesworth, Direction* 11, August 2002, 45. See note 51 below.

[36] Albert Hibbert, *Smith Wigglesworth: The Secret of his Power* (Tulsa: Harrison House, 1982); P. J. Madden, *The Wigglesworth Standard: The Standard for God's End-time Army* (Springdale, PA: Whitaker House, 1993).

[37] Basil Hall, "The Welsh Revival of 1904-5: A Critique," in G. J. Cuming and Derek Baker, eds., *Studies in Church History*, vol. 8, *Popular Belief and Practice* (Cambridge: Cambridge University Press, 1972), 292.

[38] For a very clear statement of this see Boddy's "The Pentecostal Movement: The Story of its Beginnings at Sunderland and its Present Position in Great Britain," *Confidence*, August 1910, 193.

[39] R. Hayward, "From the Millennial Future to the Unconscious Past: The Transformation of Prophecy in Early Twentieth-Century Britain," in Bertrand Taithe and Tim Thornton, eds., *Prophecy: The Power of Inspired Language in History, 1300-2000* (Stroud: Sutton Publishing, 1997), 161.

[40] J. Cynddylan Jones, "Introduction" to Jessie Penn-Lewis, *The Awakening in Wales (And Some of Its Hidden Springs)* (Poole: Overcomer Literature Trust, 1922), 9.

[41] Richard Kieckhefer, "Major Currents in Late Medieval Devotion," in Jill Raitt, ed., *Christian Spirituality: High Middle Ages and Reformation* (London: SCM Press, 1989),

exuberance"[42] is certainly in evidence, and a flavour of such ultra-"providentialist"[43] writings is afforded by the following idealised perspective:

> Wigglesworth could have been a wealthy man...He could have lived in a palace, but instead he chose to be content in a little stone house in Bradford, Yorkshire, England. That home had the atmosphere of God's throne room. The very presence of God could be felt within. I always found it a delight to visit him. It was like going into the sanctuary, into the Cloud of Glory.[44]

In the light of this general tendency, a rare disclaimer is to be found in the unlikely context of the prolegomenon to a book entitled *Reminiscences of Smith Wigglesworth*. Its author, an elderly Pentecostalist minister at the time of writing, states:

> This little book is what it claims to be. Nothing more. It is not a Biography. I am not the one to write the Biography of Smith Wigglesworth. I have not sufficient Data. I write exclusively from my own contact with him. No doubt there are others who could write more. But they have not done so. After long consideration, I have written under compulsion, feeling that something more should be made public...[45]

Hacking presents his work as that of a Pentecostal participant and practitioner, fully cognizant of the deficiency of what he has compiled as an historical document. He does not make undue or unsustainable claims on its behalf, and recognizes the imperative of undertaking a more rigorous approach, but laments the fact that a quarter of a century after Wigglesworth's death, this had not been achieved. Hacking therefore offers his *Reminiscences* as imperfect but necessary, and does so with an implicit sense of anticipation at what he feels should be forthcoming. He would have been disappointed as more than three decades later there has been little appreciable advance in the qualitative nature of what has been written on this Pentecostal pioneer. Desmond Cartwright, the

---

95-96. See also Stephen Wilson, "Introduction," to Stephen Wilson, ed., *Saints and their Cults: Studies in Religious Sociology, Folklore and History* (Cambridge: Cambridge University Press, 1987), 1-53, and Thomas J. Heffernan, *Sacred Biography: Saints and their Biographers in the Middle Ages* (Oxford: Oxford University Press, 1992).

[42] E. G. Rupp, "The Importance of Denominational History," *Baptist Quarterly* 17 (1957-58): 315. Rupp cites American Mennonite scholarship as guilty of this tendency, while otherwise producing work of merit.

[43] George Marsden and John Woodbridge, "Christian History Today," *Christian History* XX. 4 (2001): 50-54.

[44] Hibbert, *Smith Wigglesworth*, 22.

[45] W. Hacking, *Reminiscences of Smith Wigglesworth* (London: Peniel Press, 1973), 1.

founding archivist of the Donald Gee Centre for Pentecostal and Charismatic Research, has noted that "little or no use has been made of the early records in printed sources or of extant letters." Although this repository houses more than thirty of his original letters, as well as copies of others, "none of these letters have been used by any of those who have written books about Wigglesworth."[46]

Gordon Rupp has identified as a turning-point in modern historiography, the watershed which became apparent between the *annalists* and the *historians*. If the Pentecostal publications which have dealt with the life of Smith Wigglesworth had to be categorized in either of these "two worlds of historiography," they would fit most readily in the former. A prominent feature of this 'world' is the amateur historian who "like Macaulay in one century and Churchill in another, snatch time to study and write history amid other avocations."[47] Among the most commendable of this school are the American Roberts Liardon, who has both written about Wigglesworth,[48] and acted as compiler and propagator of his sermons and miscellaneous writings,[49] and the British Desmond Cartwright, a retired minister who is now recognised as the "official historian of the Elim Pentecostal Churches."[50] The latter's recent work *The Real Smith Wigglesworth*, is one of the more significant secondary sources available, although he acknowledges that it is not aimed at the scholar, but the general reader.[51]

Cecil Robeck, then editor of *Pnuema: The Journal of the Society for Pentecostal Studies*, pointed out almost two decades ago that there was "an acute need for critical, analytical biographical treatments in Pentecostal

---

[46] Desmond W. Cartwright, "The Real Wigglesworth," *Journal of the European Pentecostal Theological Association* XVII (1997): 95. The present writer gratefully acknowledges that these letters have been made available by Rev. Cartwright for the purposes of this study.

[47] Rupp, "The Victorian Churchman as Historian: A Reconstruction of R. W. Dixon's 'History of the Church of England,'" in G. V. Bennett and J. D. Walsh, eds., *Essays in Modern English Church History* (London: Adam & Charles Black, 1966), 211-212.

[48] Roberts Liardon, "Smith Wigglesworth: Apostle of Faith," in *God's Generals: Why They Succeeded and Why Some Failed* (Tulsa: Albury Publishing, 1998), 195-226.

[49] Liardon, ed., *Smith Wigglesworth: The Complete Collection of His Life Teachings* (Tulsa: Albury Publishing, 1996).

[50] Chris Cartwright, "Introduction" to Desmond Cartwright, *The Real Smith Wigglesworth: The Man, The Myth, The Message* (Tonbridge: Sovereign World, 2000), 5.

[51] D. Cartwright, "Preface" to *The Real Smith Wigglesworth*, 10. While the merit of Cartwright's approach has been acknowledged, it has also been pointed out that he writes "with the popular audience in mind," and that the "sophisticated reader may become frustrated by the lack of essential documentation." See Cecil M. Robeck, "The Use of Biography in Pentecostal Historiography," *Pneuma: The Journal of the Society for Pentecostal Studies* 8.2 (Fall 1986): 79.

historiography." The imperative of moving beyond an approach characterised by "insertions representative of the author's own piety" was acknowledged to have "for the most part...gone unheeded."[52] E. H. Carr's observation about the nineteenth century, seems apposite to Pentecostal writings that have dealt with Smith Wigglesworth: "Historians walked in the Garden of Eden, without a scrap of philosophy to cover them, naked and unashamed before the God of history. Since then we have known Sin and experienced a Fall."[53] Pentecostal scholarship in general, and Pentecostal history in particular, can no longer parade itself naked yet unashamed before the God of history. Would-be scholars can no longer perpetuate "sacred meteor themes" or convictions that Pentecostal origins were "forged outside the ordinary processes of history."[54] It must be acknowledged that what has been described as the transition "from *Logos* to Canon"[55] has taken place with respect of Wigglesworth literature, heightening the imperative that any future treatment of pioneering figures and the roles they played in the growth of the fledgling movement must, in contradistinction, adhere to credible historical conventions if it is to be taken seriously by a wider readership. Such an approach can only serve to broaden and deepen the apprehension of vital aspects of Pentecostalism's heritage, both within and beyond its boundaries.

Bournemouth/William Oliver Hutchinson

It is not difficult to enumerate the works that deal with William Oliver Hutchinson (1864-1928) and the Apostolic Faith Church which emanated from the Pentecostal Centre he founded in Bournemouth. Gordon Weeks, a retired minister of the Apostolic Church which had its origins in a secession from Hutchinson's enterprise in 1916, compiled a "History of the Apostolic Church" which in manuscript form, is available from the official website of that church body.[56] While clearly of the *annalist* school already mentioned, this work is significant in so far as it represents an unprecedented step toward the Apostolic Church's acknowledgement of their controversial pre-1916 origins. Weeks has since undertaken, primarily for the purposes of a denominational readership, to privately publish a historical survey of this Pentecostal grouping over a century

---

[52] Robeck, "The Use of Biography in Pentecostal Historiography," 77, 79.

[53] Edward H. Carr, *What is History?* (New York: Vintage Books, 1961), 21.

[54] Wacker, "Are the Golden Oldies Still Worth Playing? Reflections on History Writing among Early Pentecostals," *Pnuema* 8:2 (Fall 1986): 86, 81.

[55] In a chapter which incisively delineates this process, Heffernan observes that as the hypothetical saint's life "moves from oral through multiple written versions, it moves toward being accepted as canonical undergoing the while a subtle but sure transformation from witness to tale, to text, to history, and finally to sacred history." See *Sacred Biography*, 36.

[56] Gordon Weeks, "A History of the Apostolic Church, Part One: 1900-1919," on http://www.apostolic-church.org/History.html.

of its development.[57] While hampered by cumbersome and erratic documentation and less than satisfactory in many respects, this work also acknowledges some of the excesses and eccentricities that occurred under the early leadership of William Hutchinson and, to that extent, serves to illuminate a particularly neglected aspect of Pentecostal origins in Britain.

A comparable, but more substantive work has been produced by James Worsfold who from the position of ministerial affiliation with the Apostolic Church in New Zealand, has sought to establish the early years and vicissitudes encountered by the denomination in its country of origin. While *The Origins of the Apostolic Church in Great Britain*[58] contains useful detail and documentation, this work is distinctly reverential in tone, and asks few searching questions. Difficulties associated with Hutchinson are acknowledged and while this represents another advance in Apostolic thinking, rigorous objectivity could hardly be claimed and generous interpretations are repeatedly advanced for highly problematic issues.

A less extensive but more ideologically detached treatment has been presented in an article by Malcolm Hathaway, a minister of the Elim Pentecostal Church, whose interest has doubtless been heightened by the fact that his grandparents were, for a time, involved with Hutchinson in Bournemouth. He outlines the increasingly erratic practices and teachings adopted and promulgated by the Apostolic Faith Church and the network of congregations which initially associated themselves with it, while identifying in the organisational structures established, an initial imperfect impetus toward the formation of Pentecostal denominations in Britain.[59]

Both Hathaway and Worsfold remark on the palpable silence that surrounds Hutchinson, and his short-lived enterprise, in Pentecostal and other writings.[60] Hathaway remarkably overstates the case, however, in his assertion that in Gee's, *The Pentecostal Movement*, Hutchinson's name "is not even mentioned."[61] This is curious as Gee gives express treatment to the emergence of the Apostolic Faith Church from within the broader Pentecostal community, and states that to neglect to do so would constitute a "culpable omission."[62]

Worsfold outlines a more extensive range of writers whom he believes to have committed the injustice of such oversights. Among them are Whittaker,

[57] Weeks, *Chapter Thirty Two - Part of: A History of the Apostolic Church, 1900-2000* (Barnsley: Gordon Weeks, 2003).

[58] James E. Worsfold, *The Origins of the Apostolic Church in Great Britain* (Wellington, New Zealand: Julian Literature Trust, 1991).

[59] Hathaway, "The role of William Oliver Hutchinson and the Apostolic Faith Church in the formation of the British Pentecostal Churches," *Journal of the European Pentecostal Theological Association* XVI (1996): 40-57.

[60] Hathaway, "William Oliver Hutchinson," 40; Worsfold, "Introduction" to The Origins, xxv-xxvi.

[61] Hathaway, "William Oliver Hutchinson," 40.

[62] Gee, *The Pentecostal Movement*, 117.

whose stated ambition to reveal "the inside story of the Pentecostal movement"[63] is hampered by a "blind spot"[64] which precluded any acknowledgement of the role of the Apostolic Faith Church. David L. Edwards is criticised for being similarly silent in his *Christian England from the Eighteenth Century to the First World War*, despite an avowed attempt to write the "first ecumenical history of English Christianity" which would "do justice to Catholics, evangelicals, Anglicans, non-conformists, conservatives, radicals, poets, preachers, intellectuals, and the people."[65] This is less surprising when considered in the light of the fact that no reference to Pentecostalism generally or any of its other leaders occurs in this work, a pattern which is repeated in most of the standard histories of the period. In this respect early English Pentecostalism possesses a dubious commonality with Dispensationalism, another religious phenomenon which Prof. Alexander of the University of Manchester has described as little known "outside Church circles of a particular ecclesiastical type," and which he has observed to be "hardly mentioned in academic studies of contemporary Christianity."[66] For instance, a recent history of religion in Wales entirely overlooks the role of Hutchinson or Bournemouth in the genesis of the Apostolic Church under Daniel P. Williams (1883-1927). Its author merely states that through Williams "links were forged with other Pentecostal groups," resulting in a "loose confederation" becoming a denominational body based in Pen-y-groes in 1916.[67]

Various reasons will be advanced below for this general tendency, but a more specific rationale for Hutchinson's exclusion from Pentecostal writings must undeniably be linked to the curious nature of much of the doctrine that came to be propagated in Bournemouth and its increasingly irregular outworkings in the life of his Apostolic Faith Church. Andrew Walker has alluded to the protracted struggles of British Pentecostals in their, at times, reluctance to become "principled Christian communities." By the 1930s it became apparent that their early aspirations to "carry all before them in the power of the Spirit and in the light of an expected Second Advent," had not,

---

[63] Colin Whittaker, *Seven Pentecostal Pioneers: The Inside Story of the Pentecostal Movement and its Present-day Influence* (Basingstoke: Marshall, Morgan & Scott, 1983). Whittaker certainly presented an insider perspective to the extent that he was a member of the Executive Council of the British Assemblies of God at the time of writing. His use of primary material appears, however, to have been limited.

[64] Worsfold, "Introduction" to *Origins of the Apostolic Church*, xxvi.

[65] David L. Edwards, "Preface" to *Christian England*, vol. 3, *From the Eighteenth Century to the First World War* (London: Collins, 1984), 9.

[66] Philip S. Alexander, "Dispensationalism, Christian Zionism and the State of Israel." Presidential Lecture for the Manson Society, 2001, Department of Religions and Theology, University of Manchester, 1.

[67] D. Densil Morgan, *The Span of the Cross: Christian Religion and Society in Wales 1914-2000* (Cardiff: University of Wales Press, 1999), 13-14.

and held no immediate prospect of being realised.[68]   They thus faced the unpalatable and formidable challenge of reconciling their hitherto guiding and cherished motivations to intractable reality.   As they sought to carve out a credible and enduring niche in the wider Christian community, Hutchinson cannot have appeared an auspicious ally in the search for what was popularly termed "Pentecost with dignity."[69]

Croydon/Pastor Inchcombe

While mentioned by Gee as one of the "very few"[70] Pentecostal congregations in the capital prior to the First World War, an otherwise conspicuous absence of written material, whether popular, denominational, or scholarly, appears to indicate that no research has to this point been undertaken into Pastor Inchcombe, or Croydon's Holiness Mission Hall over which he presided.

Sources and Perspectives

Pentecostalism and the Historical Record

Christopher Hill observed that the principal headache of the historian is not too few documents, but too many predecessors.   Sufferers from this particular malady find much of their time consumed in sifting and assessing the works of previous scholars.[71]   The present writer has not had to grapple with the trials of this scholarly ailment, indeed the reverse of Hill's diagnosis would more accurately reflect the challenge encountered.   Not only is the field of Pentecostal scholarship, certainly in relation to the early history of the movement in Britain, notably uncluttered, it is also the case that the phenomenon is resolutely absent from standard religious histories of the period. For instance Hugh McLeod's *Religion and Society in England, 1850-1914* gives consideration to, and comment on, a range of small religious bodies and minority interest groups, among which the first generation of Pentecostals do not feature.[72]   Likewise Gilbert's expansive *Religion and Society in Industrial*

---

[68] Walker, "Foreword" to Kay's *Pentecostals in Britain*, vii.

[69] This phrase is commonly associated with the aspirations of British Pentecostalism in the difficult aftermath of the Second World War. See Hudson, "Worship: Singing a New Song in a Strange Land," in Warrington, ed., *Pentecostal* Perspectives, 181. This tendency is worthy of comparison with an earlier phenomenon which James Munson terms "The Nonconformists' Search for Dignity," in *The Nonconformists: In Search of a Lost Culture* (London: SPCK, 1991), 129-156.

[70] Gee, *The Pentecostal Movement*, 55.

[71] Christopher Hill, "History and Denominational History," *Baptist Quarterly*, 22 (1967-8): 65.

[72] Hugh McLeod, *Religion and Society in England, 1850-1914* (New York: St. Martin's Press, 1996).

England,[73] and Currie, Gilbert and Horsley's *Churches and Churchgoers*,[74] which has been described as "the fullest and most authoritative treatment of patterns of religious affiliation in modern England,"[75] betray no inkling of Pentecostal existence.

Two works which deal with Evangelical Christianity as integral to the fabric of British religious life have included details of the Pentecostal phenomenon. David Bebbington allocates a little more than two pages to the early stages of Pentecostalism in his detailed and comprehensive history *Evangelicalism in Modern Britain*.[76] Ian Randall's exploration of evangelical spirituality during the inter-war period includes a chapter on Pentecostalism, although its main concentration is not on its emergent years, but on the subsequent denominational phase which gathered momentum from the mid-1920s. He is particularly keen to highlight the influence of, and continuities with, the evangelical tradition.[77] He has extended this theme in his contribution to a collection of essays exploring aspects of Baptist history and influence.[78]

Grant Wacker, the foremost authority on early American Pentecostalism, has pointed out that despite Pentecostals', at times, "extravagant assessment" of their own importance, emissaries from the world of academia have typically only ventured into their domain to seek to discover how a movement perceived to be so manifestly backward could have come into existence in the sunlit progressivism of the twentieth century.[79] Walker has commented that David Martin, a sociologist who has written extensively of the contemporary Pentecostal phenomenon, is as yet one of the few in the academic world who have approached Pentecostalism "without either rancour or condescension."[80]

---

[73] A. D. Gilbert, *Religion and Society in Industrial England: Church, Chapel and Social Change, 1740-1914* (London: Longman, 1976).

[74] Robert Currie, Alan Gilbert, and Lee Horsley, *Churches and Churchgoers: Patterns of Church Growth in the British Isles since 1700* (Oxford: Oxford University Press, 1977).

[75] Richard J. Helmstadter, "Orthodox Nonconformity," in D. G. Paz, ed., *Nineteenth-Century English Religious Traditions: Retrospect and Prospect* (Westport, Connecticut, and London: Greenwood Press, 1995), 69.

[76] David Bebbington, *Evangelicalism in Modern Britain: A History from the 1730s to the 1980s* (Grand Rapids: Baker Book House, 1992), 196-198.

[77] Randall, "Old-time Power: Pentecostal Spirituality," chapter 8 of *A Study in the Spirituality of English Evangelicalism*, 206-237. See also his "Old Time Power: Relationships between Pentecostalism and Evangelical Spirituality in England," *Pnuema: Journal of the Society for Pentecostal Studies*, 19.1 (Spring 1997): 53-80.

[78] Randall, "'Days of Pentecostal Overflowing': Baptists and the Shaping of Pentecostalism," in D. W. Bebbington, ed., *The Gospel in the World: International Baptist Studies* (Carlisle: Paternoster Press, 2002), 80-104.

[79] Wacker, "Evangelical Responses to Pentecostalism," 505.

[80] Walker, "Foreword" to Kay's *Pentecostals in Britain*, vii. This observation is corroborated by another social scientist who has described Martin as "one of the very

This further parallels Alexander's observation concerning Dispensationalism which is generally considered unworthy of "serious treatment or refutation," while "those academics who do take any notice of it can usually barely conceal their contempt."[81]

There are however, less prejudicial grounds for this lack of historical consideration. A distinct absence of Pentecostal academic engagement allied with the problematic nature of much of what has been written, as already outlined, cannot have enhanced the prospects for scholarly endeavour. Also of primary significance is the fact that, as Gee has acknowledged, in contradistinction to its American and European counterparts, British Pentecostalism remained numerically negligible before the 1920s.[82] It reached the zenith of its visibility at its annual conventions, in particular those hosted by Boddy in Sunderland and Polhill in London, but beyond that it inhabited, for several years, a vague religious hinterland, resisting overt signs of organisation.[83] As McLeod has pointed out, conditions of religious pluralism and toleration which prevailed within an overall Protestant consensus resulted in the co-existence of a significant number of idiosyncratic religious denominations and groupings during the Victorian, and into the Edwardian period.[84] Kent has written of the "fantastically diversified would-be evangelization" which was a significant feature of the religious life of later nineteenth-century England. It was from among this "elaborate pattern" made up of many who were, to varying degrees, alienated from older Protestant structures that, with notable exceptions, the main body of those who came to ally themselves with the Pentecostal cause were principally drawn. The result was, to the chagrin of the historical researcher, that emerging Pentecostal leaders continued to devote their lives in this pre-denominational period to the

---

few sociologists of religion to take Pentecostalism seriously." See Bernice Martin, "The Pentecostal Gender Paradox: A Cautionary Tale for the Sociology of Religion," in Richard K. Fenn, ed., *The Blackwell Companion to Sociology of Religion* (Oxford: Blackwell, 2003), 59.

[81] Alexander, "Dispensationalism," 1.

[82] Gee, *The Pentecostal Movement*, 97, 55.

[83] Gee offered the retrospective assessment that "for many years there were very few Pentecostal assemblies of any size or importance established in the British Isles," and that this was directly attributable to the fact that the "annual Conventions were held, more or less, under the auspices of the Church of England." It was furthermore pronounced that "the spread of the Revival in the British Isles was undoubtedly hindered in this way for several years." See "The Pentecostal Movement: A Short History of its Rise and Development," *Redemption Tidings*, October 1932, 2. This one-dimensional perspective will be considered and challenged in Section 3 below.

[84] McLeod, *Religion and Society in England*, 1-2. See also Gerald Parsons, "Introduction: Victorian Religion, Paradox and Variety," in Gerald Parsons, ed., *Religion in Victorian Britain*, vol. 1, *Traditions* (Manchester: Manchester University Press, 1988), 5-8.

"unsuccessful obscurity" of the "Gospel Halls."[85]

Source Materials and Qualitative Nature of this Study

Lineham has remarked on the necessity and value of, but also the particular challenges associated with, the conduct of historical research into England's minority religious groups. Principal among the difficulties are such groups' attitudes toward historical records, which too often provided little impetus toward preservation in the past, and which can manifest inhibitive sensitivities toward the use of what has been preserved in the present.[86] In the introductory section of her study of religion in Bradford between 1880 and 1914, Rosemary Chadwick has observed that what little material survives for many minor Protestant groups is not only difficult to trace, but that it is unlikely that what could be gleaned would justify the time involved.[87] These considerations directed the main concentration of her researches away from such religious groups toward those for whom quantifiable historical records have been preserved.

The notable lack of viable and identifiable records relating to the early years of England's Pentecostal movement can only have served to deter historians such as McLeod, from including it alongside other minority constituencies. It certainly boasts no standard and recognisable holdings comparable to the repositories of Anglican Ecclesiastical Libraries or Diocesan Registries, the Methodist Archive housed in Manchester University's John Rylands Library, or the Congregational Archive located in the Dr. Williams' Library in London. Other resources in the form of publications such as Crockford's *Clerical Directory* or the proceedings and publications of the Baptist, Congregational, or United Reformed Church Historical Societies are also notable by their absence. It is telling that Pentecostal churches have not been included in Richardson's *Local Historian's Encyclopaedia* while groups such as the Bible Christians, the Free Church of England, and the Swedenborgians or New Church, all merit inclusion under the designation "Non-Conformist Sects and Other Religions."[88]

This study aims neither to avoid nor deny the marginal nature of early

---

[85] John Kent, *Holding the Fort: Studies in Victorian Revivalism* (London: Epworth Press, 1978), 301.

[86] Peter J. Lineham, "The Protestant 'Sects,'" in Paz, ed., *Nineteenth-Century English Religious Traditions*, 169-170. This bears comparison with observations made by both Cartwright in "The Real Wigglesworth," 90-92, and Brian Robert Ross, "Donald Gee: In Search of a Church; Sectarian in Transition" (Unpublished D.Th. Dissertation: Knox College Toronto, 1974), 88.

[87] Rosemary Chadwick, "Church and People in Bradford and District, 1880-1914: The Protestant Churches in an Urban Industrial Environment" (Unpublished D. Phil. Dissertation: University of Oxford, 1986), 14, 138-139.

[88] John Richardson, *The Local Historian's Encyclopaedia* (New Barnet, Herts.: Historical Publications, 1993), 191-194.

manifestations of Pentecostalism on the periphery of England's religious landscape, or the lack of empirical data which would facilitate a more statistically or demographically driven investigation. Taylor introduces his study with vast cumulative figures to bolster the claim that Pentecostalism is "the world's fastest-growing religious movement."[89] Robinson similarly justifies his examination of aspects of Pentecostal enculturation in Ulster on the basis of the "sweeping phenomenon" of almost a century later.[90] The present writer feels no inclination to appropriate grandiose religious demographics to justify or bolster an exploration of the origins and early years of the movement in England. Its underlying motivations, ambiguities, curiosities, eccentricities, and guiding principles, it is contested, would remain deserving of attention had the movement not embarked upon another phase but rather become moribund during the 1920s. The approach adopted toward the examination of another chapter in the history of religious radicalism seems apposite in this context: "Our purpose has been to identify some of the patterns of development in the more ambiguous part of their careers when the final outcome was still far from being a foregone conclusion."[91]

It has been observed that the religious historian is particularly prone to the danger of domination by a spirit of "historical fundamentalism" whereby the past under investigation becomes a "chunk of dead rock from which anachronistic, but superficially relevant proof-texts are chiselled to the required shape."[92] The present writer feels justified in claiming a certain 'imaginative sympathy' with charismatic Christianity in general, but has no interest or obligation through denominational allegiance, or otherwise, in advancing or perpetuating, what might be deemed a *Whig interpretation of history* for the Pentecostal cause.[93] Noll has commented on the discomfiture associated with, if not inherent in, progress beyond sanitized versions of received tradition when the golden ages of the past appear more tarnished than heretofore in the light of

---

[89] He offers the estimate that there were "at least half a million" Pentecostals in Britain in 1993 and that there were in the region of 500 million adherents worldwide. See Taylor, "Publish and be Blessed," 11. This is strikingly at variance with the findings of a statistical monitor of religious attendance in the U.K. which calculated a total of 208,631 Pentecostal adherents in Britain in 1995. This represented an increase from 167,006 in 1990. See *UK Christian Handbook Religious Trends No. 4*, Peter Brierley, ed., (London: Christian Research, 2003), 9.12.

[90] Robinson, *Early Pentecostalism in Ireland*, xxi-xxiv, xxvii, 296.

[91] Timothy C. F. Stunt, *From Awakening to Secession: Radical Evangelicals in Switzerland and Britain, 1815-1835* (Edinburgh: T. & T. Clark, 2000), 311.

[92] B. White, "The Task of a Baptist Historian," *Baptist Quarterly* 22 (1967-68): 404.

[93] Herbert Butterfield, *The Whig Interpretation of History* (1931; repr. London: Pelican, 1973), 69. This triumphalist and partisan approach to history has more recently been summarised in John Burrow, *A History of Histories* (London: Penguin Books, 2009), 472-475.

more detached consideration.[94] Rowan Williams has recently argued for "real engagement with the strangeness of the past" as antidotal to the "ultimate trivialising" of religious identity.[95] The present writer recognises and identifies wholeheartedly with Rupp's assessment of the Mennonite Encycolpaedia in which he laments that the "eccentricities and aberrations" of the radicals are repeatedly toned down to the detriment of the historical record. His concluding comment could be appropriated as a further guiding principle of the present undertaking which aspires to engage in history, not apologetic: "How much more striking are the facts."[96]

While the historical records relating to the first generation of English Pentecostals are in comparative terms, notably limited, its pioneers have bequeathed to posterity sources of particular merit. The paucity of personal papers relating to Alexander Boddy, while disappointing, is not insuperable as Wolffe has remarked that a whole field of research remains to be undertaken into the careers and religious ideas of Evangelical clergy who "while seldom if ever leaving personal papers," have left significant traces in other printed records and the pages of local papers.[97] It is certainly the case that early developments at Sunderland generated comment in not just local, but national print media. The most significant surviving record, however, was the periodical *Confidence* which Boddy established in 1908 and over which he presided as editor until 1926. This publication has been acknowledged as the "official organ" and "authoritative voice of British Pentecostal leadership"[98] for a decade after its inception, and occupies according to Taylor, a unique position as "*the* primary source"[99] for research related to the origins and development of the movement in Britain. Robinson has also emphasised the invaluable status of this publication, stating that in his investigation of the early history of Pentecostalism in Northern Ireland: "The monthly issues of *Confidence* are almost the only source of information about the movement in the province in its pre-denominational stage until the publication of the *Elim Evangel* which started with the December 1919 issue and was published quarterly for its first two years."[100] Other periodicals came before the Pentecostal constituency

---

[94] Mark A. Noll, *Turning Points: Decisive Moments in the History of Christianity* (Leicester: IVP, 1997), 19.

[95] Rowan Williams, *Why Study the Past? The Quest for the Historical Church* (London: Darton, Longman and Todd, 2005), 23-24.

[96] Rupp, "The Importance of Denominational History," 315.

[97] John Wolffe, "Anglicanism" in Paz, ed., *Nineteenth-Century English Religious Traditions*, 8-9. According to Robinson, Boddy's personal papers were burned on the death of his son. See "The Charismatic Anglican," 8. Certainly no evidence of extant materials are to be found in *Papers of British Churchmen, 1780-1940*, Guides to Sources for British History 6 (London: Her Majesty's Stationery Office, 1987).

[98] Gee, *The Pentecostal Movement*, 45-46.

[99] Taylor, "Publish and be Blessed," 129.

[100] Robinson, "Bibliographical Note," in *Early Pentecostalism in Ireland*, 336.

during this period, none of which enjoyed the longevity or influence of *Confidence*, but what has survived is nothing less than "invaluable"[101] in any attempt to understand the emergent movement. In the context of her exploration of the role of women in British Nonconformity during these decades, Lauer has highlighted the utility of such primary source material: "As reflectors of the trends and opinions, purveyors of news, and arbiters of taste, the religious periodical" constitutes "an ideal source."[102]

It is necessarily the case that a substantial reliance on these primary sources will result in a study which could be described as *qualitative* rather than *quantitative* in nature. No claim is made that what has been undertaken is empirical or scientific in the data utilized or the conclusions reached. Indeed it is, with due consideration, asserted that such a study would prove difficult in the light of the available materials. It is further suggested that such an undertaking, however illuminating, could not claim to have uncovered the elemental nature of the movement, nor would it have addressed the primary concerns of its principal protagonists. Emerging Pentecostals were among those whose emphasis was on "quality of belief rather than on quantity of numbers."[103] Boddy himself stated that "statistics are only poor and cold," and instead chose to emphasise that Christ "was never so loved as He is today, and many are looking for his coming again."[104] It was elsewhere stated: "We do not dare to count numbers," but rather asserted that what was of importance was that there were those who testified to having encountered "joy and the full assurance" of spiritual "freedom."[105] Hutchinson exhibited a similar bent toward spiritual rather than numerical advancement, stating: "It would be difficult to keep count of those blessed in a work like this where so many come and go. We have learned not to reckon on numbers. David made a big mistake by doing this."[106] In its earliest manifestations this movement eschewed the formalised machinery of religious organisation, and sought rather to preserve and propagate the quintessence of spiritual vitality which it believed had been vouchsafed to it for the benefit of the Christian Church. Alongside newspaper reports, correspondences, and pamphlets, its periodicals, as primary means of ideological diffusion, present us with an incomparable record of the fortunes of English Pentecostalism.

---

[101] Hudson, "The Earliest Days of British Pentecostalism," 54.

[102] L. E. Lauer, "Women in British Nonconformity, circa 1880-1920, with special reference to the Society of Friends, Baptist Union and Salvation Army" (Unpublished Ph.D. Dissertation: University of Oxford, 1997), 30.

[103] John D. Gay, *The Geography of Religion in England* (London: Duckworth, 1971), 177-178.

[104] "A Year of Blessing: September 1907 - September 1908," *Confidence*, September 1908, 5.

[105] "Halifax (Yorkshire): A Note of Praise as to the Recent Conference," *Confidence*, December 1909, 275.

[106] "Into Our Fourth Year," *Showers of Blessing*, no. 8, n.d., 6.

SECTION ONE

Origins and Emergence

Introduction

This section will begin with the presentation of an overview of the size, scale, and nature of the Pentecostal movement as it came to assume an identifiable form from 1908 onwards. Wacker has highlighted Pentecostals' tendency toward an "extravagant assessment of their own importance"[1] and while superlative claims to having attained the status of being "the elite of the universe"[2] may convey an impression to the contrary, the movement will be shown to have been diminutive in numerical terms during much of the period under consideration. An outcome of this will be that the lingering assumptions of problematic historiographies characterised by romantic leanings and triumphant outlooks will be challenged by what follows.

A recent study of the "theologies" of American Pentecostalism prior to 1925 has advanced a "spiritual biography" for each of the "theological spokespersons of the first generation" which it considers. Its author argues the necessity of this in order to understand the "attitudes and priorities" of prominent protagonists amid the "boisterous beginnings" of the religious movement.[3] While in no sense attempting to provide a comprehensive or definitive biography of Alexander Boddy, Cecil Polhill or the other early leaders under consideration, pertinent aspects of their spiritual backgrounds and formative influences will be highlighted in an attempt to enact the injunction to "take very seriously the original *Sitz-im-Leben* of the figure involved."[4] Such details are introduced for their value in elucidating the origins and emergence of a recognizable Pentecostal movement on English soil. Consideration will be given, where appropriate and practicable, to the wider religious contexts in which Pentecostal Centres emerged. This will be shown to have occurred amid burgeoning evangelical activity and frequently against hinterlands characterised by religious cosmopolitanism as well as tendencies toward fragmentation and diversification. Insights will be provided into the process whereby the congregation, grouping or mission came into contact with, or under the

---

[1] Wacker, "Evangelical Responses to Pentecostalism," 505.

[2] T. M. Jeffreys, "A Retrospect of the Sunderland Convention," *Confidence*, June 1910, 127.

[3] Douglas Jacobsen, *Thinking in the Spirit: Theologies of the Early Pentecostal Movement* (Bloomington, IN.: Indiana University Press, 2003), xiii, 235.

[4] Robeck, "The Use of Biography in Pentecostal Historiography," 79.

influence of, Pentecostal teaching, typically through the sympathies of leadership. The manner in which this message was adopted and transmitted in particular Centres will be considered, and evidences of limited adoption and uneasy transition, as well as successful and effective inculcation, will be uncovered. Furthermore it will become apparent that local, national, and even international influences and dynamics impinged upon the four contexts represented. Significant exchanges and distinct centrifugal tendencies will be shown to have been operative in the spread and transmission of the Pentecostal message.

Section1.1: Overview of the Scale and Nature of the Emerging Movement

> In September 1907, during a visit of Pastor Barratt of Norway, the Holy Spirit commenced to fall in Sunderland. In 1908 the small showers of Latter Rain blessedly became a cloudburst, and by 1910 the land was being flooded by a deluge of Pentecostal power. In Sunderland the streams became a mighty river reaching Lytham, Preston, Bradford, and various towns in Wales, Scotland, and Ireland. Thousands were baptized in the Holy Ghost and spoke with new tongues, magnifying the Lord, who had put no difference between them and those mentioned in the tarrying company in Acts 2, having given them the same gift.[5]

This is the account, offered by Pentecostal publicist Stanley H. Frodsham, of the genesis and early fortunes of this movement in Britain. It is necessary in a study of this nature to delve behind hyperbole and generalisations and, in spite of other difficulties already acknowledged, to attempt to provide an overview and approximation of the size and scale of the movement in the period under consideration. It is interesting that the opening editorial of the first issue of *Confidence* stated that while some had suggested that this self-styled "Pentecostal Paper for Great Britain" could appropriately be called *Pentecost with Signs*, its chosen title reflected a deliberate intention of providing a "means of grace and of mutual encouragement" to "lonely ones and to scattered bands." These isolated and frequently beleaguered individuals were perceived to be in need of "*Confidence* that this work is of God," and of assurance that "His Pentecostal Blessing is spreading all the time."[6] Its editor, in response to the rhetorical question "What hath God wrought?" recounted that the previous year he was only aware of "some five or six persons in Great Britain who were in the experience." By the time of writing during the spring of 1908 this had grown to in excess of five hundred.[7]

---

[5] Frodsham, *With Signs Following: The Story of the Pentecostal Revival in the Twentieth Century* (Springfield, MS.: Gospel Publishing House, 1941), 61.

[6] Alexander A. Boddy, "'Confidence': Our First Number," *Confidence,* April 1908, 3. Hereafter it can be assumed that, unless stated otherwise, articles from periodicals are to be attributed to their respective editors.

[7] "Our First Number," *Confidence,* April 1908, 3.

A list of *Pentecostal Centres in Great Britain and Ireland* was presented as early as the fourth issue of *Confidence*. At this stage these comprised one in Ireland, three in Wales, eleven in Scotland and seventeen in England, of which only three were in the greater London area.[8] Taylor points out that if from the 500 initiates cited by Boddy, 70 of these individuals were resident in Sunderland, and the rest diffused in 34 Pentecostal Centres scattered across Britain, "simple division" would indicate that the remaining Centres were "small and struggling, averaging only some 13 to 15 glossolalists each."[9] These figures, while not necessarily of the strictest accuracy,[10] convey an approximate sense of the scale and proportions of the diminutive gatherings and congregations that formed the constituent parts of the emerging Pentecostal network. Gee, in the course of a commentary on Boddy's distinction that what had transpired was "quite different to 500 conversions,"[11] remarked of what he termed the "character of the early seekers":

> Those who had thus received were almost all of them experienced Christians, and many of them active workers...Almost all those who gathered in those comparatively small early Conventions, or still smaller prayer groups, were Christians of mature spiritual experience. Many of them were missionaries or workers, and they had often tasted a previous experience of the Spirit's grace and power in connection with the Holiness and Keswick Movements.[12]

While the suggestive number of 120 visitors[13] to the first Sunderland Convention from "all over Great Britain and many other lands" had surprised the hosts in 1908, it was recorded that subsequent attendances were "much larger."[14] The following year there were "over 300 delegates,"[15] and by 1910

---

[8] "Pentecostal Centres in Great Britain and Ireland," *Confidence*, July 1908, 2. A further list was presented in "The Pentecostal Movement," *Confidence*, August 1910, 196.

[9] Taylor, "Publish and Be Blessed," 343.

[10] In September 1908 Boddy stated that "about 100" had received a "definite Baptism of the Holy Ghost" in Sunderland. The majority of these were described as "long-distance visitors" while an estimation of "from thirty to forty" local individuals were said to have undergone the experience. See "A Year of Blessing," *Confidence*, September 1908, 4-5. While the first listing of July 1908 identified 32 Pentecostal Centres in the British Isles, 70 Centres were identified in 1910, although Boddy went on to offer the following disclaimer: "We are not officially connected with all these Centres, nor are any of us responsible for the actions of the others..." See "The Pentecostal Movement," *Confidence*, August 1910, 196.

[11] "Our First Number," *Confidence*, April 1908, 3.

[12] Gee, *The Pentecostal Movement*, 48-49.

[13] According to Acts chapter 1, verse 15, 120 disciples gathered in Jerusalem prior to the feast of Pentecost. *Upper room* parallelism was commonplace among those who saw themselves as latter-day inheritors of the mantel of Peter and the early Church.

[14] "The Pentecostal Movement," *Confidence*, August 1910, 196.

[15] "Sunderland International Pentecostal Congress: General Impressions,"

they found themselves "crowded to the doors and out into the street." The Parish Hall which could accommodate 700, was "very full." Boddy indeed welcomed the fact that while in 1908 Sunderland had "stood alone," it had been joined by many other similar events, of admittedly varying sizes, which advanced the message of "a full salvation and a Pentecost for all." His personal estimate was that by 1910, "more than a thousand" had received the 'Baptism of the Holy Spirit."[16]

There were 3,000 copies of the early issues of *Confidence* magazine, though admittedly a significant proportion of these were shipped overseas, as it achieved "international penetration"[17] within a surprisingly short space of time. Its editor's claim that it represented a "far-reaching, silent Missionary of God's Pentecostal Truth"[18] was confirmed by his meeting with subscribers from Georgia while undertaking a tour of North America during 1912. Boddy encountered others in Los Angeles, the fount of international Pentecostalism, and recorded that "it seemed like meeting old acquaintances." He found a pastor of a Methodist Episcopal Church "perusing a bound copy of *Confidence*" and availed of the opportunity, when reporting this, of publishing the particulars of those who could supply the periodical to other interested parties in the U.S.A.[19] It was this international dimension that necessitated the alteration of the frontispiece which from November 1911 declared it to be "A Pentecostal Paper for Great Britain and Other Lands."[20]

At the time of the launch of the third volume, Boddy pointed out that its circulation had increased to 4,000 per month, while making a plea for increased financial assistance. It was in this context that he estimated his readership to be in the region of 20,000.[21] This figure which, as Kay has stated, "looks rather high,"[22] was based on the supposition that each copy would come into the hands of an average of five readers. That this practice did occur is corroborated by Gee's recounting of the fact that as a young Congregationalist, he frequently

---

Confidence, June 1909, 127.

[16] "About the Convention," *Confidence*, June 1910, 128; "The Pentecostal Movement," *Confidence*, August 1910, 196.

[17] Taylor, "Publish and Be Blessed," 124.

[18] "The Cost of Issuing 'Confidence,'" *Confidence*, October 1909, 240.

[19] "In the Southern States," *Confidence*, September 1912, 209; "In Southern California," *Confidence*, November 1912, 245, 247; "'Confidence' in the U.S.A.," *Confidence*, November 1912, 258.

[20] *Confidence*, November 1911, 241. This contrasts with other publications such as Hutchinson's *Showers of Blessing* which carried the subtitle "Testimonies of Pentecostal Blessing and Work from Bournemouth and other places," and *The Pentecostal Witness* which described itself as "A Paper Principally for Scotland." See Taylor, "Publish and Be Blessed," 127; Appendix 3, 368.

[21] "The Third Volume of 'Confidence,'" *Confidence*, January 1910, 12.

[22] Kay, "Assemblies of God: Distinctive Continuity and Distinctive Change," in Warrington, ed., *Pentecostal Perspectives*, 42.

found his mother reading "loaned copies" of *Confidence*,[23] however, such an optimistic extrapolation does not furnish a reliable demographic for the number of Pentecostal adherents in Britain at this stage. A broader perspective on the relative scale of the emerging movement is obtained when it is considered in the light of the "vast output" of religious periodicals during the last quarter of the nineteenth-century, the dissemination of which had enabled Nonconformity "to draw and to hold its clientele."[24] While it has been observed that Methodism "rallied its forces and made fresh conquests" by virtue of such potent mediums as *The Methodist Times*, which under the editorship of Hugh Price Hughes (1847-1902) achieved a weekly circulation of 24,000 copies,[25] General Booth's *War Cry* had attained formidable weekly sales of 350,000 in 1883.[26] In comparison *Confidence* magazine - at the peak of its popularity selling a total of 4.000 copies (home and abroad) - catered for an interest group that was dwarfed by the Methodist constituency or adherents of the Salvation Army.

Kay also found it necessary to "speculate" on the number of congregations which "accepted the experience and functioned in a Pentecostal dimension." To this end he suggests that on the basis of the number of subscribers to *Redemption Tidings* magazine, assuming it to have functioned as something of a substitute to *Confidence* from 1925,[27] and the numbers who attended the conventions held at London's Kingsway Hall from July 1925,[28] a figure of "between 4,000 and 8,000 people"[29] is arrived at. A further "admittedly arbitrary figure" of 50 individuals per congregation is advanced, and on the basis of this British Pentecostalism could be said to have constituted

---

[23] Gee, *The Pentecostal Movement*, 46.

[24] Bebbington, *Victorian Nonconformity* (Bangor: Headstart History, 1992), 38-40.

[25] Alec R. Vidler, "The English Free Churches," chapter 12 of *The Church in an Age of Revolution* (London: Penguin Books, 1990), 143.

[26] Norman H. Murdoch, *Origins of the Salvation Army* (Knoxville: University of Tennessee Press, 1994), 122.

[27] In the second issue of the periodical it was suggested that a circulation of 10,000 could be achieved if every Pentecostal household ordered one copy. Six months later its editor J. Nelson Parr, more realistically, stated that the intention was to "increase circulation to 5,000 before the end of the year. See "Items of Interest," *Redemption Tidings*, October 1924, 15, and "Items of Interest," *Redemption Tidings*, April 1925, 13. Yet even this revised figure appears ambitious in the light of comparison with the American Assemblies of God's *Pentecostal Evangel* which had a circulation of 20,000 toward the end of 1924. See Stanley H. Frodsham, "Reports from Far and Near: U.S.A.," *Redemption Tidings*, December 1924, 16.

[28] Gee reported: "The meetings were out-and-away the biggest we have ever seen at Kingsway Hall through a long succession of Whitsuntides. We can truthfully say 'approaching 2,000' at some of the meetings; 1,500 to 1,600 would be a sober estimate." See "Kingsway 1925: The London Whitsuntide Convention," *Redemption Tidings*, July 1925, 2.

[29] Kay, "Assemblies of God," in Warrington, ed., *Pentecostal Perspectives*, 42.

somewhere between 80 and 160 congregations by 1925.[30] Denominational developments from that point onwards enable more precise quantification and on the basis of that Kay concludes: "Certainly the British Assemblies of God counted 200 congregations by 1929 and Elim 70 congregations in 1928...What we may suppose is that the number of tongues-speakers rose from about 500 in 1908 to approximately ten times that figure twenty years later."[31]

William Oliver Hutchinson who, as will become apparent, fostered a separate grouping within British Pentecostalism from 1911, had by the end of that year six assemblies in Scotland, eleven in England and thirteen in Wales that were in "active fellowship"[32] with their Bournemouth mentor. Pronounced disagreement on matters of polity and church governance resulted in further secession and the establishment of the Apostolic Church (*Yr Eglwys Apostolaidd*) in Pen-y-groes, Llanelli, in 1916. This involved a defection of some 19 congregations from Hutchinson's authority, and Kay has pointed out that thereafter his theological views became "increasingly divergent" from those of the majority of Pentecostals and evangelicals, while the denomination he had founded "shrunk to a tiny remnant."[33] The Apostolic Church, whose principal concentration remained in Wales, went on to establish a "wider Pentecostal network" numbering 23 congregations by 1920.[34] However a broader perspective on its scale is afforded by a recent historian who observed that, dwarfed by the "four great Nonconformist denominations" of Wales, it retained a "small knot of churches mainly in the valleys." While diminutive in scale, Morgan acknowledges its contribution to Welsh religious life: while "unsophisticated" and appealing mainly to a working-class constituency, "it afforded ordinary people a taste of the vitality and excitement of New Testament faith at its most elemental."[35]

Frank Bartleman, a Pentecostal luminary from California described by Wacker as an "Azusa pioneer,"[36] conducted an early tour of several British Pentecostal Centres. He recounted that while in Edinburgh he "was privileged to address a little company of hungry Saints...at a private home, opened for

---

[30] By the autumn of 1924 there were 74 Assemblies of God congregations while a further 6 were "applying for fellowship." See "General Presbytery of the Assemblies of God in Great Britain and Ireland," *Redemption Tidings*, October 1924, 24.

[31] Kay, "Assemblies of God," in Warrington, ed., *Pentecostal Perspectives*, 42-43.

[32] Weeks, "A History of the Apostolic Church," 42.

[33] Kay, *Pentecostals in Britain*, 18-19.

[34] Worsfold, *Origins of the Apostolic Church*, 169-170.

[35] Morgan, *Religion and Society in Wales*, 14-15. For an overview see Henry Byron Llewellyn, "A Study in the History and Thought of the Apostolic Church in Wales in the Context of Pentecostalism" (Unpublished M. Phil. Dissertation: University of Wales, 1997).

[36] Wacker, *Early Pentecostals*, 99-100. Bartleman went on to write *Azusa Street: The Roots of Modern-day Pentecost* (1925; repr. Plainfield, N.J.: Logos International, 1980).

Pentecost."[37] The image of a small group meeting in search of *Pentecost*, or ardent to celebrate its aftermath, is far from untypical. Boddy informed his readership that "our brother, Mr. H. Mogridge writes very hopefully of the Centre which meets in his home." The hope was expressed that the "days of difficulty" had passed and the homely, if somewhat isolated, spiritual experience of one of the members was recounted who:

> ...had been victorious in standing firm when much persuasion had been brought to bear upon her to give up. She went to her room in sheer desperation. She took her Bible with her, and bowed before the Lord and called upon Him to make all clear to her. Suddenly the room was filled with the glory of the Lord, and the vessel was soon overflowing with the love of God, and she began to praise the Lord in other Tongues.[38]

Mrs. S. A. Williams wrote on behalf of a group of eleven who had begun regular meetings in Trowbridge in Wiltshire (12 miles from Bath). She enquired about conferences in the vicinity and confessed that they were "longing for the full Baptism of the Holy Ghost, that the Life of the Lord Jesus Christ in us may be manifested to others." She requested prayer "that the Holy Fire may fall on us", and concluded with the request: "Please consider the address as a Centre for Pentecostal Meetings."[39] Another notice in *Confidence* which included a statement from a "Brother Maynard" in Sussex, demonstrates that what has been described as "the ethic of the bootstrap,"[40] so characteristic of small-scale Protestant endeavours of late nineteenth-century England, was very much in evidence in the formation and functioning of many small Pentecostal Centres. It related that:

> A Pentecostal Centre has been formed at the Connaught Mission at Burgess Hill, Brother Long, the leader, having received the 'Baptism'. Brother Maynard writes: 'The Saints are not able to supply a man yet, so I am stepping out on faith lines as Pentecostal Colporteur with Books, Bibles, Texts, etc.'[41]

Another interesting feature that becomes apparent is the exercise of authority in terms of the recognition and functioning of a *de facto* membership of this emerging network. It is evident that this appears in a number of guises and operates at a number of levels. The readership was informed that a William Black from Woodhouse, Nottinghamshire, described as "our Evangelist friend," was exercising "charge of a Mission...and would like to make it a Pentecostal

---

[37] "Brother Bartleman: His Visits to British Pentecostal Centres," *Confidence*, August 1910, 185, 187.

[38] "Brief Notes," *Confidence*, April 1910, 86-87.

[39] "Pentecostal News: Wiltshire," *Confidence*, August 1910, 188.

[40] Lineham, "The Protestant Sects," in Paz, ed., *Nineteenth-Century English Religious Traditions*, 152.

[41] "Pentecostal News," *Confidence*, July 1910, 165.

Centre." His credentials for such an undertaking were conveyed in the qualification that he had "received his Baptism at Sunderland Convention two years ago."[42] Black could therefore, in the terminology employed by Wilson, be said to have satisfied "tests of merit" and performed "an act/s of subscription."[43] Similar discrimination appears under the heading "A Note as to Impulsive Giving" which states: "We would like to remind our brethren, especially where there are Pentecostal Centres, that while we are always glad to welcome accredited brethren...," caution was urged against the danger of rashly responding to emotional appeals for "financial support."[44] Another instance of this is to be seen in the publicised functioning of "Brother Mr. J. Miller's 'House of Rest' for Boarders" in Glasgow. He was, it was announced, "always glad to welcome any of God's dear Pentecostal children as they visit and pass through Glasgow (provided, of course, that they can authenticate satisfactorily their integrity)."[45]

These brief instances serve to undermine the perspective that what Robinson terms "the Boddy era" permitted "free rein to roving freelance figures" and rendered them beyond directive or accountability.[46] Interestingly, in the context of a retrospective, if veiled, reference to Boddy's experience and methodology, it was acknowledged by later denominational Pentecostals that there had been "great trouble at the beginning of this great outpouring of the Spirit" when "grievous wolves" had sought to infiltrate and sully the "pure godly testimony." Precautions remarkably reminiscent of those advanced by Boddy almost two decades previously were enjoined so that the then consolidating Assemblies of God might "be safeguarded against evil men, seducers and false teachers."[47] From its emergence in the Edwardian period, Boddy's Pentecostal conglomeration fulfilled the dual aspirations which he shared with other leaders who recognized the need for organization and the benefits of association, while simultaneously eschewing the inclination to establish a new denomination or church body. The notion of the Pentecostal Centre seemed to allow those who chose to identify themselves with the cause to do so without renouncing existing allegiances and, to that extent, the emerging network could be said to have fulfilled a para-church, or trans-denominational function.[48]

---

[42] "Pentecostal Items," *Confidence*, March 1911, 62.

[43] Bryan Wilson, *Religious Sects: A Sociological Study* (London: Weidenfeld and Nicolson, 1970), 29-30.

[44] "A Note as to Impulsive Giving," *Confidence*, August 1910, 198.

[45] "Pentecostal Items," *Confidence*, March 1911, 62.

[46] Robinson, *Early Pentecostalism in Ireland*, 70.

[47] J. Nelson Parr, "Items of Interest: False Teachers," *Redemption Tidings*, June 1926, 9.

[48] This ethos was shared by the Faith Missions whether missionary or domestic. See Klaus Fielder, *The Story of Faith Missions: From Hudson Taylor to Present Day Africa* (Oxford: Regnum Books, 1994), 173, and T. Rennie Warburton, "The Faith Mission: A Study in Interdenominationalism," in David Martin, ed., *Sociological Yearbook of Religion in Britain*, vol. 2 (London: SCM Press, 1969), 75-102.

While not without its limitations, the Centre presents a useful framework for the examination of this nascent spiritual movement in its earliest manifestations. By 1910 the union comprised of in the region of a thousand individual glossolalists drawn from a variety of churches, mission halls, and domestic fellowships across a wide geographical area, and their predominantly lay-oriented, voluntaristic association is arguably best observed in terms of this localised means of Pentecostal attachment. It is toward an appreciation of the nucleus or epicentre of this emerging movement that attention is now turned.

Section1.2: Historical Locality - Sunderland

Formative Years and Pre-Pentecostal Ministry of Rev. Alexander A. Boddy

All Saints' Church, Monkwearmouth, Sunderland, had been described in the middle of the nineteenth-century as "a handsome stone building in the early English style."[49] Erected in 1848, it had been designed by John Dobson (1787-1865) who, in addition to his work in town planning and prison building, notably specialised in churches of the "non-ecclesiological type." This designation confirms that he did not subscribe to, or derive inspiration from, a philosophy of church building which saw the enactment of the English rite as most appropriately observed in the context of long chancels, choir stalls, fonts and raised altars frontals, altar crosses - an approach which necessitated a return to the lavish ornateness of the Gothic style.[50] All Saints', in contradistinction, had been designed to fulfil a more pedestrian but pressing need which the Church of England was increasingly encountering in the early Victorian period - the imperative of maintaining a credible presence among the urban poor.[51]

That the original ideals for All Saints' had not been realised owed much to the fact that the Rev. Benjamin Kennicott, its first incumbent had "taken to drink and emptied his church."[52] It was on a November evening when he had been in Holy Orders for four years that Alexander Boddy was summoned by his "sturdy, saintly Bishop" to the "sanctum" at Auckland. There a map was unfurled, a parish was identified, and "things that were sad indeed" were brought to the attention of the prospective young vicar, who was duly informed

---

[49] William Whellan, *History, Topography and Directory of the County Palatine of Durham* (London: Whittaker and Co., 1856), 662.

[50] Basil F. L. Clarke, *Church Builders of the Nineteenth Century: A Study of the Gothic Revival in England* (1938; repr. Trowbridge: Redwood Press, 1969), 253-254, 75.

[51] On this see Geoffrey E. Milburn, "Religion in Sunderland in the Mid-Nineteenth Century," Unpublished Occasional Paper No. 3 (Department of Geography and History, Sunderland Polytechnic, 1983), 25. For a more general commentary on this phenomenon see Robin Gill, *The Myth of the Empty Church* (London: SPCK, 1993), 117-118.

[52] Jane Vazeille Boddy, *Alexander Alfred Boddy, 1854-1930* (Unpublished manuscript), 1. This posthumous *Memoir* of her father is believed to have been written c. 1970. See Kay, *Inside Story*, 40.

by J. B. Lightfoot his ecclesiastical superior that he was being thrust "in the front of the battle."[53] The young clergyman was then faced with the not insignificant challenges later pithily summarized as encompassing "an empty church, neglected grounds, and a derelict vicarage set in a slum district."[54] Boddy was quick to embark upon a course of renovation which would render his vicarage more habitable and the church pews more populated. His longstanding ecumenical disposition, something which had been encouraged by the Bishop of Durham among his clergy,[55] ensured that he had no difficulty in utilising a Chapel belonging to the United Methodist Free Church while reconstruction and repairs were carried out. Geoffrey Milburn, a religious historian with a particular interest in the locality, has pointed out that across Sunderland, but particularly in Monkwearmouth and Bishopwearmouth as they developed, Nonconformity and especially Methodism, were dominant forces in the religious and social life of the town.[56] A general mission was held in Sunderland during the autumn of 1890 and a Canon Grant from Kent conducted the campaign in the then renovated All Saints' Church. This venture was to have the unforeseen benefit of introducing Boddy to his future wife: the Rev. James Pollock who had come to serve as Boddy's curate had enlisted his sister among the "several lady workers" who came to offer assistance.[57] Herself the daughter of a Rector from Yorkshire, Mary was unaccustomed to deprived urban surroundings, yet in time she came to accept not only this but Alexander's proposal of marriage. They were married in 1891 and children followed in 1892, 1893, and 1895. Their two daughters were called Mary Vazeille and Jane Vazeille respectively, an indication of Boddy's concern for the continuity of this French Huguenot name.[58]

---

[53] "From Sunderland to Pittington: The Recent Removal of Rev. A. A. Boddy, Editor of *Confidence*," *Confidence*, January-March 1923, 64. This is probably the most detailed piece of autobiographical writing which Boddy has bequeathed to posterity. It was written as a retrospective of his almost four decades at All Saints', Monkwearmouth, on the occasion of his removal to Pittington, a country parish six miles from Durham.

[54] J. V. Boddy, *Memoir*, 1-2.

[55] Milburn observes that in his episcopal capacity Lightfoot had exerted "a profound influence" in fostering an irenic outlook among his clergy and lay leaders. To this end it is pointed out that in a speech made in Sunderland in 1886, the "saintly bishop" had advocated that the "truest Churchmen are those whose minds are most open to the lessons which can be gathered from all quarters." See "Church and Chapel in Sunderland 1780-1914," Unpublished Occasional Paper No. 4 (Department of Geography and History, Sunderland Polytechnic, 1988), 50.

[56] Milburn, "Religion in Sunderland in the Mid-Nineteenth Century," 43.

[57] "From Sunderland to Pittington," *Confidence*, January-March 1923, 66.

[58] The third son of Rev. James Boddy, Rector of St. Thomas' Church in Cheetham, Manchester, Alexander was in fact the great grandson of John Wesley's wife, Mary Vazeille. According to Lavin he was determined to bestow this French Huguenot name, and its associations, on his daughters. He also attributes Boddy's "generous spirit" in

Boddy's irenic outlook also owed much to his exposure to foreign cultures and customs which, among other things, consolidated an enduring distaste for religious intolerance. Before ordination he had travelled in "Barbary" or Tripoli and Tunisia. His first book *To Kairwan the Holy: Scenes in Muhammedan Africa*, published in 1885, describes his visit to the Mosque of Okhbah where he examined and touched the exquisite carvings and "stood actually on the holiest spot in Muhammedan Africa."[59] It was by virtue of this publication that he was made a Fellow of the Royal Geographical Society, an honour which was bestowed on him in the same year.[60] Instances of "unfortunate Israelites" condemned to die by the swallowing of molten lead, severed heads kicked through the streets, and religiously motivated stonings prompted a deep antipathy toward what he pejoratively termed "zeal for religion." While in north Africa he significantly established a rapport with a Father Angelo di Sant' Agata stating that "religious differences" were "much diminished" in that context, and expressing the developing conviction that "a conscientious servant of his Master, like Father Angelo, is deserving of all respect, even from those who look at the Truth from a different standpoint." When the self-designated "Wanderer from the Isles of the North"[61] returned to his urban parish, it was with his horizons evidently broadened and his sympathies irrevocably deepened.

As vicar of All Saints' parish, Boddy went some way toward embodying a phenomenon which McLeod observes to have been peculiar to this period of England's social and industrial evolution; the so called "slum priest," or man who devoted his life's work to an urban working-class parish and sought, in the process, to identify himself as wholly as possible with the life of its people.[62] Prior to his involvement in Pentecostal matters Boddy had particularly enjoyed gathering "young and old" on Fulwell Village green during the summer months where he would array before them "magic lantern lectures" by means of a sheet outside and a lantern inside a cottage window. He later recalled with some fondness how "old Mr. Allison and Mr. Edwin Hutchinson" would sit on their chairs in the open air, engaged by his Bible talks and frequently posing "quaint questions."[63] In 1912 Boddy sought to appraise the by then international readership of *Confidence* magazine of the situation in which he tended his flock. All Saints' stood "in the midst of industry." A "great Rope Manufactory," which employed hundreds of both men and women, extended along two sides of the church. On the other side was an iron works the furnaces

---

part at least to what he terms this "Methodist Connection." See Lavin, *Alexander Boddy*, 14. For comments on Boddy's "catholicity of spirit" see also Robinson, "The Charismatic Anglican," 19-20.

[59] Boddy, *To Kairwan the Holy: Scenes in Muhammedan Africa* (London: Kegan Paul, Trench & Co., 1885), 177.

[60] *Crockford's Clerical Directory*, 122-123.

[61] Boddy, *Scenes in...*, 244, 120, 165.

[62] McLeod, *Religion and Society in England*, 19.

[63] "From Sunderland to Pittington," *Confidence*, January-March 1923, 65.

of which blazed "night and day." Amid "great steam hammers with resounding and colossal blows, driving dross out of great masses of soft and glowing metal," Boddy revealed: "We live and worship above one of the deepest of the British coal mines - Monkwearmouth Colliery, or 'Pemberton's Pit' as it is often called."[64]

It is interesting to note that amid such circumstances, in the assessment of his daughter, "it was as a faithful parish priest that he did his best work. He loved his people and they loved him, for he never spared himself and was available day and night."[65] A potent indicator of the intensity of Boddy's social concern was his personal and protracted involvement in what he termed "the Coal Famine of 1892."[66] When the market curve of coal prices had followed a downward trajectory for some time and pit owners sought to enforce a significant wage reduction, the resultant impasse was only surmounted on the intervention of Bishop Westcott.[67] Of his role it was somewhat ironically observed:

> That Bishop Westcott should have induced the Durham mine-owners just to be content with beating the men without mercilessly punishing them for their presumption in striking, was hailed by the workers of County Durham as a marvellous and hitherto unheard-of act of Christian statesmanship.[68]

The "extraordinary sensation" caused by this act of arbitration was cited as "further proof" of the persistent "gulf between Church and Labour."[69] Yet there was scant evidence of any such gulf in All Saints' parish as Boddy entertained neither reticence nor reluctance to appeal for support for "sufferers" from the adjoining iron works. He formed a committee among the men and by virtue of this they and their families were "fed and helped" for many months. When the worst of the travail was past, what he regarded as a "remarkable gathering" was held at Mr. Lister's café on Roker's Lower Promenade. The proprietor himself made a "memorable and rousing speech" after breakfast had been consumed and the men assembled then proceeded with the presentation of a silver communion set to Alexander and a decorative urn to Mrs. Boddy. The prominence given to this episode in what was Boddy's valedictory address to his parishioners betrays his estimation of this aspect of a thirty-eight year tenure in Sunderland. This Christian statesmanship enacted at a local level was

[64] "A Church Over a Coal Mine," *Confidence*, April 1912, 87.
[65] J. V. Boddy, *Memoir*, 3.
[66] "From Sunderland to Pittington," *Confidence*, January-March 1923, 65.
[67] David Douglas, "Pit Life in Co. Durham: Rank and File Movements and Workers' Control," History Workshop Pamphlets No. 6 (1972), 59.
[68] Conrad Noel, "Organized Labour: The Working Classes," in W. K. Lowther Clarke, ed., *Facing the Facts, or An Englishman's Religion* (London: Nisbet, 1911), 104.
[69] Noel, "Organized Labour," in Lowther Clarke, ed., *An Englishman's Religion*, 103.

retrospectively deemed to have been one of his principal achievements while at All Saints' and the tokens of gratitude which had been presented were, three decades later, "very highly prized today in remembrance of those stirring times."[70] Boddy's capacity to relate across social groupings found further expression during his later Pentecostal involvement and was evidenced by the fact that he was keen to portray the Sunderland Convention as attracting "many of the artisan class" in addition to "people in well-to-do circumstances."[71]

Healing, Holiness and Revival

In his brief overview of Boddy's ministry, Wakefield describes him as "not just a great physical traveller, but also a spiritual searcher."[72] Interestingly Jane Vazeille's designation of her father as a "pioneer in the movement toward Spiritual Healing"[73] relates to a disposition which predated the advent of Pentecost by some considerable time. When *Lloyd's Weekly* reported on events at All Saints' during the autumn of 1907, Boddy was identified as a vicar who "for a long while has preached healing by faith."[74] In a paper presented to the Durham Junior Clergy Society in 1910 on the subject of divine healing, he himself stated:

> There was a time in the writer's experience when it was harder to stand for this Truth than it is today. Ten years ago he was very much alone, but today, Bishops and Christian Leaders are sympathetically examining into it. The writer is thankful that he has been kept true.[75]

Mary Boddy's healing from asthma in 1899 was probably the most instrumental influence in this direction.[76] Lavin surmises that Alexander's interest may have, at least to an extent, been aroused by the colourful American evangelist Dr. John Alexander Dowie (1847-1907) who founded a would-be religious utopia, Zion City, Illinois, in 1896.[77] Boddy certainly visited Zion City

---

[70] "From Sunderland to Pittington," *Confidence*, January-March 1923, 66.

[71] "The Pentecostal Movement," *Confidence*, August 1910, 195.

[72] Wakefield, *The First Pentecostal Anglican*, 6.

[73] J. V. Boddy, *Memoir*, 5.

[74] "Revival Scenes: Incoherent Ravings Interpreted as Heavenly Languages," *Lloyd's Weekly* October 6, 1907, 6.

[75] "Faith Healing," *Confidence*, January 1910, 15.

[76] "Pentecost at Sunderland: The Testimony of a Vicar's Wife" (Unpublished pamphlet, Donald Gee Centre for Pentecostal and Charismatic Research - hereafter DCG).

[77] Lavin, *Alexander Boddy*, 36-37. On Dowie see Grant Wacker, Chris R. Armstrong, and Jay S. F. Blossom, "John Alexander Dowie: Harbinger of Pentecostal Power," in James R. Godd and Grant Wacker, eds., *Portraits of a Generation: Early Pentecostal Leaders* (Fayetteville: University of Arkansas Press, 2002), 3-19, and Nancy A. Hardesty, *Faith Cure: Divine Healing in the Holiness and Pentecostal*

on a transatlantic visit during 1913. By this time Dowie was no longer alive, and the heady days of optimism and experiment were truly over, yet the fact that he included it in his itinerary and provided an extensive account for readers of *Confidence*, is indicative of a degree of fascination on the part of some who had gravitated toward Pentecostal things in the early years of the century.[78] Dowie had certainly attained a significant public profile on this side of the Atlantic earning himself inclusion in James Joyce's epic novel *Ulysses*.[79] Whatever the influence from this direction may have been, Boddy was not above the injection of some Anglican ceremonial into his endeavours toward the attainment of divine healing. While from February 1899 Mary Boddy was persuaded of the veracity of an inherent gift of healing and as a consequence found herself frequently ministering to the sick,[80] according to Jane Vazeille, her father never claimed to possess any such spiritual endowment. He did, however, conduct the service of Anointing the Sick as an element of regular worship in All Saints'.[81] That healing was also a feature of domestic life in the vicarage is attested by his daughter's recollection:

In our family we rarely saw a doctor. If we were sick my father would anoint, and my mother lay her hands on us for healing and we accepted this as the normal procedure...Spiritual healing was accepted in our parish as the right thing, and there were some wonderful healings.[82]

Perhaps the most significant of Boddy's pre-1907 involvements with spiritual forward movements[83] was his association with the Pentecostal League of Prayer, established by Reader Harris in 1891 in order to "spread Scriptural Holiness by unsectarian methods."[84] It has been observed that the Holiness movement "crystallized out as a distinctly organized expression of religious

---

Movements (Peabody, MS.: Hendrickson, 2003), 51-53, 67-68, 110-113.

[78] For Boddy's descriptive account of his visit to Zion City which is replete with incisive comment see "Transatlantic Experiences," *Confidence*, February 1913, 33, 36-39.

[79] In the narrative a "sombre YMCA young man placed a throwaway in the hand of Mr. Bloom" as his ambled through the streets of Dublin. Here he read "Elijah is coming. Dr. John Alexander Dowie, restorer of the Church in Zion is coming..." See James Joyce, *Ulysses* (London: Penguin Books, 2000), 190.

[80] "Pentecost at Sunderland: The Testimony of a Vicar's Wife" (DCG).

[81] Boddy outlined a methodology which he had employed "since about 1892" in an article "The Anointing with Oil: James v., 13-16," *Confidence*, April-June 1922, 21-22.

[82] J. V. Boddy, *Memoir*, 5.

[83] Hugh Price Hughes (1847-1902) had been the prime mover in Methodism's *forward movement*, a phenomenon by means of which the denomination "rallied its forces and made fresh conquests." Vidler, *The Church in an Age of Revolution*, 143.

[84] Mary Howard Hooker, *Adventures of An Agnostic: Life and Letters of Reader Harris, Q.C.* (London: Marshall, Morgan & Scott, 1959), 111.

faith" on both sides of the Atlantic from the middle of the nineteenth-century.[85] While the Keswick Holiness movement which grew around the annual convention founded by Canon Harford Battersby at his Derwent-water parish remained predominantly Anglican, a variety of lesser Holiness bodies had begun to emerge and Bebbington has located the Pentecostal League within the ambit of what he deems this Holiness "sectarian fringe."[86] Similar groups included the Faith Mission in Scotland and the Star Hall in Manchester, neither of which sought to draw members away from their own churches, but rather to function as interdenominational societies whose intention was to supplement, with a view to enhancing participants' involvement in their own church of origin. Mirroring the assessment advanced by Bebbington, Warburton has suggested that association with such groupings appealed primarily to those "on the fringe of Protestant church life."[87] Harris is unlikely to have welcomed such a designation as he conceived of his League, at least in aspirational terms, as "an undenominational society that labours equally in cathedral, church, chapel, or mission hall."[88]

Of the nuanced understandings which emerged among Holiness advocates,[89] perhaps the most significant and certainly the most pertinent to developments in Sunderland, was the association of sanctification with a *filling* or *baptism* of the Spirit.[90] According to Gee who was mindful of the significance of these categories for developing Pentecostal understandings, the term *Baptism of the Holy Spirit* was employed in Holiness parlance to convey a "sense of real

---

[85] T. Rennie Warburton, "A Comparative Study of Minority Religious Groups: With Special Reference to Holiness and Related Movements in Britain in the last 50 Years" (Unpublished Ph. D. thesis, University of London, 1966), 37. For a comprehensive treatment see Melvin E. Dieter, *The Holiness Revival of the Nineteenth Century*, 2nd ed. (Lanham, Md. and London: Scarecrow Press, 1996).

[86] Bebbington, *Evangelicalism in Modern Britain*, 178.

[87] Warburton, "The Faith Mission," 100.

[88] "Editorials: Opposers and their Objections," *Tongues of Fire*, May 1905, 6.

[89] The most incisive overview and exploration of variant, indeed at times rival conceptions, was delivered by David Bebbington in his capacity as Didsbury Lecturer in 1998. This series of lectures, delivered at the Nazarene Theological College near Manchester, was published as *Holiness in Nineteenth-Century England* (Carlisle: Paternoster Press, 2000). On this see also Jack Ford, *What the Holiness People Believe: A Mid-Century Review of Holiness Teaching among the Holiness Groups of Britain* J. D. Drysdale Memorial Lecture 1954 (Birkenhead: Emmanuel Bible College, 1954). For pertinent comments on the distinction between Keswick and Wesleyan emphases see Randall, "Relationships between Pentecostalism and Evangelical Spirituality in England," 54-57.

[90] See Donald W. Dayton, "From 'Christian Perfection' to the 'Baptism of the Holy Spirit'" in *Aspects of Pentecostal-Charismatic Origins*, ed. Vinson Synan, (Plainfield, N. J.: Logos International, 1975), 43-47. For a British perspective on this "pneumatological shift" see Randall, *Study in the Spirituality of English Evangelicalism*, 30-33.

spiritual crisis for the Christian subsequent to regeneration." The emphasis was firmly upon "cleansing from sin...the 'Baptism' was essentially a purifying baptism, and the 'Fire' was refining fire."[91] Significant impetus in this direction had followed the publication of William Arthur's *The Tongue of Fire* in 1856. This Irish Methodist had espoused the notion of spiritual baptism as requisite if the Christian Church were to rediscover "primitive power" and embark upon an "age of opportunity."[92] Among the leading figures of the Keswick constellation was Andrew Murray who came to prominently advocate a "baptism of the Holy Spirit" and deemed this the "crown and glory of Jesus' work."[93] The title chosen by Harris for both his organisation and its monthly periodical, *Tongues of Fire*, therefore, reflected a terminology increasing in vogue across the Holiness fraternity during the latter decades of the nineteenth century. Bebbington has commented on Arthur's use of "oblique genteel language" which served to "tone down the distinctiveness of the experience" in view of the fact that radically-inclined professions of perfection and instantaneous holiness might have disturbed the equanimity of Victorian suburbia.[94] Expressions of distaste and disapproval at Pentecostals' subsequent claims to having experimentally attained their spiritual ideals are at least partly illuminated by similar considerations.

Harris' daughter and biographer recorded that by 1898 Plymouth and Sunderland were "particularly flourishing" among the Pentecostal League's provincial Centres.[95] This is borne out by the sales figures for the official organ of the League. Sunderland's monthly total of 72.5 dozen repeatedly outstripped those of Manchester, which at 30 dozen, represented the League's second most

---

[91] Gee, *The Pentecostal Movement*, 4.

[92] William Arthur, *The Tongue of Fire; or the True Power of Christianity* Peoples' Edition (London: Charles H. Kelly, 1856), 208. On Arthur see Norman W. Taggart, *William Arthur: First Among Methodists* (London: Epworth Press, 1993). The significance of *The Tongue of Fire* and the evocation of such imagery has been heralded as instrumental in instigating a "symbolic turn" or "semantic cut" which would "cut...the ties" with the received "order" and "interpretations of the mainline churches." While this analysis of ecclesiological implications for Pentecostal Christianity is contendable, the highlighting of the significance of this efflorescence of 'Pentecostal' terminology is entirely apt. See Wolfgang Vondey, "The Symbolic Turn: A Symbolic Conception of the Liturgy of Pentecostalism," *Wesleyan Theological Journal* 36.2 (Fall 2001): 238-241.

[93] Andrew Murray, *The Spirit of Christ: Thoughts on the Indwelling of the Holy Spirit in the Believer and the Church* (London: Nisbet & Co., 1888), 29.

[94] Bebbington, "Holiness in the Evangelical Tradition," in Stephen C. Barton, ed., *Holiness Past and Present* (London and New York: T. & T. Clark, 2003), 307-308.

[95] Howard Hooker, *Life and Letters*, 116. Wakefield offers insights into Sunderland's religious heritage and suggests that as a locality it was positively disposed to the acceptance of "the new religious experience." See his *Pentecostal Anglican Pioneer*, 94-99.

prolific outlet.[96] During the early years of the twentieth century a general monthly meeting was held at the Subscription Library Hall, Fawcett Street, and the "Rev. Alex. A. Boddy" was publicised as one of the leading clergymen associated with the League. Indeed it would appear that he was the only local representative of Church allegiance, the other eight individuals presented being drawn from a range of Nonconformist and independent bodies.[97] An estimation of the level of Boddy's involvement, as well as the esteem in which he was held, is evident from the fact that he was invited to address the League's annual conference which was held at Speke Hall, Battersea, on May 3rd, 1905.[98]

It is also the case that the message presented on that occasion affords fascinating insights into interests and preoccupations which would predispose him toward acceptance of the Pentecostal phenomena he would encounter less than two years later. The Pentecostal League of Prayer promoted itself as "an inter-denominational union of Christian people," who employed prayer as the chief instrument toward the attainment of their three-fold aims: "the filling of the Holy Spirit for all believers," "revival in the Churches," and "the spread of Scriptural holiness."[99] In the course of an address which took Revelation chapter 22, verse 1, as its text and emphasised the "living water" which would come "via Wales, into thirsty England," Boddy spoke of how involvement with the League had brought significant "blessing" into his own church and parish. He admitted that he had initially entertained some prejudices "as a Church clergyman" against the League and its methods, but these had been more than overcome. Since his active involvement All Saints' had become "a centre of attraction for many" whose aspiration was to "go all the way" with Christ.[100]

Boddy stated his gratitude for the fact that his association with the League had brought him in contact with what he called "a larger world of Spirit-filled brothers and sisters." He spoke of the "mighty blessing" which had occurred at All Saints' only the week before under the influence of a "strong Pentecostal Leaguer," his brother-in-law and former curate, the Rev. J. M. Pollock. While the visitor conducted his mission, "the power of God began to fall," and Boddy confessed that what he had witnessed while with Evan Roberts in Wales did not compare to what occurred in his own parish on this occasion. He cited one

---

[96] See "'Tongues of Fire' Sales," *Tongues of Fire*, May 1905, 10; "'Tongues of Fire' Sales," *Tongues of Fire*, September 1905, 10.

[97] "Pentecostal League Centre Meetings," *Tongues of Fire*, January 1905, 11. This pattern was repeated across England and it has been pointed out on the basis of listings of local secretaries that Boddy was one of only five Anglican clergy to act as representatives for the League in 1905. Of the monthly listings provided see for instance "Pentecostal League Centre Meetings," *Tongues of Fire*, May 1905, 11. For comments on this lay and Free Church preponderance see Geoffrey Norman Fewkes, "Richard Reader Harris, 1847-1909: An Assessment of the Life and Influence of a Leader of the Holiness Movement" (M.A. dissertation: Victoria University of Manchester, 1995), 46.

[98] "The Annual Meetings: Rev. Alex. A. Boddy," *Tongues of Fire*, June 1905, 3.

[99] Howard Hooker, *Life and Letters*, 111.

[100] "The Annual Meetings," *Tongues of Fire*, June 1905, 3.

instance of a "refined lady," a leader of the Young Women's Christian Association in Sunderland, who had been "overwhelmed with the power of the Holy Ghost."[101] By July of 1905 gratitude was being expressed before the readership of the League's official organ "for the outpouring of the Holy Spirit upon the young men at All Saints' Church, Monkwearmouth."[102]

These fascinating insights serve to elucidate not only what was occurring at All Saints' prior to 1907, but also to uncover something of the outlook and aspirations of the League and its sympathisers. For fourteen years Harris and his associated had prayed for "the Holy Spirit" and for "revival among believers." The pages of *Tongues of Fire* are imbued with a palpable sense of expectancy: God wanted to deal not just with the Welsh but with "many others." Providential dealings with Great Britain had, it was asserted, always been preceded by revivals of religion and anticipation for the future could scarcely have been higher. "Revival is verily in the air,"[103] Harris declaimed while raising the prospect of a "sweeping" phenomenon expected by "so many earnest believers…as the immediate precursor of the Second Coming of the Lord."[104] That such aspirations had been thoroughly adopted is substantiated by Jane Vazeille's statement that it was "about 1906" that her parents began to feel the need for spiritual awakening in the parish, and established a weekly prayer meeting in the Vicarage to that end. She retained memories of the sincerity and intensity of those involved and more than six decades later wrote: "I still remember the fervour of their extemporary prayers."[105] According to Boddy, prominent among this "gathering of hungry ones at Sunderland" was a "little circle of earnest young men," as well as many who had been "helped by the writer's dear wife, who had ministered to them, especially in the healing of the sick."[106]

Boddy's sharing a pulpit with Evan Roberts in the Rhondda Valley, already mentioned in connection with his address at Speke Hall, was recounted five years later for the readers of *Confidence*. In 1910 he related how the leading figure of the Revival of 1904-5 had sent him home with a succinct if determinedly Arminianizing message for those in Sunderland: "They must fight Heaven down, they must fight it down."[107] Little is known about this encounter beyond Boddy's cursory mention of it.[108] Perhaps of greater significance than matters of detail, however, is the fact that its occurrence demonstrated Boddy to

---

[101] "The Annual Meetings," *Tongues of Fire*, June 1905, 3.

[102] "Requests for Prayer," *Tongues of Fire*, July 1905, 9.

[103] "Editorials," *Tongues of Fire*, January 1905, 6.

[104] "Editorials," *Tongues of Fire*, October 1905, 6

[105] J. V. Boddy, *Memoir*, 5.

[106] "The Pentecostal Movement," *Confidence*, August 1910, 194-195.

[107] "The Pentecostal Movement," *Confidence*, August 1910, 193. Warburton has commented on a "simplified Arminianism" which characterised Britain's Holiness sectarian fringe. See "The Faith Mission," 75.

[108] The encounter was also mentioned without elaboration in "Tongues in Norway: A Pentecostal Experience," *Leaflets on Tongues* No. 6 (DCG).

have been a clergyman of searching disposition and to locate him at the forefront of a certain type of inquisitive evangelical spirituality. In his chronicle of British Pentecostalism, Gee aptly summarized the effects of what had occurred in Wales in terms both of expectations generated, and the direction of future outcomes:

> Men justly asked 'Why Wales only?' Why not other lands? Why not a world-wide Revival? Prayer to that end received a tremendous new impetus...Faith was rising to visualise a return to apostolic Christianity in all its pristine beauty and power...In this manner the spiritual soil was prepared in the providence of God for the rise of the Pentecostal movement. Of special interest to British people is the little group that gathered around the godly vicar of All Saints' Parish Church, Sunderland.[109]

It was among this group that T. B. Barratt (1862-1940) arrived amid "rejoicing" on the evening of 31st August, 1907.[110] This British born presiding elder of Norway's Methodist Episcopal Church had visited New York during 1906, and while experiencing financial disappointment there, had undergone a Pentecostal experience which would radically alter his subsequent ministry as well as having significant ramifications for some who had hitherto involved themselves in England's Holiness fraternity. What transpired after his return to Norway would earn him the posthumous designations "spiritual father"[111] and "apostle"[112] of the Pentecostal movement in Europe. In the memoir which he compiled Barratt stated:

> Ministers and evangelists came from neighbouring lands in Scandinavia, as well as from England and Germany. One of the first to visit us was the Rev. Alex. A. Boddy, vicar of All Saints' parish, Sunderland, England. He came, not only to see the revival, but also to get a blessing for his own hungry soul. Ever since his visit he pressed me to visit his church...[113]

Spiritual hunger was a theme that was both dominant and recurring among these early writers - Boddy himself identified the *raison d'être* of the movement as "to meet and satisfy a very hungry people."[114] At this stage he described how he had heard that in Norway the "Pentecostal Gift of Tongues" was "witnessing to the incoming of the Holy Spirit in power." The deliberate and explicit association of this charismatic gift with the baptism of the Holy

---

[109] Gee, *The Pentecostal Movement*, 6.

[110] "Tongues in Sunderland: The Beginnings of a Pentecost for England," *Leaflets on Tongues* No. 9 (DGC).

[111] Gee, *The Pentecostal Movement*, 180.

[112] Nils Bloch-Hoell, *The Pentecostal Movement: Its Origins, Development and Distinctive Character* (Oslo and London: Universitatsforlaget, 1964), 75.

[113] T. B. Barratt, *When the Fire Fell and An Outline of My Life* (Oslo: Alfons Hansen & Sonner, 1927), 143.

[114] "The Pentecostal Movement," *Confidence*, August 1910, 193.

Spirit would prove to be a radical departure, but Boddy was buoyant with expectation. That his experience had again been surpassed is evident from the tract in which he declared: "My four days in Christiania cannot be forgotten. I stood with Evan Roberts at the Tonypandy meetings, but never have I witnessed such scenes as in Norway, and soon I believe they will be witnessed in England."[115] It transpired that Barratt would spend some seven weeks in Sunderland, conducting an extended mission during the course of which a significant number spoke in tongues, including Mrs. Boddy who received her baptism on September 11th.[116] Yet the primitivist impulse toward "the original doctrines and the old enthusiasm, pluck, and daring of the Pentecostal Period,"[117] so thoroughly reinforced by Harris, would result in outcomes which would not receive universal approval.

Problematic Emergence of Tongues in England

Wacker's extensive explorations of early Pentecostalism in North America have informed his observation that "the most dangerous enemies were ostensible colleagues in other parts of the Holy Ghost camp."[118] In similar vein, some of the most vociferous and vehement critics of the central feature to emerge during Barratt's campaigning in Sunderland were those who themselves shared the language of Pentecost and the Baptism of the Holy Spirit. A headline, "Speaking in Tongues - Rival Pentecostals" which appeared in the *Sunderland Echo* on Wednesday 2nd, of October 1907 encapsulated the controversy that ensued. While involved in a Pentecostal League Convention held at Sunderland's Victoria Hall, Reader Harris had heard of the phenomenon of *glossolalia* then occurring in the Parish Hall of one of the hitherto most loyal and respected members of the local branch of his organisation. Boddy confessed to having been greatly pained on being made aware of the denunciations issued by his former fellow advocate in the Pentecostal cause, who very publicly refuted this development as a deviant aberration and damned it as one which was "tainted with uncleanness, immorality and wickedness."[119] There followed a period of rhetorical exchange during which Barratt, who "led off a vigorous attack on Mr. Reader Harris,"[120] came to embody a role which in

[115] "Tongues in Norway: A Pentecostal Experience," *Leaflets on Tongues* No. 6.

[116] "Pentecost at Sunderland: Testimony of a Vicar's Wife."

[117] "Editorials: Respectable Church Fossils," *Tongues of Fire*, December 1905, 6.

[118] Wacker, *Early Pentecostals and American Culture*, 179; Wacker explores this curious tendency in some detail in "Evangelical Responses to Pentecostalism," 505-528. See also Synan, "Criticism and Controversy, 1906-20," chapter eight of *The Holiness-Pentecostal Tradition: Charismatic Movements in the Twentieth Century* 2nd ed. (Grand Rapids, MI.: Eerdmans, 1997), 143-166.

[119] "Speaking in Tongues - Rival Pentecostals," *Sunderland Echo*, 2 October 1907, 4.

[120] "Revival Scenes: The Converts Speak in Strange Tongues," *Morning Leader* 2 October 1907.

the manner reminiscent of a previous ideological apologist could, with justification, earn him the posthumous designation, *Boddy's Bulldog.*[121]

Perhaps the supreme irony of this divergence among England's "Rival Pentecostals" was the fact that the primary instrument employed in the denunciation of the practice of *glossolalia* was the periodical titled *Tongues of Fire.*[122] This publication had repeatedly urged its readership toward the attainment of "Pentecostal blessing in all its fullness,"[123] sought the "promotion and extension of Pentecostal Christianity," and encouraged sympathisers to "pray for and receive the Spirit."[124] Yet the identification of the gift of tongues as evidence of reception of the Spirit amounted to a breach that could not be countenanced. It constituted, in a manner similar to divergences of opinion in North America, "the dynamite in the crevice."[125] Furthermore Reader Harris and Oswald Chambers were not alone in their criticism of this development. Jessie Penn-Lewis, a teacher of some prominence in English Holiness circles who had been among the first women to address the Keswick convention,[126] expressed her objections in writing to Boddy before embarking on a forthright and extensive condemnation in the periodical *The Christian.* In the course of eight serialisations between January and March of 1908 she asserted that "the Adversary" had, "as an angel of light," managed to "lead astray some of the very elect."[127] In private correspondence she invoked the authority of the "mystagogue"[128] of the Welsh Revival, suggesting that Evan Roberts was in

---

[121] Victorian English biologist T. H. Huxley (1825-1895) had acquired the epithet *Darwin's Bulldog* by virtue of his strident advocacy/defence of the theory of evolution. Further evidence of Barratt's apologetic and polemical endeavours on behalf of the validity of tongues can be found in "The Truth about the Pentecostal Revival: Lecture given by Pastor T. B. Barratt in Zurich, London and elsewhere" (Unpublished pamphlet, 1908), and his published collection of pamphlets *In the Days of the Latter Rain* (1909; repr. London: Elim Publishing Company, 1928).

[122] See Oswald Chambers, "Tongues and Testing," *Tongues of Fire*, January 1908, 3. The ironies of this divergence, as well as the vehement polemics that accompanied it have been examined by the present writer in a paper presented at the Summer Conference of the Ecclesiastical History Society, 2003. This has been published as "'Signs and Wonders that Lie': Unlikely Polemical Outbursts Against the Early Pentecostal Movement in Britain," in Kate Cooper and Jeremy Gregory eds., *Studies in Church History*, vol. 41, *Signs, Wonders, Miracles: Representations of Divine Power in the Life of the Church* (Woodbridge: Boydell & Brewer Ltd., 2005), 410-422.

[123] "Editorials," *Tongues of Fire*, September 1905, 6.

[124] "Editorials," *Tongues of Fire*, May 1906, 6.

[125] Wacker, "Evangelical Responses to Pentecostalism," 509.

[126] Mary N. Garrard, *Mrs. Penn-Lewis: A Memoir* (1930; repr. Bournemouth: The Overcomer Book Room, 1947), 178, 181.

[127] Jessie Penn-Lewis, "An Hour of Peril," *The Christian*, 9 January, 1908, 12.

[128] Max Weber, *The Sociology of Religion*, trans. Ephraim Fischoff (Boston: Beacon Press, 1964), 54-55. Weber understood such a figure to function as part-magician, part-prophet in the spiritual domain, a description which seems apposite in the light of

possession of "very clear light on the whole matter," and was "greatly burdened" about Boddy's situation.[129]

It is certainly the case that emergent Pentecostalism was, at this time, at a tentative and somewhat embattled stage in England. Robinson surmises that Boddy may have entertained ambivalent feelings toward the end of 1907: a sense of fulfilment must surely have been tempered by frustration and unease at the hurtful and damaging controversies that had also taken place. It was precisely in such a situation that the qualities of this earnest Anglican vicar would come to the fore: "The movement had not found a ready acceptance. Sunderland was now both famous and notorious. Much would now depend on the leadership of Alexander Alfred Boddy."[130] Boddy informed a newspaper reporter that he had been the recipient of "an extraordinary vision" related to him by an anonymous individual, identified merely as "a young Sunderland builder,"[131] shortly before he made his exploratory journey to Norway in March 1907.[132] This communication evidently engendered a sense of involvement in something uniquely providential, and this sense of destiny would impel Bishop Lightfoot's charge toward the undertaking of a singular role on behalf of the emerging Pentecostal cause.

"The Very Acme of All Conventions"

The Sunderland Convention owed its origins to that fact that Boddy sensed that "the Lord would gather together in Conference at Sunderland many of those whom he had blessed." He initially considered holding it during September to mark the anniversary of the first "Outpouring" until a friend pointed out the appropriateness of Whitsuntide. This appears to have been a fortuitous choice and the following refrain was subsequently described as encapsulating the attitude of many who attended: "Truly, we have never known such a Whitsuntide in our lives." Of the first such event an anonymous "American sister" attested: "This Sunderland Conference has been the very acme of all

---

Roberts' short-lived, dramatic and indeed enigmatic ministry in Wales.

[129] Jessie Penn-Lewis, *Letter* to Alexander A. Boddy, November 9, 1907, (DGC). Roberts was at this time undergoing a period of protracted convalescence at the Penn-Lewis country residence near Leicester. A generous interpretation was advanced by Penn-Lewis' biographer which held that in the aftermath of eight months of daily meetings in "crowded, ill-ventilated chapels," the primary arbiter of the Revival "completely broke down." See Garrard, *Mrs. Penn-Lewis*, 230-231. Perhaps more objectively Orr commented on Roberts' forty year reclusion which rendered him "a strange mystery to the Christian public." See *The Flaming Tongue: Evangelical Awakenings, 1900-* (Chicago: Moody Press, 1975), 26.

[130] Robinson, "The Charismatic Anglican," 63.

[131] "Amazing Statement by Vicar of Monkwearmouth Church," *Lloyd's Weekly News*, 6 October 1907.

[132] "Tongues in Norway: A Pentecostal Experience," *Leaflets on Tongues* No. 6.

Conventions or Conferences I have ever attended."[133] Such an utterance was significant to the extent that it emanated from a religious constituency which already cherished the mass gathering as a mechanism for the transmission and diffusion of ideas and practices.[134] The first of the annual gatherings which would come to function as the primary forum for the exploration and promulgation of emerging Pentecostal thought and practice until the First World War, displayed many of the procedures and preoccupations that would become normative. It would also, in addition to the editorship of *Confidence* magazine and his forthcoming role in the foundation and oversight of Britain's Pentecostal Missionary Union, serve to establish Boddy as the primary arbiter and purveyor of the ideological *infra-dynamics*[135] of this emerging movement.

Foremost among these characteristics, and something which Boddy was particularly keen to celebrate, was a pervasive sense of what he described as "love of the Brethren *(philadelphia)*." The fact that delegates were welcomed by both the vicar of All Saints' and "a dear Salvation Army brother (J. Techner)" was a prelude to what would become an established feature of not only this particular gathering, but the wider Pentecostal phenomenon as envisaged by Boddy. It was to this end that Mrs. Boddy addressed one of the sessions using 1 Corinthians chapter 1, verse 10, to emphasise the importance of "no divisions."[136] A social gathering was held in the Parish Hall for the purpose of personal introduction and interaction and it was recorded that those present felt themselves to have been privileged "a glimpse of Heaven upon earth." Boddy offered this sanguine assessment on the basis of the fact that:

---

[133] "Pentecost with Signs: the Worldwide Revival," *Confidence*, June 1908, 3.

[134] Bebbington, "Evangelicalism and Cultural Diffusion," 5, 10-11. This was presented as a plenary paper at the "British Evangelical Identities: Past, Present, and Possible Futures" Conference held at King's College London during July 2004. I am grateful to Prof. Bebbington who has made a manuscript copy available prior to its publication. On the utility of the culture of the religious convention see also his *Holiness in Nineteenth-Century England*, 68, 74-77. In addition to meetings at Speke Hall in Battersea, Reader Harris regularly hired Exeter Hall for larger Pentecostal League events. Located next to the Royal Exeter Hotel on the Strand, and with a capacity for "upwards of 4,000 persons seated," this premises had routinely been used by Nonconformist ministries during the late Victorian period. See Charles Eyre Pascoe, *London of Today: An Illustrated Handbook* (London: Sampson Low, Marston, Searle, and Rivington Ltd., 1888), 225-226.

[135] Boddy's contribution is illuminated by the findings of a study of the dynamics and functioning of subsequent Pentecostal groupings. Not only does his role equate to the cultivation of "interlocking personal and group networks within the infrastructure," but he also assumed significant responsibility in the "communication of the integrating core ideology of the movement." On these see Luther P. Gerlach and Virginia H. Hine, "Five Factors Crucial to the Growth and Spread of a Modern Religious Movement," *Journal for the Scientific Study of Religion* 7.1 (1968): 29-30.

[136] "The Whitsuntide Conference," *Confidence*, June 1908, 4-6.

There was a unity which nothing but the Holy Spirit could give. We were Anglicans, Methodists, Friends, Salvationists, Congregationalists, Mission Members, etc., but 'denomination' was forgotten. All one in Christ Jesus, was true.[137]

This is revealing, not merely in affording an insight into the backgrounds of those who were aligning themselves with the Pentecostal cause, but also to the extent that it articulates Boddy's central aspiration that the movement in general could and should function as *ecclesiolae in ecclesia*. This concept, denoting "little churches within the church," was advanced by sociologist of religion, Joachim Wach, who defined it as consisting of a "loosely organised group, limited in numbers and united in a common enthusiasm, peculiar convictions, intense devotion, and rigid discipline, which is striving to attain higher spiritual and moral perfection than can be realised under prevailing conditions."[138] Cecil Polhill, an Anglican layman and Pentecostal activist, described those who identified themselves with the movement as entering what he termed "a mutual edification society in Jesus."[139] In a manner remarkably reminiscent of Reader Harris, and conforming to this model which facilitated the coexistence of a variety of religious affiliations within a collectivity, Boddy envisaged a loosely-aligned network of Centres engaging in mutual support and edification neither threatening nor undermining denominational allegiances, much less resorting to partisan or competitive positions.[140] The Sunderland Convention, held between 1908 and 1914, certainly succeeded in realising these aspirations to a significant degree and, as will be explored in Section 3, it was only in the later absence of this "scheme of diffusion"[141] that the movement came to lack the cohesion necessary for the successful implementation of such an *ecclesiolae in ecclesia* paradigm.

Another notable feature of the Sunderland Convention from its inception was the proprietary concern exercised by Boddy amid what was, from the first, a febrile atmosphere analogous to what is sociologically termed a period of *prophetic excitation*. It is in such a context that preaching, in the technical sense of collective instruction concerning religious and ethical matters, is most typically operative.[142] While the vague but injurious charges of "uncleanness, immorality and wickedness"[143] made by Reader Harris had already been

---

[137] "The Social Gathering," *Confidence*, June 1908, 9.

[138] Wach, *Sociology of Religion*, 177.

[139] "He Setteth the Solitary in Families," *Flames of Fire*, December 1916, 3. For more detail on Polhill and his involvement see p. 50 ff. below.

[140] A statement of this form of spiritual "protest within" existing religious structures (Wach, *Sociology of Religion*, 175) is to be found in his article "Unity not Uniformity," *Confidence*, March 1911, 60.

[141] Bebbington, "Evangelicals and Cultural Diffusion," 5.

[142] Weber, *Sociology of Religion*, 74-75.

[143] "Speaking in Tongues - Rival Pentecostals," *Sunderland Echo*, 2 October 1907, 4.

vigorously rebutted, Boddy remained sensitive to "unholy accusations." Beyond making general recommendations on questions of morality, he referred delegates to *Counsel to Leaders*, a document which he had formulated to specifically address this area.[144] The very existence of such a position paper at this stage of the movement's evolution is testament to the singular priestly role he had come to perform.

It must also be pointed out that Boddy, even by 1908, harboured a very real concern regarding the "matter of messages." He conducted something of a symposium on 'Prophetic Messages' where he recommended the utilisation of "letters of commendation from well-known leaders" in an effort to curb the already prevalent problem of "irresponsible workers" and other "very unsuitable persons" who were holding meetings and endangering "honest souls." It was contested that there was "no scriptural authority or precedent for making Tongues (with interpretation) into a Urim and Thummin Oracle for details of daily life."[145] He stated emphatically: "We see *no warrant* for expecting a message in 'Tongues' for details of daily life and guidance."[146] While the ramifications of such practices would become more intensely apparent in areas of the movement during subsequent years, Boddy was as early as 1909, perturbed that in "some Centres" individuals had been encouraged to seek "such messages" as had merely delivered "great shocks to their faith."[147]

Such overt pastoral realism did not imply that Boddy entertained a negative disposition with regard to the future of English Pentecostalism; in fact he declared to the contrary that the first Sunderland gathering marked the beginnings of an "entirely new plane of spiritual experience."[148] What was

---

[144] "The 'Pentecostal Baptism': Counsel to Leaders and Others" (Unpublished tract, DGC); "Open Meetings of the Conference," *Confidence*, June 1908, 18.

[145] See "Prophetic Messages," *Confidence*, June 1908, 15.

[146] "The Sunderland Conference," *Confidence*, June 1908, 13. The Urim and Thummin (approximating to "lights and perfections" or "revelation and truth") were introduced into the Mosaic tradition in Exodus chapter 28, verse 30. Somewhat ambiguous, they constituted a medium whereby divine direction and counsel were imparted to Israel when required. These apparently material objects were added to the breastplate after the stones had been set in it. They were probably lost at the destruction of the temple and were not seen after the return from captivity. It was by means of the Urim and Thummin that David and Israel "enquired of the Lord." See for instance 1 Samuel 14:3; 23:9-12; 2 Samuel 21:1; Judges 1:1-2; 20:18.

[147] "Prophetic Messages and their Trustworthiness," *Confidence*, February 1909, 42. It could be concluded from an observation made by Randall that a "maturity" which sought to acknowledge and account for human error and fallibility only emerged in English Pentecostalism "after three decades of its life." See *A Study in the Spirituality of English Evangelicalism*, 223-224. It is contested that what has been highlighted here and in particular what will be explored in pages 113-124 below, demonstrates an informed realism from the outset on the part of leaders such as Boddy and T. M. Jeffreys.

[148] The comment was made that those involved had hitherto been mere spiritual

described as a "quite unpremeditated" and "heaven-sent Doxology at the close of our convention"[149] was heralded as a positive augury for the future, and when delegates gathered for the purpose of a photograph, Boddy, bordering on the euphoric, suggested that "there never was a happier group that faced a camera."[150] This, "the very acme of all Conventions," was deemed to have been a resounding success: "In our gathering of 1908 we felt that we were knit together by a love that burst all bonds of Church organisation and social position and made us truly 'one in Christ Jesus.'"[151] This slogan had been integrally associated with the Keswick Convention for more than a quarter of a century, encapsulating its ideal of "spiritual oecumenicity."[152] Boddy elsewhere recounted that he had attended the annual gathering in 1907 where he distributed his pamphlet "Pentecost for England (and other lands)," and although "thousands" of copies were distributed,[153] his overtures were not received. It would appear that Boddy optimistically vaunted this aspect of Pentecostal involvement as another means of appeal to Keswick sensibilities.

The Role of Cecil Polhill and the Formation of the Pentecostal Missionary Union

What would transpire to be a significant arm of the emerging polity of the Pentecostal movement in England had its genesis in All Saints' vicarage on the morning of Saturday 9th January, 1909. This preliminary meeting of the Executive Council of the Pentecostal Missionary Union for Great Britain and Ireland appointed Cecil Polhill as its Treasurer and Secretary for England, while Alexander Boddy was established as its Editorial Secretary. This venture was borne of "a heart of love for the Heathen in Asia, Africa, America, and the Islands of the Sea." Each Centre was to nominate a representative and these intermediaries would convey financial donations and liaise with the Council with respect of "suitable volunteers for Foreign Service." It was envisaged that "Bible Schools with a course of some months study" would be established with

---

"babes." See "The Sunderland Conference," *Confidence*, June 1908, 12.

[149] "The Last Night of the Conference," *Confidence*, June 1908, 21.

[150] "The Photographic Group," *Confidence*, June 1908, 17.

[151] "The Sunderland Conference," *Confidence*, June 1908, 13.

[152] Orr, *The Second Evangelical Awakening in Britain* (London: Marshall, Morgan & Scott, 1949), 220. The centrality of this perspective was underscored in a Silver Jubilee address delivered in 1899 by one of the most prominent speakers of the early years of the Convention. See Herbert F. Stevenson, "Keswick and its Message," and Charles A. Fox, "Keswick's Twenty-Fifth Feast of Tabernacles," in Herbert F. Stevenson, ed., *Keswick's Triumphant Voice: Forty-Eight Outstanding Addresses Delivered at the Keswick Convention, 1882-1962* (London: Marshall, Morgan & Scott, 1963), 14, 26.

[153] "The Pentecostal Movement," *Confidence*, August 1910, 194. Boddy retrospectively refers to this pamphlet of which no copies appear to have survived. The present writer has no reason to contradict Robinson's observation that "unfortunately, to date, none are extant." See "The Charismatic Anglican," 42.

a view to instilling in candidates "a fair knowledge of every Book in the Bible, and an accurate knowledge of the Doctrines of Salvation and Sanctification."[154]

The upbringing of Cecil Henry Polhill (1860-1938) has been described as "characteristic of the landed gentry of the time."[155] His father had served as High Sheriff for Bedfordshire in 1875 and Member of Parliament for Bedford for a number of years. Cecil was sent to Eton, and from there proceeded to Jesus College, Cambridge. He went on to become a Second Lieutenant in the Bedfordshire Yeomanry in 1880. Influenced by his younger brother Arthur, he came to espouse a Christian faith in 1884. Both brothers joined five other graduates in the work of the China Inland Mission in 1885, collectively becoming known as the celebrated Cambridge Seven. Pollock has pointed out that owing to their relatively late involvement, the Polhills were not formally attached to the Mission, an expedient which enabled their mother to "speak airily of 'my sons travelling in China,' thus hiding from titled and landed friends her disgrace at being the mother of missionaries."[156]

Boddy identified Polhill as being particularly significant among the many he met for the first time at the 1908 Whitsuntide Conference. The latter had returned from China less than two months prior to this and had stopped *en route* in the U.S.A. It was in what was described as a "quiet meeting" in a house in Los Angeles that he had received his Pentecost.[157] It is notable that Polhill was already functioning as a primary representative of English Pentecostalism alongside Boddy at a conference held in Germany before the end of 1908. Analogous to the meetings that continued to be held at All Saints', Polhill informed the delegates of "Drawing-room Meetings" which he was hosting in London's West End, and the "mid-day Prayer Meetings" which he was organising in Eccleston Hall and the Cannon Street Hotel in the City of London.[158] The collaborative relationship between Boddy and Polhill would prove seminal during the formative years of Pentecostalism in England.

The association forged by these individuals bears comparison with a peculiarity of English life which survived into the Edwardian period; the singular relationship between "parson" and "old squire." A contemporary commentator observed that a keen sense of privilege frequently attuned the Edwardian "old squire" to a responsible and solicitous attitude to those committed to his care. Nowhere was the sense of conscientious involvement

---

[154] "The Pentecostal Missionary Union," *Confidence*, January 1909, 13-15.

[155] Peter Hocken, "Cecil H. Polhill - Pentecostal Layman," *Pneuma: The Journal of the Society for Pentecostal Studies* 10:2 (Fall 1988): 116. For a brief biographical sketch see also Gary B. McGee, "Cecil Polhill (1860-1938)," in Gerald H. Anderson, ed., *Biographical Dictionary of Christian Missions* (Grand Rapids, MI., and Cambridge: Eerdmans Publishing Company, 1998), 541-542.

[156] John Pollock, *The Cambridge Seven* (London: Inter-Varsity Press. 1955), 91-92.

[157] "The Pentecostal Movement," *Confidence*, August 1910, 197; "Brief Items," *Confidence*, August 1908, 12-13.

[158] "Pentecostal Conference in Germany," Special Suppl. to *Confidence*, December 1908, 2.

and benefaction more in evidence, than in the relationship between "Hall and Rectory."[159] The Pentecostal movement boasted such a fortuitous combination in the persons of Polhill and Boddy, whose activism over more than a decade, embodied the tendencies of "Hall and Rectory" beyond their parochial settings. It was merely two years after meeting him that Boddy wrote of Polhill:

> The Lord has need of him and his help as one of His Stewards, and in writing of the spread of the Pentecostal Blessing in Great Britain, we must not forget how the Lord has used His willing servant in an unceasing labour of love, in arranging and holding meetings in London, and in holding many Conferences, and in succouring the Saints.[160]

Boddy elsewhere stated that Polhill "has borne willingly the greater part of the expense of hiring halls in London and many heavy items in connection with the meetings...So the London gatherings have almost come to be known as 'Mr. Polhill's Meetings,' and many Pentecostal workers have enjoyed his hospitality."[161] These meetings were held, according to the notification that appeared in the periodical which he, in a manner similar to Boddy founded and edited, at the Institute of Journalists, Tudor Street, and at Sion College near Blackfriars Bridge.[162] Gee has recorded that the regular Sion College meetings were first held at this Anglican club in March 1909, and that they were still ongoing at his time of writing some three decades later.[163] Polhill was therefore responsible for the establishment of a tradition which outlived his involvement in the movement and continued well into the denominational phase of English Pentecostalism. In spite of otherwise ungenerous remarks in his posthumous assessment of Polhill, Gee acknowledged the "deep impression" which the conscientious benefaction and spiritual egalitarianism of this "old squire" had left on him. He related how on initial encounter he "felt this was nearer to New

---

[159] William Gascoyne-Cecil, "The Upper Classes: The Old Squire and the New," in Lowther-Clarke, ed., *An Englishman's Religion*, 30, 38. For a more recent exploration of just such a collaborative relationship see Owen Chadwick, *Victorian Miniature*, 2d. ed. (Cambridge: Cambridge University Press, 1991).

[160] "The Pentecostal Movement," *Confidence*, August 1910, 197.

[161] Advance Supplement to *Confidence*, June 1909, 2. Polhill's London home at 10 York Terrace, Regents Park, which was also used for P.M.U. correspondence, was located in a district described by Booth as the capital's "home of fashion and wealth." See "The P.M.U. Council," *Flames of Fire*, October 1915, 8; and Charles Booth, *Life and Labour of the People of London*, 3rd series, *Religious Influences*, vol. 3, (London: Macmillan, 1902), 73, 93.

[162] "The London Meetings," *Flames of Fire*, October 1913, 4. While these were venues of longstanding, Boddy also records attending meetings hosted by Polhill in the Cannon Street Hotel and the Portman Rooms near Marble Arch. See "Midday Prayer Meetings in the City," and "The West End Pentecostal Meeting," *Confidence*, February 1909, 49-50.

[163] Gee, *The Pentecostal Movement*, 53-54.

Testament Christianity than anything I had then seen."[164] He elsewhere stated that he felt Boddy and Polhill to be "ideally complementary," and acknowledged that "for the first ten years of the Pentecostal Movement in the British Isles, these two men were the most outstanding figures."[165] In the functioning of "Hall and Rectory" the parish church, in its furnishings and lay-out, reflected whether the "old squire" had felt the influence of the Oxford Movement, or conversely, that his views were more non-sacramentarian in nature.[166] Tokens of Polhill's evangelical and missionary convictions are, in similar vein, not only discernible in English Pentecostalism, but owing to the all too frequently overlooked influence he came to wield, significantly shaped its formation and development.

All Saints' and Pentecostal Involvement

Before proceeding to outline another locality for emerging Pentecostal Christianity in England, some consideration will be given to the encroachment, or otherwise, of this dimension into the life and activities of All Saints' parish. Blumhofer has stated without qualification that "there is no evidence that Boddy introduced Pentecostal practices into his regularly scheduled Anglican Services."[167] In assessing the veracity of this assertion, it is instructive to note that the initial prayer meeting which was established in 1906 in the wake of the Welsh Revival took place in the Vicarage of All Saints', and that the waiting meetings which were held during and subsequent to Barratt's mission of 1907 were situated in the Parish Hall. While Pentecostal activities appear to have augmented and enhanced aspects of the life of All Saints', without causing significant controversy or disruption, the evidence indeed suggests that such involvement retained a supplementary status to the ongoing work of the parish.

Boddy informed the readers of *Confidence* of regular meetings that were held in addition to the customary church services. Alongside open-air and Christian Endeavour events, was the weekly gathering "for those who have received the Baptism with the Sign of the Tongues" which was held on Wednesday evenings at 8 p.m. in the vicarage.[168] Boddy remarked that while it had previously proven difficult to sustain prayer meetings, this regular gathering of Pentecostal initiates had proven successful, both summer and winter. He also reported a positive influence in other areas of the life of All Saints'; their open-air campaigns had been greatly enhanced, and he stated that "Spirit-guided appeals from one young man after another, and also from young maidens, have not failed to reach many a mark." There were also improvements to report in the activities of the Sunday School and Boddy spoke generally of a

---

[164] Gee, *Personal Memoirs of Pentecostal Pioneers*, 74.

[165] Gee, *The Pentecostal Movement*, 53.

[166] Gascoyne-Cecil, "The Old Squire and the New," in Lowther-Clarke, ed., *An Englishman's Religion*, 37-38.

[167] Blumhofer, "Alexander Boddy," 32.

[168] "Meetings at Sunderland," *Confidence*, September 1908, 2.

"genuine earnestness rising higher than ever in one's ministry of nearly 24 years in this Parish."[169]

Boddy's estimation, already highlighted, that there were "from thirty to forty in this place" who had undergone the Pentecostal experience, gives an early indication of the extent of the Centre that existed within the encompassment of All Saints'. Pentecostal meetings had been, and continued to be held, "in addition to the ordinary work of the Parish and the many Sunday Services conducted."[170] Further insight can be gleaned from Boddy's brief report of an event which marked the anniversary of his own spiritual apotheosis: a "special invitation" had been issued to "those attached to the Sunderland Centre," and he stated that "between forty and fifty" attended the gathering in the Parish Hall.[171]

It seems to have been the case that the principal gatherings of the annual Whitsuntide Convention were held in the Parish Hall and were, on the whole, separate from the weekly schedule of Anglican services. This did not preclude attendance of visiting delegates at these and it appears that the Communion Service afforded visitors a particular opportunity to participate alongside regular parishioners. Jane Vazeille recounted that delegates "mostly made their Communion at the Service, whatever their denominations, whether with the permission of the Bishop or not, I do not know!"[172] An individual identified merely as an "honoured visitor" from the U.S.A., furnished an appreciative account of his or her introduction to a Eucharistic service of "unusual sweetness and solemnity" while attending the 1909 Convention:

> Brothers and sisters were present who knew nothing of the ritual of the Established Church of England, but as it was read by Rev. Mr. Boddy (assisted by a curate) in tones of deepest reverence, and in the power of the Holy Spirit, a marvellous hush fell upon us and we realized that in some cases religious training had been different, yet we were all blessedly one in Christ.[173]

Participation continued and on Whit-Sunday 1913, some three hundred "earnest Christians" attended the Communion Service. When on this occasion a prominent figure in the emerging movement had been invited to preach, Boddy remarked that it was "an unusual thing in the Church of England to have the pulpit occupied by a notable barrister, Mr. John Leech, K. C., of the Dublin Courts." While it was observed that the Communion Service had "never been

---

[169] "A Year of Blessing," *Confidence*, September 1908, *4*. It is of interest to point out that just two years earlier Reader Harris had informed those involved in the Pentecostal League that "in no realm of active Christian work is a revival more needed than among Sunday School teachers." See "Editorials: Shall Sunday Schools Remain?" *Tongues of Fire*, July 1906, 6.

[170] "A Year of Blessing," *Confidence*, September 1908, 4-5.

[171] "Sunderland: A Joyful Gathering," *Confidence*, December 1908, 7.

[172] J. V. Boddy, *Memoir*, 7.

[173] "Sunderland International Pentecostal Congress," *Confidence*, August 1909, 177.

better attended" during the Whitsuntide gathering, the mainstay of Convention proceedings were still being conducted in more peripheral locations, it being recorded that while the Parish Hall overflowed for the main events, the vestry was utilised for a Missionary Meeting, and the sick were "helped in the Vicarage by Mrs. Boddy and other friends."[174]

Geoffrey Milburn, in his historical examination of Christian representation in Sunderland, remarked that Bishop Lightfoot would have been surprised if he had lived to see the results of his appointment.[175] His successor appears to have adopted an indulgent stance toward Boddy's Pentecostal involvement. Jane Vazeille recalled that Handley Moule "was always friendly towards my father and probably sympathetic in his own mind."[176] This former Principal of Ridley Hall, Cambridge (1889-1900) was a Churchman of Evangelical persuasion, who had had a longstanding and public association with Keswick, addressing the Convention on thirteen occasions.[177] His "scholarly lectures," published under the title *Thoughts on Sanctity*,[178] are held to have significantly advanced the theological maturation of the Keswick Movement.[179] His work *Veni Creator: Thoughts on the Person and Work of the Holy Spirit of Promise*, written in 1890, was replete with the parlance of the *fullness of the Spirit* in the sense which Boddy and others understood it prior to 1907. Moule's disposition as revealed in this work was that it was not within his convictions "to deny *a priori* the possibility of signs and wonders in any age, our own or another, since the apostolic,"[180] an outlook which would have been heartily endorsed by Boddy.

The Bishop of Durham, it is reasonable to suggest, would have been impressed by the additional vitality that Pentecostal involvement had brought to this needy parish in the largest urban centre in his diocese. Other developments would have resonated with his personal desire to "moderate the spirit," to "open to new sympathy the soul," and to be "more than ever sensitive against the spirit and accent of the partisan."[181] Boddy's claim that through the genius of Pentecost "Friends, Brethren, Methodists, Salvationists, Baptists, Congregationalists and Church-folk" had been in Sunderland, "one in trusting

---

[174] "Convention Notes," *Confidence*, June 1913, 116-117.

[175] Milburn, "Church and Chapel in Sunderland," 49.

[176] J. V. Boddy, *Memoir*, 7.

[177] John Battersby Harford and Frederick Charles Macdonald, *Handley Carr Glyn Moule, Bishop of Durham: A Biography* 2nd ed. (London: Hodder and Stoughton, 1923), 197, 131.

[178] Handley C. G. Moule, *Thoughts on Sanctity* (London: Seeley & Co., 1885).

[179] On this see Pollock, *The Keswick Story: The Authorized History of the Keswick Convention* (London: Hodder and Stoughton, 1964), 71-72. See also G. R. Balleine, *A History of the Evangelical Party in the Church of England* (London: Longmans, Green and Co., 1933), 283.

[180] Moule, *Veni Creator: Thoughts on the Person and Work of the Holy Spirit of Promise* (London: Pickering & Inglis, 1890), 215.

[181] Harford and Macdonald, *Bishop of Durham*, 197.

the precious Blood,"[182] is indeed likely to have been a potent factor in enlisting the sympathy of a man of Moule's sensibilities. Yet in the absence of overt expressions or demonstrations of support it seems that his stance should be characterised as more akin to tacit approval than outright and unreserved advocacy. As an ecclesiastical superior he felt bound to warn Boddy that he "could not promote him or send him to another parish, as the clergy, as a whole, were antagonistic," and according to Jane Vazeille, "none of them ever came to the Conventions, though some Ministers of other denominations did."[183] The personal cost born by this 'priestly' father of the movement, whether in terms of isolation or lost opportunities for preferment, cannot be known or qualified. What is beyond doubt is that English Pentecostalism owes an unfathomable debt to the leadership he exercised and the sacrifices he endured.

Section 1.3: Historical Locality - Bradford

Formative Years and Pre-Pentecostal Ministry of Smith Wigglesworth

When Boddy published a list of "Pentecostal Centres in Great Britain and Ireland," merely a month after Sunderland's first Whitsuntide Convention, "Mr. Smith Wigglesworth, 70 Victor Street, Manningham" was named as the Bradford "representative" and "correspondent."[184] Wigglesworth, with the active involvement of his wife, had founded the city's Bowland Street Mission, and his personal quest and spiritual pursuits were instrumental in its being categorized among England's first Pentecostal Centres some ten years after its inception as an independent evangelical mission. While many aspects of his life might prove engaging and could benefit from more rigorous scholarly attention than has yet been undertaken, it is Wigglesworth's formative origins, gravitation toward Pentecostal experience, and resultant leadership and ministry, both at Bradford's Bowland Street Mission and further afield in these

---

[182] "A Year of Blessing," *Confidence*, September 1908, 5.

[183] J. V. Boddy, *Memoir*, 7. This level of tolerance is in contrast with figures such as Graham Scroggie, one of the leading lights of the Keswick constellation from the 1920s. When he was invited to deliver an address at All Saints' Parish Hall while minister of Sunderland's Bethesda Free Church, Boddy felt obliged to issue the following disclaimer: "We do not wish to imply that Pastor Scroggie is identified with the Pentecostal movement..." See "Is the Bible Inspired? Rough Notes of an address given by Pastor W. Graham Scroggie," *Confidence*, April 1909, 82-84. It transpired that he shared with another Baptist writer, Oswald Chambers, the distinction of being among the staunchest and, in his case, the most longstanding opponents of the Pentecostal understanding of spiritual baptism. Prominent among his writings in this vein are his published pamphlets *The Baptism of the Spirit: What is it? and Speaking with Tongues: What Saith the Scriptures?* (London: Pickering & Inglis, 1956). On this see also Randall, "Baptists and the Shaping of Pentecostalism," in Bebbington, ed., *The Gospel in the World*, 91-93, 95-97.

[184] "Pentecostal Centres in Great Britain and Ireland," *Confidence*, July 1908, 2.

early years that are most pertinent to the present study.

By the time of Wigglesworth's birth on 10 June 1859, Bradford had acquired an interesting reputation with respect of religious adherence. Its six places of worship in 1800, the Parish church and five Dissenting chapels, had increased to fifty four by the time of the census of religious worship conducted half a century later. The Census of 1851 confirmed that 68 per cent of the religious populace attended a Nonconformist place of worship, which resulted in Bradford ranking third among the urban centres of England and Wales in terms of Nonconformist dominance.[185] It had, therefore, already earned itself and would continue to merit the appellations "citadel of dissent" and "capital of religious Radicalism."[186]

Wigglesworth's spiritual propensities were evidently awakened through the influence of his grandmother who attended a Wesleyan Methodist chapel. He recounted the enduring impression on an eight year old boy of exuberant expressions of worship while his elders were "dancing around a big stove in the centre of the church, clapping their hands and singing."[187] The formative years of this Yorkshire man could indeed be said to provide some fascinating analytical material in terms of a "dynamic perspective on religious development,"[188] and among the multifarious ingredients which contributed to his spiritual *gestalt*, an Anglican influence was not absent. He subsequently informed a Pentecostal gathering that during Confirmation in an unidentified "Parish Church in Yorkshire," he had experienced a rush of the "power of the Holy Spirit," as the Bishop laid hands on him, something which he claimed to be similar to what he was to later encounter "in a fuller measure."[189] Wigglesworth's recollection of this event illustrates his abiding propensity for what Evelyn Underhill, in her masterly study of the dynamics of Christian worship termed, "vigorous spiritual realism" as opposed to the "crystallising tendencies"[190] of ceremony or ritual. This was further manifest in the ardent attraction he felt for what has been described as "the most colourful of the

---

[185] "Table F: Religious Accommodation and Attendance in Large Towns," in *Census of Great Britain, 1851: Religious Worship* (London: Her Majesty's Stationary Office, 1853), ccliii. See also "Table D" in *Voluntarism in England and Wales, or, The Census of 1851* (London: Simpkin Marshall and Co., 1854), 108.

[186] Tony Jowitt, "The Pattern of Religion in Victorian Bradford," in D. G. Wright and J. A. Jowitt, eds., *Victorian Bradford: Essays in Honour of Jack Reynolds* (Bradford: Bradford Metropolitan Council, 1982), 37, 45.

[187] Frodsham, *Smith Wigglesworth*, 3.

[188] Meredith B. McGuire, *Religion: the Social Context*, 3rd ed. (Belmont: Wadsworth, 1992), 54.

[189] "Bro. Smith Wigglesworth's Visit," *Confidence*, March 1912, 64.

[190] Evelyn Underhill, *Worship* (1936; repr. Guildford: Eagle, 1991), 228. For an appreciation of her writings and significance as an authority on the expression and enactment of Christian devotion see Ann Loades, *Evelyn Underhill* (London: Fount Paperbacks, 1997).

many new religious denominations produced by nineteenth-century Britain,"[191] - William and Catherine Booth's Salvation Army - when it arrived in Bradford in 1877.

The *Bradford Observer* conducted a census of religious observance in 1881 which affords a unique opportunity for comparison with the 1851 survey of England and Wales. One of the most immediately striking aspects of its findings was the arrival of an entirely new category of religious organisation. What have been designated Old Minority Groups had declined in numerical terms, for reasons which included the fact that bodies such as the Quakers, Unitarians, and Moravians lacked a notable evangelical impulse toward expansion.[192] In contrast the New Groups demonstrated the existence of an increasingly virulent tendency in Bradford. This category accounted for fourteen new places of worship and catered for almost five thousand individuals in terms of potential 'sittings,' the Salvation Army itself boasting a capacity of three thousand principally in the form of temporary accommodation in rented theatres and halls.[193] The identifiable presence of other small bodies which included the Catholic Apostolic Church, the New Church (Swedenborgian), German Evangelicals, and Spiritualists, reflected Bradford's increasing cosmopolitanism, as well as a tendency toward religious fragmentation and diversification.[194]

Five years after the arrival of the most audacious and colourful of these new groupings, the *Observer* offered a positive assessment of its dynamism stating that "however objectionable to refined and educated tastes may be their methods, the Army is capable of reaching and doing good to masses of men and women who are overlooked by steadier and more orthodox sects." It had apparently also secured a notable constituency among "the orderly, well dressed and respectable members of the working class."[195] It would appear that along social as well as other dimensions, the young Wigglesworth was favourably disposed to participation in the Army and its activities. It was among their ranks that he met the woman whom he described as his "helpmeet." Speaking of Mary Jane Featherstone (d. 1913), herself the daughter of a Methodist temperance lecturer, and the direction their conjoined ministry

---

[191] McLeod, *Religion and Society in England*, 31.

[192] For comments on the religious quietude of these groups, and their contentment to worship peacefully in buildings "that were growing hoary with age," see William Scruton, *Pen and Pencil Pictures of Old Bradford* (1891; repr. Otley: Amethyst Press, 1985), 21, 74.

[193] Chadwick, "Church and People," 74.

[194] Jowitt, "Religion in Victorian Bradford," in Wright and Jowitt, eds., *Victorian Bradford*, 49. What has been described as England's "remarkable growth of religious pluralism" has been examined in K. D. M. Snell and Paul S. Ell, *Rival Jerusalems: The Geography of Victorian Religion* (Cambridge: Cambridge University Press, 2000), 265-266, 405.

[195] *Bradford Observer*, 13 April, 1882, cited in Jowitt, "Religion in Victorian Bradford," in Wright and Jowitt, eds., *Victorian Bradford*, 49.

was to take beyond the Salvation Army, Wigglesworth stated:

> I encouraged her to continue her ministry of evangelising, and I continued my business as a plumber. I had a burden for the parts of Bradford that had no church, and we opened up a work in a small building that I rented...I used to carry the children to meeting and look after them while she preached. I was no preacher myself, but I was always down at the 'penitent form' to lead souls to Christ. Her work was to put down the net, mine to land the fish.[196]

The impetus and motivation that impelled a plumber to embark on the establishment and oversight of an unaffiliated mission hall was a definite product of what Kent has described as the "free, spontaneous, lay revivalist style" which had been fostered in Britain in the aftermath of the Moody and Sankey campaigns of the 1870s. What he termed a "fantastically diversified would-be evangelization,"[197] in conjunction with Bradford's "heritage of fringe religious groups,"[198] generated the conditions in which independent individuals of 'artisanal' or 'plebian' designation (approximating to the modern socio-economic category 'blue-collar') could embark upon a religious undertaking of their own instigation and devising. Commenting on a general and increasing momentum in this direction Bebbington has observed:

> The Methodist spirit of pragmatic, aggressive evangelism was spreading beyond the bounds of Methodism. A new ethos, negligent of denominational forms, emerged. The Brethren sect created much of the network responsible for the new temper and drew in many converts. All the Evangelical denominations nevertheless felt the new winds...[199]

Holiness and Healing - the Origins of the Bowland Street Mission

Further evidence of Wigglesworth's involvement with the Wesleyan school of Holiness teaching[200] is merely intimated in Whitaker's work which states without documentation that he "came under the teaching of Reader Harris" and thereby "received a deeper work of sanctification."[201] This assertion is substantiated by the official records of the Pentecostal League of Prayer. A "League Mission" had been held in Bowland Street, between December 11th and 18th 1904, and "about 24" expressed a desire to join the organisation. The missioner, a Mr. David Thomas, had impressed upon them that God could

---

[196] Frodsham, *Smith Wigglesworth*, 10.

[197] Kent, *Studies in Victorian Revivalism*, 114, 301.

[198] Jowitt, "Religion in Victorian Bradford," in Wright and Jowitt, eds., *Victorian Bradford*, 49.

[199] Bebbington, *Evangelicalism in Modern Britain*, 117.

[200] For a concise overview of the Salvation Army's Wesleyan Holiness emphasis see for instance Diane Winston, *Red-Hot and Righteous: The Urban Religion of the Salvation Army* (Cambridge, MS. and London: Harvard University Press, 1999), 19-23.

[201] Whitaker, *The Inside Story*, 22.

"deliver from all sin," and that He could likewise "baptize them with the Holy Ghost and fire." It was announced that a "League Centre" was about to be formed.[202] The Bowland Street Mission was officially publicised as such a Centre in the issue of April 1905, with Mr. S. Wigglesworth as its Secretary. According to designated instructions, a nucleus of twelve members was requisite to the formation of a Centre, although no record of names beyond that of Wigglesworth himself was provided. While it was recommended that the Secretary organise a weekly "Holiness and Prayer Meeting,"[203] Wigglesworth does not appear to have achieved this quota in Bowland Street; he hosted such a gathering on the first and third Monday of each month, at 8p.m.[204]

Active involvement in Britain's Holiness "sectarian fringe"[205] does not appear to have exhausted Wigglesworth's capacity for spiritual realism. A plumbing business that prospered during the harsh winters of England's north-east necessitated frequent trips to Leeds for supplies. There he was exposed to, and became enthralled by the activities of the Leeds Healing Home which Cartwright has identified with the international Zion Movement instigated by John Alexander Dowie.[206] Its leaders Elizabeth and Richard Paget Baxter are better known as the founders and proprietors of the *Christian Herald*.[207] They had come into contact with Dowie during conferences he had held in London during 1900. It is interesting, in the light of the rupture that subsequently occurred, that Reader Harris had in 1905 castigated "faddists and extremists...of the Dowie type," as well as those who took it upon themselves to "champion his absurd claims."[208]

---

[202] "Notes of the Month," *Tongues of Fire*, February 1905, 8. David Thomas was a layman and prominent campaigner on behalf of the Pentecostal League, yet he later seceded from this body on the grounds of the conviction that converts and those who had undergone an experience of sanctification should be afforded greater structural allegiance and support. He went on to add to what has been described as the "myriad of small evangelistic groupings and missionary societies formed at that time" in founding the International Holiness Mission (1907). In keeping with the norms of such ventures he also established and edited a monthly periodical, *The Holiness Mission Journal*. See Warburton, "Organisation and Change in a British Holiness Movement," in Wilson, ed., *Patterns of Sectarianism*, 109-110; Ford, *In the Steps of John Wesley* (Kansas City: Nazarene Publishing House, 1968), 93-116; Colin Henry Wood, "Principalities and Powers: Crises in the British Holiness Movement, 1934-1976" (M.A. dissertation: Victoria University of Manchester, 1996), 8-10.

[203] "League Centres: and How to Form Them," *Tongues of Fire*, January 1905, 7.

[204] "Pentecostal League Centre Meetings," *Tongues of Fire*, April 1905, 11.

[205] Bebbington, *Evangelicalism in Modern Britain*, 178.

[206] Cartwright, *The Real Smith Wigglesworth*, 19-21.

[207] It has been pointed out that this periodical, founded in 1866, reached weekly sales of 195,000 by 1881. See Patrick Scott, "Victorian Religious Periodicals: Fragments That Remain," in Derek Baker, ed., *Studies in Church History*, vol. 11, *The Materials, Sources and Methods of Ecclesiastical History* (Oxford: Basil Blackwell, 1975), 335.

[208] "Review of 1905," *Tongues of Fire*, January 1906, 7.

Wigglesworth alluded retrospectively to his own seminal experience of healing. He told those who attended a mission in Wales in 1925 that he had been "a weakling, helpless and dying when God in a single moment healed me. I am now sixty-six and as fresh as any of you and as ready for work as I ever was."[209] This experience was publicised by Boddy as integral to the foundation of his evangelistic activity in Bradford, and later beyond, and of initiating a fifteen year "unbroken record of God's marvellous love and power in healing."[210] Boddy's comment enables the circumvention of a distinct lack of concern for the provision of a precise date, as well as other concrete details, surrounding the opening of the Bowland Street Mission. If the assumption that Wigglesworth's embarkation on a healing ministry and the necessity for a suitable premises occurred with the same twelve month period is allowed, the inception of this enterprise could be located as occurring during 1897.

What became the Bowland Street Mission, had been built as a minor public school in 1867. Known as The Clarendon Academy, it was located just off Manningham Lane. However its tenure as an educational establishment was short-lived, its headmaster, John Barr, being reduced to the occupancy of a home for inebriates and ultimately found dead in the Leeds and Liverpool Canal.[211] Green has pointed out that until 1855 a long-standing statute forbade the assembly of more than twenty persons for religious worship in any building that was not either a church or a licensed dissenting chapel. The modification of this regulation opened a new realm of possibility for smaller religious groups, and when allied with the extensive civic building projects undertaken in the industrial centres of West Yorkshire during the 1850s and 1860s, theoretical potential was transformed into practical proposition.[212]

It should be acknowledged that there are few extraneous records of the Bowland Street Mission. It was not covered by the *Bradford Observer* survey of 1881, as the premises was not being used for religious purposes at the time, and the Mission had ceased to function by the time the Bradford Yearbook of 1928-29 compiled a comprehensive listing of places of worship.[213] It is also the case that neither the Federer, Dickons, or Empsall collections of religious material held in the Local Studies Centre of the Bradford City Library contain any reference to the Bowland Street Mission, or Wigglesworth as its leader.[214] For his part Wigglesworth was evidently more concerned to convey to posterity that a move from a previous unidentified premises was the necessary outcome

---

[209] "Home News: Remarkable Scenes at Old Colwyn," *Redemption Tidings*, September 1925, 11.

[210] "Bro. Smith Wigglesworth's Visit," *Confidence*, March 1912, 64.

[211] http://www.communigate.co.uk/brad/columbaclub/page7.phtml

[212] S. J. D. Green, *Religion in an Age of Decline: Organisation and Experience in Industrial Yorkshire, 1870-1920* (Cambridge: Cambridge University Press, 1996), 264.

[213] http://www.genuki.org.uk/big/eng/YKS/Misc/Transcriptions/WRY/BradfordChurc hes1929.html

[214] I am indebted to Peter Walker, Assistant Librarian at Bradford's Local Studies Centre for his help in this regard.

of both successful evangelistic endeavours, and the attractive nature of the divine healing message they had come to proclaim. An inescapable means of the communication of the latter took the form of a large text, displayed on a scroll behind the pulpit, which bore the inscription, "I am the Lord that healeth thee." Frodsham recorded that over the course of their tenure there many reputedly testified to having experienced healing through the inspiration of that fragment of Scripture. Certainly it confirmes the observation that for a considerable time prior to any overt Pentecostal experience, the Wigglesworths, and the Mission over which they presided had "stood for both Healing and Holiness."[215] Some eighteen months after his initial mission David Thomas returned to Bowland Street, and the report which was submitted to *Tongues of Fire* is uniquely revealing with respect of occurrences and aspirations that were being expressed by May 1906. While Wigglesworth's overt involvement with the League may have been of relatively short duration, it undeniably furthered pre-occupations which would characterise his ministry for years, indeed decades, to come:

> Mr. David Thomas has again visited the Bowland Street Mission, and we praise God that much blessing attended the meetings which he held and that since he left us, the work of soul saving and of the Spirit coming upon the Christians continues. Our prayer is that God will bless the members of the League and its leaders. We shall be glad if you will ask members to remember Bradford in prayer that a real revival may commence here. Praise the Lord, He is risen and gives us power to reign over all principalities and over all evil powers reigning in life over death.[216]

Pentecostal Initiation and its Implications

Apparently intrigued by reports of occurrences at the Centre of one of the more prominent activists of the Pentecostal League of Prayer, Wigglesworth set out for All Saints', Monkwearmouth, on 26 October, 1907. In so doing he conformed to an observed pattern of recruitment to a religious movement "along lines of pre-existing significant" relationships, with Mary Boddy acting as the "catalytic agent" in the process.[217] His experiences were recounted and propagated in a tract titled, *An Evangelist's Testimony: His Pentecost With Tongues*, which was printed by Boddy as one of the 'Leaflets on Tongues' series.[218] This particular tract had its basis in a letter which Wigglesworth wrote to "Mr. and Mrs. Boddy" on 5 November, 1907, and which had also been

---

[215] Frodsham, *Smith Wigglesworth*, 12, 2 3.

[216] Wigglesworth, "Notes of the Month: Manningham, Bradford," *Tongues of Fire*, May 1906, 8.

[217] Gerlach and Hine, "Growth and Spread of a Modern Religious Movement," 30.

[218] "An Evangelist's Testimony: His Pentecost with Tongues," *Leaflets on Tongues* no. 12 (DGC).

printed in the seventh issue of *Confidence* magazine.[219] It provides valuable insights into the perceptions of an individual who would transpire to be one of the most significant English initiates into the Pentecostal experience. Wigglesworth claimed that for three months prior to his pilgrimage to Sunderland he had been "exercised about the full Pentecost." Despite the fact that he inhabited circles where the language of Pentecost was clearly in evidence, he highlighted a sense of dissatisfaction in attending meetings where those gathered "were not seeking Pentecosts." He felt himself to have encountered "a great deal of letter, but very little of the spirit that would give the hungry and needy a Baptism of Fire." It is interesting to note that in his estimation the effects of such a "Baptism" would be to "burn up distinctions and officiousness, and appearance of Pride, and evidences of social standing."[220]

It is possible that this last aspiration reflects a sense of exclusion which Wigglesworth may have felt from the Nonconformist mercantile classes keenly in evidence in his immediate locality. Alleged hypocrisies of Bradford's Nonconformist manufacturers and their allies in chapel pulpits had certainly been the subject of frequent public denunciation.[221] It is also conceivable that his antipathy toward "distinctions," "officiousness," and "evidences of social standing" could be attributed, at least in part, to what Wigglesworth had encountered in the Pentecostal League of Prayer. Charles Booth, in his invaluable survey and exploration of religious life in the capital at the turn of the century, had observed that Reader Harris made a feature of regaling his congregations with lengthy lists of well-known people who had expressed sympathy with the League and its objectives. Wigglesworth may also have felt a sense of unease at the preponderance of sermonettes, of which there were according to Booth, a veritable "armoury" offered for sale at gatherings. In his public addresses, Harris routinely made reference to the usefulness of his own pamphlets and publications, which included photographic portraits of himself.[222] It is not unreasonable to assume that Bradford's preaching plumber was unimpressed by such devices, and that he had come to the persuasion that a Pentecostal baptism would "burn up" such objectionable elements. In contrast to his previous experiences, wherever encountered, he appears to have found a more congenial and egalitarian environment at All Saints.

Gerlach and Hine have highlighted the role of real as well as perceived opposition in the consolidation and the intensification of commitment to

---

[219] "Testimony of Smith Wigglesworth," *Confidence*, October 1908, 11, 15-16.

[220] "An Evangelist's Testimony," *Leaflets on Tongues* no. 12 (DGC).

[221] Jowitt, "Religion in Victorian Bradford," in Wright and Jowitt, eds., *Victorian Bradford*, 41. See also Munson, *The Nonconformists*, 14ff. The unsavoury alliance of business and chapel was subjected to a spirited attack in Robert Tressell's *The Ragged Trousered Philanthropists* (1914; repr. London: Flamingo, 1997).

[222] Booth, *Life and Labour*, 3rd series, *Religious Influences*, vol. 5, 223-225.

emerging religious movements.[223] Wigglesworth interestingly, concluded his *Testimony* with the assertion that he was "praying for those that fight this truth." Even at this early stage of Pentecostal evolution, ideological demarcations and delineations are evident in the concluding statement that he had been "clearly given to understand" that it was incumbent on him to "come out of every unbelieving element."[224] In the light of the recriminatory exchanges that had been issued between the platforms of Sunderland's Victoria Hall and the Parish Hall of All Saints', Wigglesworth was evidently mindful of the implications of his association with this emerging strain of Pentecostal Christianity. It is not surprising that inclusion among those who had succumbed to what was deemed a "deviation from the Way of Holiness" and a "Satanic counterfeit,"[225] rendered Wigglesworth and the Bowland Street Mission unfit for continued association with the Pentecostal League of Prayer. Accordingly before the end of 1907, after an involvement of some two and a half years, Manningham Lane, Bradford, as well as All Saints', Monkwearmouth, ceased to be listed among the League's nationwide Centres.[226]

It is also pertinent to point out that the leaders of the Bowland Street Mission appear to have assumed peripatetic preaching and teaching roles within a relatively short space of time, and in the process, established themselves as leading figures at a trans-local level in the expanding network of Pentecostal Centres. Reports of their increasing travel and influence throughout Britain frequently appeared in the pages of *Confidence*. Its editor, for instance, professed himself "most thankful" to learn that both "Mr. & Mrs. Smith Wigglesworth" had "been a blessing" in a range of localities before the end of 1908.[227] The November 1910 issue recorded that among the leaders present at a Convention which had been held at Leeds were "Brother and Sister Smith-Wigglesworth," "Mr. Stanley Frodsham," and "Mrs. A. A. Boddy." This report stated laconically: "Sick were healed, baptisms in the Holy Ghost (with tongues); and deeply spiritual teaching given."[228] What was publicised as the Preston Devotional Convention of 1911 was also addressed by the Bradford preacher, and it was noted that, coinciding with Bowland Street's long-standing

---

[223] Gerlach and Hine, "Growth and Spread of a Modern Religious Movement," 36-37.

[224] "Testimony of Smith Wigglesworth," *Confidence*, October 1908, 16.

[225] "The Gift of Tongues," *Tongues of Fire*, November 1907, 2.

[226] "Pentecostal League Centre Meetings," *Tongues of Fire*, December 1907, 11. Interestingly while Sunderland's sales of *Tongues of Fire* still topped the monthly 'league table,' the figure fell from its customary 72 to 65.5 dozen. See "'Tongues of Fire' Sales," *Tongues of Fire*, December 1907, 10. Harris indeed acknowledged that during 1907 League Centres had "decreased in number," while suggesting that those who had "lapsed" had been "the weakest." He asserted that the organisation had as a whole "distinctly increased in spiritual power." See "Review of 1907," *Tongues of Fire*, January 1908, 7.

[227] "Yorkshire: From Brother Smith Wigglesworth," *Confidence*, December 1908, 9.

[228] "Pentecostal Items," *Confidence*, November 1910, 251.

aspirations, "sick were healed and many passed into a life of holiness in Christ Jesus." The meetings took place in the Lancaster Road School-room, and the convenor of the occasion was Mr. Thos. Myerscough, of 134 St. Thomas Road, described as "the leader of the Pentecostal band in Preston."[229] In the aftermath of the death of his wife in 1913[230] Wigglesworth's itinerary was not only resumed, but significantly expanded. His first venture across the Atlantic saw him address camp meetings and conventions as he traversed Canada and North America "like a victorious warrior"[231] for a period of six months during 1914. Increasing exposure on a wider Pentecostal platform propelled him toward the attainment of the status of *religious virtuoso*.[232] The literature subsequently generated by his persona and exploits suggests that he has embodied just such an iconic function in the Pentecostal psyche throughout intervening decades.

The Bradford Convention and an Uneasy Transition

In addition to the leadership role Wigglesworth was increasingly playing throughout the cohering movement, Bradford's Bowland Street Mission came to prominence as a Centre of some note. A group of visiting delegates convened there for the first Easter Conference which took place between Good Friday and Easter Monday 1909. This marked the beginning of an annual fixture on the English Pentecostal calendar for the next decade. At this inaugural event those gathered were addressed by Pastor Hutchinson of Bournemouth, Pastor Niblock of Paddington, and Mr. and Mrs. J. Miller of Glasgow. All of the above were described in the "Notes of one who was there" as having "assisted" Smith and Mrs. Wigglesworth[233] who by no means relinquished the Bowland Street platform to visiting speakers. The observation was made that delegates encountered "dear ones from distances who had never looked into one another's faces," yet seemed "to know one another in the Spirit."[234] This serves to illustrate the fact that the phenomenon of the convention, which came to form a pivotal constituent of what might be deemed a Pentecostal liturgical cycle, was characterised by the culture of the visiting delegate. Local attendees appear to have been habitually outnumbered by visiting guests, and the prominence of the Bradford Convention ensured it

---

[229] "Pentecostal Items," *Confidence*, March 1911, 61. What became known as the Preston Assembly later moved to another premises on Lancaster Road. Hacking recorded that it was necessary to negotiate a "dingy stairway of forty-five steps" to gain access to this "Upper Room." It was situated over "Starkie's the Wire Shop" and had an entrance which he described merely as "uninviting." See, *Reminiscences*, 7.

[230] *Confidence*, January 1913, 19-20.

[231] "Westward Ho!," *Confidence*, December 1914, 223.

[232] Weber has written of a tendency whereby religious traditions produce figureheads that appear to the faithful to have been "placed in the world as an instrument of God." See *Sociology of Religion*, 162-163.

[233] "Easter Conference at Bradford," Special Suppl. to *Confidence*, April 1909, 4.

[234] "Easter Conference at Bradford," Special Suppl. to *Confidence*, April 1909, 4.

fulfilled a broader propagating function within the emerging Pentecostal constituency. It is likewise the case that, in time, the preoccupations of its host would gravitate decisively toward the macro- as opposed to micro- dimensions of leadership and ministry.

Myerscough provided Boddy with an account of the next year's proceedings. He reported that "a great number (about 40)" acquired "the clear Scripture evidence as in Acts x, 46."[235] A Baptismal Service, which would form an integral part of this annual event at Bradford,[236] was held on the Monday evening and seventeen individuals "went under the water in the name of the Father, of the Son, and of the Holy Ghost." Myerscough's concluding remarks reveal something of the tenor of the event:

> The harmony of the meetings was truly 'one accord,' and the love and fellowship amongst the brethren was a great joy to my heart. It is also a great pleasure to me to record that in all the meetings there was a sense of Godly control, and never did I see or hear anything to offend or hurt the most sensitive seeker or onlooker. Praise God![237]

This observation of a manifest concern for the maintenance of decorum and the adoption of sensitive and inoffensive methods is interesting on two levels. Firstly it represents a divergence from the characterisation of, and methodology commonly attributed to, Wigglesworth who has frequently been presented as more likely to incline toward insensitivity and offensiveness.[238] It also provides valuable intimations of the early stages of the Bowland Street Mission, in transition from its original status as an independent evangelical body to that of an emerging Pentecostal Centre. Such an evolutionary trajectory was a typical means of progression within the movement in the years prior to the First World

---

[235] "Easter Convention," *Confidence,* April 1910, 90.

[236] The Knights of St. Columba, who utilised the building from 1931, believe that the Mission's "baptismal bath" was buried under their club stage. See http://www.communigate.co.uk/brad/columbaclub/page5.phtml. This practice and indeed the very existence of such a bath is of greater significance than might first appear: in 1922 it was lamented that for two years there had been "only one baptistery available in Pentecostal circles in London." See "Home News," *Things New and Old,* January 1922, 7.

[237] "Easter Convention," *Confidence,* April 1910, 91.

[238] Hacking comments that Wigglesworth was "always courteous and kind" and only seemed harsh "when he knew he was dealing with Satanic forces of evil." See *Reminiscences,* 5. The "preaching plumber" is reputed to have on occasion, when engaged in his healing ritual, punched or otherwise struck the suppliant. Hibbert has sought to make a virtue of this and cites what is held to be a response by Wigglesworth to the charge of objectionable and potentially dangerous techniques: "I don't hit people, I hit the Devil. If they get in the way, I can't help it...You can't deal gently with the Devil." See, *The Secret of His Power,* 18-19. No direct evidence of such overtly physical behaviour has been found in the primary materials consulted in relation to the period under investigation.

War. Yet the picture that emerges from extant evidence indicates that in Bradford this transition was far from smooth, and that it was ultimately equivocal in outcome. A visiting "brother from Canada," identified simply as "A. W. F.,"[239] provided interesting insights into this process following a visit to Wigglesworth's mission. A respected observer of the growing international Pentecostal phenomenon, his commentary is worthy of consideration:

> Bowland Street Mission is an old-established mission with a good record - souls saved and bodies healed, but now there is an element of opposition. Brother Smith Wigglesworth is a faithful, hard worker, and is praying that those who do not see the Baptism of the Holy Ghost may be won over. He is ably seconded by his wife. They have a fine brass band, and the members do good open-air work. This is a splendid feature of the work. They are not in sympathy as a body with Pentecost, and personally one feels they may be a source of weakness in meetings...The brethren need our prayers.[240]

It is interesting to note that the month after this report was published a clarification appeared in *Confidence* which had been requested, if not insisted upon, by Brother Smith Wigglesworth:

> The Editor regrets that, in last month's issue, expressions occurred as to the Bowland Street Mission which the Leader feels should be re-adjusted. They admit that nothing remarkable transpired whilst the correspondent was there. Since then many have been Baptized according to Acts ii., 4, and in every case they pleaded the Precious Blood as led by the Holy Spirit. The Leader reports that they are in true sympathy with all Pentecostal work that is according to Scripture. Acts ii., 38.[241]

A. W. F.'s observations, taken in conjunction with the riposte hastily issued from Bradford, and implicitly endorsed by Boddy, are indicative of a number of matters pertinent to the organic functioning of the movement. Wilson has categorised Pentecostal groupings among those religious collectives which exhibit a strong sense of self-identification and definite boundaries. Associated sensitivities typically imply a recognition that integrity might be "impugned by the careless or insufficiently committed member."[242] It would appear that a distinctively Pentecostal identity had progressed beyond the elementary stages of its evolution, even by the early months of 1910. The notion of "an old-established mission with a good record" measured in terms of "souls saved and bodies healed...a fine brass band" and "good open-air work," was not perceived as adequate to mark such a body as necessarily or satisfactorily "in sympathy

---

[239] Arthur, brother of Stanley Frodsham, with whom he shared a common interest in travel and writing. See, for instance, A. W. Frodsham, "A Pentecostal Journey in Canada, British Columbia and the Western States," *Confidence*, May 1911, 139.

[240] "Two Visits to Pentecostal Centres: Bradford," *Confidence*, February 1910, 35.

[241] "Pentecostal News: Bradford,"*Confidence*, March 1910, 67.

[242] Wilson, *Religious Sects*, 27, 31-32.

with Pentecost." Wigglesworth's response which emphasised that "many" had since then experienced the Baptism in the Spirit according to what was held to be the normative pattern of the Book of Acts, was made in the light of a perceived need to assert increasingly recognisable credentials of full participation in the consolidating Pentecostal fraternity.

Evidently Wigglesworth's retort as leader of the Mission implied an underlying concern that misrepresentation on the part of a respected visitor could precipitate a real, if informal, ostracism from the cohering movement. He was keen to show that in terms of emerging *tests of merit* or *act/s of subscription*,[243] Bowland Street was not to be found wanting. Boddy's willing endorsement of the corrective advanced, could be seen as an act of reinstatement, if such were required, or certainly as an affirmative gesture toward this developing Pentecostal Centre. This episode also underscores an exigency commonly faced by mission and Centre leaders who sought to identify themselves with the emerging Pentecostal cause: the task of transmitting this to, and thereby transforming, their distinctive congregations. While Conventions and mass gatherings might serve as "powerful agents of innovation," functioning as "media for the dissemination of the latest views of doctrine and practice,"[244] the integration of Pentecostal ideals into specific localities was to prove a challenge which not all would surmount. This will be revisited when the outcome for the Bowland Street Mission is considered in Section 3 below.

Section 1.4: Historical Locality - Bournemouth

Formative Years and Pre-Pentecostal Ministry of William Oliver Hutchinson

William Oliver Hutchinson was born into a Primitive Methodist family in County Durham on 11 January, 1864. It was as a young Grenadier Guardsman that Hutchinson went to hear the celebrated Charles H. Spurgeon preach at the London Metropolitan Tabernacle, where he underwent an evangelical conversion. Hutchinson was sent to South Africa in March 1900, but was "invalided out" of the Boer War the following year.[245] His first occupation after medical discharge from Netley Military Hospital in 1903 was as an inspector for the Society for the Prevention of Cruelty to Children, a role which took him to Bournemouth. During this time he engaged in evangelistic activity as a Methodist lay preacher. He then affiliated himself to the Baptist cause in Winton, Bournemouth. Kent White, a later acolyte of Hutchinson, wrote a memoir which recorded that his leader had also, during this period, become intrigued by the teachings of Reader Harris and his Pentecostal League of Prayer. According to this account he "received great blessing in the teaching of a clean heart before God. This experience he then took to be the baptism of the

---

243 Wilson, *Religious Sects*, 29-30.
244 Bebbington, "Evangelicalism and Cultural Diffusion," 10-11.
245 Hathaway, "William Oliver Hutchinson," 42.

Holy Ghost. Later, he came to see that the baptism should be accompanied by the speaking in tongues."[246]

Neither Harris in the detailed records published in *Tongues of Fire*, nor Hutchinson in his later writings, have left quantifiable evidence of the latter's involvement in the League. Harris, as has been observed, disseminated his ideologies by virtue of a network of local branches or outlets and, in the early years of the century, the Bournemouth Centre convened a Sunday afternoon meeting at the Primitive Methodist church on Commercial Road.[247] Attendance here and consequent encounter with "the teaching of a clean heart" would have been consistent with Hutchinson's spiritual eclecticism and leanings during these years. That Harris' influence could be regarded as qualified is attested by Weeks' "History of the Apostolic Church" which identifies ten men who, after nineteen centuries of Christian history, were held to have functioned as latter-day apostles. Alexander Boddy, T. B. Barratt, and Smith Wigglesworth were among those who "began to build a church, a movement, which continues to expand world-wide to this day."[248] These were included despite the fact that they came to suffer disjuncture from Hutchinson and his later emphases and innovations, while Reader Harris was not in the first instance among those deemed to have been providentially chosen. The long-term significance of exposure to his teaching would therefore seem to have been preparatory in nature, engendering an expectation of spiritual rites of passage subsequent to conversion, and the overt association of this category of experience with Pentecostal terminology and parlance.

It would appear that Hutchinson declined an offer of a position as assistant pastor in a local Baptist church, a move construed by Worsfold as an option for the path of faith, an heroic stance against the lure of financial support and security.[249] It was in the context of a period of isolation and hardship induced by this ongoing and tenacious conviction that he was to function independent of denominational affiliation or support, that Hutchinson received an invitation to attend the first Whitsuntide Convention at Sunderland.[250] In common with many others whose lives had followed a similar trajectory in terms of spiritual interests and inclinations, he found what was being propagated there to be the fulfilment of his personal odyssey to that point.

When Boddy produced a list of "Pentecostal Centres in Great Britain and Ireland" merely a month after this first Convention, "Mr. W. Hutchinson, Beulah, Talbot Road, Winton," was designated as "representative" for the fledgling Centre in Bournemouth.[251] Identification with what was as yet a

---

[246] Kent White, *The Word of God Coming Again: Return of Apostolic Faith and Works Now Due on Earth. With a Sketch of the Life of Pastor W. Oliver Hutchinson* (Bournemouth: Apostolic Faith Church, 1919), 44-45.

[247] "Pentecostal League Centre Meetings," *Tongues of Fire*, February 1901, 11.

[248] Weeks, "History of the Apostolic Church," 4-5, 81-82.

[249] Worsfold, *The Origins*, 33.

[250] White, *The Word of God*, 47-48.

[251] "Pentecostal Centres in Great Britain and Ireland," *Confidence*, July 1908, 2.

loosely aligned and organic conglomeration of congregations, if one which was rapidly becoming a "body with a sense of its own integrity,"[252] afforded Hutchinson the dual-benefit of conferring a sense of purpose and involvement with others who shared common ideological convictions and aspirations, while allowing considerable scope for individual development - something which Hutchinson would avail of without delay. While Boddy sought to issue a gentle reproach to Centres "near Derby and Shrewsbury" who had "not sent in their latest reports,"[253] there is no suggestion that Hutchinson was remiss in this respect. A month after the formal acknowledgement of this Centre at Winton appeared in *Confidence*, Boddy printed an extract of a report from its leader:

> The Lord is leading us along very sweetly here. My daughter has had her Baptism (as the dew) with only a few words in the 'Tongues.' The meetings are carried along in such deep silence, praise the Lord! I find that the Spirit gets a good chance to consume the flesh.[254]

A Singular Development for the British Pentecostal Movement

Three months later this Centre would witness a dramatic development, unprecedented within English Pentecostalism. The eighth issue of *Confidence* included a substantial article which began with the announcement that "A new hall for Evangelistic and Pentecostal Services has been erected at Winton, Bournemouth, and was opened on November 5th with two services." Boddy described what was to be called "Emmanuel Mission Hall" as an "elegant little structure of brick and slate, with pitch pine roof relieved with dark oak" which was capable of accommodating "about 250" people. The individual responsible for the venture was "Mr. W. Hutchinson," and both he and Boddy were pleased to publicise the fact that all the necessary monies had "come in in answer to prayer," and that he had not "knocked at anyone's door for a penny."[255]

On the contrary, the cost incurred in the construction of the Hall, £382, precisely paralleled the donations received.[256] It would appear that in comparative terms the venture undertaken by Hutchinson was a modest one. It has been observed that in this period the "simplest school chapel" cost in the region of £1,000 to construct, and a church cost at least £3-4,000 and often considerably more.[257] The Alma Road Methodist society had erected a corrugated iron chapel in Winton, just two years prior to Hutchinson's undertaking. The fact that they had purchased a site for £250, and then faced a further expenditure of £1,080 for the building of what they fondly described as

---

[252] Wilson, *Religious Sects*, 27.

[253] "News of Pentecost," *Confidence*, April 1908, 7.

[254] "Brief Items," *Confidence*, August 1908, 12.

[255] "Bournemouth," *Confidence*, November 1908, 23. White likewise highlighted the providential nature of the funding of the Hall. See *The Word of God*, 49-52.

[256] *Showers of Blessing*, January-February 1910, 1.

[257] Chadwick, "Church and People," 182.

their "Tin Tabernacle,"[258] affords a revealing perspective on what was the first purpose-built Pentecostal meeting place anywhere in Britain.

The publication of the fact that the financial costs had been met in so timely a fashion was indicative of a very definite concern for frugality and financial rectitude. That the requisite amount was acquired in a providential manner further conveyed an implicit message that this enterprise enjoyed divine favour and was not of merely human origin. In recounting and promulgating the genesis of the Emmanuel Mission Hall in this manner, both Boddy and Hutchinson were engaging in a process of "plausibility-generation"[259] for those most immediately concerned in Bournemouth, as well as for those involved throughout the emerging network. It had earlier that year been suggested to the readers of *Confidence* that if all were attentive to, and acted upon, genuine divine inspiration and suggestion, "there would be no need for Bazaars or 'Sales of Work' to raise money for God's work."[260]

The increase in church building in the latter half of the nineteenth century has been documented by Gill who has advanced some interesting findings in his study *The Myth of the Empty Church*. It would appear that Free Church building was so vigorous during these decades that empty chapels paradoxically preceded a decline in the church-going rate.[261] This was a significant factor in a widespread fear and abhorrence of the incursion of debt in the opening of a building for religious worship. Early Pentecostals harboured a general antipathy towards what Miss Sissons, a visiting American who addressed the Sunderland Convention, described as "religious mendicancy."[262] In the aftermath of what had occurred in Sunderland, the conviction was expressed that "there ought not to be a debt on a Room where the Holy Spirit had come down." On the completion of his own Parish Hall on Fulwell Road, Boddy erected a commemorative stone which stated: "September, 1907. When the fire of the Lord fell, it burnt up the debt."[263] A preoccupation with pecuniary matters, was therefore by no means unique to Hutchinson or the Emmanuel Mission Hall, but was a common and commendable feature of the early

---

[258] http://paulct.webspace.fish.co.uk/history.htm

[259] Berger, *The Social Reality of Religion*, 188.

[260] "Prophetic Messages," *Confidence*, June 1908, 15.

[261] Gill, *The Myth of the Empty Church*, 10.

[262] Elizabeth Sisson, "Foregleams of Glory," *Confidence*, March 1913, 50. Munson has observed that "strenuous self-reliance" was central to the Nonconformist ethos. See *The Nonconformists*, 61ff.

[263] "About All Saints' Parish Hall (Sunderland)" *Confidence*, May 1908, 6. For other examples of pecuniary concerns see "Restitution," *Confidence*, April 1908, 10. Polhill expressed acute dissatisfaction with Pastor Niblock's negligent or inept handling of P.M.U. resources and this resulted in his short tenure as custodian of the Men's Missionary Training Home. See P.M.U. Council Minutes of 21 March 1910, Book I, 52-53.

Pentecostal ethos.[264]

White recorded that the dedication services were attended by "many of the foremost Pentecostal leaders of the country."[265] The advertised speaker for the event was Cecil Polhill, and his choice as the candidate for this role may have had more to it than his prominence and popularity in the movement at this stage. Chadwick has pointed out that it was common for religious bodies to capitalise on opening formalities inviting likely, or at least potential, donors to lay foundation or memorial stones.[266] Boddy recorded that in addition to Polhill's presence, there was an "unexpected pleasure" for those gathered when they found that he was accompanied by Pastor Polman from Amsterdam who introduced himself as "a Dutchman happy in Jesus." Boddy recounted their respective messages in detail and the overriding theme was a sense of providential instigation and approval of the Pentecostal cause.[267] Polhill, airing his perennial concern, emphasised the international dimension of the then-spreading movement. The belief that "the Lord was doing a wonderful work in every part of the world" was presented as assurance that in like manner "he would do a wonderful work in Bournemouth." Suggestive of a mindfulness and appreciation of continuity with their various evangelical backgrounds, those gathered were reassured that God was "bringing a fresh young bud on an old tree, a young bud fresh nourished from heaven." The unprecedented nature of this, the first purpose-built Pentecostal meeting place on English soil was presented as corroborative of divine favour: Here was "a new building for a new work."[268]

Hutchinson, for his part, appears to have been entirely reconciled to the fact that he was the individual to oversee this departure for the movement in England. Doubtless his personal sense of involvement in a divine undertaking buoyed him in this pioneering role. It would appear that he held such convictions in common with many North American counterparts who frequently displayed what has been described as "a kind of swashbuckling entrepreneurialism that left many observers amazed when they were not appalled."[269] Such tendencies were also evident within the wider English religious context with men being, according to David Bebbington, particularly susceptible to what he terms the "virile, independent image of Nonconformity."

---

[264] It has been observed of Pentecostal groupings generally that divinely-inspired activists frequently take "moderate-to-large risks" in advancing their cause and, in so doing, exhibit propensities which "economists and psychologists find so conducive to economic development." See Gerlach and Hine, "Growth and Spread of a Modern Religious Movement," 35.

[265] White, *The Word of God*, 51.

[266] Chadwick, "Church and People," 193-194. For further exploration of Nonconformist fund-raising see Jeffrey Cox, *The English Churches in a Secular Society: Lambeth, 1870-1930* (Oxford: Oxford University Press, 1982), 111ff.

[267] "Bournemouth," *Confidence*, November 1908, 23-24.

[268] "Bournemouth," *Confidence*, November 1908, 24.

[269] Wacker, *Early Pentecostals and American Culture*, 15.

The upper echelons of this sector of English Protestantism were populated by merchants and manufacturers, the "typical entrepreneurs of their age" and these individuals were "attracted by the Nonconformist dynamism that they, in turn, helped to sustain."[270] Profound personal convictions and notable entrepreneurial and organisational abilities certainly coalesced within the complex personality of William Oliver Hutchinson, and these would ensure that this was not his last pioneering endeavour. His willingness and ability to venture beyond the already-established would see him innovate in various directions over the next few years, not all of which would be generally welcomed or accepted as furthering the cause of England's Pentecostal movement.

Hutchinson as a Prominent Figure in the Emerging Network

"Elites," according to Wilson, tend to emerge at the local level of religious movements when centralised agencies have arisen and local leaders, often "self-recruiting," are those who interpret, explain and rationalise the activity of the "central group."[271] Hutchinson appears to have been recognised, certainly as a local, and to a considerable extent as a 'central' leader in his own right from the latter half of 1908. Three months after the official opening, Boddy reported that "God continues to bless at Emmanuel Mission Hall" where "about 28 have been saved, and about 21 have received the Baptism of the Holy Ghost with the Sign of Tongues."[272] At the same time it was announced that a "Three Days' Conference" would be held there between February 26th and 28th, 1909.[273] This event was significant for visitors such as Frank Trevitt who went on to function in a missionary capacity, and whose dramatic healing was recounted in an article entitled "Bournemouth: Pentecost Returned."[274] White stated that within a short space of time, Emmanuel Mission Hall "became well known among the Pentecostal assemblies throughout the country."[275]

Evidence of the esteem in which Hutchinson was held is apparent from the eminence he enjoyed as a speaker across a variety of Pentecostal platforms. While rank or seniority were not explicitly discussed it could be argued, such was his prominence, that Hutchinson was the principal visiting speaker at the first Easter Convention to be held at Bradford during 1909.[276] He also made a significant impact in Sunderland when his address to the Whitsuntide Conference of 1910 on the subject of divine healing inspired half of the "600-

---

[270] Bebbington, *Victorian Nonconformity*, 31-32.

[271] Wilson, "An Analysis of Sect Development," in Wilson, ed., *Patterns of Sectarianism*, 35.

[272] "Brief Items," *Confidence*, February 1909, 39.

[273] "Bournemouth," *Confidence*, February 1909, 51.

[274] "Bournemouth: Pentecost Returned," *Confidence*, April 1909, 86-87. See pages 104-105 below.

[275] White, *The Word of God*, 51.

[276] "Easter Conference at Bradford," Special Supplement to *Confidence*, April 1909 5-7.

"700 persons" present to stand and "put their trust in the Lord for healing."[277] Hutchinson was among the signatories of the "London Declaration" which was issued in November 1909. This affirmative doctrinal statement had been formulated in response to the fact that many had been unnerved and "stumbled by the printing in the English religious papers of the Berlin 'Declaration against the so-called Tongues Movement.'"[278] Further evidence of identification with the centralised agency that emanated from Sunderland is to be found in the context of Boddy's acknowledgement of "other Pentecostal papers in Great Britain" that had appeared since the advent, and probably indebted to the influence, of *Confidence*. Merely two months after Hutchinson founded *Showers of Blessing*,[279] Boddy, in spite of the at times precarious position of his own publication, generously recommended it to his readership as containing "much helpful matter."[280]

Hutchinson's place among the upper echelons of the emerging fraternity is further apparent from his prominent listing among Pentecostal dignitaries at an official ceremony. The event in question was the opening of a "Home of Rest" at 18 Herne Hill, London, S. E. This Home for the "Healing of Body, Soul and Spirit," which aimed to accommodate up to thirty visitors at a time, was the enterprise of "Pastor Alex. Moncur Niblock" and his "devoted helpmeet." It was described by Boddy as a "noble-looking residence, standing well back from the road, almost hidden by the trees...three stories high, with a comely little Chapel and a large conservatory...," and was situated in relative seclusion from the city of London. On the afternoon of Wednesday, 29th of June, 1910, "some fifty guests" met in the Chapel to hear Boddy's inaugural address. Amongst them were "Mr. Cecil Polhill, Rev. A. A. Boddy, Pastor Inchcombe (Croydon), and Pastor Hutchinson (Bournemouth)..."[281] The latter's ranking among the leadership of this movement at both local and central levels was therefore beyond doubt in the summer of 1910.

An entry which appeared in *Confidence* six months later stated that "Bro. A. Murdoch" reported a "time of great blessing" at a conference he had hosted in Kilsyth. Foremost among the speakers were Mr. and Mrs. Smith Wigglesworth, and Mr. and Mrs. Hutchinson of Bournemouth. It was noted that "the addresses were given in great power, and many were stirred to seek for the Gifts of the Spirit."[282] It is curious that this is the last reference to Hutchinson in Boddy's

---

[277] "Sunderland Convention: 'Day by Day,'" *Confidence*, June 1910, 138.

[278] "A London Declaration," *Confidence*, December 1909, 286-288.

[279] This periodical, which appeared at the beginning of 1910, was not published with the same regularity or precision as *Confidence*. Its first five issues were dated, appearing every two months, but a lapse then occurred which was attributed to the increasing demands of the ministry in Bournemouth. When it appeared the sixth issue was numbered but not dated, and this erratic pattern recurred in subsequent years. See, "Our Paper Overdue," *Showers of Blessing*, no. 6, 1910, 4.

[280] "Other Pentecostal Papers in Great Britain," *Confidence*, March 1910, 61.

[281] "The New 'Peniel' at Herne Hill, London, S. E.," *Confidence*, July 1910, 157.

[282] "The Kilsyth Conference," *Confidence*, January 1911, 17.

publication; the hitherto esteemed leader from Bournemouth vanished forthwith from the pages of *Confidence*. What could be described as the first significant deviation from England's consolidating Pentecostal movement can be attributed to a number of factors which merit exploration. Hutchinson's innovative and entrepreneurial bent was not limited to the erection of buildings or the establishment of publications. Considerable effort as well as editorial space had been, and continued to be given, to the establishment of what might be deemed a Pentecostal orthodoxy. While Hutchinson proved to be a fertile source for the formulation of Pentecostal theory and practice, it will become apparent that in the search for "forms of legitimacy,"[283] some of his emerging emphases ventured beyond what was deemed acceptable or could be endorsed by the cohering mainstream of the movement.

Section 1.5: Historical Locality - Croydon

Croydon's Holiness Mission

In introducing the results of the 1902 survey of religious attendance in London, Mudie-Smith stated that "the most difficult portion" of the undertaking had been locating, to a satisfactory degree, all places of worship throughout the various districts. Particularly problematic in this respect were the missions of the metropolis, many of whom remained wholly absent from the either the Registrar-General's return, or available directories, official or otherwise. He stated that this challenge had necessitated the individual investigation of every street in the twenty-nine boroughs in order to discover hitherto unaccounted for "mission-rooms, mission-halls, and houses of God of the humbler sort."[284] One such which did not evade the attention of the investigators was entered as the "Holiness Mission, Gloucester Road." Categorised among "Other Services" held in the borough of Croydon, the mission recorded fifty-four attendances at its morning service, and seventy-three in the evening. This total of 127 amounted to c. 0.52% of a total of 2,430 attendances at 'other services' in Croydon.[285]

Morris, in his more recent analysis of patterns of religious observance in Croydon has pointed out that not only had its Anglican-bias been overturned in the half century between 1851 and 1902, but that many of the principal guises of Nonconformist worship had undergone unwonted expansion in this period.

---

[283] Wacker, "Reflections on History Writing," 97.

[284] Richard Mudie-Smith, "The Methods and Lessons of the Census," in Richard Mudie-Smith, ed., *The Religious Life of London* (London: Hodder and Stoughton, 1904), 4.

[285] "Greater London – Croydon: 'Other Services,'" in Mudie-Smith, ed. *The Religious Life of London*, 385, 387. A recent study, following Horace Mann's categorisation of 1851, has employed the term "other isolated congregations." See Snell and Ell, *Geography of Victorian Religion*, 404, 424, and *Census of Great Britain, 1851: Religious Worship*, cxiii-cxv.

Indeed many denominations exhibited levels of growth far in excess of their national averages; Wesleyan Methodists, for instance, expanded by some 967 per cent locally, but only 50 per cent nationally, and Croydon's Primitive Methodists grew by a staggering 1,633 per cent as opposed to 81 percent nationally.[286] In addition to such exceptional rates of growth, the context in which the Holiness Mission Hall functioned was also characterised by a very definite tendency toward religious diversification. It was during the 1880s that what Morris terms "unorthodox" groups came to intrude upon the district which demonstrated itself to be "particularly susceptible" to them.[287] This coincides with a wider development characteristic of the last decades of the nineteenth-century whereby the larger and more established Nonconformist denominations found themselves unable to check the growth of a burgeoning "evangelical dissidence."[288]

It was therefore in a context of religious foment, similar to that observed to have occurred during this period in Bradford, that a solicitor and his family moved to Gloucester Road in 1881, and the following Sunday held what was to be the first of many meetings in an "upper room" over his place of business. There were seven participants in all - the wife of this solicitor, four young children and their maid. That evening "three dear friends" who had heard they had come to Croydon, attended the first evening meeting, and the congregation swelled to ten individuals. Inchcombe, the solicitor in question, later recounted that both he and his wife had been converted eleven years prior to this, in 1871, and had for some time been "in the enjoyment of sanctification." Their venture

---

[286] Jeremy Morris, *Religion and Urban Change: Croydon 1840-1914* (Woodbridge: Boydell Press, 1992), 39-44, 205, 209. For rates of growth see also A. D. Gilbert, *Religion and Society in Industrial England* (London: Longman, 1976), 188-189. These observations are corroborated by "Number of Places of Worship, Sittings and Attendants Connected with the Various Religious Bodies in England and Wales: Division II South-Eastern Counties, Table 46 Croydon," in *Census of Great Britain, 1851: Religious Worship*, 11, and "Borough of Croydon," in Mudie-Smith, ed., *Religious Life of London*, 382-387.

[287] Morris, *Religion and Urban Change*, 40. Mudie-Smith had himself observed what he termed an "astonishing blossoming out of offshoots and branches of the main stream of Christian life into all kinds of quaint minor sects each with its specific doctrine and place of meeting." See *Religious Life of London*, 206. The designation unorthodox is, however, potentially misleading as it essentially refers to what Chadwick has termed New Groups identified as having established a significant presence in Bradford from the 1880s. See "Church and People," 73-74. Morris' choice of terminology may have been influenced by certain religious commentators of the last quarter of the nineteenth-century who employed similar designations. For instance an Anglican writer claimed to have traversed "Unorthodox London" from "the North Pole of Nonconformity to the most torrid regions of Romanism." See C. Maurice Davies, *Unorthodox London: Phases of Religious Life in the Metropolis* 2nd ed. (London: Tinsley Brothers, 1876), 1.

[288] Kent, *Studies in Victorian Revivalism*, 300-301.

grew steadily as souls were "saved and sanctified" and in time the premises became too small for the numbers that assembled, even when the staircase was utilised to provide additional capacity.[289]

Morris highlights two principal schemes of growth discernable within Croydon's Nonconformist and minority churches. The first of these can be identified in the fissiparous nature of Congregationalism in Croydon which was "particularly susceptible to schism." Secondly there existed a pattern of growth which, owing to its informal and unplanned nature, has proven difficult for the historian to trace. According to this pattern a "small cause" might be started by a preacher or layman with a tiny following which typically developed into a circle of worshippers who would, in time, seek to accumulate the capital necessary for a permanent building. Meetings might initially be held in the open air, in a house or cottage, and then progress to a small hall or an iron church. This means of growth thrived on lay interest and participation as well as on a relaxed and informal attitude to structure and organisation. The "small cause" which could suddenly spring up in a house or a room over a shop, and perhaps just around the corner from a parish church, was at the heart of the Anglican *contagion theory* of the spread of dissent. The arrival and spread of the 'contagion' of Pentecostalism in Croydon conforms most readily to this model of growth. In the light of the observation that the informal pattern of expansion typical of the "small cause" is singularly difficult to document,[290] invaluable insights into the inception and development of this mission hall, which became one of London's first Pentecostal Centres, are to be found in the pages of the Pentecostal periodicals.

Inchcombe's account of events proves revealing in that the terminology he employed assists in the task of locating his independent mission on the religious continuum. Prior to their arrival in Croydon he and his wife had been "in the enjoyment of sanctification," and their avowed aim was to conduct their subsequent ministry "on Scriptural holiness lines."[291] No prior association with the Pentecostal League of Prayer has been detected, although the latter did have a Centre in Croydon which was based at Addiscombe Gospel Hall, on Lower Addiscombe Road.[292] While irrecusable evidence of involvement with individual Holiness groupings is not available, it is certainly the case that Inchcombe and the mission over which he presided, were in definite sympathy with the general tenor of the emphases of this strain of English evangelicalism. Croydon's Holiness Mission Hall appears to have been among the

---

[289] H. Inchcombe, "Croydon: Times of Blessing," *Confidence*, March 1912, 66.

[290] Morris, *Religion and Urban Change*, 72-75.

[291] Inchcombe, "Croydon: Times of Blessing," *Confidence*, March 1912, 66.

[292] "Pentecostal League Centre Meetings," *Tongues of Fire*, January 1905, 11. Sales of *Tongues of Fire* in Croydon were typically buoyant at 15 dozen per month, and in the light of Harris' inducements toward vigorous and widespread dissemination, the ideas conveyed therein may have found sympathy and influence among those associated with the Holiness Mission Hall. See "'Tongues of Fire' Sales," in *Tongues of Fire*, January 1905, 10, and May 1905, 10.

"indeterminate number of small independent gospel and mission halls" observed to have constituted the bulwark of the Holiness movement in Britain in the early years of the Edwardian period.[293] After three years of existence this "small cause" had made its own contribution to the church building of the period by erecting a hall, again on the same street, which boasted a capacity of 250 seatings. Apparently with a predilection for the qualitative over the quantitative, Inchcombe recounted that the "best of all" was to come a decade after this development. Inspired by the Welsh Revival of 1904-5 and in similar manner to those in Sunderland, a "Waiting Meeting" held on each Wednesday afternoon at 3 p.m. was established. None other than Mrs. Boddy, who was so instrumental among the "hungry souls" who met at All Saints' Vicarage, visited these gatherings on several occasions.[294]

Introduction of the Pentecostal Message

It was after the experience which Mary Boddy underwent on September 11th, 1907, that those in Croydon "noticed and felt a difference with her." Inchcombe recorded that "four or five of our dear people came graciously under the power when she met with them."[295] The Whitsuntide Convention of 1916 was addressed by one of the members of the Holiness Mission, a Mrs. Hodges, who recounted how she had "received her Baptism" thanks to the ministrations of Mrs. Boddy and Mrs. Price in a drawing room in Croydon in 1908.[296] Mrs. Price, of 14 Akerman Road, Brixton, was reputed to have been the first person in Britain to have spoken in tongues.[297] It is therefore not surprising that what Boddy deemed "the band" at Brixton, would find common cause with "the hungry ones"[298] at Sunderland, and others of similar propensity in Croydon. Emerging Pentecostals had evidently not departed from Harris' commendation of "drawing-room meetings" as a "most effective and inexpensive method of diffusing knowledge concerning God's truth and God's work," and one which was deemed particularly apt to appeal to "many lady friends."[299]

---

[293] Warburton, "Organisation and Change in a British Holiness Movement," in Wilson, ed., *Patterns of Sectarianism*, 110.

[294] Inchcombe, "Croydon: Times of Blessing," *Confidence*, March 1912, 67.

[295] Inchcombe, "Croydon: Times of Blessing," *Confidence*, March 1912, 67.

[296] Mrs. Hodges, "How to Seek the Holy Spirit," *Flames of Fire*, July 1916, 6-7. This address is mentioned in Boddy's summary of the same conference, see "The Whitsuntide Convention," *Confidence*, August 1916, 128.

[297] "A Pentecost at Home (Tongues as a Sign): Testimony of a Busy Mother" (Unpublished pamphlet, DGC). This had been reported to a North American Pentecostal readership in "Many Witnesses to the Power of the Blood and of the Holy Ghost: In London," *The Apostolic Faith*, April 1907, 1. Fred T. Corum's collection *Like As of Fire: A Reprint of the Old Azusa Street Papers* (Willington, MS.: n. p. 1981) has been utilized in this study. See also Frodsham's memoir *With Signs Following*, 59-60.

[298] "The Pentecostal Movement," *Confidence*, August 1910, 195.

[299] "Editorials: Drawing-room Meetings," *Tongues of Fire*, December 1905, 6.

Inchcombe's venture was first officially publicised as a Pentecostal Centre in August 1910,[300] and at the beginning of 1912 Boddy described the solicitor as among those "intimately connected with the 'Pentecostal Movement.'"[301] Their Wednesday afternoon meeting of 16th November, 1910, was addressed by both Mrs. Boddy and T. H. Mundell and the latter's theme went under the heading, 'That in all things He might have the pre-eminence.'[302] Mundell, a layman, was a figure of some prominence and influence during the early years of the movement in Britain. When the P.M.U. was founded in 1909, Mundell, who was described as a "well-known London Solicitor," was among the seven members of its Executive Council, and was indeed listed third following Cecil Polhill and Alexander Boddy.[303]

The solicitor's role within these early years was varied, but significant in each area of involvement. He engaged in polemical forays on behalf of the Pentecostal cause and these included his *Letter to a Friend*, which was essentially an exposition on the relationship of the "gift of Tongues" to the baptism of the Spirit,[304] and his treatment of one of the movement's most problematic and contentious issues in an article titled "False Prophets and Messages."[305] In addition to such writings Mundell was prominent on the conference platform. He addressed Cecil Polhill's Bedford Conference of 1910[306] and it is recorded that at the Whitsuntide Conference of that year, "Mr. Mundell of South Croydon and London," testified to "Pentecostal Blessings."[307] He was also among the speakers at the "Eight Days' Mission for the Deepening of Spiritual Life" that was held at Holborn Hall, in Gray's Inn Road, London between April 24th and May 2nd 1912.[308] Further evidence of the esteem in which he was held is apparent in that fact that while Polhill was overseas in China during 1911, enquiries and other business relating to "those who are called to the Mission Field" were to be directed to Mr. Mundell.[309]

An interesting feature of the developing Pentecostal movement was the recognition of the need for adequate and credible training which was faithful to the central rubric of the baptism of the Holy Spirit. This was forthrightly expressed by a visiting leader from the Netherlands where similar challenges were being encountered. He enjoined the movement to consider that "since God is calling such fine people into His work, and is giving them in the Pentecostal Baptism such a wonderful spiritual equipment, it seems to me we ought to do our very best to add the very best training that human learning is able to

---

[300] "The Pentecostal Movement," *Confidence*, August 1910, 196.

[301] "The London Conference," *Confidence*, February 1912, 36.

[302] "Pentecostal Items," *Confidence*, December 1910, 278.

[303] "The Pentecostal Missionary Union," *Confidence*, January 1909, 13.

[304] "This is of God: A Letter to a Friend," *Confidence*, October 1909, 233-235.

[305] "False Prophets and Messages," *Confidence*, January 1911, 11, 14-15.

[306] "Brief Notes," *Confidence*, April 1910, 86.

[307] "Day by Day at the Convention," *Confidence*, June 1910, 129.

[308] "The Pentecostal Meetings in London," *Confidence*, May 1912, 106.

[309] "The Pentecostal Missionary Union," *Confidence*, January 1911, 24.

afford." His express intention was to impress upon English Pentecostals the necessity of taking a "deep interest not only in the missionaries out in the field, but also in those who are being prepared for the holy war."[310] A Bible School was established and placed under the directorship of Pastor Niblock at 7 Howley Place in Paddington. By the autumn of 1909 it was catering for "about ten students" whose daily schedule was outlined in *Confidence*.[311] A Training Home for female missionaries, located at 116 King Edward Road, Hackney, was established the following year. Among the prominent functionaries present at the opening service were "Pastor Niblock, Pastor Jeffreys and Mr. Mundell."[312] It worth noting that early engagement in the Pentecostal cause facilitated the conjoined efforts of otherwise diverse individuals; in this instance we see the collaboration of an independent peripatetic preacher, a Welsh Nonconformist, and a professional Anglican layman.

Mundell also addressed those who gathered for the opening of the re-constituted Men's Training Home in 1913.[313] Involvement at the organizational level in Pentecostal training was to continue; in 1920 he invited a young pastor recently moved to the capital from Birmingham, to his home for afternoon tea. The proposition put to Howard Carter was that he take over as principal of the Hampstead Bible School, an eventuality to which the prospective incumbent was by no means immediately inclined. Yet according to Whittaker's depiction Mundell overcame Carter's reluctance and persuaded him to undertake a position which he would occupy for twenty-seven and a half years and which would constitute "his life's main work."[314]

The picture that emerges of this well regarded London solicitor who was based in south Croydon, is of an individual exercising leadership beyond the local level in the emerging Pentecostal movement. His membership of the first Executive Council of the P.M.U., his proximity to Boddy and Polhill, his prominence on Conference platforms, his involvement in training, in addition to his polemical forays on behalf of the Pentecostal cause, confirm his place among the first coterie of leaders to emerge at the upper echelons of English Pentecostalism. In an era when, according to Gee, there were "only a few little Pentecostal Assemblies" in the capital city, the fact that a Holiness Mission in

---

310 "The P.M.U. Training Home," *Confidence,* October 1909, 219; See also "P.M.U.," *Confidence,* November 1909, 253-254.

311 "Pentecostal News: London," *Confidence,* September 1909, 206.

312 "The P.M.U. Bible School at Hackney," *Confidence,* February 1910, 32-33.

313 "The Men's Missionary Training Home," *Flames of Fire,* October 1913, 4.

314 Whitaker, *The Inside Story,* 108-109. When considered in the context of a period of organisational foment which will be explored further in Section 3, Carter's initial uncertainty is more comprehensible. His reluctance is intimated in the P.M.U. Council Minutes of 19 May 1921, Book II, 337, and 4 May 1923, Book III, 135. Insights into Carter's oversight of the Bible Training School as well as his Pentecostal involvement generally are to be found in the biographical memoir written by his brother. See John Carter, *Howard Carter: Man of the Spirit* (Nottingham: Assemblies of God Publishing House, 1971).

South London "had embraced the Pentecostal testimony"[315] was rendered the more significant by virtue of its association with this solicitor and godson of Dean Tait who would later become Archbishop of Canterbury.[316]

A Stable and Developing Mission

Inchcombe, the other notable Croydon solicitor who aligned himself with the emerging Pentecostal cause, did not exercise comparable influence or attain this degree of prominence throughout the movement. Rather his energies appear to have been principally directed toward the oversight and welfare of his immediate congregation. While regularly attending the London conferences and numbering among the speakers on more than one occasion,[317] Inchcombe does not appear to have engaged in a peripatetic ministry or asserted himself as a leader in other institutional spheres.[318] He was, in reality, more likely to seek to secure the ministry of others for the benefit of his own congregation. In addition to visits from such influential figures as Mrs. Boddy and Brother Niblock, T. B. Barratt and Alexander Boddy also made their way to Croydon.[319] The latter wrote of the "privilege of visiting Pastor Inchcombe," and of "kneeling with him in prayer in that place of blessing."[320] The next time Boddy travelled to Croydon it would be to visit the new hall to which the Holiness Mission had relocated. Inchcombe reported that this building which he regarded as "much more suitable for the work" had opened for its first service on Whit-Sunday 1916. Divine favour of a numerically modest nature was held to have attended the event in which "one soul professed to be saved, another

---

[315] Gee, *The Pentecostal Movement*, 55.

[316] It seems that this ecclesiastical association was vaunted by later Pentecostals. Mundell's obituary in the official organ of the Assemblies of God, the denominational body with which he later involved himself, stated that his parents had been "intimate friends" of Dean Tait and that it was by virtue of this that he became godfather to the infant Mundell. Beyond this observation little detail of the solicitor's Anglican background is uncovered. See "Home-Call of Mr. T. H. Mundell," *Redemption Tidings*, 1 December 1934, 1, and Gee, *The Pentecostal Movement*, 55. This seems to be in keeping with an activist orientation among denominationalists who were more intent upon the construction and development of their fledgling organisations than upon exploring or documenting the churchmanship or previous allegiances of Pentecostal protagonists.

[317] "The National Convention at Westminster," *Confidence*, July 1916, 112. Both Inchcombe and Mundell were among the speakers at the Conference that was held in Caxton Hall, Westminster in 1915. See "The Whitsuntide Conference in London," *Flames of Fire*, May 1915, 8. Two years later Inchcombe addressed the conference on what Boddy described as "his special theme of Holiness." See "The Whitsuntide Convention," *Confidence*, July-August 1917, 57.

[318] McGuire, *Religion: The Social Context*, 154.

[319] "Pentecostal Items," *Confidence*, December 1910, 278.

[320] "Pentecostal Items," *Confidence*, October 1910, 227.

sanctified." On the following Sunday the new hall was visited by Polhill and Wigglesworth, of whom it was stated that the latter was "quite at home, although he had never visited us before."[321]

On the occasion of his previous visit to "that place of blessing," Boddy, without conveying specific details, informed his readership that Mrs. Inchcombe had "for some time been fighting a fight of faith, and is glad to have the prayers of God's people for perfect Victory."[322] The inclusion in *Confidence* of an account of his visit to the new premises shed retrospective light on the nature of this lady's particular trial of faith. Boddy described Wednesday 30th August, 1917, as a "day of privilege." This began with his participation in a Morning Service in Christ Church, close to Kew Gardens. On arrival at No. 95 Sydenham Road, the visitor was ushered into a large vestry at the rear of the platform. Employing his pragmatic and descriptive propensities, the editor of *Confidence* informed his readership that the building had a large basement hall, "dry and well heated," which was primarily used for young people. The main meeting space had a "handsome high panelled roof and good lighting arrangement." It is recorded that the entire property, which included the house, cost £1,700, of which £500 remained outstanding at that point. Boddy, in line with an early Pentecostal preoccupation already highlighted, added the comment that "much prayer goes up for the speedy reduction of this sum."[323] Mudie-Smith's survey had despairingly highlighted South London's "whole collection of shabby, dilapidated mission-halls of tin or drab brick." It is clear from Boddy's description that the new premises at 95 Sydenham Road could not be numbered among these "lamentable erections" which were too frequently "offered as homes for the spiritual nourishment of the poor."[324]

When Boddy entered the Hall in the company of his hosts he was impressed to discover it to be "completely filled" to its two hundred and fifty seat capacity. The occasion of this gathering was the weekly afternoon waiting meeting - still being conducted in 1916 - and he was pleased to note the number of "brothers" present, despite the time of commencement. He was to encounter one of these "brothers" in his regular capacity as tram driver later that afternoon. The observation was made that the "Sisters (members) of this Holiness Mission all wear a distinctive bonnet, which is neat and becoming."[325]

---

[321] "Croydon: Opening of New Holiness Hall," *Confidence*, September 1916, 152.

[322] "Pentecostal Items," *Confidence*, October 1910, 227.

[323] "A Holiness Mission at Croydon," *Confidence*, September-October 1917, 76.

[324] Charles F. G. Masterman, "The Problem of South London," in Mudie-Smith, ed., *The Religious Life of London*, 202.

[325] "A Holiness Mission at Croydon," *Confidence*, September-October 1917, 76; Phoebe Palmer, influential in America as an itinerant evangelist, editor of the periodical *Guide to Holiness*, and host of the *Tuesday Meetings for the Promotion of Holiness* in New York, spent five years in Britain during the 1860s. Among other things, she inspired Catherine Booth to preach, and through this influenced the Salvation Army bonnet-ministry. See Orr, *The Second Evangelical Awakening*, 106, and Harold E. Raser, *Phoebe Palmer: Her Life and Thought* Studies in Women and Religion, 22

Commenting on the background and pedigree of this Pentecostal Centre Boddy stated:

> For some 36 years Pastor Inchcombe and his gifted wife have taught in this neighbourhood the deeper truths of Sanctification, the Baptism in the Spirit and Divine Healing. They are a people who are accustomed to advanced deeper truths. Our Brother's reverent and incisively impressive mode of conducting the opening portions of the meeting was worthy of special note. His lengthy and beautiful prayer had so much of deeply reverent but arresting thought in it.[326]

Boddy preached on the theme of "Earthen Vessels" (2 Cor. 4:7), in addition to giving personal testimony. During his oration a Sister "intervened" with a message in tongues which was described in approbatory terms as being "in a very clear language."[327] Mrs. Inchcombe conducted the latter stages of the meeting, both thanking the visitor and speaking of the history of their work in the Holiness Mission. In common with other wives of pastors and leaders involved in emergent Pentecostalism, she appears to have played an active and visible role in the ministry being undertaken. Her aforementioned "fight of faith"[328] is elucidated seven years on in the comment that "Mrs. Inchcombe has been raised up to a new life from being a helpless invalid. Faith in the atoning work of the Lord has done it."[329]

Further insight into the dynamic momentum of the wider Pentecostal phenomenon is furnished by Boddy's recollection of the time of refreshment that took place in the lower hall at the close of the meeting. He expressed his gratification at encountering many who had been to the Sunderland Convention, its London counterpart, or the regular meetings hosted by Polhill at Sion College, close to the Embankment.[330] Evidently the movement retained a significant degree of cohesiveness, ideological and structural, as it approached the twilight of its first decade in England, with the ethos instilled by Boddy and Polhill via their Whitsuntide Conferences, and other channels of influence, remaining operative. Croydon's Holiness Mission Hall, as a particular historical locality, appears to have positively assimilated Pentecostal emphases and to have translated these into prominent features of the life and growth of this longstanding independent religious community.

Conclusion

This section presented an overview of the size, scale, and nature of the Pentecostal movement, identifiable from 1908, which was initially formed

(Lewiston, NY.: Edwin Mellen Press, 1987).

[326] "A Holiness Mission at Croydon," *Confidence*, September-October 1917, 76.
[327] "A Holiness Mission at Croydon," *Confidence*, September-October 1917, 76.
[328] "Pentecostal Items," *Confidence*, October 1910, 227.
[329] "A Holiness Mission at Croydon," *Confidence*, September-October 1917, 77.
[330] "A Holiness Mission at Croydon," *Confidence*, September-October 1917, 77.

under the solicitous oversight of the Vicar of All Saints', Monkwearmouth, Sunderland. While the difficulties associated with the application of strict statistical accuracy to this pre-denominational era have been acknowledged, it has been established that during the years under consideration, the number of those associated with the Pentecostal cause grew from several hundred toward a constituency in the region of 5,000 individuals. Perhaps more importantly, and certainly more in tune with the priorities of those whose emphasis was on "quality of belief rather than on quantity of members,"[331] insights have been offered into the rationale for, and elemental nature of, the movement that emerged. Churches, mission halls, and even domestic fellowships which were part of a dynamic and diversified evangelical sector, embarked upon a form of voluntary association whose primary aim was the provision and furtherance of mutual support and edification without impugning or imperilling existing denominational (or indeed non-denominational) allegiances.

This *collegia pietatis* model, apparent from the earliest editions of *Confidence* magazine, betrays notable similarity to that adopted by Reader Harris in the formation of the Pentecostal League of Prayer as a trans-denominational body in 1891, and the prior involvement of emerging Pentecostal leaders with his cause has been amply demonstrated. Boddy, as Harris had done, evidently envisaged a *Gesellschaft* form of association which would allow participants to co-operate in the pursuit of the shared aim of renewal across a range of traditions, and to do this while maintaining pre-existing allegiances and functions.[332] Identification with a loosely-aligned and organic conglomeration afforded Wigglesworth, Hutchinson, and Inchcombe, as well as other leaders and their disparate congregations, a sense of purpose and belonging alongside others who shared similar convictions and aspirations. Such benefits were conveyed without any attempt to encroach upon or undermine the essential autonomy of the eclectic and independently constituted ventures that chose to associate under the aegis of the Pentecostal message.

Consideration of the specific contexts in which Centres of Pentecostal activity emerged has proven fruitful. Each of those examined has demonstrated prior interest in and involvement with England's Holiness fraternity. Hinterlands of religious growth, diversification, and evangelical activism have been shown to have provided contexts amenable to the reception and propagation of the Pentecostal message. Moreover each of the pivotal leaders identified has exhibited a propensity, at times pronounced, for intensity of devotion within the parameters of recognizable forms of evangelical spiritual experience.

What has been outlined in this section concurs with the observation that "face-to-face recruitment along lines of pre-existing significant social relationships" is central to the spread of modern religious movements. Wigglesworth, for instance, travelled to Sunderland in person to witness phenomena then occurring in the parish of a Vicar of whom he had previously

---

[331] Gay, *Geography of Religion in England*, 177-178.
[332] Martin, *Sociology of English Religion* (London: SCM Press, 1967), 105-106.

read in the pages of *Tongues of Fire*, the official organ of the organisation of which they were both members. Mrs. Boddy, it would appear, had been in the habit of visiting and participating in meetings for spiritual edification in Croydon, and she proved to be the *catalytic agent*[333] in the introduction of the Pentecostal message to the Holiness Mission Hall. At another level the Sunderland Whitsuntide Convention not only functioned as an effective mechanism for the transmission and diffusion of Pentecostal ideology, but served as a nexus for the furtherance of significant interpersonal relations, interaction, and exchange.

The unique collaboration between Alexander Boddy and Cecil Polhill, English Pentecostalism's most prominent leaders until c. 1920, was itself instigated by their meeting at the Convention of 1908. Their combined internationalist perspectives, evident in the pages of their respective and singularly influential magazines, as well as on the platforms of the gatherings they convened, provided hitherto disparate and isolated congregations with a sense of involvement in a spiritual awakening of global proportions, as well as of ultimate significance. Their balanced and measured approaches, which will become further apparent in Sections 2 and 3, also served to establish mores which those who would function under the auspices of their leadership would not just abide by, but come to imbibe as normative. Never, it would appear, as imposing of authority or personality as Reader Harris had been in the context of his League of Prayer,[334] Polhill, and especially Boddy, came to fulfil statesman-like as well as sacerdotal roles across the Pentecostal constituency. Their presence at the opening of a mission hall, as in Bournemouth, or the bestowal of an *imprimatur* as occurred with respect of the Bowland Street Mission in the aftermath of perceived criticism, represented instances of a centrifugal tendency which conveyed authority, affirmation, and influence from the emerging elite toward the localised Pentecostal context.

---

[333] Gerlach and Hine, "Growth and Spread of a Modern Religious Movement," 30.

[334] Ford has highlighted Harris' combative propensities and in particular his aptitude for controversy and polemic in defence of his version of Holiness orthodoxy. See *What the Holiness People Believe*, 51. Firsthand evidence of a tendency toward self-aggrandizement, as well as what were perceived to be unappealing proclamations of spiritual and moral authority, were recorded by Charles Booth who attended Pentecostal League gatherings at both Exeter and Speke Halls in London for the purpose of his religious survey. See *Life and Labour*, 3rd series, *Religious Influences*, vol. 5, 223-225.

SECTION TWO

Ideological Developments

Introduction

Why Spirituality?

It is no longer the case that an article reviewing recent writing on Christian spirituality, such as that which appeared in the *Scottish Journal of Theology* in 1975,[1] would not include some treatment of the Pentecostal and/or Charismatic dimension. The ensuing decades have witnessed considerable alteration, and what has been acknowledged by some as an unprecedented and unexpected emergence of a *Third Force in Christendom*,[2] has been described as a recovery of a "primal piety" whose "archetypal modes of worship" present the key to how Pentecostalism acquired its capacity to "root itself in almost any culture."[3] It has become normative for general works to include reference to Pentecostal religious expression as it emerged during the twentieth-century, and to acknowledge this to represent a vibrant and distinctive contribution to the varieties of Christian spirituality.[4] A recent synoptic study indeed stated that "one of the most distinctive features of English spirituality in the twentieth-century is the growth of the Pentecostal movement."[5]

It is contested that for the purposes of the present undertaking, spirituality as a category for the study of early Pentecostal lived religion, is preferable to the related areas of theology or doctrinal formulation. In spite of possessing an

---

[1] Robert M. Yule, "Recent Writing on Christian Spirituality: An Article Review," *Scottish Journal of Theology*, 28.6 (1975): 588-598.

[2] Synan, *The Holiness-Pentecostal Tradition*, 280.

[3] Cox, *The Rise of Pentecostal Spirituality*, 99, 101.

[4] See for instance Steven J. Land, "Pentecostal Spirituality: Living in the Spirit," in Louis Dupre and Dan E. Saliers, eds., *Christian Spirituality: Post-Reformation and Modern* (London: SCM Press, 1990), 479-499; Walter J. Hollenweger, "Pentecostals and the Charismatic Movement," in Cheslyn Jones, Geoffrey Wainwright and Edward Yarnold, eds., *The Study of Spirituality* (London: SPCK, 1996), 549-554; Bradley P. Holt, *A Brief History of Christian Spirituality* (Oxford: Lion Publishing, 1997), 124-127. A recent work which charts "the unexpected resurgence of religion" has alotted particular attention to "the remarkable case of Pentecostalism." See Alister McGrath, *The Twilight of Atheism: The Rise and Fall of Disbelief in the Modern World* (Rider: London, 2004), 192-197, 214-216, 277-278.

[5] Gordon Mursell, *English Spirituality: From 1700 to the Present Day* (London: SPCK, 2001), 405.

L.Th. from Durham,[6] and being the most theologically literate of Britain's first generation of Pentecostal leaders, Robinson has described Alexander Boddy as undertaking "fairly primitive attempts at theological interpretation"[7] on behalf of the movement of which he was a primary architect. Gee himself described the phenomenon as "a movement emphasising an experience rather than a merely abstract doctrine."[8] If as Macquarrie has stated, theology and spirituality are two paths "by which men seek God," then the latter path was certainly the one most frequently trodden by England's emerging Pentecostals. However as he also pointed out, these paths are not mutually exclusive, but rather they tend towards a convergence which he designates "dynamic theology."[9] It is this dynamism which elicits Sheldrake's description of spirituality as *lived theology*.[10] If, as a recent commentator has suggested, this "essentially oral, musical and experimental movement" is by virtue of its essential nature "less susceptible to neat academic assessment,"[11] then it is contested that the development of its practical spirituality during the period under consideration offers not just a viable but an essential mode of investigation.

In advancing a rationale for the basis of his exploration of Pentecostal spirituality, Land has stated that while acknowledging the imperative of critical history, as opposed to the ritualized or romanticized versions of some participants, neither these nor psycho-social deprivation[12] approaches are capable of yielding the most comprehensive and satisfactory appreciation of the phenomenon. Such methodologies do not adequately explore what he terms the "depth and inner logic of Pentecostal spirituality."[13] Indeed it is the case that while its earliest English manifestation eschewed defining itself in overtly

---

[6] *Crockford's Clerical Directory*, 122.

[7] Robinson, "The Charismatic Anglican," 108, 114. It is instructive to note that a theological sluggishness has been observed to have been common among Nonconformist bodies of the late nineteenth-century. According to Reardon, British Congregationalists represented an exception to this general tendency. See Bernard M. G. Reardon, *Religious Thought in the Victorian Age: A Survey from Coleridge to Gore*, 2nd ed. (Longman, 1995), 15.

[8] Gee, "The Pentecostal Movement: A Short History of its Rise and Development," *Redemption Tidings*, August 1932, 3.

[9] John Macquarrie, *Paths in Spirituality* 2nd ed. (London: SCM Press, 1992), 72.

[10] Philip Sheldrake, *Spirituality and Theology: Christian Living and the Doctrine of God* (London: Darton, Longman and Todd, 1998), 3ff.

[11] Mursell, *English Spirituality*, 405.

[12] Prominent studies which have adopted the latter approach include Robert Mapes Anderson, *Vision of the Disinherited: The Making of American Pentecostalism* (Oxford: Oxford University Press, 1979), and Cheryl Bridges Johns, *Pentecostal Formation: A Pedagogy Among the Oppressed* (Sheffield: Sheffield Academic Press, 1993).

[13] Land, "Pentecostal Spirituality," 481. This point has also been made by Gerlach and Hine in the context of their examination of the dynamics observed in the growth and spread of Pentecostalism. See "Growth and Spread of a Modern Religious Movement," 38.

organisational or structural terms, its claim to an essentially spiritual identity was repeatedly advanced. Programmes and strategies were regarded as subservient to "the intensive work of the Holy Spirit"[14] among those who described themselves as an "advance-guard of earnest Christians,"[15] and who took upon themselves the restoration of "whole-meal Christianity"[16] in the religious world of their day. Such a revolution could only be accomplished by the Holy Spirit taking, not only "possession of the faculties of the soul," but also of the "members of the body to the glory of the Triune God."[17] It is suggested that any attempt to investigate the ideological development of this movement must come to terms with the depth and inner logic of these uncompromisingly spiritual preoccupations.

The term ideological as employed in this context, encompasses the interaction and exchange of ideas and convictions, theory and practice, that suffused the Pentecostal movement during its first two decades. Neither its theoretical formulations nor its patterns and practices of behaviour and expression took shape in isolation. It is rather the case that, as in other evangelical movements characterised by practical Christianity and religious devotion, "convictions both shaped and were shaped by concrete experience."[18] As will be amply demonstrated, the early years of this movement represent a period of foment and fertility in the exchange and refinement of ideas, the modification of practice, and the overall construction of an identifiably Pentecostal spirituality. Ideological is to be understood as embracing the different elements of this developmental process.

Historico-Thematic Approach

It is perhaps the case that in approaching the rich and varied material that constitutes the historical record of early Pentecostals' lived religion, a denominationalist writer might fall prey to the temptation to seek to unravel the seemingly intractable ambiguity surrounding the identification of tongues as the *sine qua non* of the baptism of the Spirit. This issue is indeed discussed below, although the primary material uncovered will do little to satisfy those in search of a definitive resolution, and it is not accorded more attention than it merited in the priorities of the original protagonists. The present writer has sought to avoid anachronistic interpolation[19] and instead endeavoured to highlight and

---

[14] "The Pentecostal Movement," *Confidence*, July 1915, 124.

[15] "The Pentecostal Movement," *Confidence*, August 1910, 196.

[16] Arthur S. Booth-Clibborn, "The Why and How of this Revival," *Confidence*, June 1910, 143.

[17] Barratt, *In the Days of the Latter Rain*, 197.

[18] Randall, *A Study in the Spirituality of English Evangelicalism*, 2.

[19] It is difficult to avoid the conclusion that a recent writer has approached the early years of the phenomenon in order to bolster the case for women in contemporary Pentecostal ministry. See Diana Chapman, "The Rise and Demise of Women's Ministry in the Origins and Early Years of Pentecostalism in Britain," *Journal of Pentecostal*

concentrate on aspects of emerging Pentecostal religion that would have been most pertinent and recognisable to participants in the movement. The five resultant categories represent issues and concerns that were prominently aired and discussed in periodicals, as well as on conference platforms, and it is contested that they encompass salient aspects of this evolving and developing strain of religious expression.

In the preamble to his study of specific manifestations of evangelical spirituality in England during the inter-war period, Randall identifies three principal modes of investigation. These are the examination and categorisation of spirituality in terms of denomination or churchmanship, in terms of themes or dominant *motifs*, and lastly according to typology based on theological orientation or world-view.[20] Each of these is represented in the forthcoming exploration of the ideological developments that occurred within English Pentecostalism between 1907 and 1925. This section is presented in the form of an essentially thematic approach which outlines and examines five aspects of Pentecostal spirituality, the first four of which follow a broadly chronological narrative. Beginning with patterns of entry into Pentecostal experience which are evident from 1907, these progress from individual to collective preoccupations and then outwards toward the consideration of large-scale revivalistic endeavours which, in the 1920s, came to illuminate the Pentecostal cause across a broader historical canvass. The fifth and final category departs

---

Theology 12.2 (2004): 217-246. This undercurrent is made explicit in the rallying-cry issued as a final flourish at the end of the paper. I would suggest that the *rise* of women's ministry was far from being as "radical" as Chapman suggests (p. 234) – prominent and active roles occupied by women across Holiness movements being an obvious case in point - and that its posited *demise* is likewise overstated, at least at this point in Pentecostal development. A discussion among leaders at the last Sunderland Convention is cited by Chapman as marking the beginnings of deliberate diminution, if not determined suppression, of a perceived hitherto unrestricted role for women. It is ironic that the only documented female contribution to this debate saw Mrs. Polman extol the fact that women "had great liberality in this Pentecostal movement." See "Woman's Place in the Church," *Confidence*, November 1914, 214. I would contest that this publicised discussion was most notable for its singularity, and that the question of women in ministry or woman's role in the church was not a vexed, contentious, or even a prominent issue for the first generation of English Pentecostals. On the contrary the 1914 debate, which reached no formal conclusions and issued no decrees, shows leaders of conservative evangelical persuasion seeking to accord women a more dynamic and pnuematic role than was typically the case within their respective traditions. While denominational bodies may have curtailed the role of women in subsequent decades, to attribute this to deliberations that took place in Sunderland prior to the First World War is to fall prey to anachronism.

[20] Randall, *A Study in the Spirituality of English Evangelicalism*, 6-7. These "frameworks" of investigation are expounded in more detail in Sheldrake, *Spirituality and History*, 196-218. A collection of essays which adopts the churchmanship approach is to be found in Frank C. Senn, ed., *Protestant Spiritual Traditions* (New York: Paulist Press, 1996).

from chronological progression to examine a pervasive and broadly consistent theme which underwent little refinement during the period under consideration. Of notable interest in its own right, it also offers an interesting and necessary contrast to the previous themes, while elucidating the analysis of early Pentecostal spirituality along the dimensions of churchmanship and theological world-view.

Churchmanship

Those who initially came to sympathise with, and participate in, the Pentecostal dimension as it came to be promulgated from Sunderland in 1907 were drawn from a variety of demoninational and non-denominational backgrounds. As has already been pointed out, Gee observed that far from being recently proselytized converts these were "almost all of them experienced Christians, and many of them active workers." These "Christians of mature spiritual experience" were linked, if not denominationally, then certainly by conservative evangelical persuasion. His further acknowledgement that pioneering Pentecostals had "often tasted a previous experience of the Spirit's grace and power in connection with the Holiness and Keswick movements,"[21] provides further clarification of churchmanship and orientation.

While prior involvement in Wesleyan-Holiness endeavours has already been demonstrated in Section 1, further aspects of the disjuncture that occurred with proponents of such views will be explored in Section 2. In the course of each of the five themes or categories to be considered, inherited traits will be acknowledged and highlighted, while distinctive Pentecostal nuances and departures will also be identified. Much will be uncovered which will demonstrate that Pentecostal theory and practice did not develop *sui generis*, but was forged at the heart of an evangelical *milieu* whose influence proved longstanding and pervasive. In short, the veracity of the statement that "the evidence from developments in England is that the spirituality of Pentecostalism forms part of the wider story of the evangelical search for spiritual experience"[22] will be amply explored with respect of the years 1907 to 1925 in the pages that follow.

Theological World-View

Methodist scholar Geoffrey Wainwright, in an analysis of typologies of spirituality adopted from a seminal work by Richard Niebuhr, has categorised Pentecostalism alongside martyrdom and primitive monasticism as an embodiment of the *Christ against Culture* world-view.[23] Niebuhr's original

---

[21] Gee, *The Pentecostal Movement*, 48-49.

[22] Randall, "Pentecostalism and Evangelical Spirituality in England," 80.

[23] Wainwright, "Types of Spirituality," in Jones, Wainwright and Yarnold, eds., *The Study of Spirituality*, 595.

study which did not directly address Pentecostal piety, was based on an exploration of a recurrent religious dynamic which he termed an "infinite dialogue" observed to have characterised the course of Christian history. This involved a "double movement from world to God and from God to world" and something of a perpetual oscillation between these poles, he averred, could be expected as long as Christians continue to be "challenged to abandon all things for the sake of God," while "being sent back into the world to teach and practise all the things that have been commanded them."[24]

While in certain respects conforming to the essentials of the *Christ against Culture* world-view, emergent Pentecostal spirituality, as thematically presented here, displays notable evidence of a world-affirming disposition more readily associated with *Christ above Culture*. The limitations inherent in this mode of analysis were acknowledged by Niebuhr and while "historically inadequate," it has the merit of drawing attention to the "continuity and significance of the great *motifs* that appear in the long wrestling of Christians with their enduring problem."[25] England's early Pentecostals will be shown to have wrestled with this enduring problem in their pursuit of the presence of the divine and their quest to actualise the sacred in the temporal realm, not merely recoiling from the perceived vanities of the world, but straining to "shout out the midnight cry throughout the whole world."[26] Alongside other modes of categorisation, the theological world-view will provide an enlightening analytical tool for the study of emerging Pentecostal religion.

Historiography

Finally elements of what is explored in this section will present a challenge to existing Pentecostal historiographies. Three aspects of this challenge will be highlighted. What follows will offer a critique of the *sacred meteor* theory, or the notion that the Pentecostal phenomenon arrived fully-formed, "suddenly from heaven." This phrase derives from an influential denominational history dating from the 1960s of which it has recently been observed: "Perhaps more than he realised, Brumback's main title exemplified one of the revival's deepest assumptions."[27] As has been made apparent in the Introductory Section it was not only North America which generated a corpus of literature which, largely uninformed by modern historical methodology, was content, even pleased, to portray the origins of their movement as having been "forged outside the

---

[24] H. Richard Niebuhr, *Christ and Culture* (London: Faber and Faber Limited, 1952), 53, 43.

[25] Niebuhr, *Christ and Culture*, 56-57.

[26] P. Edel, "Behold, the Bridegroom Cometh!" *Confidence*, January 1914, 9.

[27] See Carl Brumback, *Suddenly...From Heaven: A History of the Assemblies of God* (Springfield, Missouri: Gospel Publishing House, 1961), and James R. Goff, JR. and Grant Wacker, "Introduction," in Goff and Wacker, eds., *Portraits of a Generation: Early Pentecostal Leaders*, xvii.

ordinary processes of history."[28] While commendable historical practitioners have come to acknowledge and counteract this tendency,[29] the present investigation represents a further opportunity to secure its demise, while being one among very few to have done so with respect of Pentecostal origins and evolution in England. Secondly it will also undermine the insinuation present in later denominational writings, notably those of the uniquely influential Donald Gee, which suggests that English Pentecostalism's incipient phase was characterised by weak leadership, irresolution, and a stultifying of the inspirational dimension. Thirdly it will present a challenge to an unhelpful historiographical tendency which Anderson has termed "the made-in-the-USA" assumption.[30] In support of a recent observation that Pentecostalism has had many beginnings and that there are many "Pentecostalisms,"[31] significant light will be shed on the emergence and ideological and practical moulding of its distinctly English embodiment by distinctly English practitioners.

Section 2.1: "This Fiery Baptism": Pentecostal Initiation

In the first issue of *Confidence* magazine its founder and editor posed the rhetorical question, "What hath God wrought?" By way of response Boddy related that while only "some five or six persons in Great Britain" had been *"in the experience"* in the first half of 1907, by April 1908 there were believed to be in excess of five hundred. He deliberately pointed out that in making this claim, he was attesting to something that was "quite different to 500 conversions." This, it was solemnly announced, was a subsequent and "deep work, from which it would be terrible to turn back."[32] Remarkable insights into what this experience entailed can be gleaned from the numerous personal testimonies that are to be found in the pages of *Confidence* during its early years.[33] One such took the form of a letter from a John Martin of Motherwell, dated 6th of March, 1908, which stated:

---

[28] Wacker, "Reflections on History Writing among Early Pentecostals," 81.

[29] In addition to the writings of Grant Wacker, an exemplar of the historical method, see for instance Augustus Cerillo Jr., "Interpretative Approaches to the History of American Pentecostal Origins," *Pnuema: The Journal of the Society for Pentecostal Studies* 19.1 (Spring 1997): 29-52.

[30] Anderson, *Introduction to Global Pentecostalism*, 170.

[31] Everett A. Wilson, "They Crossed the Red Sea, Didn't They?: Critical History and Pentecostal Beginnings," in Dempster, Klaus, and Peterson, eds., *The Globalization of Pentecostalism*, 107.

[32] "'Confidence': Our First Number," *Confidence*, April 1908, 3.

[33] Peter Hocken has observed that the earliest Pentecostal understandings of baptism in the Holy Spirit are "best grasped from testimonies which abound in all their broadsheets and magazines." See *The Glory and the Shame: Reflections on the 20th Century Outpouring of the Holy Spirit* (Guildford: Eagle, 1994), 53.

I know you will be glad to learn that I have received my Pentecost with its seal of the New Testament evidence. You will remember I was with you for a week-end and enjoyed it very much...I know I ought to have come through when I was with you, I do not know what hindered, unless that I limited the power of the atoning blood of Christ...I *came through* as it is called, not unaptly...in the kitchen of our dear brother, Mr. Andrew Murdoch, the Leader of the Westport Hall, Kilsyth, where perhaps 200 have been sealed. Not two of us come through alike, I was three hours on my back, and when I was in that lowly position, I stripped myself of every hindrance...and offered my vows unto God, at any cost or any price...I said, 'Lord, I mean what I say, You will lift a corpse off this floor, but I will see you face to face in this Fiery Baptism.[34]

Martin went on to recount how while in this state of supplication he began to "plead the blood of Christ," and felt his capacity to speak in English severely impaired; he could only utter the word "Blood." An overwhelming sense of inner compulsion resulted in utterances in what he claimed to be three languages. These he identified as "a few words in Hebrew, more in an East African Bantu tongue like Swahelli, and what was taken to be an Indian dialect." He further recounted a loss of mobility, but after an unspecified time, "as the night (or early morning) wore on, I got up, staggering like a drunken man."[35] Some of the practical ramifications for the life of this individual will be recounted in the treatment of Pentecostal otherworldliness below, but at present, Martin's concluding statements in relation to what he had undergone are worthy of consideration:

This Baptism is the one cure for all weak Christianity under whatever name it may shelter itself. No wonder Jesus charged His disciples to tarry until they were endued with power from on high. Hallelujah! The Fire has fallen, and now, Dear Brother, go on. You have been helping us all, even when you stood almost alone. This work no one can stay, God is marching on and sealing His own people. Yours under His Seal, till He comes, John Martin.[36]

Tongues and Pentecostal Initiation

While as has been noted, notions of a baptism in the Holy Spirit were commonly espoused by Holiness advocates,[37] the reason that Boddy had found himself "ostracised"[38] from such and "almost alone,"[39] was its identification

---

[34] John Martin, "Testimony from Motherwell," *Confidence*, April 1908, 12-13.

[35] Martin, "Testimony from Motherwell," *Confidence*, April 1908, 12-13.

[36] Martin, "Testimony from Motherwell," *Confidence*, April 1908, 13.

[37] Contemporary instances in English periodicals include A. Pierson, "God's Chosen Vessels," *Tongues of Fire*, October 1905, 7; R. Harris, "The Gospel of the Comforter," *Tongues of Fire*, November 1905, 1-2; C. J. Fowler, "The More Excellent Way," *The Way of Holiness*, June 1911, 4; D. Thomas, "Editor's Notes: The Baptism," *The Holiness Mission Journal*, June 1911, 66.

[38] "Amazing Story by Vicar of Monkwearmouth Church: Mr. Boddy Ostracised,"

with what Martin termed "its seal of the New Testament evidence." When Reader Harris asserted that "the man or woman who is born again," can legitimately "seek and claim the mighty Pentecostal baptism with the Holy Ghost," he did not envisage an outcome such as had been recounted by the correspondent from Motherwell. According to Harris, the devil was, at the close of 1907, "making a strange attack upon true believers." This manifested itself in the form of teachers who were propagating the "devilish lie" that "unless God's people speak with tongues they are not baptized with the Holy Ghost." This infernal ploy would only succeed in "dragging the saints down from their excellency by making them seek for material evidence of the truth of God's Word, which God invites them to accept by faith."[40]

It is interesting to note that even within the emerging Pentecostal constituency, some ambiguity surrounded the status of the seal or sign of tongues as evidence of initiation into the experience. A direct correlation had been made in 1906 in the first issue of the influential *Apostolic Faith* magazine which was edited by William J. Seymour,[41] the leader of the Asuza Street Mission in Los Angeles. It stated: "Pentecost has surely come and with it the Bible evidences are following, many being converted and sanctified and filled with the Holy Ghost, speaking in tongues as they did on the day of Pentecost."[42] Another publication subsequently reported that across North America during the summer period, "the revival season for all tent and outdoor meetings...thousands have been baptised with the Holy Ghost." The claim was made that "every one reported to have spoken with other tongues as the Spirit of God gave them utterance as in Acts 2:4."[43]

When this sign was first manifested at Sunderland during Barratt's 1907 mission, the special correspondent of the *Daily Chronicle* learned from the host: "More than 20,000 people throughout the world are now so filled with the Holy Ghost that they are speaking in tongues. Of these Mr. Boddy informs me, about twenty are to be found in his parish."[44] Boddy had himself set out for Norway during March of that year having heard that "the Pentecostal Gift of

---

Lloyd's Weekly, 6 October 1907.

[39] Boddy himself referred to having been "very much alone" in his early espousal of this conception of the baptism of the Holy Spirit. See "The Pentecostal Movement," *Confidence*, August 1910, 196. His daughter subsequently highlighted the isolation he encountered within the Anglican communion. See J. V. Boddy, *Memoir*, 7.

[40] "A Slave, or a King?" *Tongues of Fire*, December 1907, 2.

[41] Wacker points out that Seymour never explicitly stated or acknowledged his editorship. See *Early Pentecostals and American Culture*, 286. This approach appears to have been inspired by the express notion that "there is no man at the head of this movement. God himself is speaking in the earth." See *The Apostolic Faith*, January 1908, 1.

[42] "Pentecost Has Come," *The Apostolic Faith*, September 1906, 1.

[43] "God Working Still in the Land," *Word and Witness*, December 1912, 3.

[44] "Alleged Healing: North Country Stirred by Strange Signs," *Daily Chronicle*, 5 October 1907.

Tongues was witnessing there to the incoming of the Holy Spirit in power."[45] The general impression conveyed by the literature of these early years was that the Holy Spirit "announces His arrival by speaking in other Tongues."[46] Yet it was not long before qualifications and modifications of this view began to be expressed and explored. Evidently mindful of criticisms that had been advanced, the opinion leaders of the movement in England were alive to the limitations of propounding this empirical sign as the *sine qua non* of the baptism of the Holy Spirit.

Boddy informed those gathered at a Men's Service at St. Gabriel's, Bishopwearmouth, in 1910 that "the Holy Spirit gives evidence of having taken possession of the believer's body by worshipping through the yielded tongue." Yet he went on to state that "the Lord Jesus is much more to us than the Speaking in Tongues."[47] He elsewhere stated that while "the Lord" was "vouchsafing in these days to true believers seeking Him with pure hearts, the Sign of Tongues," his experience was such that he could not necessarily or incontrovertibly say of a stranger: "This man is baptized in the Holy Ghost because he speaks in Tongues." In response to "many letters" and queries on this matter, Boddy had come to conclude that while *tongues* were "a sign of His mighty entrance," *love* was "the evidence of His continuance in controlling power."[48] Mary Boddy, whose brother Rev. James M. Pollock, former Missioner-in-chief at All Saints' had subsequently renounced the Pentecostal experience he had had during Barratt's initial mission,[49] confessed herself "more and more convinced" that "to speak in Tongues only is not, I can see, a sufficient sign of the Baptism." She had, by the end of 1909, observed that an exclusive emphasis on 'tongues' alone, to the neglect of personal

---

[45] "Tongues in Norway: A Pentecostal Experience," *Leaflets on Tongues* No. 6.

[46] "The Baptism of the Holy Ghost with the Sign of Tongues," *Confidence*, May 1909, 122.

[47] "Speaking in Tongues: What is It?" *Confidence*, May 1910, 99.

[48] "Tongues: The Pentecostal Sign," *Confidence*, November 1910, 260-261. Boddy appears to have had some sympathy with the logic of the position expressed by Reader Harris: "What shall we say of the millions of saints and martyrs throughout the dispensation who never spoke in Tongues? Were they not filled with the Spirit? Of course they were." See "The Gift of Tongues," *Tongues of Fire*, November 1907, 2.

[49] Robinson, "The Charismatic Anglican," 62-63. On the occasion of Boddy's removal from All Saints' he recounted the involvement of his brother-in-law soon after his first arrival in Sunderland. See "From Sunderland to Pittington," *Confidence*, January-March 1923, 66. Pollock was not mentioned in *Confidence* magazine until Boddy had become tangential to the movement. During the autumn of 1922 Boddy spent a month at 9 Brondesbury Road, Kilburn, while the incumbent vicar, "a very earnest preacher of the Gospel," enjoyed "a well-earned holiday." While there he visited the Rev. J. M. Pollock, M. A., who was "overseeing a church" in Wallington, near Croydon. While providing little other personal detail, Boddy pointed out that his erstwhile curate had become "identified with the Japan Evangelistic Band." See "An Autumn Month in North-West London," *Confidence*, October-December 1922, 50, 57.

transformation had already resulted in "many" instances in which "much dishonour and damage" had been visited upon "God's work."[50]

A note of equivocation was sounded by Barratt who, while suggesting that tongues "may attend every real infilling of the Holy Spirit," found himself "obliged to suppose that many have been thus filled, without the tongues, owing to ignorance or a definite resistance of this physical sign."[51] Further ambiguities are to be found in the proceedings of the Executive Council of the Pentecostal Missionary Union. Minutes of a meeting held on 23 May, 1916, recorded that after protracted deliberations, "the Council expressed the unanimous opinion that whilst all who are...so baptized do speak in tongues, more or less, yet this is not the only evidence of this Baptism, but the Recipient should also give clear proof by his life and magnify God, Acts 10:46."[52] It is perhaps not surprising that the latitude allowed by this statement, promulgated in *Confidence* magazine,[53] was not wholly appreciated by the wider Pentecostal constituency. It was Wigglesworth, appointed to the Executive Council during 1915,[54] who reported that the statement had been "considered very unsatisfactory by several of the Assemblies."[55] The subsequently revised statement proved revealing:

> The Members of the P. M. U. Council hold and teach that every Believer should be baptized with the Holy Ghost and that the Scriptures show that the Apostles regarded the speaking with Tongues as evidence that the Believer had been so baptized. Each seeker for the Baptism with the Holy Ghost should therefore expect God to give him a full measure of His sanctifying Grace in his heart and also to speak with Tongues and magnify God as a sign and confirmation that he is truly baptized with the Holy Ghost.[56]

It would appear that unspecified but significant purveyors of the Pentecostal experience throughout the wider movement were not content with indeterminate and accommodating statements regarding the nature of the baptism of the Holy Spirit. A more definite association of tongues with the baptism was sought and issued. It is not the intention in this context to engage in an extensive, much less a comprehensive analysis of the theological nuances of such positions, and indeed it is acknowledged that no easy resolution has been attained in the course of the intervening century.[57] The salient point for the

---

[50] M. Boddy, "The Real Baptism of the Holy Ghost," *Confidence*, November 1909, 260-261.

[51] Barratt, *In the Days of the Latter Rain*, 190. A similar rationale is to be found in his pamphlet, "The Truth about the Pentecostal Revival," 12-13.

[52] P. M. U. Council Minutes of 23 May 1916, Book I, 464.

[53] "The Pentecostal Missionary Union," *Confidence*, August 1916, 137-138.

[54] "The Pentecostal Missionary Union," *Confidence*, June 1915, 116.

[55] P. M. U. Council Minutes of 7 November 1916, Book I, 493-494.

[56] P. M. U. Council Minutes of 5 December 1916, Book I, 501-502. This was publicised in "The Pentecostal Missionary Union," *Confidence*, December 1916, 197.

[57] After almost a century Pentecostal leaders are still seeking to assert this as "the

exploration of early Pentecostal spirituality is that there existed a very definite advocacy of signs, foremost among which was the gift of tongues. The notion that "Full Salvation" necessarily entailed a "Baptism of the Holy Ghost with Signs,"[58] broadened the horizon of expectation beyond that of glossolalic experience to incorporate a range of supernatural manifestations. It was this development which aroused the ire of those who condemned any reliance on "signs," "wonders," or "manifestations"[59] as a departure "stamped unmistakably with the cloven hoof." Harris therefore asserted that the prudent would resist the "attractions of the 'Tongues movement,'" and thereby avoid being "entangled in the coils of this error," which had been "raiding the Churches and carrying captive silly women."[60]

Yet beyond the vexed question as to whether tongues could or should be regarded as the seal of Pentecostal baptism, there lurked a further problematic issue, albeit one which attracted less attention. Martin's claim to having spoken "a few words in Hebrew, more in an East African Bantu tongue like Swahelli, and what was taken to be an Indian dialect,"[61] was by no means unique among Pentecostal initiates during the early years of the phenomenon. The first issue of *The Apostolic Faith* claimed that "the gift of languages" had been granted to "the unlearned." This seemingly logical extension of Acts chapter 2, verses 4-11, whereby Galileans proclaimed "the wonderful works of God" in a variety of dialects, was heralded as "the divine plan for missionaries." It was held that the languages in question were not to be learned, but would become operative as "the Lord takes control of the organs of speech" and effects a "sign to the heathen" that the "Holy Ghost speaks all the languages of the world through His children."[62]

Boddy published, for the benefit of his readership, the claim that a Professor of Latin, Greek and Hebrew from a Mennonite College in Indiana, had attended

---

great hallmark of authentic Pentecostalism," while admitting that "some Pentecostals" do not insist upon it as "the initial evidence." See Colin Dye, "Are Pentecostals Pentecostal?: A Revisit to the Doctrine of Pentecost," *Journal of the European Pentecostal Theological Association* XIX (1999): 60.

[58] "Across the Channel," *Confidence*, November 1909, 263.

[59] Chambers, "Tongues and Testing," *Tongues of Fire*, January 1908, 3; Penn-Lewis, "An Hour of Peril: Part 8," *The Christian*, 5 March 1908, 13.

[60] "Editorials: The Truth Denied Encourages Satanic Counterfeit," *Tongues of Fire*, February 1908, 6. For a discourse against "seeking of signs" see Mrs. Reader Harris, "Editorials: The Age of His Silence," *Tongues of Fire*, June 1913, 6. Randall has commented on Pentecostal distinctiveness in this regard in "Pentecostalism and Evangelical Spirituality in England," 62-66.

[61] Martin, "Testimony from Motherwell," 12-13. This practice which has been given the technical designation *xenolalia*, has been succinctly defined as a phenomenon whereby individuals "speak and understand languages of which they have no normal knowledge." See David Christie-Murray, *Voices from the Gods: Speaking with Tongues* (London and Henley: Routledge & Kegan Paul, 1978), 12.

[62] "Pentecost Has Come," *The Apostolic Faith*, September 1906, 1.

a Pentecostal convention where he heard a "sister" deliver a "message of some length in the Hebrew language." The impact of this was deemed more potent as this woman had previously not known "a single character or sound of the Hebrew alphabet."[63] While early leaders were sufficiently prudent to avoid excessively dogmatic assertions in relation to this practice, the conviction was widespread that glossolalic experience incorporated not merely tongues "of angels," but that at times and in certain circumstances, tongues "of the nations" had also been attested.[64] While the apostolic experience was repeatedly invoked in this respect, it came to be admitted that in terms of "definite human language...nothing like so many" had been manifest, nor had the impact been as potent.[65] Boddy, as early as 1909, made the following poignant observation: "I feel it is only right to say that among the very many who have gone abroad after the Pentecostal blessing we have not yet received one letter stating that they have this miraculous gift. I long to receive or see such a letter."[66]

An early sanguine disposition which indulged the notion that missionary enterprise could be utterly reconfigured,[67] was being questioned within a few years by figures such as Barratt. While not denying the veracity of *missionary tongues*, he cautioned that the "call to any field among the heathen must not be guided by the language given." The admission that some had been "bitterly disappointed" by "mistakes" that had been made on account of xenolalia,[68] confirms Wacker's assessment that the pragmatic impulses that had inspired such notions among Pentecostal pioneers, had just as readily contributed to their demise. While *primitivist determination* secured the status of this curious phenomenon as a cherished "artifact of first-century signs and wonders," *pragmatic calculation* served to relegate it to the "hazy realm of Pentecostal mythology"[69] on both sides of the Atlantic.

Initiation Narratives

The importance of external signs or manifestations was nowhere greater than in relation to the act or process of initiation into the Pentecostal dimension. Martin's recounting of his "coming through" in the kitchen of the leader of Westport Hall was broadly typical of what might be deemed Pentecostal *initiation narratives*. Something of a prototype or template for such initiation narratives was provided by Barratt who thereby enhanced his already seminal influence on early developments in England. Having been intrigued by reports of "Pentecost Afresh" which were emanating from Los Angeles in 1906, he

---

[63] "Brought to God through 'Tongues,'" *Confidence*, January 1916, 15.

[64] W. T. Dixon, "About Tongues: A Word in Season," *Confidence*, February 1914, 27; "The Gift of the Chinese Language," *Things New and Old*, June 1922, 5.

[65] "A Well-known Missionary on 'Tongues,'" *Confidence*, September 1915, 175.

[66] "The 'Pentecostal Baptism': Counsel to Leaders and Others," 4.

[67] Jacobsen, *Theologies of the Early Pentecostal Movement*, 49-50.

[68] Barratt, *In the Days of the Latter Rain*, 45, 87.

[69] Wacker, *Early Pentecostals and American Culture*, 45, 51.

embarked on a fervent and protracted quest to explore the experience for himself. He subsequently reported how on 15 November, 1906, "nothing interfered with the workings of the Divine Spirit, and as a result the same outward sign of the Spirit's presence was seen and heard as on the Day of Pentecost in Jerusalem."[70]

This breakthrough came in the wake of "days and hours" spent "before the Lord." The potent motif of struggle and travail was not without its diabolical aspect: "Once the presence of the devil was so near to me that I shook my fist at him in the Name of the Lord, though I did not see him." Doubts and personal misgivings had also proven "sufficient to hinder the work of the Spirit." "Tarrying" continued until what he reported as "a remarkable sensation" that passed through his "whole body," and he believed himself to have reached a point where he was fully "prepared for the outward evidences of the Power, and not at all anxious..."[71] Then came the awaited moment of epiphany:

> My being was flooded with light and an indescribable power, and I began to speak in a foreign language as loudly as I could. For a long time I was lying upon my back on the floor, speaking...then at last I sat on a chair, and the whole time I spoke in 'divers kinds of tongues' (1 Corinthians 12: 10) with a short interval between...I am sure that I spoke seven or eight different languages...[72]

Barratt stated that he had "entered into details" because "different questions" would "arise in many a heart." He directed his readers to one authority alone: "Dear friends, read your Bibles!" This recourse was to be undertaken because "the unbelief of centuries, and the expositions of those who are not led by the Word of God, are no longer an authority in this matter." His further commentary betrayed a perceived disjuncture with aspects of Christian tradition:

> You may be sure when the power of God falls upon people, old traditions and rules will not be followed exactly. Here was a movement and life which would not have fitted in with High Mass in a cathedral, but it would not hurt the cathedral, nor those who attend the services there, if this light and life should break in on them.[73]

These comments are interesting in the light of Chan's observations regarding the difficulty encountered by those of "low church" persuasion who find themselves without adequate conceptual tools to delineate the nature and mechanisms of spiritual progress. While participants in the sacramental communions enunciate Christian beginnings and subsequent development in the distinct rites of baptism and confirmation,[74] pioneering Pentecostals forged

---

[70] Barratt, *When the Fire Fell*, 103, 126.

[71] Barratt, *When the Fire Fell*, 127-128.

[72] Barratt, *When the Fire Fell*, 129-130.

[73] Barratt, *When the Fire Fell*, 131, 128.

[74] Simon Chan, *Pentecostal Theology and the Christian Spiritual Tradition*, Journal

their own narrative accounts in an attempt to encapsulate the complex realities of the Christian growth process. Such accounts of initiation into the Pentecostal dimension, encompassing both *crisis* and *process*,[75] were primary in terms of significance as well as chronology among what have been termed "Pentecostal worship rites."[76] Their propagation indeed served to establish patterns or practices which would, in vital respects, become normative.

A notable aspect of this was the fact that while engaged in protracted pursuit of Pentecostal experience in New York during 1906, Barratt had sought the advice and assistance of a lady who he identified merely as a doctor's wife. He subsequently informed a reporter that the devil had "taunted" him on this account in ridiculing "the idea of a minister going to ask a women to pray for him." But his riposte was swift: "I bade the devil be gone."[77] While the avatar of Pentecostal awakening in England had felt the assistance of a woman in such matters to be somewhat beneath him, he had more significantly felt himself compelled to overcome this reluctance. Others evidently followed Barratt's paradigmatic experience as expressions of gender prejudice are rare in early Pentecostal literature and, furthermore, the attribution of such a disposition to malign spiritual forces does not recur. On the contrary female figures, perhaps most notably Mary Boddy, became prominently involved in the assistance towards, and initiation into, the baptism in the Holy Spirit as has been demonstrated in the cases of both Smith Wigglesworth and Holiness Mission Hall.[78]

Dunn has ventured that R. A. Knox committed "a surprising error of judgement" in omitting Pentecostalism and its worship from his "brilliant study" as, in his estimation, Knox's delineation of *enthusiasm* and *ultrasupernaturalism*, "fits Pentecostalism very well."[79] Knox does deal with "symptoms" of revivalism which he deems to be "not seldom its concomitants," and as Dunn has suggested, these correlate closely with salient aspects of Pentecostal practice. This is particularly the case in relation to

---

of Pentecostal Theology Supplement Series, 21 (Sheffield: Sheffield Academic Press, 2000), 89-90, 92-93.

[75] Land employs the term "crisis-development dialectic." See *Pentecostal Spirituality*, 117.

[76] Daniel E. Albrecht, *Rites in the Spirit: A Ritual Approach to Pentecostal/Charismatic Spirituality*, Journal of Pentecostal Theology Supplement Series, 17 (Sheffield: Sheffield Academic Press, 1999), 13. Albrecht applies the insights and approaches of ritual studies or ritology to an examination of three contemporary Pentecostal/charismatic contexts of worship. While he does not address their historic antecedents, his categories and terminology are conducive to an analysis of early Pentecostal *praxis*.

[77] "Marvellous Life Story of a Religious Enthusiast," *Morning Leader*, 4 October 1907.

[78] See pages 62 and 78 above.

[79] James D. G. Dunn, "Spirit-Baptism and Pentecostalism," in *Scottish Journal of Theology* 23.4 (Nov. 1970): 402.

phenomena frequently recounted in initiation narratives. Among such "symptoms" Knox identifies religious "ecstasy" which encompasses "a mass of abnormal phenomena, the by-products...of 'convincement.'" Such "by-products" are said to include "unintelligible utterance, or utterance identified by expert evidence as a language unknown to themselves; people remaining destitute of their senses in a holy trance, or more often, shaken by convulsive movements from head to foot, for hours at a time..."[80] Religious rituals have been defined as "symbolic actions that strengthen and reaffirm a group's beliefs" which are "often accompanied by a sense of awe, mystery and wonder."[81] It would appear that as a primary worship rite, initiation into the Pentecostal experience as practised during the early years of the movement in England, had a profound and cohesive effect on this, as yet, diminutive religious grouping. Overt and attestable forms of initiation came to perform, as in other traditions, an "ontological function" involving a "radical change in the initiand's mode of being" amid a "desacralized world" and a "degraded religion."[82]

In his general analysis of Pentecostal spirituality, Land has stated that its first generation advocated "neither a smooth continuity with tradition, nor a complete discontinuity." Something of this "continuity in discontinuity"[83] is appreciated when typical Pentecostal initiation phenomena are considered alongside what Knox has termed "Methodist paroxysms."[84] He described Wesley as having "set an enormous value on those sensible consolations in which (it seems) his followers abounded." He went on to make the interesting observation that it would be difficult to find a perspective "more absolutely opposed" to that of the Quietists. While for advocates of this school such as Madame Guyon, the very adventure of religion implied "adhering to God by naked faith, disregarding consolations and even welcoming the absence of them," the Wesleyan perspective regarded a religion whose love resided solely

---

[80] R. A. Knox, *Enthusiasm: A Chapter in the History of Religion* (Oxford: Clarendon Press, 1950), 4.

[81] Simon Coleman and Peter Collins, "The 'Plain' and the 'Positive': Experience and Aesthetics in Quakerism and Charismatic Christianity," *Journal of Contemporary Religion* 15:3 (2000): 317. In terms employed by Gerlach and Hine, such manifestations represent evidence of "commitment by experience." See "Growth and Spread of a Modern Religious Movement," 33.

[82] Mircea Eliade, *Birth and Rebirth: The Religious Meanings of Initiation in Human Culture*, trans. Williard R. Trask (London: Harvill Press, 1958), 127-128.

[83] Land, *Pentecostal Spirituality*, 119. This is in contrast with Vondey who portrays an acute disjuncture between Pentecostal Christianity and "tradition" and "the mainline churches." See "The Symbolic Turn," 240-244.

[84] Knox, *Enthusiasm*, 520-528. Gordon Wakefield has explicitly likened what was witnessed among some early Methodist Societies to "manifestations of enthusiasm" that have been associated with twentieth-century Pentecostals. See *Methodist Spirituality*, (Peterborough: Epworth Press, 1999), 24-25.

in the will, as "a dead, dry carcase."[85] Hempton has commented on the "sensuous and subversive dimension" which, in spite of a definite emphasis on discipline and order characteristic of Methodist spirituality, "lay at the heart of the raw emotions" described in accounts of Methodist revival from South Carolina to Yorkshire. He observes that "what is particularly striking about such accounts is the sheer vitality and variety of oral and bodily expression that onlookers at the time and religious historians ever since, have struggled unsuccessfully to interpret."[86] The readership of *Flames of Fire* was in this vein informed, quite unequivocally, of affinities with "the early Methodist preachers" who, according to Cecil Polhill, attained a high degree of effectiveness on the basis of a depth of conviction induced by "their own spiritual experiences."[87]

Parallels with Pentecostalism abound, not merely in the similarities of the "paroxysms" and "sensible consolations," but in the significance which was attributed to them. Painfully aware of the growth of infidelity during the eighteenth-century, for those of Wesleyan disposition "every invasion from the other world" served as something of an ideological "counterblast." Knox describes Wesley as observing "the *energumens* who lay on the floor crying for mercy," and inwardly congratulating himself "that this was a stick to beat the Deists with." But the benefits of such consolations were also of more immediate effect: they constituted "the spectacle of a spiritual conflict and a spiritual victory externalized, translated into terms of flesh and blood."[88] Hall has pointed out that the Welsh Revival - viewed by Boddy as a divine preparation for and precursor to his own movement[89] - had "gloried" in "physical effects," and that those who underwent them both "demonstrated divine power" and furnished "a focal point and a catharsis."[90] Such interpretation could readily be transferred to Pentecostal phenomena generally, and those associated with its emerging rites of initiation in particular. They functioned not merely as sensible consolations or corroborations for initiates,

---

[85] Knox, *Enthusiasm*, 537. See David Lyle Jeffrey, ed., *English Spirituality in the Age of Wesley* (Grand Rapids, MI.: Eerdmans, 1994), 241-242. One aspect of this tendency has recently been examined in Robert Webster, "Seeing Salvation: The Place of Dreams and Visions in John Wesley's *Arminian Magazine*," in Cooper and Gregory, eds., *Studies in Church History*, vol. 41, 376-388, while an extensive exposition on the general theme is to be found in Wilfred R. Wilkinson, *Religious Experience: The Methodist Fundamental* (London: Holborn Publishing, 1928).

[86] David Hempton, *The Religion of the People: Methodism and Popular Religion c. 1750-1900* (London and New York: Routledge, 1996), 12-13. David Martin has briefly considered this aspect of what he terms the "Methodist linkage" in *Pentecostalism: The World Their Parish* (Oxford: Blackwell, 2002), 7-11.

[87] "The Early Methodist Preachers," *Flames of Fire*, December 1914, 3.

[88] Knox, *Enthusiasm*, 588.

[89] "The Pentecostal Movement," *Confidence*, August 1910, 192-193.

[90] Hall, "The Welsh Revival," in Cuming and Baker, eds., *Studies in Church History*, vol. 8, 293.

but fulfilled an apologetic capacity as "convincements" in the face of critics, sceptics and detractors. These occurrences also represented a "counterblast" against the perceived rationalism and reductionism of the "New Theologians" against whom Barratt's "spirit burned with indignation," as well as against the culpability of a Christian Church perceived to have "laid aside this great blessing in lukewarmness and unbelief."[91]

The Release of Spiritual Energy

A further aspect of the crisis-development dialectic is apparent from the account of Smith Wigglesworth's Pentecostal initiation. Its notable features ranged from the inclusion of dire warnings against proceeding to a reputed spiritual swooning which he likened to the experience of Daniel "in his tenth chapter."[92] Such elements exhibit a tendency toward interior struggle which contemporary William James, in his celebrated Gifford Lectures of 1901-2, identified as recurrent in the history of Protestant Christianity. Processes of this order reveal the inner realm to have been a recurrent "battle-ground" for what the individual felt to be "two deadly hostile selves, one actual, the other ideal."[93] Wigglesworth perceived himself to have conquered and gained mastery of a spiritual dimension to which he would subsequently admit others; that of "actually living the Acts of the Apostles' time."[94] Continuities with the "element of crisis in Keswick teaching" could reasonably be postulated in this context. This crisis, according to Bebbington's observations, exhibited a penchant for "dramatic moments" and "the highly charged juncture, the *kairos*"

---

[91] Barratt, *When the Fire Fell*, 106, 125. Until the rise of the Neo-Orthodox school in the aftermath of the First World War, classical Liberal theology had assumed a dominance for almost half a century. Synonymous with figures such as Albert Ritschl and Adolf Harnack, this post-Enlightenment attempt to reconstruct Christian theology in the light of advances in knowledge would attract vehement criticism on a number of fronts, particularly from traditionalists. It was perceived that the Liberal venture necessitated fundamental diminution/adulteration of Christian essentials, the implications of which were memorably summarized: "A God without wrath brought men without sin into a kingdom without judgement through the ministrations of a Christ without a cross." See H. Richard Niebuhr, *The Kingdom of God in America*, 193, quoted in Stanley J. Grenz and Roger E. Olson, *20th Century Theology: God and the World in a Transitional Age* (Carlisle: Paternoster Press, 1992), 62. Views such as those expressed by Barratt are considered in more detail in Section 2.5 below.

[92] "Testimony of Smith Wigglesworth," *Confidence*, October 1908, 15.

[93] William James, *The Varieties of Religious Experience: A Study in Human Nature* (London: Longmans, Green and Co., 1922), 171. This pioneering psychologist is probably best remembered for the insights he offered into the dynamics of religious experience and mysticism.

[94] "Testimony of Smith Wigglesworth," *Confidence*, October 1908, 15.

which suggested a tendency "marked in various ways by Romantic affinities."[95] The transformative potential of such narratives, as exemplified in the case of the Bradford preacher, was maximised in so far as the very act of narrating or recounting such occurrences implied what has been described as an "apocalyptic *telos*" which acted on the testifier as he or she told of miraculous happenings or providential events. In this manner both addressor and addressee became participants in salvation history as "stories merged with *the* story."[96]

Land has also written of the release of "spiritual energy" amid the "ensuing fission" of an individual entering into the Pentecostal fellowship. While *fission* denotes separation, disjunction, and polarising tendencies, *fusion* represented the integrative and cohesive aspects of the encounter. If aspects of the self and its propensities would necessarily be abandoned and forsaken by virtue of this progression, the integration of the superior or idealised self with the Holy Spirit resulted in an outcome where "everyday time is *kairos* for those upon whom the end of the ages has come."[97] Reflecting elements of what has been identified as the "classic scenario of all traditional initiation," the purpose of such depictions of "total crisis" is to underscore the attainment of a "definite and total *renovatio*, a renewal capable of transmuting life." England's emerging Pentecostals thereby became *"proteges* of the Supernatural" who functioned within the realm of "the sacred primordial."[98]

Such dynamics are vividly portrayed in the account of the experience of a young man who attended Emmanuel Mission Hall for a "Three Days' Conference" that was held there between 26-28 February, 1909. While visiting Bournemouth, Frank Trevitt read an advertisement in a local paper for "a conference in connection of a revival of Pentecostal power." He had been sent to the south coast from Birmingham, a "physical wreck." Suffering from "copious hemorrhage, apparent consumption, and general breakdown," Trevitt could do little more than "crawl with the aid of a stick." The opinion of "several eminent medical specialists" had been that unless "something very extraordinary occurred," he would be "under the soil in six weeks."[99] White described this pilgrim as "on the verge of the grave" with "only hope for a few days more of life."[100] What transpired was the more extraordinary in that it occurred while those in attendance were waiting for tea and engaged in "pleasant conversation" between the afternoon and evening meetings. It was recorded that "a sister, in the Spirit, rose and began to adore God." Others fell to their knees where they were, as did Trevitt, who claimed that his body was "mightily moved as by electrical shocks." Presently his lips and tongue were

---

[95] Bebbington, *Holiness in Nineteenth-Century England*, 79, 80. It could be surmised that such associations were also at work in Wigglesworth's brand of healing-evangelism. See pages 143-147 below.

[96] Land, *Pentecostal Spirituality*, 112.

[97] Land, *Pentecostal Spirituality*, 104, 98.

[98] Eliade, *Religious Meanings of Initiation*, 124, 128-129, 135.

[99] "Bournemouth: Pentecost Returned," *Confidence*, April 1909, 86-87.

[100] White, *The Word of God*, 51.

"used by the Holy Spirit to pour forth a volume of speech in some foreign language." In what can only have presented itself as an unusual sight, he "shot his arms upward and outward, and hammered his chest with his fists, loudly declaring that he was in perfect health, and felt as fit as any man." Boddy concluded that Trevitt had received "the Pentecostal gift of the Holy Ghost, and healing at the same time," and added that he "rose to his feet a new man."[101]

The transformation undergone by Trevitt, containing variations on the constituent elements recounted by other Pentecostal initiates, could be said to have elevated him to "an altogether new level of spiritual vitality, a relatively heroic level, in which impossible things have become possible, and new energies and endurances are shown."[102] As the seeker after sanctification had typically done so by means of an experience of dereliction followed by the deliverance of "an extraneous higher power,"[103] the Pentecostal neophyte found him/herself resurrected from an abject condition and vitalised in a manner that surpassed former experience or expectation. James described such processes, which he identified as integrally associated with the Methodist and revivalist traditions, as not only "the more interesting dramatically," but also "the more complete" psychologically.[104]

The Locus of Divine-Human Convergence: The Waiting Meeting

While moments of initiation into Pentecostal reality could theoretically occur at any moment and in any place, as had been experienced during afternoon tea in Bournemouth, particular foci emerged for the enactment of this spiritual rite of passage. The primary focus of "human-divine convergence"[105] during the initial phase of the movement in England was undoubtedly what came to be known as the "waiting meeting."[106] This practice, based on the injunction issued in Luke 24:49, displayed recurrent characteristics or *semantic guidemarks*[107] which became integral to the process. These are apparent in accounts such as that offered by a correspondent from Clydebank in Scotland. Having heard of developments in Sunderland, and closer to home in Kilsyth's Westport Hall, a

---

[101] "Bournemouth: Pentecost Returned," *Confidence*, April 1909, 87.

[102] James, *Varieties of Religious Experience*, 241.

[103] James, *Varieties of Religious Experience*, 228. See for instance Andrew Murray's account of the experience of Canon Harford Battersby of St. John's Church, Keswick, in *The Coming Revival*, Evangelical Heritage Series (London: Marshall Pickering, 1989), 83-87, and Mrs. Howard Hooker's retelling of that of her father in "Snap-shots from the Life of the Late Reader Harris, K. C.," *Tongues of Fire*, May 1915, 7.

[104] He attributed this to what he observed to be "the admirable congruity of Protestant theology with the structure of the mind as shown in such experiences." See *Varieties of Religious Experience*, 227-228.

[105] Albrecht, *Rites in the Spirit*, 133.

[106] "Testimony of a Seeker after God," *Confidence*, October 1908, 4-5.

[107] Jean Borella, *The Sense of the Supernatural*, trans. G. John Champoux (Edinburgh: T. & T. Clark, 1998), 101-102.

series of after-meetings were instigated: "It was settled to have three nights in the week set apart to wait upon God and night after night we met, expecting God to work in a new way. But no outward manifestations were witnessed in those waiting times, only the hunger was deepening..."[108] A breakthrough occurred when during one such meeting a young man "was raised to his feet and then laid on his back on the floor." For a time he lay "under the power" until "God took his tongue and he began to speak and sing in an unknown tongue, whether of angels or men we cannot tell, but he went on in this way for fully three hours."[109] The waiting meetings were continued but "no more received any manifestation in this way" until a deputation arrived from Kilsyth. The presence of more established purveyors of "Paracletic initiation,"[110] here as elsewhere, proved instrumental: "We were three hours before God, and the hungry were filled to the full. In that one weekend nearly a dozen received the New Tongue." Those described as merely a "little band" consisting of the "very young" were buoyed by the conviction that "truly God does take the weak things to confound the mighty."[111]

It is appropriate, before turning to a consideration of the general tone and tenor of developing Pentecostal worship in England, to mention particular objections that were raised against the waiting-meeting phenomenon, as well as some of the responses they elicited. While the general charge had been advanced that "dangerous supernatural forces" had been emanating from "the Californian movement,"[112] this focus of inauguration into the Pentecostal baptism was highlighted as the fulcrum of malign influence. Jessie Penn-Lewis held the primary danger of the waiting-meeting to be its propensity to degenerate into something akin to a séance to the detriment of unwitting and "innocent Christians gathered." It was attested that "workings of Satan, peculiar to Spiritualism have taken place in such gatherings."[113] Such "motor automatisms"[114] as were commonplace were likened to forms of levitation, a "distinctly spiritualistic" practice. Groanings and other audible articulations were denounced as corresponding with "the 'inflation' of the Python oracle at Delphi" and advanced as potent evidence of "the danger of Spiritualism stealthily entering and misleading the very elect of God."[115] Interestingly, Barratt himself acknowledged that a rationale against the advocacy of tongues as the *sine qua non* of Pentecostal baptism was the fact that "even Spiritualists

---

[108] Robert Gibson, "Scotland: Clydebank," *Confidence*, December 1908, 10.

[109] Gibson, "Scotland: Clydebank," *Confidence*, December 1908, 11.

[110] Borella, *The Sense of the Supernatural*, 120.

[111] Gibson, "Scotland: Clydebank," *Confidence*, December 1908, 11.

[112] Penn-Lewis, "An Hour of Peril: Part 4," *The Christian*, 6 February, 1908, 12.

[113] Penn-Lewis, "An Hour of Peril: Part 6," *The Christian*, 20 February, 1908, 11. Extensive evidence of the incidence of tongues among nineteenth- and twentieth-century Spiritualists is presented in Christie-Murray, *Voices from the Gods*, 68-90, 129ff.

[114] James, *Varieties of Religious Experience*, 478.

[115] Penn-Lewis, "An Hour of Peril: Part 6," *The Christian*, 20 February, 1908, 11.

speak in tongues."[116]

Boddy, characteristically sensitive to such criticism, issued a pamphlet with the express purpose of advising those who were seeking to bring others "through into their Pentecostal Blessing." In this he warned against "false fire" and "fleshly energy;" "fleshly importunity" on the part of leaders as well as seekers; "the workings of the unconscious mind," which were described as "very, very deep;" and "fleshly extravagancies." In the face of such difficulties he enjoined vigilance and discernment on the part of leaders, adherence to Scripture in all matters, and the exercise of open rebuke where necessary.[117] It is of significance that both morning and afternoon sessions on the Monday of the first Sunderland Convention were "fully occupied with an important and deeply interesting discussion as to our Waiting Meetings." In this context it was transparently acknowledged that "unscriptural methods" would "naturally provoke great opposition, give the adversary cause to reproach, strengthen those who oppose, and stumble weak believers."[118]

An evident concern for decorum and rectitude in the manner in which these gatherings were conducted in no sense implied a questioning of the validity of the phenomenon. In Polhill's estimation, an "occasional sigh" or "a languid interest" on part of a would-be seeker would prove ineffectual.[119] Instead he asserted "earnestness is essential; there must be a real hunger, a consuming desire." Nothing less than "complete surrender and holiness of life" were required in addition to an "earnest unceasing cry in the heart." Christ's observation that "the Kingdom of Heaven suffereth violence, and the violent take it by force" (Matt. 11:12), was taken as a normative disposition for the Pentecostal initiate. It was pointed out: "'Tarry until ye be endued' is the Scripture injunction" in pursuit of the "luminous sign" of the "tongue of fire." If at Pentecost "it came with rushing mighty wind," while at Samaria "it was gloriously apparent,"[120] nothing tame could be constituted sufficient to the "overpowering, overwhelming, empowering, enveloping, mysterious, divine, unquestionable, enduement of the Baptism of the Holy Ghost."[121]

Polhill expressly addressed that fact that there existed what he regarded as "some misconception as to the utility and character of waiting meetings." In his estimation it was only those personally unacquainted with the practice that could deride them as "orgies of fanaticism or wild manifestation." The waiting-meeting was, to his mind, akin to the Salvationist "penitent form" or the

---

[116] Barratt, "An Urgent Plea for Charity and Unity," *Confidence*, February 1911, 31.

[117] "The 'Pentecostal Baptism': Counsel to Leaders and Others," (Unpublished tract, DGC).

[118] "Opening Meetings of the Conference," *Confidence*, June 1908, 8.

[119] "How to Receive the Baptism of the Holy Ghost and Fire," *Flames of Fire*, January 1916, 1-2.

[120] "How to Receive the Baptism of the Holy Ghost and Fire," *Flames of Fire*, November 1911, 1.

[121] "What is the Baptism of the Holy Ghost and Fire?" *Flames of Fire*, October 1911, 1.

Keswick "after meeting."[122] He also averred that John Wesley had received his spiritual breakthrough "at a prolonged waiting meeting in Fetter Lane."[123] The practice represented a "definite setting oneself to obtain and experience" and he likened it to "the 'standing before God' of Abraham that will not be denied," or the "'I will not let Thee go unless Thou bless me' of Jacob." He did acknowledge that "unbalanced and highly strung nervous people" were to be found "in almost every meeting," and therefore enjoined that "false or unseemly manifestations" be suppressed. Yet he resolutely endorsed the practice which he deemed "a valuable auxiliary to the general plan of campaign as a means of clinching the utterance of Truth."[124]

It is suggested, in summary, that much of what has been outlined with respect of emergent and developing paradigms of inauguration into Pentecostal experience in England belies the statement that "Spirit baptism" was in its early form "a symbol with no tradition" and "no ritual."[125] In the light of a succinct description of spirituality as "the composite of invocation of, and response to, the divine presence,"[126] much of the essence and inner logic of Pentecostal spirituality is to be observed in its norms and processes of initiation.   Both invocation and response were abundantly in evidence in the process whereby novitiates embarked on their Pentecostal pilgrimage. While critics decried the tendency to seek or rely on sensible consolations as characteristic of "faddists and extremists...of the Dowie type,"[127] or regarded them to be, at best, "in a very elementary condition of grace,"[128] emerging Pentecostals were resolute in conviction and prolific in practice to the contrary. Even before other aspects of Pentecostal worship and ideology are considered, what has been outlined in relation to their inaugural rites serves to demonstrate that the typical early initiate could be described as having been something of an empiricist in matters of religion. A correspondent who claimed to have been divinely led "through physical exercises" which included "strong crying, joyous laughter, holy song and heavenly vision," was not perturbed at having undergone a two-hour marathon of ecstatic experience. Only something of this magnitude was deemed adequate to affect the breaking forth of the "artesian springs" of the soul.[129]

---

[122] "Waiting Meetings," *Flames of Fire*, October 1914, 2.

[123] "When the Fire Fell," *Flames of Fire*, October 1914, 1. It was not merely coincidental that the same issue of *Flames of Fire* advertised the fact that "earnest seekers of the truth" were invited to attend a meeting held weekly on Friday afternoons at an auspicious London address, Newton Hall, 17 *Fleur-de-lis* Court, Fetter Lane. See "The London Meetings," 4.

[124] "Waiting Meetings," *Flames of Fire*, October 1914, 2.

[125] Vondey, "The Symbolic Turn," 241-242.

[126] Cheryl Sanders, "Disciplined Spirituality," in Mark A. Noll and Ronald F. Thiemann, eds., *Where Shall My Wond'ring Soul Begin?: The Landscape of Evangelical Piety and Thought* (Grand Rapids, MI.: Eerdmans, 2000), 62.

[127] "Review of 1905," *Tongues of Fire*, January 1906, 7.

[128] Chambers, "After God's Silence - What?" *Spiritual Life*, January 1923, 4.

[129] Gerard A. Bailly, "God's Sovereignty in Diversity: A Testimony," *Flames of*

Such visible convincements were deemed befitting to the "new epoch"[130] which both individual and Church were believed to be encountering. The *affective chemistry*[131] attendant upon the conjunction of apocalyptic vision and transcendent presence was issuing in palpable and observable demonstrations of the fact that participants were involved in "the throes of a great convulsion."[132]

Section 2.2: The Tenor of Emerging Pentecostal Worship in England

Colourful Christianity in Britain

It has been observed of English Pentecostalism's trans-Atlantic counterpart that "the Holy Ghost revival epitomized the uninhibited expression of raw religious emotion." Yet Wacker goes on to make the point that this religious grouping held no monopoly in matters of spiritual intensity.[133] That this can be extrapolated across the Atlantic is demonstrated by commentators and analysts of the British context. T. H. Huxley had derided the Salvation Army's charismatic emphases as "corybantic Christianity,"[134] while a more sympathetic categorisation described them as sounding "the Elizabethan note in religion."[135] This, the most successful form of religious primitivism in late nineteenth-century England, was described by Horton Davies as having broken through "the cordons of reserve and decorum in a riot of joyous righteousness."[136] Underlying this outpouring of religious exuberance was the conviction that "the damned could only be drawn from hot sin by hot religion."[137] This tendency was, however, by no means limited to the "most colourful of the many new religious denominations produced by nineteenth-century Britain,"[138] as Victorian Nonconformist religion was generally a more colourful affair than is popularly supposed.[139] Charles Booth, in his magisterial survey of patterns of

---

Fire, October 1913, 3.

[130] Bailly, "God's Sovereignty in Diversity: Post-Pentecostal Evidences and Blessings," *Flames of Fire*, December 1913, 2.

[131] Land, *Pentecostal Spirituality*, 137.

[132] Bailly, "God's Sovereignty in Diversity: Post-Pentecostal Evidences," *Flames of Fire*, December 1913, 2.

[133] Wacker, *Early Pentecostals and American Culture*, 99.

[134] Horton Davies, *Worship and Theology in England*, vol. 4, *From Newman to Martineau, 1850-1900* (Grand Rapids, MI.: Eerdmans, 1996) 168.

[135] John Ervine, *God's Soldier: General William Booth*, vol. 1 (London: Heinemann, 1934), 260.

[136] Davies, *Worship and Theology in England*, vol. 4, *From Newman to Martineau*, 169.

[137] Ervine, *God's Soldier*, 264.

[138] McLeod, *Religion and Society in England*, 31.

[139] On this see Kenneth Young, *Chapel: The Joyous Days and Prayerful Nights of the Nonconformists in their heyday, c.1850-1950* (London: Eyre Methuen, 1972), 18, 51-53; McLeod, *Religion and Society in England*, 144-145. For insights across the

worship in the metropolis at the turn of the twentieth-century, observed that "the general movement of taste and habit in religion, as well as in life generally, has been in the direction of greater brightness."[140] Contributors to the *Daily Telegraph* religious survey of 1904 had complained of "flitting scenes of spiritual phantasmagoria,"[141] and what were described as "the outbursts of Mr. Evan Roberts and the Welsh revivalists"[142] came to prominent notoriety. This latter phenomenon, characteristically "visionary and ecstatic," was described by one contemporary commentator as having "deteriorated into an orgy of singing and praying, like a pagan feast."[143] Even a more reverential observer allowed that "extravagances of excitement" had "spasmodically broken out" and that in this manner "distressing features" had come to prominence during the Revival.[144]

Alexander Boddy, by virtue of his involvement with the Pentecostal League of Prayer, had for some time sought to foster what was arguably its central aim: "revival in the churches."[145] If paradigms of revival can be said to broadly correspond to either spiritual *quickening* or revitalisation within the parameters of existing religious bodies, or the attempted attraction and conversion of those without,[146] Boddy tended toward the former. His expressions, at the League's annual gathering of 1905, of appreciation for the vivifying effects of this association in his own parish amply demonstrate his sympathies in this direction.[147] This found him therefore inhabiting, in the first years of the century, a religious culture which heralded the intensification of "fervour," and "spiritual hunger and thirst," as valid and welcome indicators of the fact that England was "on the threshold of a religious revolution."[148] While, as will

---

religious spectrum see Gerald Parsons, "Emotion and Piety: Revivalism and Ritualism in Victorian Christianity," in Parsons, ed., *Religion in Victorian Britain*, vol. 1, *Traditions* (Manchester and New York: Manchester University Press, 1988), 213-234.

[140] Booth, *Life and Labour of the People of London*, 3rd series, *Religious Influences*, vol. 7, 53.

[141] From CREDENTI NIHIL DIFFICILE, *Do We Believe?: A Record of a Great Correspondence in 'The Daily Telegraph,' October, November, December 1904* (London: Hodder and Stoughton, 1904), 146.

[142] From Lousi Hervey D'Egville, of 19 Baker Street, London, *Do We Believe?*, 259.

[143] J. Vyrnwy Morgan, *The Welsh Religious Revival 1904-5: A Retrospect and a Criticism* (London: Chapman & Hall Ltd., 1909), 82-83, 112-113.

[144] H. Elvert Lewis, *With Christ Among the Miners: Incidents and Impressions of the Welsh Revival* (London: Hodder and Stoughton, 1906), 180-181, 34-35.

[145] Howard Hooker, *Life and Letters*, 111. Similar statements abounded in the League's monthly publication. Examples are to be found in "Revival: *The* Church Question," *Tongues of Fire*, January 1905, 1-2, and "Editorials: Revival or Extinction," *Tongues of Fire*, October 1905, 6.

[146] For comments on this distinction see Janice Holmes, *Religious Revivals in Britain and Ireland, 1859-1905* (Dublin: Irish Academic Press, 2000), 193.

[147] See "The Annual Meetings," *Tongues of Fire*, June 1905, 3.

[148] "Editorials: The Welsh Revival," *Tongues of Fire*, February 1905, 6.

become apparent, leading figures within emerging Pentecostalism shared reservations with respect to some of the problematic aspects of revival that had been witnessed in Wales, it nonetheless functioned as a whetstone for future aspirations. Barratt had written to Evan Roberts early in 1904 claiming, "I have often experienced the power of the Holy Spirit in my work as a minister, and now as leader of the Christiania City Mission...I want a Fuller Baptism of fire."[149] It was the subsequent fulfilment of this desire that caused Boddy to write in 1907:

> My four days in Christiania cannot be forgotten. I stood with Evan Roberts at the Tonypandy meetings, but never have I witnessed such scenes as in Norway, and soon I believe they will be witnessed in England.[150]

Scenes were certainly witnessed from the moment Barratt arrived at his first waiting-meeting at All Saints' on 31 August, 1907. The following night three individuals "entered right in and went through into Pentecost with the signs following." To this Boddy added that "to encourage others God allowed them to be dealt with very tenderly."[151] However not all of the spiritual transactions conducted in Sunderland would prove as apparently innocuous and inoffensive as these initial instances. Individual initiations, personal encounters, and corporate expressions of Pentecostal worship would involve intensity and exuberance that would prove exhilarating, as well as disconcerting, even to some of those most closely involved.

Emotional Outbursts and Pentecostal Paroxysms in Sunderland

It is the case that external sources afford some of the most detailed and descriptive accounts of these initial Pentecostal meetings in Sunderland. Reports of local and national press offer unique and revealing insights into the tone and tenor of the gatherings which would prove formative in the emergence and development of the *orthopraxy* and *orthopathy*[152] of English Pentecostalism. One of the first reports announced that a "certain happy portion" of the population of Monkwearmouth was to be found "in the throes of a joyful and inspired excitement," while "strange things in the name of religion" were "happening in its midst."[153] The *Daily Chronicle* pronounced it "not an ordinary revival," but remarked that it was being accompanied "by some of the more commonplace phases of - dare I say! - hysteria which made

---

[149] Barratt, *When the Fire Fell*, 96-97.

[150] "Tongues in Norway: A Pentecostal Experience," *Leaflets on Tongues* No. 6.

[151] "Tongues in Sunderland: The Beginnings of a Pentecost for England," *Leaflets on Tongues* No. 9.

[152] Land uses these terms to describe a consensus or orthodoxy in terms of "right practice" and "right affections." See *Pentecostal Spirituality*, 13.

[153] "Northern Revival Fervour: Extraordinary Scenes at the Meetings," *Morning Leader*, 3 October 1907.

such a strange figure of Evan Roberts in Wales." The reporter was, in this instance, succinct in his account: "To reduce some of the phenomena with which I am about to deal to their lowest common denominator: there have been groanings and grovellings, visions and tears, laughter and visions."[154] In the estimation of the *Morning Dispatch*, an "orgy of prayer" was the only term adequate to encompass the "extraordinary scenes" that were witnessed in the meeting that was conducted after the regular evening service. According to this descriptive report:

> Women sobbed convulsively, or cried aloud till their hysterical weepings mingled with the agonised moanings of the men...The eeriness was soon forthcoming. Above all the sobs, sighs, groans and table-thumping arose the silvery notes of a weird chant which resembled nothing so much as the mourning chants with which old-fashioned Irish people still lament their dead. Upon the people the effect was electrical. It seemed to drive them into every kind of extreme.[155]

It is interesting to note that in emerging Pentecostal parlance the "weird chant" transmogrified into an eminently more reverential "Heavenly Anthem." What would become a feature of Pentecostal gatherings was described by proponents as characterised by "wonderful tones, prolonged cadences," and the "sweet bell-like tones" of those "adoring the Lamb" in their newly acquired heavenly language.[156] It would appear that on this occasion the general exuberance was surpassed by a university student from Wales "who had been more than usually noisy." His spiritual perturbations were recounted with a realism of detail that would not have found its way into any of the Pentecostal publications:

> The Welshman shrieked. He yelled out 'Glory' in long protracted yells, until the neighbours must have turned in their beds and wondered what kind of wrack could be extracting such agony. He writhed like an animal in pain, but nothing came of his ravings.[157]

Lloyd's Weekly expressed surprise that in a building consecrated by the Bishop of Durham, services were being marked by such "extraordinary scenes." It was observed that the language spoken "is certainly not English, and in some cases it sounds more like farmyard imitations than anything human." The

---

[154] "Alleged Healing: North-Country Stirred by Strange Signs," *Daily Chronicle*, 5 October 1907.

[155] "Revival Scenes: Weird Chants and Frenzied Appeals," *The Morning Dispatch*, 7 October 1907.

[156] "Tongues in Sunderland," *Leaflets on Tongues* No. 9. This phenomenon was described by Pastor Paul of Germany as "a song of praise" which "starts in the audience - nobody can exactly say where. It begins with a low murmur, but gradually swells into a grand *diapason*." See "The Sunderland Convention: A Synopsis of the Meetings and Addresses," *Confidence*, June 1913, 113.

[157] "Revival Scenes: Weird Chants and Frenzied Appeals," *The Morning Dispatch*, 7 October 1907.

correspondent seemed astonished by the fact that the vicar's wife "interprets passages from it as messages from God," and furthermore that the clergyman hosting these unusual proceedings was indeed a Fellow of the Royal Geographic Society.[158]

While it had initially been reported that "those who attend the meetings are mostly women,"[159] within a matter of days "the number of men present equalled for the first time the number of women." This development was heralded by both Boddy and Barratt as "a magnificent sign" which impelled them on with "increased energy for their spiritual labour."[160] Male involvement in, and masculine expressions of, religious fervour certainly appear to have made an impression on visiting correspondents. The *Daily Chronicle*, for instance, reported that the focal point of the sparsely furnished Parish Hall in which the mission was conducted was a plain table on which an open Bible had been placed. At this table knelt the missioner, "a strong, rugged man, his head bowed." When prayer commenced Barratt "hurled his tremendous voice" and was followed by a Salvation Army captain who in like fashion "flung out his chest and joined in the chorus."[161] It was, for instance, recorded that when Barratt gave out the hymn, "his sonorous voice rolled over the meeting like a giant roaring in a cave." Thereafter "men groaned aloud" and Barratt did so "as if wrestling with some well-nigh overpowering force." It was observed that "the muscles on his neck stood out like knots" while he clenched his fist. This was followed by his flinging his arms upward and shouting "strange words."[162] Boddy appeared "more composed" and having "buried his face in a large handkerchief," he admonished those present to guard against "doubt and unbelief." In "quiet, unemotional words" he expressed the conviction that the "Pentecostal manifestations" being witnessed were of the utmost significance: they "foreboded the end of the present order - the dawn of the Second Coming."[163]

"Good Under the Rubbish": Uses and Utilisation of Press and Other Reports

It must be pointed out that neither Boddy nor Barratt were wholly averse to the

---

[158] "Revival Scenes: Incoherent Ravings Interpreted as Heavenly Messages," *Lloyd's Weekly*, 6 October 1907.

[159] "Revival Scenes: Weird Services in Sunderland Mission Hall," *Daily Chronicle*, 2 October 1907.

[160] "Amazing Story," *Morning Leader*, 4 October 1907.

[161] "An Israelite's Passion," *Daily Chronicle*, 7 October 1907.

[162] "An Israelite's Passion," *Daily Chronicle*, 7 October 1907. For comments on a late nineteenth-century "spiritual realignment" whereby emotion, strength, and spirituality were not regarded as incompatible see Alison M. Bucknall, "Martha's Work and Mary's Contemplation? The Women of the Mildmay Conference and the Keswick Convention 1856-1900," in R. N. Swanson, ed., *Studies in Church History*, vol. 34, *Gender and Religion* (Woodbridge: Boydell Press, 1998), 415-416.

[163] "An Israelite's Passion," *Daily Chronicle*, 7 October 1907.

attention which these initial exuberant meetings attracted. Barratt recorded on 10 October, 1907, that "the papers are alive with the Movement all over England." He claimed to have received a letter from a proprietor of a 'Palace of Amusements' who had been converted while reading these accounts in the daily newspapers.[164] According to Gee, Boddy had on his return from Norway, sought to utilise the press as a vehicle for the dissemination of the Pentecostal message.[165] It was certainly attested by a gentleman of the press that he welcomed correspondents and reporters "in the friendliest way"[166] while he sought to offer a rationale for the curious phenomena they were witnessing. He would later admit that while these reports were "often grotesque," they undoubtedly "raised deep interest." Having read these accounts many traversed "long distances to meet God and to be helped by His servants" before returning home "to spread the Flame."[167]

It is of course the case that such widespread and vivid reportage was not without its problematic aspects, which for Boddy appear to have lain in the less welcome attentions they attracted. In addition to genuine seekers, the prospect of religious euphoria also appealed to "cranks and mischief-makers" who would cause "much pain and anxiety...strange people with strange spirits" who "brought great trials of faith to simple souls."[168] It is certainly the case that when he came to publicise the first Sunderland Convention some six months later in the first issue of *Confidence* magazine, considerable thought had been given to the restriction of the potential for "trials of faith," whether emanating from those who would deliberately oppose or from the unsettling influence of "strange spirits."

Boddy was evidently keen to not only avoid "extravagant proceedings and deplorable exhibitions,"[169] but to promote and foster a sense of propriety and decorum in what would be England's and Britain's largest Pentecostal gathering to date. The simple and pragmatic guidelines he advanced enjoined punctuality, quietness prior to the meeting, and respect for the leader as "confusion is not always edifying." To this it was added that the Chairman's ruling was to be "promptly and willingly obeyed in cases of difficulty."[170] It would appear that as Chairman and general custodian Boddy was keen to advance the development of Pentecostal worship beyond initial "wild scenes,"[171] "orgies of prayer" and unseemly intrusions into, and interruptions

---

[164] Barratt, *When the Fire Fell*, 152.

[165] Gee, *The Pentecostal Movement*, 22.

[166] "Northern Revival Fervour: Extraordinary Scenes at the Meetings," *Morning Leader*, 3 October 1907.

[167] "The Pentecostal Movement," *Confidence*, August 1910, 195.

[168] "The Pentecostal Movement," *Confidence*, August 1910, 195.

[169] A charge levelled by Pentecostal League founder and former associate Reader Harris in his condemnatory article "The Gift of Tongues," *Tongues of Fire*, November 1907, 2.

[170] "Whitsuntide Conference at Sunderland," *Confidence*, April 1908, 2.

[171] "Revival Scenes: The Converts Speak in Strange Tongues," *Morning Leader*, 2

of, the sermon or address from the platform.[172] In agreement with prominent criticisms he too disapproved of "unwarranted extremes," "extravagant proceedings," "extravagances and worse," and was endeavouring to ensure that such behaviour would not become normative. However, unlike the implacable Reader Harris, he never doubted that there was "good under the rubbish."[173]

A defence of empirical expressions of religious fervour in the context of the nineteenth-century North American camp meeting had asserted that:

> Something of an extraordinary nature was necessary to arrest the attention of a wicked and sceptical people, who were ready to conclude that Christianity was a fable and futurity a dream...(it) brought numbers beyond calculation under the influence of experimental religion and practical piety.[174]

McLeod has observed that what he terms the "ultra-Evangelical view of average human nature" has historically sought to promote a clearly marked hiatus in the lives of individuals under divine influence.[175] Beyond individual initiation, Pentecostal worship was held to embody visible attestations of the fact that, as Boddy informed a newspaper reporter, "the Spirit comes in strange ways"[176] and to offer arresting evidence of genuine encounter and transformation in the lives of participants. It was Boddy's estimation that when authentic this would provoke fundamental questions: "Am I a true child of God? Am I all my Heavenly Father wishes me to be, and all He can and will make me if I yield to Him? Have I really received the Holy Spirit?"[177] It was toward the task of both the generation and reinforcement of acceptable norms of Pentecostal expression that much of this urban clergyman's energies were directed in the context of the Sunderland Convention which functioned as the *magisterium* of the movement[178] during its first seven years.

Control Exercised in the Form of the "Visible Leader"

Integral to this formidable task was the avoidance, if not, outright suppression of the wayward, the indulgent, and the unnecessarily bizarre. It has been

---

October 1907.

[172] "Revival Scenes: Weird Chants and Frenzied Appeals," *The Morning Dispatch*, 7 October 1907. This report presented a picture of erratic proceedings, punctuated by a variety of unpredictable and distracting interruptions.

[173] "The Gift of Tongues," *Tongues of Fire*, November 1907, 1-2.

[174] G. W. Henry, *Shouting: Genuine and Spurious* (Chicago: Metropolitan Church Association, 1903), 287.

[175] McLeod, *Class and Religion in the Late Victorian City* (London: Croom Helm, 1974), 71.

[176] "Northern Revival Fervour: Extraordinary Scenes at the Meetings," *Morning Leader*, 3 October 1907.

[177] "Our Faithful God," *Confidence*, May 1908, 3.

[178] Bebbington, "Evangelicalism and Cultural Diffusion," 10.

observed of religious collectives that an interdenominational, as opposed to undenominational pose, necessitates a concern for respectability as it demands that the movement be acceptable to a range of groups.[179] Such considerations were doubtless present as evidenced by Boddy's statement after the first Sunderland convention that although "the Lord was our Leader," there had also been a "visible leader" in "all gatherings." Referring in the third person to his own role, he related that although "he sought not to be in evidence, he was just ready if needed." By way of explication it was added that "the Lord has always had overseers, whom He uses to guide under His control, that all things may be done becomingly and in order." He held that there were liable to be "restive spirits in every large gathering" as well as those "only content if they dominate," but it would appear that the warnings and injunctions issued in advance had proven effective. In a comment which indicated a perception of progress and development in this matter, the leader of the event concluded: "We are learning...to detect the flesh in some extravagances, in some messages, in some manifestations, but to go forward fearlessly and to exalt Jesus far above all."[180]

An unnamed visitor to the Sunderland Convention remarked that the times of prayer had "proved very powerful," and had not been "stiff in any way," or "merely mechanical." Such were the contrary tendencies, potentially even more unpalatable to Pentecostal sensibilities, to which collective worship could succumb. An insight is afforded into the directive approach adopted by Boddy as he sought to regulate, but not constrain, the spontaneity held to accompanying genuine inspiration. A notice was placed at the front of the platform which sought to restrict without offending or devaluing "the long-praying folk" who were "nearly always at such meetings." It read: "Friends who are praying at a considerable length will not, we trust, take it unkindly if we sing quietly some helpful chorus. This may apply also to prayers which cannot be heard and joined in by the audience." The German commentator concluded this to be "a very good example" and "worthy of imitation."[181]

Whatever difficulties attended the organisation and conduct of the Sunderland Convention appear to have been overshadowed, certainly in the perceptions of key protagonists, by the challenge of staging a similar gathering in Wales. In a Special Supplement to *Confidence* which appeared in the spring of 1909, T. M. Jeffreys, himself a pastor from South Wales, stated with forthright candour: "We expected the Welsh Conference to be a difficult one. Our expectations have been fully realized." In an interesting reflection on the

---

[179] It would appear that in a manner akin to Boddy, John G. Govan, founder of the Faith Mission, established an official organ which was sober and respectable in format and few of whose articles betrayed "the inflammatory evangelical language found among the publications of many Holiness and revivalistic groups." See Warburton, "The Faith Mission," 94.

[180] "The Whitsuntide Conference," *Confidence*, June 1908, 4.

[181] "German Thoughts About the Sunderland Convention," *Confidence*, July 1913, 137.

perceived legacy of the Revival of 1904-5, it was regretted that although "hundreds" had been "going on in the divine life...they have had no shepherds." The paucity of effective leadership had had, it was asserted, a deleterious effect: "deluding spirits have crept in; the gifts and manifestations have been exalted...and sad havoc has 'the wolf' wrought among the little bands." Apprehensions in advance of the Conference were attributed to the assessment that "the Welsh character lacks restraint."[182] Without making explicit reference to specific works of psychology of religion, the emerging coterie of Pentecostal leaders intimated an awareness of, and sympathy with, contemporary thinking in this field of investigation. While in his Gifford Lectures, James had remarked on "how native the sense of God's presence must be to certain minds,"[183] Jeffreys identified the Welsh character as exhibiting a particular "sensitiveness to all psychic influence." In his estimation it was not immediately apparent to this Celtic race that "the wonderful emotions liberated in the soul by the Spirit of God, must needs also be controlled by the same Spirit, and not indulged in riotously to the mere gratification of the animal senses."[184]

Jeffreys also betrays an affinity with analytical critiques of the Revival such as that published by Congregationalist minister J. Vyrnwy Morgan in the same year. Certainly their assessments of Celtic characteristics bear striking similarity. In the aftermath of the Revival, Morgan highlighted the Welsh capacity for *Dwysder*, imperfectly translated as *gravity* or *intensity*, as a significant factor in the predisposition of the ethnic group toward religion and associated exuberant expression. In addition to this the Welsh were said to be "particularly endowed" in the direction of "superstition." This manifested itself in the fact that "from time immemorial the Welsh mind has familiarized itself with the mysterious and incomprehensible," to the extent that it was to be found "surrounded by clouds of miraculous encumbrances." The ultimate conclusion drawn was that "there is no race that possesses this type of imagination in so marked degree as the Welsh," a circumstance which rendered them uniquely sensitive to "those fluctuations of feeling to which all forms of religion are subject."[185]

---

[182] T. M. Jeffreys, "The Cardiff Conference," Special Supplement to *Confidence*, April 1909, 1.

[183] James, *Varieties of Religious Experience*, 69.

[184] T. M. Jeffreys, "The Cardiff Conference," Special Supplement to *Confidence*, April 1909, 1. An application of the concept of the *crowd*, then current in the field of social psychology, had recently been made to the study of religious revival. The Celtic *crowd* had been identified as particularly prone to "sympathetic outbreak" of exaggerated "extent, intensity, and character." See Frederick Morgan Davenport, *Primitive Traits in Religious Revivals: A Study in Mental and Social Evolution* (London: Macmillan & Co., 1906), 25, 30.

[185] Morgan, *The Welsh Religious Revival*, 33-35, 43, 48. A correspondent from *The Times* advanced a similar assessment: "What an interesting fellow the Celt is!...Warm-hearted and wayward, intelligent and superstitious, impulsive and obstinate, anarchic

The positive aspects of this disposition resulted in the observation that when "150 souls" met in the Long Room of the Park Hotel, Cardiff, during the spring of 1909: "Surely never did hostelry ring with such glad and sanctified song as filled the building." Yet these propensities also necessitated Jeffreys, "right at the very commencement, to lovingly but firmly denounce the ecstasies of the flesh which some were indulging in, and also to silence one or two brothers, who were giving vent to vehement ejaculations of Tongues, manifestly not of God." Cecil Polhill presided at the afternoon meeting which was "thrown open for questions." This proved "most profitable" to the extent that it "served to bring difficulties to light, and enabled one to see how some of God's best children were carried away into delusions by the 'enemy of souls.'"[186]

The evening meeting was addressed by "Vicar Boddy," who in addition to "stirring accounts" of "gracious visitations at Sunderland," also pointedly issued "solemn warnings...against all extravagance, strange teaching and insidious sins." "Fresh from victories won at Bradford," Wigglesworth's contribution generated "a keen hunger for Pentecost" with the outcome that "dozens flocked forward to definitely seek." Yet Jeffreys reported an unfortunate degeneration as "this part of the meeting culminated in quite an unnecessary outburst of riotous emotion and extravagance, such as, if encouraged, must surely hinder the pure and blessed workings of the Holy Spirit." In a statement which affords insights into not only the tone of the Cardiff Conference, but also the acceptable norms of worship and expression which the leaders of the movement were seeking to engender, Jeffreys concluded:

> Welshmen do not need any inciting to shout, they are only too ready to do this. Praise should be free and unstinted. Hallelujahs must not be quenched, but there is no necessity to work up a shouting competition to an extent that the cries become screams and yells. This may seem hard, but God must not be dishonoured...and while under the power of the Holy Ghost, it is to be expected that newly liberated emotions will find free vent, yet praise should always be...rendered as if in the very presence of a Holy, Holy God.[187]

At the conclusion of this account Boddy felt it necessary to add his own commentary which lamented any attempt to "work up manifestations."[188] This statement is highly suggestive in the light of the criticism advanced by Reader Harris in his condemnation, while in Sunderland, of "the deadly dangers

---

and easily lead, he has always shown a certain instability of character...his religion always the chief interest of his life. The year now ended illustrates his temperament." From "The Welsh Revival," *The Times*, 3 January 1905.

[186] T. M. Jeffreys, "The Cardiff Conference," Special Supplement to *Confidence*, April 1909, 1-2.

[187] T. M. Jeffreys, "The Cardiff Conference," Special Supplement to *Confidence*, April 1909, 2-3.

[188] "Note by the Editor," Special Supplement to *Confidence*, April 1909, 4.

accompanying much of the present-day desire for manifestations."[189] Such concerns echo the fascinating observations made by Evan Roberts who retrospectively identified "the mistake at the time of the Revival in Wales," as having been an increasing preoccupation with "the effects of the Revival," rather than its larger purpose.[190] Emerging Pentecostal ideologues, it is clear, exerted considerable efforts toward ensuring that what had begun in Sunderland during the autumn of 1907 would not be remembered as merely another "wave of intense religious emotion" or "blaze of glory" which had proven to be "as brief as it was excessive."[191]

Transatlantic Perspectives

In his treatment of "cataleptic" occurrences in early American Pentecostal worship, Wacker quotes an anonymous reporter who described the proceedings at a Maria Woodworth-Etter meeting in Connecticut in 1913 during which the interior of the tent "resembled a veritable madhouse." While some of those present shook "to and fro in a 'tango' movement," others executed something approximating to a "'turkey-trot' sway" as they might have done in a "cabaret or hootchy-kootchy show." The overall impression was that "the scene in the tent resembled the fabled confusions of Bedlam."[192] Wacker goes on to make the following observation: "Pentecostal meetings overseas followed the same script. Though the British might have preferred to think they remained free of such excesses, they did not."[193]

What has been outlined in the present study has demonstrated that while English contemporaries might indeed have preferred to have been free of "such excesses," they entertained no illusions as to the realities of what they were confronting. Indeed painfully aware of the problematic nature of tendencies in

---

[189] J. Dixon Johnson, "Sunderland Convention," *Tongues of Fire*, November 1907, 4.

[190] Penn-Lewis and Evan Roberts, *War on the Saints: A Text Book on the Work of Deceiving Spirits among the Children of God, and the Way of Deliverance*, 3rd ed., (Leicester: The Overcomer Book Room, 1922), 283. While this may indicate a point of convergence, it is the case that grave reservations were expressed with regard to the overall tenor of this unusual joint publication. *War on the Saints* was in effect a compendium of demonology reminiscent of a seventeenth-century *genre* epitomized in works such as Reginald Scot's *The Discoverie of Witchcraft* (London: A. Clark, 1665). Boddy issued a measured but definite rebuttal in "A Book about Demons," *Confidence*, January 1913, 20. Two articles appeared immediately after the publication of the second edition and offered further clarification of the issues involved. See "Our Victory in the Heavenlies," *Confidence*, July 1916, 116-119, and "Our Victory over Demons and Disease," *Confidence*, November 1916, 180-183.

[191] Hall, "The Welsh Revival," in Cuming and Baker, eds., *Studies in Church History*, vol. 8, 291-292.

[192] *Bridgeport Herald*, 15 June 1913, cited in Wacker, *Early Pentecostals and American Culture*, 101-102.

[193] Wacker, *Early Pentecostals and American Culture*, 102.

this direction, the movement's custodians went to considerable lengths to address and counteract these difficulties. Furthermore it is noteworthy that in making allusion to what Pentecostals in Britain might have regarded themselves as superior to, Wacker refers, without specific quotation, to an article by Boddy. This article represents the concluding part of the latter's account of his final tour of North America before the outbreak of war. Offering a "Summary of the Journey," Boddy commended the "Pentecostal people" he had encountered for their orthodoxy in relation to "the Scriptures, the Atonement, the Coming of Christ, Hell and Heaven, etc." While there was elsewhere "much apostasy in Christendom," those he described as "our people" were "always true and loyal to these truths." He commended them for their spiritual "keenness" and their ready appreciation of "a live message." Then in a comment far from shocked by, or condemnatory of what he had observed on the other side of the Atlantic, and much less implying an exemption from, or immunity to, similar tendencies at home, Boddy stated:

> I noticed that in U. S. A. there is a love of physical 'manifestations.' Many find them stimulating and strengthening. That which shocks some does not seem irreverent at all to others who wish to be very true to God. There is a great danger in judging. We know that in suppressing what we think is the 'flesh,' there is a danger of 'quenching the Spirit.'[194]

An unabashed realism is evidenced in Boddy's candid remarks to Darlington's *North Star* who acknowledged that in addition to "remarkable manifestations" in Sunderland, "of course there have been extravagances which I do not approve."[195] He elsewhere claimed that God was "working mightily in this Pentecostal Movement in spite of our extravagancies and foolishness."[196] It was, in similar vein, admitted at the last Sunderland Convention that Pentecostals had at times earned themselves the ridicule of other Christians "because they missed in the Pentecostal assembly the sound mind" enjoined by the apostle Paul in 2 Timothy 1:7.[197] Boddy was seemingly alive to the charge that some had "abandoned the life of faith to seek signs," and that some of the more "deplorable accompaniments"[198] had served to "reduce the religion of Jesus Christ to a farce."[199] This spiritual movement was, with the help of correctives and injunctions advanced by its leadership, to pursue instead the

---

[194] "Westward Ho!: The Conclusion of the Journey," *Confidence*, December 1914, 226-227.

[195] "Pentecostal Conventions at Sunderland: Interview with Rev. A. A. Boddy," Reprinted from *North Star*, Darlington, 24 May 1915, in *Confidence*, June 1915, 106.

[196] "Pentecostal Work in the Metropolis," *Confidence*, February 1910, 31.

[197] "Woman's Place in the Church," *Confidence*, November 1914, 212.

[198] "Review of 1907," *Tongues of Fire*, January 1908, 7.

[199] "Editorials: The Truth Denied Encourages Satanic Counterfeit," *Tongues of Fire*, February 1908, 6.

attainment of a higher goal: "Let us lose ourselves in Him."[200]

The perspective advanced by "Azusa pioneer"[201] Frank Bartleman proves enlightening with regard to Pentecostal worship and expression as it was developing in England. Visiting London in 1910, Bartleman found "a company of very able, precious saints," of whom he offered the opinion that they were "not quite as free as one might wish." This was attributed, in part at least, to the fact that their surroundings in the "busy, worldly...immense metropolis" were "affecting them somewhat." Yet in addressing a number of meetings he confessed to having "never met a more hearty welcome or been better treated anywhere." Those he encountered were not only "the most precious people all around," they were observed to "love their Bibles," a trait which he wished was more in evidence in his homeland. This feature of the spirituality he witnessed was deemed to have had a stabilizing effect, ensuring that "the work" was "kept very steadily here on the whole." Although those observed "may swing a little to the conservative extreme," he confessed that this "furnished a somewhat delightful contrast to some things we have experienced elsewhere."[202]

Another form of "delightful contrast" was attested by a German visitor who recorded a positive impression of both the surroundings and atmosphere in which Pentecostal worship was conducted in England. Of the several churches and chapels visited it was stated that they were "not dark like some old churches where one is afraid to shout a good 'Hallelujah!' In Pastor Boddy's church someone shouted: 'Glory be to God,' and it fitted in very nicely with Bro. Boddy's sermon. What would have been said if someone had said that in Germany? They would have called that a disturbance."[203] Evidently the tenor of emerging English Pentecostal worship, while deemed somewhat conservative from a trans-Atlantic perspective, was hailed as refreshingly bright and buoyant by European counterparts.

Correctives Employed - Sanity Enjoined

It is obvious that during the formative years of Pentecostal expression, those overseeing the process were attempting to pursue a median and moderate position amid a welter of contrary tendencies, seeking to promote and maintain order and spiritual sobriety while sustaining what has been described as "the irrigation of a movement constantly in need of the refreshing waters of religious experience."[204] It is pertinent to point out that amid such challenges

---

[200] "Pentecostal Work in the Metropolis," *Confidence*, February 1910, 31.

[201] Wacker, *Early Pentecostals and American Culture*, 99-100.

[202] "Brother Bartleman: His Visits to British Pentecostal Centres," *Confidence*, August 1910, 185.

[203] "German Thoughts About the Sunderland Convention," *Confidence*, August 1913, 157.

[204] Margaret Poloma, "The Millenarianism of the Pentecostal Movement," in Stephen Hunt, ed., *Christian Millenarianism: From the Early Church to Waco* (Bloomington and Indianapolis: Indiana University Press, 2001), 186.

the emollient repeatedly applied was the *Word of God*. Periodicals proclaimed that it was by means of "the instrumentality of His Word" that the "life of Christ" was "injected" or "engrafted" into the individual,[205] while it was a departure from the "all sufficiency of the Word of God" which had resulted in the fanaticism, extremism, and "pretended inspiration of the false prophets" associated with the radical elements of the European Reformation.[206] Reflecting a longstanding and cherished disposition within the evangelical tradition,[207] Polhill stated that "men cannot do despite to the written Word of God with impunity." For those who embarked on such a course, "a dangerous and slippery path is entered upon, fraught with subtle and terrible dangers." In his estimation "the newly baptised one" should not scorn "old, methodical, well-learned habits of quiet prayer and diligent Bible study." Otherwise there remained the potent danger that those elated by "wonders" and "new revelations" could find themselves enticed by the subtle allurements of "an unbalanced and fanatical live."[208] The biblical injunction: "In quietness and confidence shall be your strength" (Is. 30:15) was hailed as nothing less than the enunciation of "a vital law." Truly "devout saints" should neither "harass themselves nor God by importunate cries to Him." Simple obedience to the plain injunctions of Scripture would result in the attainment of an inner spiritual unification[209] or holism which would enable the individual to "walk unfalteringly in God's appointed way."[210]

Boddy made the observation in 1910 that "extravagance and excrescences are dying down, leaving the British Pentecostal people standing steadfast and immovable."[211] He was pleased to announce that a seasoned Primitive Methodist minister, while attending the London Convention of 1912, was heard to proclaim: "This is the old fire that the Primitive Methodists used to have."[212] Polhill was eager to report that the gifts of the Spirit had been "beautifully in evidence" at a colloquy that had been held earlier that year. These had included messages in tongues and interpretations which were delivered "without a trace of disorder or wildfire."[213] In the estimation of T. M. Jeffreys, "increased liberty" was being enjoyed "because of increased control. There was freedom

---

[205] George D. Watson, "The Engrafted Word," *Flames of Fire*, October 1911, 2.

[206] Bartleman, "Extracts from the Reformation," *Flames of Fire*, October 1911, 3.

[207] Evangelical utilisation of, and recourse to, Scripture has been examined by D. K. Gillett in his study *Trust and Obey: Explorations in Evangelical Spirituality* (London: Darton, Longman and Todd, 1993), 129-157.

[208] "After the Baptism of the Holy Ghost," *Flames of Fire*, January 1912, 3.

[209] James had addressed the quest for the attainment of such a condition, commenting on difficulties encountered even by exemplars of the Protestant tradition. See *Varieties of Religious Experience*, 183-188.

[210] May Mabbette Anderson, "Quietness and Confidence," *Flames of Fire*, November 1911, 2.

[211] "The Pentecostal Movement," *Confidence*, August 1910, 196.

[212] "The Pentecostal Meetings in London," *Confidence*, May 1912, 107.

[213] "Editorial," *Flames of Fire*, March 1912, 1.

for the Spirit's manifestations because the flesh was quietened."[214] He reported demonstrable progress:

> Evidently the Lord is teaching His children deportment. The heavenly people, the elite of the Universe are learning how to behave themselves, even under transcending joys. There was an absence of hysterical excitement, and Pentecost was recommended by the spirit of a sound mind. Would that dozens of little assemblies which were not represented could have witnessed so splendid an object-lesson in Spirit-control as this Conference afforded.[215]

It would appear that the first custodians of Pentecostal expression in England perceived themselves to have, before the First World War, attained a degree of success in the management of divergent tendencies. A movement whose worship merited inclusion among those characterised by a demand for "first-hand experience," a passion for "simplicity and sincerity of expression," and an over-arching "vigorous spiritual realism,"[216] was achieving an amalgam described by Polhill as "a quietness combined with power."[217] Participants were being "brought face-to-face with the inwardness of Pentecost" and were thereby realising that this encompassed "something more than 'Tongues' and delightful sensations for the soul."[218] The enduring nature of the ethos that such pioneers sought to inculcate is attested by the fact that later denominational leaders, using very similar terms, reiterated the imperative of "spiritual warning" against "spurious" and "soulish manifestations."[219] The notion that

---

[214] T. M. Jeffreys, "A Retrospect of the Sunderland Convention," *Confidence*, June 1910, 127.

[215] T. M. Jeffreys, "A Retrospect of the Sunderland Convention," *Confidence*, June 1910, 127. The self-designation "the elite of the Universe" lends credence to Wacker's comment that in their early years Pentecostals exhibited an "extravagant assessment of their own importance." See "Evangelical Responses to Pentecostalism," 505. Further consideration will be given to aspects of this self-conception which to the outside observer has all the appearance of megalomania on pages 130-131 below.

[216] Underhill, *Worship*, 228-229.

[217] "Editorial," *Flames of Fire*, March 1912, 1.

[218] T. M. Jeffreys, "A Retrospect of the Sunderland Convention," *Confidence*, June 1910, 127.

[219] See P. Correy, "The Baptism in the Holy Spirit," *Redemption Tidings*, January 1925, 3. Terminology remarkably similar to that used by Boddy *et al* is to be found in George Jeffreys, *Pentecostal Rays: The Baptism and Gifts of the Holy Spirit* (London: Elim Publishing Company 1933), 244. Furthermore detailed observations made by Walker and Atherton with respect of conventions, the "'Dionysian' highlights in the Pentecostal calendar" some six decades later, corroborate Hudson's more recent conclusion: "If the Welsh Revival and its aftermath would mark future Pentecostalism in its tendency to emotionalism, the Sunderland Conventions would bring an order and sense of purpose...that the denominations would bear right up to the present day." Andrew G. Walker and James S. Atherton, "An Easter Pentecostal Convention: the Successful Management of a 'Time of Blessing,'" *Sociological Review* 17.3 (1971):

"Pentecost" consisted of "ecstasy first and ecstasy last with ecstasy in between" had been repeatedly and effectively challenged and an alternative paradigm for collective expression - again betraying the motif of spiritual hunger/appetite - was instead asserted: "Praise and joy in the Holy Ghost from the beginning to the end, but wholesome strong meet of the Word generously sandwiched between."[220] It is significant that while critics were apt to deride the Pentecostal phenomenon as appealing to and "carrying captive silly women,"[221] it was Mrs. Walshaw, a prominent female leader of a Pentecostal Mission in Halifax, who enjoined the movement to function "soberly" and to strive to be "a sane people, free from fads, fancies and extravagances."[222] The disposition of the most influential pioneering leaders could be said to have been characterised by a sobriety which was suffused with a cognizance of the fact that "the rankest fanaticism runs closely along the line of the deepest spirituality."[223]

Section 2.3: Pentecostal Apocalypticism

Overview

The first issue of *Confidence* in April 1908 stated: "Never since the day when that initial outpouring of the 'Promise of the Father,' with heavenly gifts and signs caused the wondering people to ask 'What meaneth this?' has that question of old become the new and absorbing question of so many minds as in the past year of restored signs and gifts." It was further claimed that there had hitherto not been such a "swift and strategic marshalling of forces" as was to be witnessed at the closing years of the nineteenth and the opening of the twentieth centuries, with each year "speeding more intensely toward the predicted consummation." Not since the Church had been promised "Behold, I come quickly," had there been "such sublime and supernatural preparations for that coming."[224] Boddy opened the first Sunderland Convention on the evening of 10 June, 1908, with a reading from Luke 12:32-40 and reminded those gathered of the timeliness of the injunction: 'Be ye also ready; for the Son of Man

---

367, 372-375, and Hudson, "Worship," in Warrington, ed. *Pentecostal Perspectives*, 179.

[220] T. M. Jeffreys, "Sunderland International Pentecostal Congress: Teaching," *Confidence*, June 1909, 134.

[221] "Editorials: The Truth Denied Encourages Satanic Counterfeit," *Tongues of Fire*, February 1908, 6.

[222] Mrs. Walshaw, "Prayer in the Holy Ghost," *Flames of Fire*, June 1915, 6. Lydia Walshaw was the wife of a Yorkshire solicitor, but it was she who took the more prominent and proactive role in their Emmaus Mission Hall. Gee included her as an honourary man in his *These Men I Knew* where he stated: "Mrs. Walshaw was one of those personalities that seem to flourish in the early years of a Revival Movement before it has had time to solidify into a denomination." See *Personal Memoirs of Pentecostal Pioneers*, 86.

[223] J. M. Pike, "The Coming Revival," *Flames of Fire*, August 1915, 2.

[224] "The Bridegroom Cometh," *Confidence*, April 1908, 19.

cometh at an hour when ye think not.'[225] These statements not only reveal pronounced eschatological preoccupations, but also betray a self-understanding which gave purpose and cohesion to this fledgling spiritual movement. England's emerging Pentecostals were aligning themselves with what has been described as a "proto-foundationalist myth" where traditional and ancient elements combined with history, psychology, customs, and ideals to explain the totality of human society.[226] The breadth of humanity, its past, present, and future, and in particular their own role within this grand scheme, was thereby imbued with ultimate meaning.

The Pre-Millennial Paradigm

The origins of this all-encompassing outlook it must be pointed out, significantly predated the advent of Pentecostal ideology. It is perhaps not surprising that the first generation of Pentecostals in England adhered to an eschatological system that has been described as "perhaps the most significant flowering of apocalypticism in Christianity in the past two centuries."[227] The aftermath of the French Revolution and the Napoleonic Wars which witnessed an efflorescence of radical political thought and writings, in addition to the social and economic upheavals associated with the industrial revolution, created an unease from which the religious world was not immune. A resort to prophecy was largely undertaken by Protestants who belonged to the upper middle classes and lower aristocracy,[228] an anxious intelligentsia who were engaged in the self-interpretation of the "revolutionary residues"[229] of their era. It was such considerations which inspired the Right Honourable Henry Drummond (1786-1860) to terminate his careers in banking and the House of Commons, and summon clergy and interested lay people to his Albury Park estate for the purpose of the examination of prophetic truth. The outcome of a series of convocations was the formulation of an eschatological system which would exert appeal and influence significantly beyond the immediate scope of this original Circle. The principal "ingredients of the Albury response" have

---

[225] "The Near Coming of the Lord," *Confidence*, June 1908, 17.

[226] Mark Patterson, "Creating a Last Days' Revival: The Premillennial Worldview and the Albury Circle," in Andrew Walker and Kristin Aune, eds., *On Revival: A Critical Examination* (Carlisle: Paternoster Press, 2003), 100.

[227] Philip S. Alexander, "Dispensationalism, Christian Zionism and the State of Israel", Presidential Lecture for the Manson Society, University of Manchester, 2001), 1. For insights into the variations of apocalyptic expectation that constituted the millennial dawn of the late eighteenth, and early nineteenth-centuries, see J. F. C. Harrison, *The Second Coming: Popular Millenarianism, 1780-1850* (London and Henley: Routledge and Kegan Paul, 1979).

[228] Patterson, "The Premillennial Worldview and the Albury Circle," in Walker and Aune, eds., *On Revival*, 89-90.

[229] Henri Descroche, *The Sociology of Hope*, trans. Carol Martin-Sperry (London: Routledge & Kegan Paul, 1979), 133.

been summarized as postulating:

> The apostate nation, inter-related social, political, religious and moral disorders, despair at the present situation, hope only over the bridge of calamity, judgement, wrath and purification, the saving role of a faithful remnant, and the millennium as the ultimate righter of wrongs.[230]

The dissemination and inculcation of this teaching continued throughout the nineteenth-century and, according to Sandeen, it had attracted able and winning advocates in the evangelical wing of the Churches of England and Scotland by the 1870s.[231] Wesley Myland, one of North American Pentecostalism's most prominent purveyors of eschatological thinking, highlighted the infiltration of this school of interpretation into the Anglican constituency. He commented that "we have some grand teaching coming out of the Church of England, the best mother of theology I know of in the world." He identified G. H. Pember's *The Great Prophecies* as a "most comprehensive work" among those that had emanated from this historic communion which, in the latter half of the nineteenth century, had "brought down rivers of truth from God's Word."[232]

Bebbington has pointed out that a Keswick stalwart, Prebendary Webb-Peploe, when addressing an Islington Clerical Meeting in 1901, assumed that all his hearers adhered to the notion of a premillennial advent. It is evident that such prophetic teaching had not only become firmly established by the turn of the new century, but that its futurist guise was the predominant form of advent hope by the onset of the First World War.[233] Historicist premillennialists held that prophetic Scriptures present in symbolic form, the history of the Christian Church to the millennial reign of Christ predicted in Revelation chapter 20, and contested that with scrutiny significant developments could be deciphered. Those of the futurist school, among whom John Nelson Darby (1800-1882)[234]

---

[230]W. H. Oliver, *Prophets and Millennialists: The Uses of Biblical Prophecy in England from the 1790s to the 1840s* (Auckland: Auckland University Press, 1978), 141.

[231] Ernest R. Sandeen, *The Roots of Fundamentalism: British and American Millenarianism, 1800-1930* (Chicago and London: University of Chicago Press, 1970), 89.

[232] D. Wesley Myland, *The Revelation of Jesus Christ: A Comprehensive Harmonic Outline and Perspective View of the Book* (Chicago, Ill.: Evangel Publishing House, 1911), 21; G. H. Pember, *The Great Prophecies of the Centuries* (1881; repr. London and Edinburgh: Oliphants Ltd., 1941).

[233] Bebbington, *Evangelicalism in Modern Britain*, 192.

[234] On Darby and his singular influence see Timothy C. F. Stunt, "Influences in the Early Development of J. N. Darby," in Crawford Gribben and Timothy C. F. Stunt, eds., *Prisoners of Hope? Aspects of Evangelical Millennialism in Britain and Ireland, 1800-1880* (Carlisle: Paternoster Press, 2004), 44-68; Harold H. Rowdon, *The Origins of the Brethren, 1825-1850* (London: Pickering & Inglis Lts., 1967), 41-53; Sandeen, *Roots of Fundamentalism*, 59-80; Timothy P. Weber, *Living in the Shadow of the Second Coming: American Premillennialism, 1875-1925* (New York and Oxford: Oxford University Press, 1979), 16-24.

had been eminent, contended that none of the outcomes depicted in these writings had yet been fulfilled, and that this would only occur within a condensed period prior to the return of Christ.[235] What had attained a significant following within the evangelical constituency by the final quarter of the nineteenth-century, received further impetus with the publication of the Scofield Reference Bible in 1909, which sold in excess of two million copies by the end of the second decade of the century. Its *Authorized Version* text was annotated in a manner designed to lucidly and persuasively present the dispensationalist schema.[236]

Significantly, the central tenets of this interpretive system had been routinely propounded in the official publication of the Pentecostal League of Prayer prior to the disassociation of Boddy, Wigglesworth and others post-1907. Prominent among these were a firm adherence to the notion of spiritual epochs or dispensations; a preoccupation with Israel and the spiritual reinstatement and repatriation of the Jewish people; spiritual deterioration characterised by the "lukewarmness and worldliness of the Churches;" an anticipated "gathering up" of the saints prior to the "anguish and awfulness of the great tribulation;" and ultimately Christ's second coming with the "body of saints" to inaugurate the Millennium.[237] In what was probably his most comprehensive expository treatment of this recurrent subject, Boddy himself expanded upon characteristically premillennialist "signs of His coming."[238] As I have explored these elsewhere,[239] fascinating and unique features that arose among emerging Pentecostals, frequently exercising significant influence into the longer term, will be highlighted in this context.

Divine Imminence: Salient Ramifications

The remarkable sense of urgency and imminence with which the *Parousia* was anticipated in the early years of Pentecostal experience, while of interest on several levels, will here be considered in the light of salient implications for the fledgling movement. The conviction that the emergence of "Pentecostal manifestations" in October 1907 "foreboded the end of the present order - the

---

[235] Weber, *Living in the Shadow of the Second Coming*, 9-11; Sandeen, *Roots of Fundamentalism*, 36-37.

[236] Peter E. Prosser, *Dispensationalist Eschatology and Its Influence on American and British Religious Movements* (Lampeter: Edwin Mellen Press, 1999), 74-75. For an appreciation of this singularly influential volume see Frank E. Gaebelein, *The Story of the Scofield Reference Bible, 1909-1959* (New York: Oxford University Press, 1959).

[237] "Things to Come: The Order of Events," *Tongues of Fire*, September 1906, 1-2; "Things to Come: Signs Among the Nations," *Tongues of Fire*, August 1906, 1-2; "Things to Come: The Story of Noah," *Tongues of Fire*, October 1906, 2.

[238] "Seven Signs of His Coming," *Confidence*, December 1910, 282-288.

[239] For more on this see my article "Eschatology and the Fortunes of Early British Pentecostalism," *Theology* 113.871 (January-February 2010): 31-43.

dawn of the Second Coming,"[240] would be emphasised and re-emphasised throughout subsequent years. In an editorial piece which reflected on 1909 as it drew to a close and surmised about prospects for the future, Boddy stated:

> If 1910 be our last year, then let it be our best...He has put a great expectancy into many hearts. Those who are ready for the coming of the Lord are the only safe ones. These are they who are ready for Halley's Comet, for a sudden home-call of any kind, but especially for the coming of our Friend and Saviour in the Clouds (1 Thess. iv., 14-18).[241]

The advance notification of a subsequent Convention was imbued with a similar sense of anticipation: "If the Lord tarries still, we shall hold, God willing, our Sixth International Pentecostal Convention in the Parish Hall of All Saints...We feel that each Convention may be our very last, as the Lord's Coming draws so nigh."[242] It would be difficult to overstate the implications of such pervasive convictions for the aims, methods, and structures of this religious movement. Such a profound sense of imminent intrusion into history coheres with what Stackhouse terms "apocalyptic vision,"[243] and tends toward the preclusion of social concerns or involvement. When leaders and key protagonists operated from the persuasion the "history will not take us further,"[244] the ramifications in terms of the structures they put in place, or of potentially greater significance, left in abeyance, could not but be considerable. Certainly in the pre-war period this conviction appears to have remained undimmed. Polhill's confident utterance in 1913 that "the blessed hope of the Coming of the Lord grows brighter day by day, and we are really planning to meet Him almost any time,"[245] demonstrates that during their early years English Pentecostals unflinchingly anticipated what has been described as "the ultimate religious 'solution.'"[246]

The tendency toward *apocalyptic* as opposed to *prophetic vision* does not seek to engage and challenge the reality it finds in the light of religious ideals, but instead foresees nothing but destitution and cataclysm for all but a spiritual elite.[247] Apocalyptic pronouncements anticipating "the early passing of the old society and the coming into history of a new divine order," allows the categorisation of these Pentecostal pioneers among those of *Christ against Culture* disposition. Yet in keeping with Niebuhr's acknowledgement that this radical stance "cannot itself exist without the counter-weight of other types of

---

[240] "An Israelite's Passion," *Daily Chronicle*, 7 October 1907.

[241] "Peace upon Earth among Men of Goodwill," *Confidence*, December 1909, 276.

[242] "The Sunderland International Convention," *Confidence*, January 1913, 12.

[243] Reginald Stackhouse, *The End of the World? A New Look at an Old Belief* (New York: Paulist Press, 1997), 28.

[244] "Seven Signs of His Coming," *Confidence*, December 1910, 283.

[245] "Missionaries," *Flames of Fire*, July 1912, 1.

[246] McQuire, *Religion: The Social Context*, 47.

[247] Stackhouse, *The End of the World*, 10-28.

Christianity,"[248] early Pentecostalism generated another strain of thinking which served to mitigate against the harsher implications of adherence to what has been termed a "catastrophic view of eschatology."[249] What some commentators have regarded as an unlikely conjunction of the "joyless trappings" of apocalyptic and dispensational fundamentalism with a religious disposition so open to spiritual ecstasy and the overtly miraculous,[250] was rendered possible in this period of foment and upheaval by the interjection of a concept known as the *Latter Rain*. It has been observed that so sharp a break with the conventional order as millennialism typically implies has, in its recurrence through the course of Christian history, frequently been associated with *charisma* and inspirational leadership.[251] It was certainly the case that emerging Pentecostalism advanced its apocalyptic emphases by means of an essentially charismatic message - one for which a distinctive rationale was devised and then widely propounded.

A Pentecostal Development: The Latter Rain

This notion was presented to the readers of *Confidence* as the final, and most persuasive, of the seven "Signs of His Coming." It manifested itself in an, at times, curious admixture of literal and metaphorical interpretations. While passages of scripture such as Zechariah 10:1, "Ask the Lord for rain, in the time of the latter rain," were taken as representations of "the mighty outpouring of the Holy Ghost towards the close of this Dispensation,"[252] patterns of literal precipitation over Palestine were scrutinized as further corroboration of the fulfilment of these biblical prefigurations. Boddy alleged that the spring rains which had historically aided the ripening of arable crops had not been observed for some time, but that an average fall had been measured from 1861 when some 21 inches had fallen. This was reputed to have steadily increased until

---

[248] Niebuhr, *Christ and Culture*, 76.

[249] Orr, *The Second Evangelical Awakening*, 253-254. It is interesting to note that several decades later some who otherwise claimed an indebtedness to the Pentecostal tradition, came to repudiate what was perceived to be a characteristically Pentecostal *eschatology of disaster*. This was replaced by what was held to be a more enlightened *eschatology of victory*. See Arthur Wallis, "Appendix 1," in Andrew Walker, *Restoring the Kingdom: The Radical Christianity of the House Church Movement*, 2nd ed. (Guildford, Surrey: Eagle, 1998), 377-378.

[250] Prosser, *Dispensationalist Eschatology*, 275. For comments on Pentecostalism's "questionable alliance" with dispensationalism see Chan, *Pentecostal Theology and the Christian Spiritual Tradition*, 11.

[251] Roy Wallis, "Introduction: Millennialism and Charisma," in Roy Wallis, ed., *Millennialism and Charisma* (Belfast: Queens University Press, 1982), 1-2. This observation is borne out against a broad historical backdrop by Norman Cohn's *The Pursuit of the Millennium: Revolutionary Millenarians and Mystical Anarchists of the Middle Ages* (London: Paladin Books, 1978).

[252] Barratt, "The Truth about the Pentecostal Revival," 9.

1891 when a "latter rain" to the depth of 29 inches had been measured. The corollary of this was that "the Lord has been pouring out His Spirit phenomenally in many lands," with spiritual indices exhibiting a similar trajectory:

> He has baptized with such an intense baptism that the Holy Ghost has actually spoken through the human instruments controlling the vocal organs. We have heard again and again those who were thus overwhelmed by the 'coming upon' of the Spirit cry with the intensity of an inward forcing power, 'JESUS IS COMING SOON.'[253]

Pentecostal advocates believed that their restorationist interpretation of events was being miraculously confirmed by evidence from nature, and alleged changes in weather patterns in Palestine functioned "as a kind of barometer indicating parallel changes in the spiritual realm."[254] What was early Pentecostalism's nuanced contribution to standard dispensational teaching, was not original to English adherents, although it found enthusiastic advocates among their ranks. The second issue of *The Apostolic Faith* published in Los Angeles had proclaimed the beginning of the end of this dispensation of history, as "the promised Latter Rain" was "now being poured out on God's humble people."[255] The concept was perhaps most comprehensively codified and promulgated in *The Latter Rain Pentecost*, a work by D. Wesley Myland. What was publicised by Boddy as "a remarkable book" to which he had had the "privilege" of contributing an introduction,[256] had originally been preached as a series of sermons in Chicago's Stone Church, and demonstrated what has been described as the "poetic theology" of its author.[257] It encapsulated the essential themes of the Latter Rain motif in its avowal of "the significant fact that simultaneously the Jews are returning to their native land; the literal rain is falling upon Palestine, and the spiritual latter rain is falling upon God's expectant people."[258]

It is evident that Boddy fulsomely endorsed this perspective, which amounted to much more than adherence to a particular eschatological schema, but served to bestow upon his movement a unique place in providential dealings. The wider Christian Church was increasingly regarded by the first generation of Pentecostals as "Laodicean"[259] in character, a "church of wealth and yet of poverty because of carelessness and ignorance in spiritual

---

[253] "Seven Signs of His Coming," *Confidence*, December 1910, 287-288.

[254] Jacobsen, *Theologies of the Early Pentecostal Movement*, 124.

[255] "The Pentecostal Baptism Restored," *The Apostolic Faith*, October 1906, 1.

[256] "The Latter Rain Pentecost," *Confidence*, November 1910, 258.

[257] Jacobsen, *Theologies of the Early Pentecostal Movement*, 110.

[258] "The Latter Rain Pentecost," *Confidence*, November 1910, 258.

[259] Polhill contrasted "Laodicean lukewarmness" with "red hot holiness." See "The Whitsuntide Pentecostal Conference," *Flames of Fire*, March 1915, 8.

matters."[260] It was this condition that necessitated the Latter Rain which amounted to a Copernican Revolution in the spiritual domain, an upheaval destined to overturn what was regarded by premillennialists generally as an "age of compromise between the Church and the world."[261] Faupel has aptly summarized the implications of such a concatenation of ideas: the Latter Rain motif was used "to disclose the Pentecostal movement as standing at the apex of history."[262] Jeffreys' proclamation at the London Convention of 1910 betrays nothing less than the enormity of this sense of destiny: "This is the battle of the universe! We are called to participate in THE SUPREME EVENT."[263]

The notion of a second and ultimate "Pentecostal Age" occurring as the "times of the Gentiles" came to a close, and immediately prior to the Rapture of the Church,[264] cannot but have provided considerable ideological respite to a movement that was, as yet, numerically insignificant and had incurred opposition entailing a degree of estrangement for many of its adherents. The effect, it is suggested, approximated to the generation of what Desroche has termed a "shared messianic or paramessianic consciousness."[265] Claims indeed emanated from English Pentecostal platforms to the effect that Christ truly "cannot do without his saints,"[266] and that initiates had progressed beyond both "old dispensation Christians" and the "gifts of the old dispensation."[267] The self-designation "Enoch Church,"[268] which indicated those who at the close of the Pentecostal dispensation would "walk with God" and "not be found,"[269] certainly betrayed a remarkable leap in ideological fortitude. Within the parameters of the present study it is argued that it was the early crystallisation of a collective consciousness of this order which both galvanised and inspired

---

[260] Wesley Myland, *The Revelation of Jesus Christ*, 104-105.

[261] A. R. Fausset, *The Signs of the Times in Relation to the Speedy Return of Our Lord Jesus in Person to Reign* 2nd ed. (London: J. Nisbet & Co., 1896), 15.

[262] D. William Faupel, *The Everlasting Gospel: The Significance of Eschatology in the Development of Pentecostal Thought*, Journal of Pentecostal Theology Supplement Series, 10 (Sheffield: Sheffield Academic Press, 1996), 34

[263] T. M. Jeffreys, "The *Parousis*, or 'Appearing' of the Lord," *Confidence*, June 1910, 151.

[264] See chart "The Seven Ages of the World's History and the Soon Coming of the Lord," *Confidence*, October 1911, 229. Boddy later presented his readership with "A Chart of the World's Ages," *Confidence*, April 1914, 70. Alexander has observed that dispensationalists were "very fond of charts, which, though their naivete raises a smile, are a remarkable attempt to make visible the vivid imagery of the apocalyptic imagination." See "Dispensationalism, Christian Zionism and the State of Israel," 7.

[265] Desroche, *The Sociology of Hope*, 87.

[266] M. Boddy, "The Coming Rapture," *Confidence*, July 1911, 155.

[267] E. Beyerhaus, "The Spirit of Pentecost and His Gifts," *Confidence*, December 1910, 291.

[268] T. M. Jeffreys, "The *Parousia*, or 'Appearing' of the Lord," *Confidence*, June 1910, 150.

[269] "The Coming of the Lord," *Confidence*, June 1914, 116.

England's Pentecostals in their novitiate years, and would in time furnish their release from the strictures of *apocalyptic* to engage in the expansiveness of a more *prophetic vision*.[270] Impetus in this direction was provided by the exigencies and vicissitudes encountered during the years 1914-18.

Reaction to War-time Upheavals

Speculation Regarding Antichrist and World Events

It is the case that within weeks of the outbreak of war in 1914, many in British society sought solace and refuge, if not meaning, in a range in sources of a mystical or esoteric nature.[271] It was certainly the case that within the parameters of their particular spiritual cosmology, Pentecostals exercised, and further developed, their own mechanisms for comprehending or co-existing with the unprecedented eventualities then being encountered. While the basic tenets of the premillennialist position were never fundamentally abandoned, changes of emphasis are detectable from the time the international conflict became a reality with which those involved in the movement had to contend.

At the outset of the War, Mrs. Boddy presented her own reflections which were arrived at by the consideration of sources as varied as "the fine speech of our Prime Minister," the contents of daily newspapers, and apocalyptic writings contained in the sixth chapters of the books of Zechariah and Revelation. After a process of what she described as "prayerful comparison" she was led to conclude "that this terrible time of war is the Word of God going forth in judgement." The "awful spirit of death" associated with the red horse was no longer confined within the pages of John's *Apocalypse*, and the European conflagration was interpreted as "a spiritual warfare, the instruments being nations, men and women."[272]

---

[270] That such a teleology was espoused in these early years serves to elucidate the fact that by the third decade of its existence, subsequent British Pentecostal leaders could, without irony, suggest that some of its most prominently public activities were without parallel in Christian history. Randall has highlighted the ambitious nature of some of these later claims in *Evangelical Experiences*, 211, 216.

[271] A contemporary observer, described by Horton Davies as possibly "the most quoted clergyman of his time," commented on the widespread recourse to occult and paranormal avenues. See Dean Inge, *Lay Thoughts of a Dean* (New York and London: G. P. Putnam's Sons, 1926), 304, and Davies, *Worship and Theology in England*, vol. 5, *The Ecumenical Century, 1900-1965* (Grand Rapids, MI.: Eerdmans, 1996), 136. An historian of the Anglican response to the Great War has observed that within church paramaters "clergymen of all parties, but especially Evangelicals, turned to their Bibles, seeking to predict the future." See Albert Martin, *The Last Crusade: The Church of England in the First World War* (Durham, North Carolina: Duke University Press, 1974), 137.

[272] M. Boddy, "The War: Zechariah's Horses," *Confidence*, September 1914, 170-171.

Albert Weaver of Springfield, Massachusetts, contributed an article in which he ventured beyond the received identification of Antichrist with the papacy. The traditional foe of dispensationalists, and indeed the larger Protestant cause, had been displaced in favour of one more germane to contemporary circumstances; he was yet to emerge as "a world-wide ruler, a military genius, a dictator surpassing all others heretofore."[273] Hill has commented on the malleability and utility of the Antichrist motif in Protestant thought - by virtue of its vagueness it could usefully conceal attacks on more than one target while encompassing "confusion and shifting opinions" in uncertain times.[274] Other presentiments and predictions relating to this figure bear standard hallmarks of premillennialist foreboding: rebellious humanity would accept the blandishments inherent in apparent advancements such as democracy and would thereby become inured against the blasphemy of a "coming Millennium of man."[275]

A Scottish correspondent, Alice M. Watt of Athol Terrace, Dunfermline, introduced another perspective in the question she posed: "Is it not possible that out of this great international war, God means to fulfil this ancient covenant...?" A characteristic preoccupation with the Holy Land was given an inflection that had to that point been rare in the pages of *Confidence*. It was suggested that "so many of God's loved ones" were of the conviction that "the British nation is the birthright tribe of Ephraim," that Egypt's having recently "become a British possession" was being heralded as constituting a significant advance toward the fulfilment of the "everlasting covenant" of Genesis 17:19.[276] These observations intimate an emphasis which would be adopted by some within the Pentecostal constituency, a development which would prove problematic. During the period under consideration, it was to the increasingly "divergent"[277] propensities of William Oliver Hutchinson that the theory known as British Israelism made its most noteworthy appeal. Described by Horton Davies as a "racialist distortion of the faith," this school of thought regarded the British Commonwealth of Nations and the United States of America as the descendants of the ten lost tribes of Israel and as such, the inheritors of the divine promises made to the people of Abraham. Davies observed that this theory was maintained on the basis of an ethnology that was "fanciful," and a philology

---

[273] Albert Weaver, "Antichrist and His System," *Confidence*, September 1914, 167.

[274] Hill, *Antichrist in Seventeenth-Century England* (London: Oxford University Press, 1971), 66.

[275] Marr Murray, "The Career of the Antichrist," *Confidence*, March 1916, 46. While commenting on a popular symbolic interpretation of "Daniel's image" (Dan. 2:31-35) Boddy stated: "In this twentieth century we have very clearly come down to the democratic age when the people (*demos*) are ruling...history will not take us further..." in "Seven Signs of His Coming," *Confidence*, December 1910, 82-83.

[276] Alice M. Watt, "Signs of the Times: A Scripture Study," *Confidence*, April 1915, 72.

[277] For comments on the distinction between *convergent* and *divergent* thinking in the religious domain see Walker, *Restoring the Kingdom*, 119.

that was "fantastic."[278] It is undeniable that if scant appreciation of, or allowance for, the metaphorical was a hallmark of British Israelist reading of scripture, this approach found ready acceptance with the methods of exegesis that came to emanate from Winton, Bournemouth.

Hutchinson claimed to have been significantly influenced in this direction by the thoughts of Max Nordon, President of the Congress of Zionists, as expressed in the national press as well as the *National Message*, the weekly paper of the British Israel World Foundation.[279] From May-June 1922 his own periodical adopted a new format which, amid patriotic symbolism, exuded a distinct air of imperial splendour. This he claimed was "more representative of our teaching, showing the national as well as the spiritual side of the truth."[280] London, it was held, had by then undergone "a wonderful cleansing" in the course of the travails of war and was equated with the New Jerusalem. It was asserted that "the throne and the Lamb are present in the midst of the City."[281] These convictions which saw both the Union Jack and the Stars and Stripes hang from the rostrum and adorn conference venues alongside other quasi-sacramental emblems of empire,[282] rendered Hutchinson and his supporters among those described by Inge as characterised by "a very crude mentality."[283] It is certainly the case that these emphases were not to be found in the pages of *Confidence* or *Flames of Fire*, nor were they in evidence on Boddy's Sunderland or Polhill's London conference platforms. The amalgamation of these eschatological leanings with other idiosyncratic tendencies, therefore, conspired to confirm Hutchinson and his loyalists as denizens of "the boundaries"[284] of England's Pentecostal movement.

---

[278] Davies, *Christian Deviations: Essays in Defence of the Christian Faith* (London: SCM Press, 1957), 20, 83-84.

[279] "God's House," *Showers of Blessing*, May-June 1922, 2; "Editorial Notes," *Showers of Blessing*, May June 1922, 4. It is interesting to note that although he is unacknowledged as in influence in this direction, Reader Harris had himself espoused the "romance of a God-loved race" in both the official organ of the Pentecostal League of Prayer and a book first published in 1907. See "The Lost Tribes of Israel," *Tongues of Fire*, November 1906, 1-3, and *The Lost Tribes of Israel* 6th ed. (London: Covenant Publishing Company, 1921), 5.

[280] "Our New Frontispiece," *Shower of Blessing*, May-June 1922, 4. The timing of this development is confirmed by the fact that British Israelism had not yet been enshrined in the *Articles of Belief* of the Apostolic Faith Church as delineated in 1919. See "Appendix – Doctrines and Articles of Belief," in White, *The Word of God*, 286-292.

[281] "The Mountain Top of the British Empire: Jacob's Ladder," *Showers of Blessing*, September-October 1924, 129-130.

[282] G. Gordon Dennis, "Apostolic Faith Church: Annual New Year Scottish Conference 1924" (Unpublished manuscript, DGC), 2.

[283] William Ralph Inge, *Protestantism* (London: Ernest Benn, 1927), 158-159.

[284] In his exploration of the North American context, Jacobsen has suggested that the boundaries of the Pentecostal faith have not always been as clear or precise as loyalists or commentators may have wished them to be. He deliberately includes in his study the

In an effort to maintain eschatological speculations within acceptable parameters, the advice of Mr. E. J. G. Titterington M.A., who had been appointed by Polhill as residential superintendent of the London Training Home for men in 1915,[285] was promulgated to the readership of *Confidence* magazine. Titterington, who had previously presented an authoritative and irenic perspective on contentious matters,[286] recognised that many had enquired into and speculated about whether the war was of "dispensational or prophetic significance." While he granted that this was understandable, he expressed the opinion that it did not appear plausible "to identify the present struggle with any that is predicted in Scripture," beyond a generic inclusion among those referred to as "the beginning of sorrows" (Matt. 24: 6-8). Titterington informed the readers in a manner which was notably balanced, moderate, and lucid, that their greatest need was to "read, mark, learn, and inwardly digest all that God has caused to be written for our learning upon these important matters." A sober and cerebral antidote was presented to the "traps and pitfalls that will beset the path of the child of God in the latter days" - the bulwark of adherence to Scripture again being advanced against the encroachment of extremist tendencies. In this vein he concluded: "It is increasingly important that we do not neglect the Word of God, for herein alone lies our safety."[287]

Strange Providences and Uncanny Phenomena

It is necessary to draw attention to a variant of eschatological preoccupation that emerged during the war years, albeit one which was predominantly, but not wholly associated with the pages of *Confidence* magazine. This development had its basis in a series of curious incidents which were held to have occurred during the course of the War, and which exercised some fascination for Pentecostals, as indeed for others. Early in 1916, Boddy published an account of an occurrence which, in his estimation, "had probably seized the public imagination more than any other episode of the war." He reported how the meeting place of the Lune Street Brotherhood, Preston, had been filled to capacity to hear an address delivered in "simple, soldier fashion" by a Corporal Rogers of the Essex Regiment. He described how during a critical period of the Mons retreat on August 25th, 1914, a light had appeared in the sky which

---

work of some who functioned "within the fuzzy penumbra of the movement" but whose influences, positive and negative, were considerable on a more readily recognisable mainstream. See *Theologies of the Early Pentecostal Movement*, 286, 290. It is contested that Hutchinson occupied a comparable role at and from the boundaries/margins of the English Pentecostal scene.

[285] P.M.U. Correspondence, Letter from Mundell to Thomas Myerscough, 27 February 1915, 63.

[286] Boddy had commended Titterington as the author of a helpful pamphlet which addressed the exercise of spiritual gifts. See "Pentecostal Items," *Confidence*, June 1915, 116.

[287] E. J. G. Titterington, "The War and Prophecy," *Confidence*, September 1915, 175-176.

seemed to grow in size and brightness. Troops were apparently rendered spellbound as three angels became visible, and any attempt at combat was futile. The conviction was clearly expressed that, as at other vital junctures in history, an otherwise inexplicable reversal in fortunes had been providentially instigated and this resulted in the opposing army being "thrown back."[288]

Boddy, with characteristic zeal, embarked on something of a crusade on behalf of this cause, publicising a booklet for which there was in his own words "great demand" and addressing gatherings at, among other venues, the Salvation Army Hall, Monkwearmouth.[289] Open-air meetings were held at the Detention Hospital which was located in the transformed All Saints' parish hall, for the benefit of injured soldiers and any others which wished to attend. One such gathering attracted "a large number" of passers-by and Boddy informed them that while attached to the British Expeditionary force in France he had had opportunity to investigate the story of the vision at Mons. He sought to establish a cumulative case consisting of newspaper reports, letters, personal interviews and other means of eye-witness account from "decent, plain-speaking fellows" who were deemed to be "not at all imaginative or highly strung."[290] This public relations offensive was not limited to localized endeavours as Boddy had also undertaken to lay his case before the highest in the land. He prefaced his disquisition on the *Vision of Mons* with the statement that "our Gracious Queen Mary" had expressed "great interest in the incidents referred to in this article." The readers of *Confidence* could scarcely have been other than impressed when informed that "the Editor received Her Majesty's sincere thanks for sending her the account of his investigation. A letter from Windsor Castle (Sept. 3rd), closes with the words, 'the Queen has read your sketch with much interest.'"[291]

Alexander Boddy had been impelled to these lengths by virtue of deep convictions regarding the ultimate significance of these occurrences. He averred that through such visitations "the Divine Voice" was addressing mankind "as rarely before." The "National need, the sorrows of the battlefield, the sorrows of the mourning ones, or the signs in the Heavens" were all being used to draw individuals "to a truer spiritual plane." He concluded that angels were being used "to turn our thoughts heavenwards and to draw our hearts to Himself."[292] The pattern of an earlier era where "ministers and pastors were at the forefront of efforts to record and interpret apparitions and other inexplicable phenomena," was clearly recurring amid the disequilibrium of the period. Fascination with such auguries was yet again not confined to the "credulous poor" as interest in "heavenly spectacles" transcended barriers erected by

---

[288] "Angels at Mons: Soldier's Testimony at a Preston Church," *Confidence*, March 1916, 48.

[289] "Pentecostal Items," *Confidence*, March 1916, 55.

[290] "The Vision at Mons," *Confidence*, September 1915, 166.

[291] "The Vision at Mons," *Confidence*, September 1915, 165.

[292] "The Visions at Mons," *Confidence*, September 1915, 169.

wealth, education, and social rank.[293] So significant was Boddy's publicizing of these angelic epiphanies that a recent reassessment of the phenomenon identifies him as having made a singular contribution among various figures from across the spectrum of Christian denominations, as well as the world of Spiritualism, Theosophy, and the occult.[294] What has been described as Boddy's "emotional telling of the tale" of the Real Angel of Mons[295] can be regarded as potent evidence of his desire to present a Christian and evangelical alternative to more heterodox schools of interpretation. It is evident that supernaturalist practices and persuasions which had engaged him for some years had acquired heightened significance amid these unprecedented circumstances.

That Boddy was not the sole arbiter of fascination with unusual providences within Pentecostal circles was made apparent in the address of Welsh evangelist Stephen Jeffreys to the London convention of 1916. Jeffreys presented a message on Christ's transfiguration (Luke 9:28-35) to those gathered in Westminster's Central Hall on 13th June. He related how during the course of what he called "a mountain top meeting," there had appeared on the wall directly behind his pulpit a face which he identified as "the Man of Sorrows."[296] The phenomenon which took place in the Island Place Mission Room at Llanelly had generated some interest when it occurred two years previously, yet it would transpire that it was only when the War had fostered different expectations and outlooks, that it would come to exert a wider fascination among Pentecostal adherents. This was certainly the case for Boddy who reported the event in considerably more detail, and attributed greater significance to the incident than Jeffreys himself had done. The editor of *Confidence* informed his readership that he was in a position to "endorse the story, as one who knows the Welsh Revivalist." Having bestowed his *imprimatur*, Boddy proceeded to outline what had transpired. At first the "supernatural picture" had revealed the head of a lamb, but it gradually transformed into "the face of the Man of Sorrows." Some of the congregation stated that the head was crowned with thorns, but Jeffreys did not claim to have seen this. He did attest to "ineffable love and compassion" in the eyes, while it had been suggested by others that the eyes seemed to be "alive and moving." The vision was said to have approximated to the size to an average man's face, and was reputed to have lasted for some six hours.[297]

It is interesting to note that in the immediate aftermath of the event, Jeffreys told the representative of the local paper that "it was a proof to us that the Lord is with us in our work, and it will inspire us to more wholehearted consecration

---

[293] Alexandra Walsham, "Sermons in the Sky: Apparitions in Early Modern Europe," *History Today*, 51.4 (2001): 59, 57.

[294] David Clarke, *The Angel of Mons: Phantom Soldiers and Ghostly Guardians* (Chichester: Wiley, 2004), 131-134, 142.

[295] Martin, *The Last Crusade*, 137.

[296] Stephen Jeffreys, "A Mountain Top Meeting," *Flames of Fire*, August 1916, 6.

[297] "The Face of Christ: A Miraculous Appearance," *Confidence*, July 1916, 113-114.

to His service."[298] Yet two years later the occurrence was subjected to nuanced and broader ranging interpretations. He stated to those gathered in Westminster: "We did not understand it at the time, but today many are asking me, 'Don't you believe there was something in that vision in relation to the present war?' I believe there was. I believe it indicated the sorrows that were coming over the whole world."[299] What would previously have appeared extraordinary in terms of Pentecostal praxis, more readily approximating to miraculous occurrences associated with the Catholic *cultus*,[300] was less outlandish when viewed alongside such providences as had regularly been arrayed in the pages of *Confidence* magazine since the onset of war. In this retrospective evaluation it was imbued with eschatological significance:

> It was surely in some way a warning as to that terrible thing that was coming on the earth...It reminded us that He was indeed the slain Lamb, and that that Lamb was identical with the Crucified Saviour bearing the sin of the world. He seemed to be sorrowing with His people over the things which were coming upon the earth.[301]

All of the above displays Boddy portraying, and the readership of *Confidence* imbibing, a perspective of immanence that was "willingly thaumaturgical."[302] It would however, seem to be the case that when compared with the veneration of "mystic elements" such as occurred in Wales during 1904-5, Pentecostalism under Boddy's direction succeeded in avoiding an outcome where "sensationalism was actually consecrated."[303] The attestation of "uncanny phenomena" which were without obvious scriptural precedent appears to have been construed almost exclusively as "curiosities presaging the imminence of the Second Coming."[304] Yet it is also interesting to note that the "Pulpit of the Heavens" was on this occasion not simply declaiming "sinister portents of impending calamity,"[305] as providential undercurrents characterised the interpretive framework employed by contemporary Pentecostals. While heightened adventist imminence may have impelled toward an arraignment of *Christ against Culture*, rendering the present order "obsolete and

---

[298] "The Face of Christ," *Confidence*, July 1916, 114.

[299] S. Jeffreys, "A Mountain Top Meeting," *Flames of Fire*, August 1916, 6.

[300] Protestant polemicists against the miraculous would not have applauded Pentecostal association with a dimension derided as "one of the proudest boasts of the church of Rome." See Benjamin B. Warfield, *Counterfeit Miracles* (1918; repr. London: Banner of Truth Trust, 1972), 74. For further development of this theme see pages 151-159 below.

[301] "The Face of Christ," *Confidence*, July 1916, 113-114.

[302] Desroche, *The Sociology of Hope*, 94-95.

[303] Lewis, *Incidents and Impressions of the Welsh Revival*, 231; Morgan, *The Welsh Religious Revival of 1904-5*, 140.

[304] Wacker, *Early Pentecostals and American Culture*, 93-94.

[305] Walsham, "Sermons in the Sky," 57-58.

superfluous...a site that at best seeks only to be liquidated,"[306] extrapolations of the Latter Rain perspective on history served to further a redemptive-conversionist motif.[307] This, the most unique aspect of early Pentecostal apocalypticism, forged the potential for the perception of Christ as *Transformer of Culture*, or certainly as a deity that was not averse to immanent interventions beyond the boundaries of the self-designated "Enoch church"[308] as will be seen in the pages that follow.

Polhill and an Altered Eschatological Emphasis

It is notable that while Polhill in the pages of his periodical displayed comparatively little interest in the propagation of uncanny phenomena, his opening address to the Whitsuntide Conference of 1915 demonstrated considerable reflection on, and engagement with the spiritual implications of the single great issue of the day. Delegates were greeted with the declaration that war was "a scourge," albeit one which "opens up paths for the fulfilment of God's purposes." In a manner reminiscent of the 'muscular' tenor of much of late Victorian religion, Polhill declared that war could serve as something of a divine gadfly to a recalcitrant nation, "bracing it up, making sacrifice...increasing manliness, patriotism, then righteousness, holiness and godliness." While the religious grouping which had come into being seven years before the onset of hostility was described as having been to that point "essentially a prayer revival," he went on to extol the "wise and far-seeing provision" which had orchestrated "such a movement for the present emergency." The expectation was expressed that a "reconstituted Europe" would prove "ready and open for a time of religious work" and a vast tableau was depicted across which Pentecostalism could "increase its influence and efficiency a hundredfold."[309]

The man who occupied the singularly influential position of convenor and chairman of the National Whitsuntide Pentecostal Convention from 1915,[310] was at the forefront of a discernable shift in eschatological emphasis among Britain's Pentecostals. He posited the Pentecostal phenomenon and its message as the panacea to the ills and traumas of an international situation "for which history affords no parallel."[311] A tangible development in this direction was an event billed as a United Evangelistic Rally which was to be held in Westminster's Central Hall between 3rd and 17th of October 1915. The

---

[306] Desroche, *The Sociology of Hope*, 94.

[307] For comments on the potential for the conjunction of both tendencies see Niebuhr, *Christ and Culture*, 205-206.

[308] T. M. Jeffreys, "The *Parousia*, or 'Appearing' of the Lord," *Confidence*, June 1910, 150.

[309] "The Great European War and Great Spiritual Revival," *Flames of Fire*, June 1915 1-2.

[310] "Pentecostal Convention," *Flames of Fire*, July 1916, 1.

[311] "Reapers or No Reapers: The Harvest," *Flames of Fire*, July 1915, 1.

missioners were John Leech, K. C., of Dublin and Polhill himself, and the participation of "singers from Wales" was also publicised. The hope was fervently expressed that "the old time gospel truths preached by Paul, Luther, Wesley and Whitefield - of forgiveness by faith in the crucified and risen One - of eternal life and eternal condemnation - be preached in the power of the Holy Ghost send down from Heaven."[312] Anecdotal evidence was provided of what appears to have been a modest number of conversions, prominent among which, unsurprisingly, were soldiers travelling to the front.[313] Yet the significance of this departure lay not in its scale but rather in the change of emphasis which it embodied.

Polhill sought to advance a paradigm for the spread of the Christian message in his assessment that in the apostolic period individuals "filled with the Holy Ghost" had been granted such an effectiveness in preaching that they witnessed "the Gospel spreading as a prairie fire over a whole region."[314] The accuracy, or otherwise, of this understanding of the diffusion of first century Christianity cannot be examined in this context, but the pertinent point is that this line of thinking represented a more outward-looking and expansionary dynamic than had hitherto been evident within English Pentecostalism. Randall has observed that much of the wider evangelical constituency sought refuge and inspiration in premillennial advent hope in the aftermath of the Great War. As such an emphasis tended to foster a disposition toward withdrawal from, rather than involvement in society, it was, according to Randall, only in the latter half of the century when this theme had become less prominent, that British evangelicalism began once again to meaningfully engage with the culture in which it found itself.[315] England's Pentecostals, by virtue of eschatological emphases heightened during the 1914-18 period would, in contrast, come to engage their surrounding society in a very definite if distinctive way during the subsequent decade.

Section 2.4: Pentecostal Revivalism - Planned and Providential

Postwar Prospects

The early Pentecostal notion of the Latter Rain could be interpreted as a magnified and nuanced representation of the paradoxical fact that despite assessments and prognostications to the contrary, those of evangelical persuasion have never irretrievably abandoned the hope that Christ might infiltrate and dramatically redeem elements of their culture. As a commentator has related: "Revival is always at least a distant possibility lurking in our souls

---

[312] "United Evangelistic Rally," *Flames of Fire*, August 1915, 8.

[313] "The London United Evangelistic Rally," *Flames of Fire*, October 1915, 2.

[314] "Revival Notes," *Flames of Fire*, October 1915, 2.

[315] Randall, "Cultural Change and Future Hope: Premillennialism in Britain Following the First World War," *Christianity and History Newsletter* 13 (June 1994): 25.

and the evangelical scheme. At the first hint of an opportunity to exercise cultural influence, the revivalist motif emerges and tends to become a formative influence in our thinking."[316] This motif did indeed emerge and assert itself within English Pentecostalism toward the end, and certainly in the aftermath of the First World War. Those who had spent several years initiating into the Pentecostal dimension and developing acceptable parameters of related practice, were to seek revival of another category which would involve a significantly expanded field of endeavour.

Polhill opened the Whitsuntide Convention of 1916 with an address which lauded "the great Irish Revival of 1859." While it was acknowledged that they were themselves participants in "a remarkable movement" which was evident across national boundaries, the prospect of "a still more pronounced repetition of that which happened fifty-seven years ago" was laid before his auditors.[317] These utterances identified proponents of Pentecostal Christianity with the sizeable stratum of the evangelical community who had come to regard revival, in the form of an idealised version of the events of 1859, as both goal and inspiration. Polhill and those persuaded by him were therefore among those who heralded this prospect as a panacea confidently expecting it to "revolutionise society and reorder it according to spiritual guidelines."[318]

Similar expectations were unequivocally expressed at the penultimate convention to be held at the Bowland Street Mission. What was described as a "voluntary offering on the Bible" amounted to in excess of £200, a significant advance on the comparable offering during previous years. This was interpreted as denoting "the hopefulness of the future," and throughout the ten-day gathering considerable expression was given to aspirations for the post-war period, and in particular, to the role which it was envisaged Pentecostals would play in what was to follow. It was recorded that "a prayer came forth from all to God for our poor, broken world, in its present chaos of war, and a cry was raised for deliverance for our land." Wigglesworth, as convenor, impressed upon those present that "nothing could meet the need of the day like the Baptism with the Holy Ghost and fire." He developed this logic further stating:

> We now see the Pentecostal future of unlimited success, when the war ceases and railway fares and food are as before...our present experience in these hard times clearly proving to us that Acts ii. is going to be fulfilled in a fuller measure.[319]

A Heritage of Planned Revivalism

It can be stated without exaggeration that what in many ways represented a seismic shift for the Pentecostal movement would come to represent another

---

[316] Richard Mouw, "Evangelical Ethics," in Noll and Thiemann, eds., *The Landscape of Evangelical Piety and Thought*, 80.

[317] "The Wonder Touch of Prayer," *Flames of Fire*, July 1916, 1.

[318] Holmes, *Religious Revivals in Britain and Ireland*, 167.

[319] Wigglesworth, "The Bradford Convention," *Confidence*, April-June 1918, 22-23.

chapter in the history of revivalism in England. Oscillation between phases or categories of revival has been observed to have occurred periodically since "the paradigm of all revivals,"[320] the Evangelical Awakening of the eighteenth century. Two principal paradigms of religious revival have been identified by analysts as relating either primarily to a spiritual *quickening* or revitalisation of existing church members, or to concerted and deliberate efforts toward the conversion of the uninitiated.[321] The early years of the Pentecostal movement in England were, as noted, chiefly characterised by an inclination toward the former in terms of the initiation into, and subsequent development of, the Pentecostal baptism in its individual and corporate dimensions. In this vein the London Convention of 1912 was publicised as "An Eight Days' Mission for the Deepening of the Spiritual Life."[322] In line with such aspirations it was adjudged that the movement had attained "the deepest spirituality" and had "witnessed results" which "angels rejoiced over,"[323] yet developments during the Great War precipitated a shift toward a more noticeably outward orientation.

Statements such as those made on London and Bradford conference platforms which conjured images of "a Pentecostal future of unlimited success,"[324] are testament to what has been described as an "old evangelical self-confidence." The recitation of former glories demonstrates continuity with, and a definite sense of adherence to, an "effective and emotive paradigm" for religious life which could accommodate a coalescence of "evangelical planning and divine initiative."[325] Reference to the "great Irish Revival of 1859," in conjunction with the prospect of "a still more pronounced repetition of that which happened fifty-seven years ago,"[326] and the invocation of D. L. Moody in the form of deliberate parallelisms drawn with "his great work in London,"[327] constitute what Chan terms a "primary traditioning act."[328] Pentecostals, having spent several years in the exploration and delineation of their essential and distinctive message within their own immediate constituency were attempting to affirm and further continuity with a strain of English religious life that had reached its highwater mark during the late nineteenth-century.[329] This had been

---

[320] Bebbington, "Revival and Enlightenment in Eighteenth-Century England," in Walker and Aune, eds., *On Revival: A Critical Examination*, 71.

[321] Holmes, *Religious Revivals in Britain and Ireland*, 193. On the conjunction of these tendencies see Christopher Ben Turner, "Revivals of Popular Religion in Victorian and Edwardian Wales" (Unpublished Ph. D. dissertation: University of Wales, 1979), 45. See also page 110 above.

[322] "The Pentecostal Meetings in London," *Confidence*, May 1912, 106.

[323] J. M. Pike, "The Coming Revival," *Flames of Fire*, August 1915, 1-2.

[324] "The Bradford Convention," *Confidence*, April-June 1918, 22.

[325] Holmes, *Religious Revivals in Britain and Ireland*, 180, 194.

[326] "The Wonder Touch of Prayer," *Flames of Fire*, July 1916, 1.

[327] "The Welsh Revivalists in London," *Confidence*, April 1913, 78.

[328] Chan, *Pentecostal Theology and the Christian Spiritual Tradition*, 32.

[329] Kent, *Studies in Victorian Revivalism*, 153.

characterised by deliberate efforts toward the orchestration of mass evangelism, the most salient examples being the strategically planned campaigns of Dwight L. Moody and Ira Sankey between 1873 and 1875, and Reuben Torrey between 1903 and 1905.[330]

Revivalist as Showman and Shaman - Wigglesworth

Yet as the Latter Rain motif has been demonstrated to have differentiated Pentecostal eschatology from classical dispensational premillennialism, from so too in certain unmistakable respects did emerging Pentecostal revivalism venture beyond the approach which characterised the received Moody/Sankey tradition. In assessing the nature and grounds for some of the criticism that had been advanced against the style and methods employed during their 1873-5 campaign, Kent observes that according to this pattern "the revivalist was a *showman*, not a *shaman*."[331] The more prominent of the emerging Pentecostal revivalists, while retaining and employing the stratagems of the *showman*, also went on to develop and enact facets of revivalism which in anthropological terms would earn them the designation, religious *shaman*,[332] prophet or *mystagogue*.[333]

It is certainly the case that Smith Wigglesworth functioned along both dimensions in the itinerant capacity he came to fulfil throughout the movement. Whether addressing delegates at the Whitsuntide Convention in London, or officiating at the opening of a small Mission Hall, he typically combined "earnest, fiery delivery"[334] with methods that were at times "quite unconventional."[335] An ability to enthral gatherings for durations often considerably in excess of an hour relied upon fervent gesticulation and

---

[330] For Moody's activities in Britain see W. R. Moody, *The Life of Dwight L. Moody* (London: Morgan and Scott, 1900), 138-227, and W. H. Daniels, *D. L. Moody and His Work* (London: Hodder and Stoughton, 1875), 353-381. Prescriptions and guidelines for the organisation and execution of revival meetings and events were codified by the Principal of Moody Bible Institute in Chicago. See R. A. Torrey, *How to Work for Christ: A Compendium of Effective Methods* (London: Nisbet & Co. Ltd., 1901), 280-290. The cherished notion that revival could solely be attributed to "an interposition of Divine power" had previously been decried by a celebrated Anglo-Saxon revivalist - in a publication which acquired something approaching text-book status, Charles G. Finney issued a broadside against such "absurdity" with the declaration: "God has overthrown generally, the theory that revivals are miracles." See *Lectures on Revivals of Religion*, 12th ed. (Halifax: Milner and Sowerey, 1860), 21-22.

[331] Kent, *Studies in Victorian Revivalism*, 143.

[332] Piers Vitebsky, *The Shaman: Voyages of the Soul, Trance, Ecstasy and Healing from Siberia to the Amazon* (London: Duncan Baird Publishers, 1995), 132-134.

[333] Weber, *The Sociology of Religion*, 46-59.

[334] "Opening of a Pentecostal Mission Hall Near Portsmouth," *Confidence*, September-October 1917, 73.

[335] "Notes on the London Conference," *Confidence*, June 1915, 109.

animated delivery. In no sense aspiring toward a cultivated Atticism, Wigglesworth had little in common with, for instance, the flamboyant homiletics of what has been described as the Golden Age of the English pulpit, an era which "glittered in the etymological analysis and patristic learning" of preachers such as Lancelot Andrews.[336] Possessing limited homiletical and exegetical abilities, he in contrast, delivered repetitive and one-dimensional sermons replete with "remarkable stories"[337] and "Wigglesworthisms."[338] These were augmented by what Boddy described as an "unhesitating and free" use of "the Chairman and others on the platform." Attentions were retained, if for no other reason, because "no one knows what may happen next, or whose turn it may be to be embarrassed by being made use of as an object lesson."[339]

While Wigglesworth's capacities as revivalistic *showman* may have been characterised by an unpretentious and unsophisticated approach, his enduring and distinctive appeal appears to have come from a consolidating reputation as something of a revivalistic *shaman*. A study of ecstatic religion has described the "inspired priest" or shamanic figure as appearing to possess, among other attributes, privileged access to supernatural powers, capacities of discernment and diagnosis, and the ability to convey or prescribe the appropriate spiritual remedy,[340] a profile readily observed in the expanding ministry of the plumber from Bradford. His own experience at the hands of an individual unidentified for posterity appears to have had a formative and enduring influence on the man who within a short period became identified as a healing evangelist and went on to exert an influence far beyond the North East of England. As the utterance "Come out, you devil!" had apparently proved the nemesis of his own acute appendicitis,[341] similarly abrupt and audacious injunctions became

---

[336] Davies, *Worship and Theology in England*, vol. 2, *From Andrewes to Baxter and Fox, 1603-1690* (Princeton: Princeton University Press, 1975), 134, 142.

[337] "Opening of a Pentecostal Mission Hall Near Portsmouth," *Confidence*, September-October 1917, 73.

[338] A term used by Hacking to describe some of his idiosyncratic manners of expression. See *Reminiscences*, 13. Wigglesworth's style bears comparison with certain inner-city missionaries of the Edwardian period, observed to relate messages and experiences "with the conviction and naivety of a medieval." Booth, *Life and Labour*, 3rd Series, *Religious Influences*, vol. 7, 290.

[339] "Opening of a Pentecostal Mission Hall Near Portsmouth," *Confidence*, September-October 1917, 73.

[340] I. M. Lewis, *Ecstatic Religion: An Anthropological Study of Spirit Possession and Shamanism* (London: Penguin Books, 1971), 34.

[341] "Bradford Man's Testimony," *Confidence*, June 1912, 131; "Deliverance to the Captives," *Confidence*, October-December, 1923, 105. Alexander Dowie, whose influence had been transmitted to him via the Leeds Healing Home, had himself launched a "Holy War" against "Doctors, Drugs and Devils" during the 1890s. He had declared that the most dreaded disease of all was *"bacillis lunaticus medicus."* *Leaves of Healing*, June 14, 1895, 563, cited in Wacker, *Early Pentecostals and American Culture*, 191. See also Hardesty, *Divine Healing in the Holiness and Pentecostal*

characteristic of Wigglesworth's healing ritual. For instance a young girl whose movement was severely impeded was instructed: "Throw your stick away; burn it. You will not want it again."[342]

A repeated attribution of sickness to malevolent supernatural entities with whom spiritual warfare was to be waged in order that the oppressed person be relinquished was another integral if inflammatory feature of his ritual. What could be perceived as akin to a form of Manichean dualism[343] inspired assertions such as: "All fevers are spirits,"[344] "Consumption is of the devil,"[345] and "Get the devil out of you and you will have a different body."[346] The allied conviction that "the Spirit...prepares us to be more than a match for Satanic forces,"[347] reveals something of the self-perception of an individual who felt himself called upon to enact such "dualistic theodramas."[348] As has been observed of a similarly inclined North American pioneer, "not all Pentecostals since then would share his metaphysics,"[349] yet Wiggleworth had by the First World War secured a singular position both within and beyond the English Pentecostal constituency. It is curious to note that Boddy, over the period under consideration, displayed patently deep and longstanding loyalty to

---

Movements, 51-54, 67-68.

[342] "Healings in Australia," *Confidence*, April-June 1922, 28. In the light of what has been noted regarding the small but established body of Wigglesworth literature on pages 11-15 above, it is also of interest that the attribution of both physical healing and exorcism to spiritual *virtuosi* has proven a recurrent theme in the Christian tradition. See Richard Kieckhefer, "Imitators of Christ: Sainthood in the Christian Tradition," in Richard Kieckhefer and George D. Bond, eds., *Sainthood: Its Manifestations in World Religions* (Berkeley: University of California Press, 1990), 21-22.

[343] Andrew Louth, "Augustine," in Jones, Wainwright and Yarnold, eds., *The Study of Spirituality*, 137-138. For an historical perspective on this tendency see Clarke Garrett, *Spirit Possession and Popular Religion: From the Camisards to the Shakers* (Baltimore and London: John Hopkins University Press, 1987), and Henry D. Rack, "Doctors, Demons and Early Methodist Healing," in *The Church and Healing*, ed. W. J. Sheils, *Studies in Church History* vol. 19 (Oxford: Blackwell, 1982), 137-152.

[344] "Bradford Convention," *Confidence*, April-June 1920, 22.

[345] "Mr. Wigglesworth at the Antipodes," *Confidence*, July-September 1922, 44

[346] Wigglesworth, "Divine Life and Divine Health," *Confidence*, April-June 1924, 129.

[347] Wigglesworth, "Deliverance to the Captives," *Confidence*, October-December 1923, 104.

[348] Anton Houtepen, *God: An Open Question*, trans. John Bowden (London: Continuum, 2002), 35.

[349] Land makes this observation with regard to William J. Seymour. See *Pentecostal Spirituality*, 151. For an overview of the life and significance of this first generation leader see Rufus G. W. Sanders, *William Joseph Seymour: Black Father of the 20th Century Pentecostal/Charismatic Movement* (Sandusky, OH.: Xulon Press, 2003), and "William J. Seymour and the Beginnings of Pentecostalism," in Cecil M. Robeck, Jr., *The Azusa Street Mission and Revival: The Birth of the Global Pentecostal Movement* (Nashville: Thomas Nelson, 2006), 17-52.

Wigglesworth. This is evident from the prominence, indeed preponderance, of the latter's sermons in the pages of *Confidence* during its years of steady decline, and serves as a vivid indicator of the esteem in which the *high priest* of English Pentecostalism held its most visible prophet or *shaman* during years of transition.

Wigglesworth not only transmitted Pentecostal rhetoric in an effective manner to a wider audience, but he also translated and dramatically conveyed this into a seemingly incontrovertible experimental reality. At the time of the last Convention to be held in Bowland Street, for instance, he made the claim: "I am being much used and God is helping me to rebuke the 'Flu' demons. Many are healed who apparently were dying."[350] While many antidotes and remedies were pedalled against what was poetically described as the "plague of the Spanish lady" which claimed some 21.5 million lives worldwide,[351] Wigglesworth offered a singularly Pentecostal solution. He subsequently stated that some "would have passed away with influenza if God had not intervened."[352] His forthright conviction that New Testament miracles had not merely been intended "for the privileged few in the first century," and his emphatic and relentless proclamation of Christ as "Saviour" and "Healer,"[353] saw him appropriate a function as mediator and nexus of spiritual power. It was by virtue of a pronounced awareness of this role that he could advance the claim: "I have left hundreds saved and healed in Sydney. Australia has been moved."[354]

It is appropriate to point out at this juncture that this brand of revivalism serves to illuminate the observation that men who underwent evangelical conversion in this period found their masculinity both challenged and affirmed. If the stereotypical language of penitence and surrender which was redolent of female vocabulary and experience, represented the antithesis of received conceptions of masculinity,[355] the militaristic language of "Power within," slaying Satan, and "victory assured"[356] suggests that it would be mistaken to suppose that the male Pentecostal participant found himself on an inevitable path toward emasculation. Boddy's characterisation of Wigglesworth as traversing America "like a victorious warrior"[357] and another editor's feting of

---

[350] "The Bradford Convention," *Confidence*, April-June 1919, 26.

[351] Malcolm Brown, *The Imperial War Museum Book of 1918: Year of Victory* (London: Sidgwick & Jackson, 1998), 168-169.

[352] Wigglesworth, "Faith Based Upon Knowledge," *Confidence*, October-December 1919, 60.

[353] Wigglesworth, "Deliverance to the Captives," *Confidence*, October-December 1923, 103, 105.

[354] "Mr. Wigglesworth at the Antipodes," *Confidence*, July-September 1922, 43.

[355] Margaret Lamberts Bendroth, *Fundamentalism and Gender, 1875 to the Present* (New Haven and London: Yale University Press, 1993), 22, 52.

[356] Wigglesworth, "The Place of Victory," *Flames of Fire*, February 1916, 2-3.

[357] "Westward Ho!" *Confidence*, December 1914, 223.

"the forceful style of which Brother Wigglesworth is a past master,"[358] are evidence of the fact that developing Pentecostalism was generating avenues of religious expression within which emotion, strength and spirituality were not incompatible. If men were, as among Salvationists, called upon to repudiate some of the hallmarks of "traditional all-male associational cultures,"[359] this did not imply the offering of any concession to "the poison of effeminacy." It is interesting to note that while Evangelicals regarded Victorian Ritualism as "tainted" by aestheticism and sensuality and therefore perilously opposed to "manly" virtues,[360] this tendency was singled out for particular criticism at the National Whitsuntide Pentecostal Convention of 1916 which was held in London's Westminster Central Hall. E. W. Moser informed those gathered that one of the primary tasks of the movement was the waging of a sustained spiritual onslaught on malign forces. He stated: "Satan rules this world and the 'principalities and powers and hosts of wickedness in heavenly places'...Ritualism is one of his strongholds...These strongholds are going to be brought down beneath the feet of God's people."[361] This disposition and the pugilistic terminology which accompanied it, found particular resonance with the "hero *mythos*"[362] which came to surround Smith Wigglesworth, and would inform not only the developing Pentecostal lexicon, but a gender perspective worthy of deeper consideration. It is only possible in this context to state that this tendency is also to be observed in prominent Pentecostal women such as Mrs. Crisp who had founded and overseen a branch of the Y.W.C.A. in Hackney prior to her involvement in the movement. Known for a characteristically "bold, aggressive testimony," she had informed a congregation in Croydon in 1923 that she would "rather go home a scarred warrior than not go home a warrior at all."[363]

Revivalistic Planning and Showmanship of the Jeffreys Brothers

That the brothers Stephen and George Jeffreys developed and cultivated a

---

[358] "Home News," *Things New and Old*, January 1922, 7.

[359] Laura Lauer, "Soul-Saving Partnerships and Pacifist Soldiers: The Ideal of Masculinity in the Salvation Army," in Andrew Bradstock, Sean Gill, Anne Hogan and Sue Morgan, eds., *Masculinity and Spirituality in Victorian Culture* (London: Macmillan, 2000), 198.

[360] John Shelton Reed, *Glorious Battle: The Church Politics of Victorian Anglo-Catholicism* (Nashville and London: Vanderbilt University Press, 1996), 216-223.

[361] E. W. Moser, "Praying in the Holy Spirit," *Flames of Fire*, July 1916, 4.

[362] John Lash, *The Hero: Manhood and Power* (London: Thames and Hudson, 1995), 27.

[363] "Mrs. Crisp: A Mother in Israel," *Confidence*, January-March 1924, 114-115. It is likely that Mrs. Crisp, in common with other English Pentecostals, did not merely esteem, but had been influenced by Catherine Booth's espousal of *aggressive Christianity*. The latter's book with this title had been extolled by Cecil Polhill who cited it at length in "Holding forth the Word of Life," *Flames of Fire*, July 1912, 1-2.

distinctively revivalist paradigm is undeniable. Possessing an evangelical precociousness which was a marked and often criticised feature of the Welsh Revival,[364] George would claim that "from the earliest days of childhood there was that consciousness borne with me that I was called to preach the Gospel."[365] He had enjoyed the patronage of Cecil Polhill during the months he spent in the Men's Training Home in Preston,[366] a beneficence which can only have conferred considerable affirmation on a hitherto unknown Co-operative Store worker. The attentions of Alexander Boddy, who was sufficiently impressed when he travelled to observe the evangelistic preaching of the Jeffreys brothers at the beginning of 1913, cannot but have further augmented an already crystallising sense of calling and destiny. His comments on the occasion of their first meeting at the "Penybont Revival Meeting" are highly significant, expressing the felt need for a departure into an area of endeavour which had not to that point been significantly undertaken by any segment of the British Pentecostal constituency. He recorded:

> Bro. Stephen and Bro. George and I had a long heart-to-heart talk. They feel that the Lord needs evangelists in Pentecostal work today. There are many teachers and would-be teachers, but few evangelists. The Lord is giving an answer through this Revival to the criticism that the Pentecostal people are not interested in Evangelistic work, and only seek to have good times. (May the Lord shake this out of His people. Amen.)[367]

In addition to such positive endorsement in the pages of *Confidence*, an invitation to address the Sunderland Convention was forthcoming from its host. The effect of the latter has been intimated by Gee: this annual gathering exerted a "formative influence in attracting and helping to mould not only the immediate leaders of the multitudinous little Pentecostal meetings," but of more long-term significance, "the younger men who were destined to become leaders of the Movement."[368] George Jeffreys was prominent among such and he came to embody a new emphasis which would exert a singular influence upon future developments of Pentecostalism across the British Isles. Of fundamental significance was his meeting with a group of enthusiastic associates in what was later described as "solemn conclave" in Monaghan in January 1915, to

---

[364] Morgan, *The Welsh Religious Revival 1904-5*, 189. For a recent assessment of this phenomenon see R. Hayward, "From the Millennial Future to the Unconscious Past: The Transformation of Prophecy in Early Twentieth-Century Britain," in Bertrand Taithe and Tim Thornton, eds., *Prophecy: The Power of Inspired Language in History 1300-2000* (Stroud: Sutton Publishing, 1997), 170-171.

[365] George Jeffreys, *Healing Rays* (London: Elim Publishing Company, 1932), 56-57.

[366] E. C. W. Boulton, *George Jeffreys: A Ministry in the Miraculous* (London: Elim Publishing Company, 1928), 12; "An Apostolic Welsh Revival," *Confidence*, February 1913, 27.

[367] "The Welsh Revivalists Visited," *Confidence*, March 1913, 48.

[368] Gee, *The Pentecostal Movement*, 41.

discuss and plan a strategy which would enable the evangelisation of Ulster.[369] Amid the feverish activities that followed, it was announced that "our Bro. George Jeffreys" would conduct a month-long Camp Meeting in Ballymena, which was described as nothing less than the fount of "the great Ulster Revival" of 1859. This was followed by a further Camp Meeting which would be held in Bangor throughout July.[370] It was enthusiastically reported that at another gathering, an elderly man who claimed to have been converted in 1859, had asserted "with much emphasis that the Power manifested at Victoria Hall, Portadown" was "*the same power* as was displayed at that wonderful, never-to-be-forgotten time."[371]

Claims to effectiveness among "strangers to salvation," if not unprecedented, had certainly not been prominent during the pre-war years of the movement anywhere in Britain. The significance of such a development was underscored by the clarifying statement of a loyal assistant of Jeffreys: "There is nothing like the salvation of souls to convince the people that God is really pouring out His Spirit in Pentecostal fullness."[372] The implication of this is that it was held that visible and credible effectiveness in terms of conversion would confer on Pentecostal practitioners a creditability they had not hitherto enjoyed from the wider evangelical constituency. Such revivalist activities also served a particular and novel function within the Pentecostal fraternity itself, propelling it beyond its initial solipsistic orientation revolving around quickening and revitalisation. In the light of such considerations it is difficult not to detect a note of reproach in an observation made in the official organ of Jeffreys' Elim Pentecostal Alliance during 1921:

> The Pentecostal brethren of London have the privilege of hearing a great variety of well-known speakers from all parts of the United Kingdom and of the world, and it has been said that the time has arrived when we who are so favoured should be up and doing something for the Lord by passing on to the unsaved the glorious message of salvation instead of keeping the good things to ourselves...[373]

A movement which, according to Gee, experienced something of a leadership vacuum in the immediate aftermath of the war,[374] had issued an "increasing stream of appeals" to Jeffreys, with the result that his evangelistic activities would, from 1920, no longer be confined to Ireland.[375] The chronicle of these

---

[369] Boulton, *George Jeffreys*, 23-24. For his own account see George Jeffreys, "A Prophetic Vision Fulfilled, or How the Elim Work in Ireland Began," *Elim Evangel*, December 1920, 5-7. The evolution, from these beginnings, of a Pentecostal denomination which would establish a notable presence in Ulster has received extensive attention in Robinson, *Early Pentecostalism in Ireland*, 120-232.

[370] "Camp Meetings in Ireland," *Confidence*, June 1916, 106.

[371] Florence Vipan, "What Hath God Wrought!" *Elim Evangel*, December 1919, 12.

[372] R. E. Darragh, "The Ballymena Convention," *Confidence*, March-April 1917, 19.

[373] "Open-Air Work in London," *Elim Evangel*, June 1921, 51.

[374] Gee, *The Pentecostal Movement*, 121-123; *Memoirs of Pentecostal Pioneers*, 82.

[375] Boulton, *George Jeffreys*, 83. This development is discussed in "News of

early years of foment compiled by his associate E. C. W. Boulton, provides valuable insights into the methods employed to combat the spiritual "obstinacies" of, among other places, "Gospel-hardened London." At East Ham those gathered engaged in the singing of "Elim Revival hymns with intense fervour and feeling" while awaiting the appearance of the evangelist.[376] Evidently replete with elements of revivalistic *showmanship*, Boulton's description of Jeffreys' 'performance' when he took to the platform, even allowing for obvious sympathies, is highly revealing:

> His address was given with the same deep fervour that marked everything connected with the service. As he spoke he walked about the platform and gesticulated, at times furiously. He had a trick of suddenly leaning over the table in front of him and pointing at the audience, speaking in rapid tones the while. He was lucid and voluble and was never at a loss for a word. At times he would speak of the Bible, or the portion from which he took his text, and at another he would speak scathingly of certain present-day habits.[377]

This convert of the Welsh Revival, had it would appear, departed considerably from the methods and ethos that had characterised that phenomenon. It has been observed that "those who felt the impact of the Welsh Revival ('bent like corn before the wind') were addressed by no great preachers like Jonathan Edwards, Charles Finney or Howell Harris. It was not prepared for, and carefully organised by professional revivalists on the lines of Torrey and Alexander, working at that very time in London." Likewise the almost scientific methodology delineated by Finney was "either ignored or used only occasionally and haphazardly."[378] In contrast to 1904-5, insights into the deliberately organisational and methodological aspects of Jeffreys' revivalism are afforded by Boulton's deliberate drawing of parallels with political campaigners active prior to the election of 1924:

> Shall we be any less devoted and determined in our prosecution of this campaign to establish and extend the empire of Christ and secure his enthronement in the lives of those around us? Not an evanescent enthusiasm that speedily evaporates, or a fluctuating fervour which is as inconsistent as the wind, will be sufficient to accomplish this. The condition of Christless souls is desperate indeed, and demands that drastic measures should be employed to encompass their deliverance...Their sorry state constitutes an imperative call to *consecrated action.*[379]

As former campaigns such as those of Torrey and Alexander had employed

---

Blessing," *Things New and Old*, April 1922, 2-3.

[376] Boulton, *George Jeffreys*, 92-93.

[377] Boulton, *George Jeffreys*, 94.

[378] Hall, "The Welsh Revival of 1904-5," in Cuming and Baker, eds., *Studies in Church History*, vol. 8, 295-296.

[379] "Editorial," *Elim Evangel*, January 1924, 2.

"splendid organisation and advertising," and it was to this that their "huge success" had been attributed,[380] Jeffreys' aptitude for revivalistic *showmanship* marked another phase in the history of planned revivalism in Britain. It was this that allows his categorisation among those described as "specialists in the engineering of mass consent."[381] Meticulous preparation, the employment of hymnody at once didactic and emotive (the "sacred simulacra of the music hall songs,"[382]) the skilful utilisation of homiletical techniques and deliberate affectations (termed "revivalistic blandishments,"[383]) all combined to qualify the Jeffreys brothers as admirable inheritors of the paradigm described as "the last popular religious culture of British Nonconformity."[384]

Shamanistic Proclivities of the Jeffreys Brothers

Pentecostal proponents were by no means content to merely replicate this religious tradition. Evidences of mystical *shamanism* in the context of an orchestrated evangelism abound throughout their publications and literature. In contradistinction to Quietist spiritualities, Pentecostal praxis appears to have substantially endorsed what Underhill described as "the apparatus of visible religion." Theirs was not an exclusive mysticism which enacted wholesale distinctions between sense and spirit, but instead demonstrated itself by means of a pronounced "supernaturalist panoply"[385] to be amenable to the "generous realities of an incarnational faith."[386] During the course of a Nine Weeks' Mission conducted by Stephen Jeffreys for the Pentecostal Mission at Grimsby's Welcome Hall it was, for instance, reported that his "preaching of the Full Gospel was followed by many cases of healing."[387] The most remarkable and certainly the most publicised of these was the dramatic recovery of a woman who had been immobile for eleven years, confined to a spinal carriage:

> It was a strange scene. Standing on the platform alongside Pastor Jeffreys, this frail, little woman, looking supremely happy, told her story with a calm deliberation. Her testimony was supported by the spectacle of the spinal carriage which was suspended from the wall nearby, and bore upon it in chalk the words: 'She is not here, but is risen.' The narrative was punctuated here and there with

---

[380] "Editorials," *Tongues of Fire*, March 1905, 6.

[381] William G. McLoughlin, *Modern Revivalism: Charles Grandison Finney to Billy Graham* (New York: Ronald Press Company, 1959), 455.

[382] Andrew Walker and Neil Hudson, "George Jeffreys, Revivalist and Reformer: A Revaluation," in Walker and Aune, eds., *On Revival: A Critical Examination*, 145.

[383] Wilson, "The Pentecostalist Minister," in Wilson, ed., *Patterns of Sectarianism*, 148.

[384] Kent, *Studies in Victorian Revivalism*, 153.

[385] Randall, *A Study in the Spirituality of English Evangelicalism*, 225.

[386] Underhill, *Worship*, 238.

[387] "Pentecostal Items," *Confidence*, April-June 1922, 18.

deep-throated 'Hallelujahs' and 'Glorys' from the members of the audience.[388]

It was in this manner that the Pentecostal revivalist tradition as propounded by the Jeffreys brothers sought, in its propagation of what was termed the "Full" or "full-orbed Gospel,"[389] to serve the religious needs and satisfy the spiritual appetites of a humanity "poised between the worlds of spirit and sense, and participating in both."[390] The persuasive force of this emphasis should not be underestimated. An anonymous female correspondent from Bournemouth related how her inherent scepticism had been overcome: "I went to see if the wonderful cures of which I had heard were really taking place and to decide...I went, I saw and I was conquered."[391] Boulton's eulogy, however partial, is itself suggestive of the genius inherent in miraculously-infused or *shamanistic* revivalism:

> Listen to the catalogue of cures!...What an argument for the Gospel's claims! What an eloquent and adequate answer to the question of agnosticism and infidelity, 'Where is God?' Let those fifteen hundred freed sin-slaves sing out their thrilling reply to the challenge of Modernism and Materialism. Let the halt, the maimed, the blind and the deaf, be brought into the witness and add their authentic attestation in defence of the Calvary message...Is the old-time Gospel still a living power in the world? Such scenes answer, yes![392]

This genius, which culminated in mass gatherings of thousands in venues such as Bingley Hall in Birmingham and the Royal Albert Hall, consisted of a masterful augmentation of revivalistic *showmanship* with potent and arresting Pentecostal *shamanism*. The fact that a mission to Leeds was being unashamedly and unapologetically announced as "the greatest feat of modern Evangelism,"[393] demonstrated an unmistakable alignment with the "professional version of revivalism"[394] in the tradition of D. L. Moody whom Polhill revered as the "Prince of Evangelists."[395] It furthermore supports Randall's observation that Pentecostals conceived of themselves as possessing extraordinary capacities which allowed them to surpass others in evangelical

---

[388] "Woman, Helpless for Eleven Years, Walks About Cured," *Confidence*, April-June 1922, 28.

[389] Boulton, *George Jeffreys*, 85.

[390] Underhill, *Worship*, 283.

[391] Boulton, *George Jeffreys*, 112.

[392] Boulton, *George Jeffreys*, 220-221.

[393] T. H. Jewitt, "Over 2,000 Converted in Two Weeks," *Elim Evangel*, 2 May 1927, 129.

[394] Parsons, "Revivalism and Ritualism in Victorian Christianity," in Parsons, ed., *Religion in Victorian Britain*, vol. 1, *Traditions*, 219.

[395] "When the Fire Fell," *Flames of Fire*, October 1914, 1. Moody had previously been accorded this title in a biography written by a Scottish Presbyterian minister. See William Ross, *D. L. Moody: The Prince of Evangelists* (London: Pickering & Inglis, 1900).

effectiveness.[396] According to Polhill, the preacher who had undergone a baptism of the Spirit took an exponential leap forward and became a "fully-fledged, useful and powerful evangelist, coming behind in no good thing."[397] Barratt wrote of the experience of the apostles in the upper room and the first Pentecost: "Before this their evangelistic efforts were feeble; afterwards they were *dynamos*."[398] Wigglesworth similarly extolled and celebrated what he called "the mighty unctionising power of God."[399] The Elim Evangelistic Band held that its initial successes in Ulster were the result of God "graciously saving souls" by means of "EMPOWERING believers." The outcome was that they held themselves to be "an aggressive Evangelistic work."[400]

Perhaps the most telling indicator of the paradigm shift that had occurred in Pentecostal notions of revival was embodied in the reporting of Stephen Jeffreys' campaign conducted in Sunderland's Victoria Hall during 1927. While it was prominently proclaimed that "3,000 accept Christ," and reference was made to Sunderland's heritage as a focal point of spiritual awakening, (the "stirring days of Wesley" were recalled), allusions to Alexander Boddy or the seminal nature of his Whitsuntide Conventions were markedly absent.[401] The platform from which Boddy and the earliest Pentecostal phenomena had been so vehemently denounced during the autumn of 1907 may have been colonised for the Pentecostal cause,[402] but two decades later little acknowledgement would be made of the role he had played in the consolidation of the incipient movement. While the culture of the religious convention had in no sense been relinquished, the Pentecostal mass gathering had acquired different connotations under its revivalist hierophants. The original *collegia pietatis* conception of the movement, so integrally associated with Boddy's Whitsuntide Convention, was not something which early denominationalists sought to perpetuate or for which they entertained evident fondness. On the

---

[396] Randall, "Baptists and the Shaping of Pentecostalism," in D. W. Bebbington, ed., *The Gospel in the World: Studies in Baptist History and Thought*, vol. 1 (Carlisle: Paternoster Press, 2002), 91.

[397] "The Evangelist," *Flames of Fire*, October 1915, 1.

[398] Barratt, *In the Days of the Latter Rain*, 191.

[399] Wigglesworth, "The Place of Power," *Confidence*, June 1916, 104.

[400] "While Peter Yet Spake," *Elim Evangel*, December 1919, 9. Gee corroborated this in his comment that the "virile Elim work," which he deemed "the brightest element" of British Pentecostalism at the beginning of the third decade of the century, was characterised by "an aggressive evangelism." See *The Pentecostal Movement*, 123.

[401] Donald Timmins, "Home News: Full Report of Sunderland Revival," *Redemption Tidings*, November 1927, 8. This was reported in somewhat sensational fashion, again without reference to previous Pentecostal associations, in the memoir compiled by Jeffreys' son. See Edward Jeffreys, *Stephen Jeffreys: The Beloved Evangelist* (London: Elim Publishing Company, 1946), 73-74.

[402] Comments on the irony of this change of fortune are to be found in my essay, "Unlikely Polemical Outbursts Against the Early Pentecostal Movement in Britain," in Cooper and Gregory, eds., *Studies in Church History*, vol. 41, 421-422.

contrary, as will be made more readily apparent in Section 3, it was something which in the hands of commentators and opinion leaders such as Donald Gee, became the object of pronounced criticism. The invocation of Wesley while deliberately overlooking much more immediate indebtedness is indicative, not only of this tendency, but of a desire to associate with a figure and a movement of consequence and pedigree within the evangelical pantheon.

By virtue of the incorporation of a thaumaturgical or *shamanistic* dimension into events that were otherwise professional, planned, and performed to considerable effect, Pentecostal revivalists succeeded in avoiding the appearance of severing the remaining link with the notion of spontaneity. Torrey had not only been accused of this, but some had suggested that the spontaneous and erratic nature of the Welsh Revival was a divine rebuke against such "over-organisation."[403] The distinctive aspects and emphases of Pentecostal revivalism, appear to have not only enabled its purveyors to retain an apparent priority of divine initiative over human effort, but to have done this so successfully that subsequent Pentecostals have been reluctant to acknowledge the professional and organisational aspects of this expansionary period.[404] It was the masterful coalescence of revivalist as both *showman* and *shaman* which facilitated the successful propagation of a virulent form of popular religion amid the challenging contingencies of post-war Britain. The aspirations that had previously been articulated on platforms in London, Bradford, and elsewhere, had in vital respects been realised.

Pentecostal Re-enchantment of the World

Overt and, at times, arrestingly thaumaturgical demonstrations serve to locate early Pentecostals in an interesting position on the continuum of the Christian spiritual tradition. Berger has observed that as a primary religious constellation of the Christian world, Protestantism could, with justification, be regarded as embodying an "immense shrinkage in the scope of the sacred in reality" when compared with its Catholic counterpart. The Catholic could be said to inhabit a world in which the sacred is mediated by means of a variety of channels which

---

[403] Holmes, *Religious Revivals in Britain and Ireland*, 192. On this tension see also Turner, "Revivals and Popular Religion," 303-305.

[404] Aspects of this have been acknowledged by Walker and Hudson who write of the "cognitive dissonance" associated with the "nostalgic need to recapitulate revival and rally behind a new dynamic leader" in the face of the more prosaic structural necessity to "maintain an established community of Christians." Britain's Pentecostals have repeatidly succumbed to the persistent inclination to "sacrifice all on the altar of revival." See "George Jeffreys, Revivalist and Reformer: A Revaluation," in Walker and Aune, *On Revival: A Critical Examination*, 152. Comments on the "negative side" of Jeffreys' healing campaigns are also to be found in David Allen's "Signs and Wonders: The Origins, Growth, Development and Significance of the Assemblies of God in Great Britain and Ireland, 1900-1980" (Unpublished Ph. D. dissertation: University of London, 1990), 164-165.

include the sacraments of the Church, the intercession of the saints, sacred images, statues and relics, and the recurring eruption of the supernatural in miracles, and together these constitute a "vast continuity of being between the seen and the unseen." In contrast the Protestant approach, with its emphasis on the polarities of divine transcendence and human fallenness, resulted in a reduction to essentials, a "radical truncation," a process which has been termed "disenchantment of the world."[405] In his monumental study *Religion and the Decline of Magic* which undertakes an extensive exploration of this theme, Thomas comments that in depreciating the miracle-working aspects of religion and elevating the importance of individual faith in God, the Protestant Reformation "helped to form a new concept of religion itself."[406] This watershed has recently been explored by Alexandra Walsham who has observed how Humanist embarrassment about popular credulity combined with emerging strands of evangelical polemic to pour "venomous scorn on notorious manifestations of the miraculous." By the Elizabethan period the combined force of these related critiques had crystallized into the precept that miracles had ceased.[407] By the middle of the nineteenth-century this ideological position was still being proclaimed as exemplified in the summarization of an eminent Glasgow Congregationalist:

> We Protestants believe in the miracles of the Old and New Testaments...But while we hold them to have been wrought, and wrought in marvellous magnitude and profusion...for the purpose of introducing and establishing Christianity - of settling it on a divine basis; we hold, at the same time, that having fully served that all-important end, they ceased.[408]

Of primary concern to emerging Pentecostals, Booth-Clibborn bemoaned the relegation of the "return of the Divine gifts" to an anticipated millennium. He

---

[405] Berger, *The Social Reality of Religion*, 117-118. Berger expands on a distinction which is to be attributed to Max Weber. See *From Max Weber: Essays in Sociology*, trans. and ed. by H. H. Gerth and C. Wright Mills, (London: Routledge & Kegan Paul, 1964), 51, 155, 350.

[406] Keith Thomas, *Religion and the Decline of Magic: Studies in Popular Beliefs in Sixteenth- and Seventeenth-Century England* (London: Penguin Books, 1973), 88-89.

[407] Walsham, "Miracles in Post-Reformation England?" in Cooper and Gregory, eds., *Studies in Church History*, vol. 41, 277. For further exploration of this theme see her *Providence in Early Modern England* (Oxford: Oxford University Press, 2001).

[408] Ralph Wardlaw, *On Miracles*, 2nd ed. (Edinburgh: Fullarton and Co., 1853), 53. Wardlaw, who had been elected Professor of Systematic Theology at the foundation of the Glasgow Theological Academy, delivered a series of lectures between 1851-52 which formed the basis of this treatise. While his primary purpose was to vindicate the miracles of the New Testament, particularly in the light of Humean criticism, he refuted the hypothesis that miracles could be performed by "inferior agencies" among whom he included both Spiritualists and faith healers of Britain and America. See William Lindsay Alexander, *Memoirs of the Life and Writings of Ralph Wardlaw D. D.* (Edinburgh: A. C. Black, 1856), 124-125, 458-459.

regarded this as an error "in the Protestant sphere" of comparable magnitude to the perceived departure from *justification by faith* in the pre-Reformation Church. The originator of such a mistaken perspective was clearly identified: "Satan himself has always been the advocate of pure, authentic Christianity, provided it was placed in the distant past or the distant future. Safely relegated there, it simply produces that discouragement and hopelessness so useful to his cause."[409]

Pentecostal pioneers were acutely aware that they were not alone in this supernatural resurgence.[410] The veracity of the Latter Rain was, to their way of thinking, further attested by "counterfeit workings"[411] and few opportunities of denouncing these remained unexploited. Even at the height of the acrimonious controversy with Reader Harris, Barratt identified an area of common feeling between rival factions: an antipathy towards Spiritualism.[412] This was not sufficient to achieve a moratorium, much less solve the internecine conflict, but its introduction was significant. Pentecostals would not follow the example of their Protestant predecessors in resigning the propensity for religious "magic" to spiritualists, astrologers, or the twentieth-century answer to the "cunning men" of the early modern period.[413] It was as a result of this powerful impetus that Alexander Boddy found himself in contemporaneous propagation of the Angel of Mons with Ralph Shirley, editor of the *Occult Review*.[414] What has been described as the "unlikely combination of an evangelical priest and an occultist"[415] was the outcome of the pursuit by both parties of Phyllis Campbell, a nurse alleged to have witnessed an angelic apparition. This evangelical priest was of course keen to enlist her testimony for the cause of Christ and the

---

[409] Booth-Clibborn, "The Why and How of this Revival," *Confidence*, June 1910, 144.

[410] Pastor Humburg, "Miracles of Today," *Confidence*, August 1911, 184-185.

[411] "A Letter to an Opposer of the 'Pentecostal' Baptism," *Confidence*, September 1912, 202; "The Pentecostal Revival," *Confidence*, March 1912, 61.

[412] "Speaking in Tongues - Rival Pentecostals," *Sunderland Echo*, 2 October 1907, 4.

[413] Thomas has observed that during the late Victorian period in Britain, "every kind of religious enthusiasm - mystical healing, millenarian prophecy, messianic preaching - made its periodic return." See *Religion and the Decline of Magic*, 795-796, 798-799. This efflorescence has been the subject of a recent collection of essays, Nicola Brown, Carolyn Burdett and Pamela Thurschwell, eds., *The Victorian Supernatural* (Cambridge: Cambridge University Press, 2004). Its continuation into the Edwardian period has been underscored in J. M. Winter, "Spiritualism and the First World War," in R. W. Davies and H. J. Helmstadter, eds., *Religion and Irreligion in Victorian Society* (London and New York: Routledge, 1992), 185-2000, and Samuel Hynes, *The Edwardian Turn of Mind* (London: Oxford University Press, 1968), 134-148.

[414] Shirley's fascination with such phenomena caused him to write *Prophecies and Omens of the Great War* (London: William Rider, 1914). His propagandising is apparent from other volumes such as his *Occultists and Mystics of All Ages* (London: William Rider & Son, 1920).

[415] Clarke, *The Angel of Mons*, 134.

miraculous cosmology he had come to espouse.

The fact that the attribution of the term *Mesmerist* to George Jeffreys at the height of his evangelistic endeavours in the 1920s elicited so little concern and, if anything, a notable degree of pride among Pentecostals, demonstrates the extent of the movement's progress by the middle of that decade. In the aftermath of Barratt's 1907 mission in Sunderland, Jessie Penn-Lewis had averred that he had been exhibiting "a strong force of animal magnetism," rendering him "almost like a galvanic battery." She suggested that through his ministrations, "evil spirits enter the bodies of the children of God, and are able to produce spiritistic visions and manifestations."[416] Less than two decades later Jeffreys' eulogist paraded this designation as evidence of his effectiveness, and as a vindication of the broader advocacy of a restoration of the miraculous.[417] According to Gee, the human constitution could never entirely succumb to "pure materialism," and he lamented the "almost frenzied attempt" to deny "every element of the miraculous and supernatural" that had, in his estimation, characterised the English pulpit "for several decades past." Critique and condemnation of Spiritualism was not deemed an adequate response, and it was held that Pentecostal Christianity could not just deliver, but embody the answer to this challenge:

> Something more is needed than an unmasking of the false - we need to bring forth the real...Herein lies the supreme opportunity of the Pentecostal testimony in this hour; we can bring forth a positive witness both as to doctrine and experience on the line of legitimate, scriptural, spiritual manifestation...a truly Apostolic outpouring of the Spirit with 'signs and wonders' provides a positive answer - the only effective one - to the impudent claim of Spiritualism.[418]

---

[416] Letter of J. Penn-Lewis to A. A. Boddy, 9 November 1907. These charges are redolent of what Wilson has termed some of the prominent "institutionalised paranoias" of the Edwardian period. In the purview of Mary Baker Eddy and Christian Science, the *animal magnetism* constituted a from of *mesmerism* whereby an individual could alter the condition of another by means of conscious or unconscious thought. Penn-Lewis appears convinced that Barratt was unwittingly exercising an *animal magnetism* of "malicious" character. On this phenomenon see Wilson, *Sects and Society: The Sociology of Three Religious Groups in Britain* (London: William Heinemann Ltd., 1961), 349, 126-127, 130.

[417] Boulton, "Veritable Pageant of Pentecostal Power at the Royal Albert Hall," *Elim Evangel*, 16 May, 1927, 145-147. See also *George Jeffreys*, 233, 241-242. Insights into the previous association of *mesmerism* and *animal magnetism* with healing and, by extension, something of the significance of Pentecostal propagandist acceptance of what was being attributed to Jeffreys, can be found in Stephen Gottschalk, *The Emergence of Christian Science in American Religious Life* (Berkeley and Los Angeles: University of California Press, 1973), 142-149.

[418] Gee, "Pentecost and Spiritualism," *Things New and Old*, August 1921, 8. Gee explored this theme further in "Spiritual Gifts or Spiritualism: A Challenge Examined," *Elim Evangel*, September 1924, 198-204. It is of interest to note that the Apostolic Faith strand of English Pentecostalism similarly denounced Spiritualism as "the opposite of

English Pentecostals, it is apparent, believed themselves to be the latter-day custodians of quintessential aspects of true Christianity that had atrophied, or otherwise been lost, to the detriment of the Church. Highlighting several groups thought to have manifested *charismata* since the apostolic period, Boddy ventured that the fact that "the Blessing" had not continued could not be attributed to providential design. Rather cessation had occurred because of human fallibility and the fact that "the Dragon" of Revelation 12 was always poised to "devour any movement specially born of God in His Church."[419] The London Declaration, formulated in November 1909 in direct response to criticisms of explicitly Pentecostal phenomena, was plain in its assertion:

> There is no hint in Holy Scripture that signs and miracles were to cease, or that gifts were to be withdrawn from the Body of Christ. It is more than possible that the weakness and unbelief of the Christian Church is the reason for these not being more generally manifested in these latter days.[420]

The implications of this provoked Cecil Polhill to a "sense of deep solicitude" as well as "sorrow and shame." He lamented the fact that weakness and inability were "writ large over Conference and Church," and that Christendom was as a whole characterised by a spiritual failure which was "blank, appalling, unalleviated."[421] Barratt deplored not only "formalism, materialism, rationalism, spiritualism, and bigotry," but included alongside these "the worldly state of many ministers and divines" which he remarked had been "denounced by the spirit of this movement all over the world."[422] Boulton spoke of "these days of spiritual declension" when the Church had "fallen into a state of Laodicean indifference and Corinthian carnality." The outcome was that "unbelief" had "distorted her vision of the truth."[423] In contrast the stated "aim and hope" of England's first Pentecostals, indeed their *raison d'être* as they perceived it, was the attainment and propagation of "a first-century grade of Christian experience."[424]

While as will be made apparent in the next section, early Pentecostals remained, in certain respects, content to inhabit the "evangelical sparseness of

---

the Holy Spirit's Life." See White, *The Word of God*, 281-282.

[419] "The Gifts of the Spirit in the Light of History," *Confidence*, January 1909, 11, 16.

[420] "A London Declaration," *Confidence*, December 1909, 288.

[421] "The Next Great Revival," *Flames of Fire*, January 1913, 2.

[422] Barratt, *In the Days of the Latter Rain*, 97.

[423] Boulton, "Divine Healing," *Elim Evangel*, September 1921, 62.

[424] T.L.W., "Separation and Revelation," *Elim Evangel*, September 1921, 65. An expository article which advances the case for the reinstatement of the miraculous dimension, while considering objections, is to be found in Theodore Booth-Clibborn, "The Supernatural in Pentecost," *Elim Evangel*, March 1924, 56-61.

Protestantism,"[425] their reinstatement of the miraculous or *magico-religious*[426] dimension represented a significant return to a spiritual *pleroma* more typically associated with the pre-modern world. This ideological development could be described in Niebuhr's terms as advocating a perspective of "history as the present encounter with God in Christ."[427] Pentecostal revivalism - at once both planned and providential - which became a potent force in England in the aftermath of the First World War embodied a "virile" and even "aggressive"[428] demonstration of Christ *above*, yet by virtue of a pronounced conversionist *motif*, condescending to reach out to, embrace and ultimately redeem *Culture*.

Section 2.5: Pentecostal Otherworldliness

Introduction

Mouw has identified three characteristics central to what might be termed an evangelical ontology which also closely relate to emerging Pentecostal conceptions of reality. The first two of these - a *remnant ecclesiology* in which the true church is perceived to be a "cognitive minority," and an *apocalyptic eschatology* that understands the wider society as gravitating, if not hurtling, toward inevitable destruction - have already been shown to loom as prominent themes in the early literature. It will become apparent that the third characteristic, an *antithetical epistemology* which insists on a radical disjuncture between genuinely Christian and non-Christian interpretations of reality,[429] was also not only present, but pervasive throughout the movement. These combined tendencies could be expected to contrive to engender an otherworldliness redolent of the *Christ against Culture* disposition and it will become apparent that this was indeed an inescapable feature of the emerging Pentecostal world-view. Salient practical and ethical outworkings of the stance which "uncompromisingly affirms the sole authority of Christ over the Christian and resolutely rejects culture's claims to loyalty,"[430] will now be considered in order to allow a representative portrayal of an inner logic and ideological identity of early English Pentecostalism.

Emerging Pentecostals, Education and the Spiritual Life

Wacker has observed that among the leadership credentials of early American Pentecostals, "education ranked especially high." He goes on to point out, lest

---

[425] Berger, *The Social Reality of Religion*, 117.

[426] Wilson, *The Noble Savages: The Primitive Origins of Charisma and Its Contemporary Survival* (Berkeley: University of California Press, 1975), vii.

[427] Niebuhr, *Christ and Culture*, 197.

[428] Gee, *The Pentecostal Movement*, 123.

[429] Mouw, "Evangelical Ethics," in Noll and Thiemann, eds., *The Landscape of Evangelical Piety and Thought*, 78.

[430] Niebuhr, *Christ and Culture*, 58.

there be any misunderstanding, that this did not involve "worldly education," but rather "mastery of the King James text of the Bible and the body of Christian doctrine peculiar to the radical evangelical and Pentecostal traditions."[431] What were regarded as "worldly" schools provoked suspicion and at times, outright hostility such as became apparent in the thoughts of T. K. Leonard who denigrated traditional forms of education and learning: "We are sure we should miss the thought of God were we to add another institution to the many, all over the land, to educate men in the accepted sense of the word." This disposition was based on the succinctly stated conviction that "time is too precious, Jesus is coming too soon, and education has proven too futile."[432] Wacker further observes that "in England, too, formal education fell under the gun." In support of this he referred to an utterance of Hutchinson in the first issue of *Showers of Blessing* to the effect that the only preparation a man or woman needed for ministry was an "upper-room experience."[433]

Central to this perception was a conviction which has not merely historically accompanied evangelical belief, but has "often been the essence of it"; the notion that "the less encumbered this truth is with reference to the past and to academic speculations, the better everybody will be."[434] A contributor to an American periodical asserted that only the "Spirit-enlightened soul" could hope to "detect the venomous allurements of the age and escape them." Yet such a positive outcome was by no means assured. The "germs of worldly delights and satanic counterfeits" were not eradicated at conversion or even after sanctification. Such "germs" were held to be "located especially in the intellect." Consequently thought and the mental faculties were to be regarded with circumspection:

> We know of people who have had a very victorious experience of heart purity, and were real channels of blessing to other souls, but through Satan's cunning were imperceptibly drawn away by the desires of the mind through music, reading, or other high mental attainments. God warns against drunkenness by which the body becomes a dirty sot and the mind imbecile. He warns us against intellectual intoxication whereby the mind becomes infidel.[435]

A. S. Copley, described by Wacker as "among the most thoughtful of first

---

[431] Wacker, *Early Pentecostals and American Culture*, 151.

[432] T. K. Leonard, "The Gospel School Department: For Bible Study and Divine Equipment for Worship and Service," *Word and Witness*, August 1914, 3.

[433] *Showers of Blessing*, January 1910, 4; Wacker, *Early Pentecostals and American Culture*, 151.

[434] David F. Wells, "Living Tradition," in Noll and Thiemann, eds., *The Landscape of Evangelical Piety and Thought*, 87.

[435] A. S. Copley, "The Seven Dispensational Parables," *The Pentecost*, December 1908, 9.

generation writers,"[436] went on to conclude that in the light of Ephesians 2:3, the "desires of the flesh and of the mind" were in fact closely aligned. "Intellectual intoxication," regarded as inducing, if not synonymous with a state of "infidelity," was certainly no better, and perhaps considerably worse, than a condition of alcoholic inebriation.[437] Similar suspicions were frequently articulated in the British context. For instance, the first issue of *Confidence* contained the testimony of an initiate which has already been considered who had found himself swept "right into the sea of Pentecostal Fullness," and thereafter experienced what he described as "a complete and utter separation from the world." In practical terms this had the effect of dealing "radically with the thought-life, every imagination being brought into captivity." Integral to this was a ruthlessly ascetic attitude toward "levity, idle talking, undue newspaper or book-reading to the neglect of the Word of God." In short it was asserted that "this Baptism is the one cure for all weak Christianity under whatever name it may shelter itself,"[438] and its efficacy was demonstrated in the suppression of the offending pursuits identified.

Comparable notions of "weak Christianity," and its root causes, were expressed by speakers on the Sunderland Convention platform. In highlighting a lack of impetus toward personal evangelism among Pentecostal adherents, a German visitor averred that it was not to their credit that individuals were wont to "tremble just like an aspen leaf" when an opportunity arose to "say something for Jesus." The source of such weakness was clear: "When Pentecostal people have such a great deal of time to read the newspaper, and so little time to read the Bible, it seems as though their speaking in tongues had not helped them very much. We ought to see what a wonderful blessing lies in reading the Word of God."[439] The advocacy of an unadulterated spiritual diet of the *Word of God* was similarly enjoined from the conference platform in Bradford. A Rev. William Reid, cited by Wigglesworth as "a great inspiration," instructed those present: "Devour your Bibles, live on your knees, be wisely mad for the salvation of the perishing."[440] Such sentiments bore remarkable similarity to opinions concurrently being expressed by Pentecostals' "pnuematological cousins"[441] in the British Holiness community who were convinced that "the curse of the churches has been intellectualism." It was lamented:

---

[436] See Wacker, *Early Pentecostals and American Culture*, 143. Copley was associated with the Kansas City branch of North America's emerging Apostolic Faith sector of the movement.

[437] Copley, "The Seven Dispensational Parables," *The Pentecost*, December 1908, 9.

[438] Martin, "Testimony from Motherwell," *Confidence*, April 1908, 13. Aspects of John Martin's Pentecostal initiation have already been highlighted in Section 2.1, p. 92ff. above.

[439] Prediger Humburg, "Isaiah Twelve," *Confidence*, October 1912, 235.

[440] Wigglesworth, "The Bradford Convention," *Confidence*, April-June 1918, 22.

[441] Randall, *Evangelical Experiences*, 219.

The sad fact stares us in the face that the Colleges and Universities of our land manufacture men to fight the Bible truth of Scriptural Holiness, instead of manufacturing men to go forth as flames of fire for God to proclaim it...Instead of that what do we see and hear in the pulpits, but the opinion of French infidels, and German philosophers, and higher critics who proclaim a salvation so broad and so long that makes one think that the Devil himself will be saved one day. Not a word about sin and its remedy, about the awful sufferings of the damned souls who by choice are going through the churches in shoals to an open gaping hell.[442]

When Elizabeth Sisson made the transatlantic journey to address the first Sunderland Convention in 1908, Boddy recorded how she left leaders with the impression that they "had never heard such an incisive, spiritual, and clever speaker." It is interesting to note that such an esteemed figure would represent the basis of her ministry in the following fashion: "A course in a theological seminary could not have equipped me for...this venture on God, and the revelation of His power, bounty and love, which came to me in this strait place." The *coup de grace* of this devotional article published for the edification of readers of *Confidence* was that "God knows how to train His souls, and often thinks as man-made institutions do not."[443]

Books, Thought, and Modernity as Enemies of the Spiritual Life

Knox has observed that the *ultrasupernaturalist* typically harbours a deep distrust of "human thought processes." For the religious *enthusiast*, "you must not think; that would be to use the arm of the flesh and forsake your birthright."[444] This perceived mutually exclusive status of divine and human forms of wisdom, knowledge, and advancement was reinforced by prominent conference speaker Mrs. Polman with respect of the question of divine healing. She claimed to have been something of a "great medicine box" at the time of her conversion at the turn of the century. Afterwards, however, she "didn't dare to touch any more medicines," a departure which was attributed to supernatural prompting. Instead her solution was "to think about divine healing" and she maintained that "the simpler I was, the quicker the answer." This was, in her estimation, evidence of progression "deeper into the resurrection life."[445] The authentic approach to spiritual well-being, therefore, lay in a form of unadorned fideism:

> Let us be simple in all things - about Salvation, about Divine Healing, about the coming of Jesus, simple about everything. Believe the Word as it is. You will find the Spirit will work immediately through the Word. I believe the time will come when God's children will put aside all other kinds of books. The time will come

---

[442] "Editor's Notes: Counteracting Holiness," *The Holiness Mission Journal*, January 1911, 6-7.

[443] Sisson, "Foregleams of Glory," *Confidence*, March 1913, 49-51.

[444] Knox, *Enthusiasm*, 585.

[445] Mrs. Polman, "The Victory of the Lord," *Confidence*, November 1911, 250-251.

when we shall live by the Word of God...and our life and preaching will be accomplished by the demonstration of the Spirit, and signs and wonders will be given, not because of us, but because of the Word of God.[446]

That foremost among the enemies of this idealised religious state were "all other kinds of books," was further demonstrated during the course of a gathering hosted by Cecil Polhill in London's Portman Rooms. Alighting from the "Electric Underground," Boddy made his way via Baker Street to the venue where he found "a good number of ladies and gentlemen" in "very comfortable" surroundings. This group of devotees was addressed by Mrs. Polman who related how she was at first "much opposed to this work of God." Implying a connection with this innate and nefarious resistance, she further related how she had had a penchant for the works of Leo Tolstoy, but she was pleased to inform those present that "the Lord had mercy" and the Holy Ghost had "delivered her." Thenceforth she read only "her Bible and the Pentecostal papers."[447]

Such limited prescriptions for literary consumption were not merely iterated among a select few or those who occupied conference platforms, but they appear to have permeated the movement. In 1913 Alfred Lewer, a twenty-two year old butcher from Bayswater, made formal application to join the P.M.U. According to Gee, he had been a contemporary of his while both were children at North London's Finsbury Park Congregational Church.[448] Lewer stated in the schedule he submitted that he had been converted on June 14, 1904, at a Pentecostal League event in Exeter Hall on the Strand.[449] In the company of Gee and others he attended gatherings at the home of Mrs. Cantel where the association of the Pentecostal baptism and the gift of tongues was clearly promoted.[450] He himself underwent such an experience toward the end of 1912 and thereafter expressed the conviction of a "clear call" to missionary activity. Having spent twenty months in the meat trade with his father, he responded to the question: "Of the books you have read, name some you most esteem; name also what periodicals you usually read," with the brief but emphatic reply: "Bible. Bible. *Confidence*."[451]

It is evident that across a range of social and educational backgrounds, exposure to printed matter, whether by innate limitation or definite conviction,

---

[446] Polman, "The Victory of the Lord," *Confidence*, November 1911, 251.

[447] "The West End Pentecostal Meeting," *Confidence*, February 1909, 49-50.

[448] Gee, "Alfred G. Lewer: A Pioneer Missionary" (Unpublished pamphlet, n. d., DGC), 1. Gee wrote this brief tribute to his former friend in the aftermath of his untimely death by accidental drowning while close to the borders of Tibet. The Donald Gee Centre retains a *Confirmation of Death Cable* addressed to Cecil Polhill, dated 16 October, 1924.

[449] Alfred George Lewer, "'Candidates' Schedule' for the Pentecostal Missionary Union of Great Britain and Ireland" (DCG).

[450] Gee, "Alfred G. Lewer," 1-2.

[451] Lewer, "Candidates' Schedule."

was highly restrictive for Pentecostal adherents. Even those who possessed both the capacity and predilection for literary fiction, such as that of Tolstoy, harboured reservations about the appropriateness of such a pursuit. The depth of this conviction is made explicitly manifest in a communication to the Rev. Allen Swift, a P.M.U. missionary stationed in Yunnan, China. Having informed him of precautions that would be taken to preserve the health and well-being of female missionaries, Mundell proceeded to address a concern which had been raised which impinged upon the perceived spiritual welfare of those in the mission field. He related how the members of the Council had been "much surprised" at the substance of a communication from Swift, and that they "had not the slightest idea that anyone of their missionaries would indulge in what you state as a phase of worldliness in reading novels." Mundell gave solemn assurance "on behalf of every member of the Council" that there was not one of them which would "sanction or encourage the reading of novels or any such literature."[452]

Swift had evidently suggested or insinuated that this practice had been permitted or condoned in the Missionary Training Home and that those commissioned had then pursued the reprehensible practice abroad. Mundell gave particular assurance that "no such books" were available in the Home. The reading material that was available, he was keen to point out, included "several good lives of Missionaries as well as biographies, and other standard books." The gravity of the matter was such that Swift's statement had brought "under suspicion all the lady Missionaries in the Field," and in the light of this it was deemed reasonable to request the names of the "offending Missionaries together with the names of the novels which they are supposed to have been reading." While it could be surmised from the correspondence record that Mundell may not have been wholly convinced by the charge laid by Swift, what is beyond dispute is the gravity with which such an eventuality appears to have been regarded. Mundell went on to express gratitude on behalf of the Council who were "most thankful" to him for being "so alive to the real interests and spiritual welfare of the Missionaries over which you have charge." Alluding to Matthew 13:25, he complimented him on his assiduousness and vigilance as "it was when man slept that the enemy sowed tares, and it is quite evident that you, my brother, are in no way asleep."[453]

Such expressions betray a continuity with an established disposition within evangelical Christianity which was notably antipathetic toward literature and what was pejoratively termed "novel-reading." Rosman has pointed out that the renaissance of the novel during the 1820s had been regarded as "symptomatic of a prevalent worldliness" which "attested to the need for religious revival."[454] These preoccupations seem to confirm Wainwright's

---

[452] P.M.U. Correspondence, Letter from Mundell to Mr. Swift, 18 July 1918, 555.

[453] P.M.U. Correspondence, Letter from Mundell to Mr. Swift, 18 July 1918, 555.

[454] Doreen M. Rosman, "'What Has Christ to do with Apollo?': Evangelicalism and the Novel, 1800-1830," in Derek Baker, ed., *Renaissance and Renewal in Christian History*, vol. 14, *Studies in Church History* (Oxford: Basil Blackwell, 1977), 301, 311.

designation of Pentecostalism among "non-monastic world-renouncing" spiritualities.[455] To this extent early Pentecostals shared in an ethic which has been observed to have characterised much of Protestant history. Practitioners of "this-worldly asceticism," according to Weber, "strode into the market-place of life, slammed the door of the monastery," and sought to fashion "a life in the world but neither of nor for this world." Moral and ascetic rigors and strictures were no longer undertaken as *opus supererogationis*, but often in the wake of sudden spiritual transformations, as furthering the *certitudo salutis*.[456] Kierkegaard's description of speaking in tongues as "the very peak of insanity"[457] is elucidated in the related observation that *glossolalia* can be understood as a "counter-cultural protest against the rationalistic and materialistic language of late Western Christendom."[458] Not merely tongues but the whole apparatus of emerging Pentecostal spirituality tended toward a renunciation of the values and standards of a fallen cosmos.

Modernising tendencies in general and the encroachment of modernity across the range of departments of life were no more welcomed by Pentecostals than they had been by earlier premillennialist adherents.[459] It might profitably be borne in mind that similar concerns were being voiced across the religious world at this time. In 1904 the Rev. H. Gresford Jones, then incumbent of St. John's, Keswick, warned those gathered for the annual Convention against the "declension" associated with this encroaching menace.[460] On September 1, 1910, Pope Pius X issued his *Sacrorum Antistitum*, or "Oath Against Modernism" which was to be sworn by "all clergy, pastors, confessors, preachers, religious superiors and professors in philosophical-theological seminaries."[461] While early Pentecostals may not have issued decretals of this nature, their antipathy was no less forthright. Arguably their most potent invective and vituperation was reserved for the perceived corrosive tendencies

See also her more expansive study *Evangelicals and Culture* (London and Canberra: Croom Helm, 1984).

[455] Wainwright, "Types of Spirituality," in Jones, Wainwright and Yarnold, eds., *The Study of Spirituality*, 595.

[456] Weber, *The Protestant Ethic and the Spirit of Capitalism*, trans. Talcott Parsons (1930; repr. London and New York: Routledge, 1992), 154, 140-141.

[457] S. Kierkegaard, *Gospel of Sufferings: Christian Discourses*, trans. A. S. Aldworth and W. S. Ferrie (London: James Clarke & Co., 1955), 139-140.

[458] Wainwright, "Types of Spirituality," in Jones, Wainwright and Yarnold, eds., *The Study of Spirituality*, 595.

[459] "Seven Signs of His Coming," *Confidence*, December 1910, 283; "The Coming of the Lord," *Confidence*, June 1914, 116.

[460] H. Gresford Jones, "In a Day of Departure from God," in Stevenson, ed., *Outstanding Addresses Delivered at the Keswick Convention*, 39-45.

[461] http://www.fordham.edu/halsall/mod/1910oathvmodernism.html. See also J. B. Lemius, *A Catechism of Modernism, Founded on the Encyclical PASCENDI DOMINICI GREGIS* (On Modernism) by Pope Pius X (1908; repr. Rockford, Ill.: Tan Books and Publishers, 1981).

of the *acids of modernity*:

> Has not modern theology assured us that there is no real danger - that the notions
> of hell and a righteous God...were the mere crudities of thought belonging to
> former days, which have been dispelled by the enlightenment of the twentieth
> century? Have not the church-goers of this day been taught upon the authority of
> 'science' and scholarship, to discard with pitying contempt the 'narrow' doctrine
> that God has one only way of salvation?[462]

The "wanton, open sacrilege" of the "so-called 'higher critics'" was certainly
the subject of relentless and vehement polemic. These were "the men who
broke Spurgeon's heart, the Isaachers of the nineteenth and early twentieth
century" who entertained the deplorable assumption that they "knew better than
God."[463] England's early Pentecostals evidently not merely applauded, but saw
themselves, in vital respects, continuing Spurgeon's heroic stand as something
of a "latter-day Mr. Valiant-for-Truth"[464] in the "Down Grade Controversy."[465]
Their prognosis was that society was permeated by "a spirit of a system of evil"
whose leaven was "working its way through and through," and the religious
domain was far from exempt from this baleful influence.[466] It was in accordance
with their characteristic *modus operandi*, that a "word" had been given at the
Apostolic Faith Church during December of 1918 which proclaimed: "The War
came out of Higher Criticism."[467] Portentous visions of Sabbath desecration,
"the most wanton, hideous licentiousness," and the pitchforking of Bibles were
advanced as eventualities with which the believer might yet have to contend.[468]
The blandishments of human progress were not to be entertained as its first

---

[462] "Echoes of the 'Titanic' Disaster" (extracts from Philip Mauro's "The Titanic
Catastrophe and its Lessons") *Confidence*, September 1912, 202.

[463] Sydney Watson, "After the Rapture" *Confidence*, April 1912, 86. While
somewhat oblique this appears to draw parallels with Isaac's mendacity recorded in
Genesis 26.

[464] On the *heroic* nature of Spurgeon's isolated stand for orthodoxy as he understood
it see Andrew Bradstock, "'A Man of God is a Manly Man': Spurgeon, Luther and
'Holy Boldness,'" in Andrew Bradstock, Sean Gill, Anne Hogan and Sue Morgan, eds.,
Masculinity and Spirituality in Victorian Culture (London: Macmillan, 2000), 209-221.
For a more general perspective on these issues see Parsons, "Biblical Criticism in
Victorian Britain: From Controversy to Acceptance?" in Parsons, ed., *Religion in
Victorian Britain*, vol. 2, *Controversies*, 238-257.

[465] In an address to the Baptist Union at the height of the controversy Spurgeon had
himself lamented that "modern-thought advocates," and purveyors of "anti-Christian
literature," were "striking at the life of our religion." They were not merely "cutting off
its horns, but tearing out its heart." See "The Evils of the Present Time," in C. H.
Spurgeon, *An All-Round Ministry: Addresses to Ministers and Students* (1900; repr.
London: Banner of Truth Trust, 1972), 286, 288.

[466] Vipan, "The Bradford Convention," *Confidence*, April-June 1920, 23.

[467] White, *The Word of God*, 275.

[468] Watson, "After the Rapture," *Confidence*, April 1912, 83.

fruits were deemed to amount to "cultivated civilised madness" and "perfected carnal blindness." Christians should not be lured away from their "tragic blood-red beliefs" and must remain vigilant against any *rapprochement* with the "views, maxims and schemes" of the surrounding culture.[469]

While the pejoratively termed *New Theology* was said to have embarked upon "a perilous course" which would inevitably "end in outer darkness," it was asserted that "the present outpouring or revival is one which brings forth all the characteristic features of primitive Christianity."[470] The goal was the vitality and purity of the "white heat of Pentecost" which alone could "shake the inner being and penetrate to the soul."[471] A return to this would negate and overcome the spiritual accretions of centuries. The expected triumph of the recrudescence held to be underway in the early years of the twentieth century was encapsulated in the triumphant cry: "We are touching the beginning!"[472] This emphasis shows English Pentecostals to have, in fact, shared common cause with a significant drift in national religious life, the observation having been made that following the Oxford movement, the dominant trend of worship in the nineteenth century was toward a return to the historic faith of the first centuries of the Christian Church. This tendency found expression in a "simpler and naïver form of Protestant primitivism which aimed at a return to the supposedly less institutional and more charismatic worship of the New Testament Church." The impetus in this direction was, according to Davies, rooted in a pervasive dissatisfaction with the existing communions as well with the "rationalism and sophistication of the age."[473]

Wacker's designation "other-worldly primitivists" bent on a "backward quest" for the apostolic and "the infinitely pure,"[474] is substantially appropriate, if not encompassing the totality of the English Pentecostal outlook. Certainly little meaningful time or attention was given to the intervening years of Christian heritage or history, except when seeking vindication for evidence of the continuity of *charismata*. Faupel's statement that "the records of church history were scoured" toward this end seems something of an overstatement, certainly with regard to literature emanating from England. The principal example he presents was that of Barratt,[475] who cited isolated passages from figures such as Origen and Irenaeus, and who drew simplified parallels with

---

[469] Booth-Clibborn, "The Final Great Rejection," *Confidence*, July 1911, 151.

[470] Booth-Clibborn, "The Why and How of this Revival," *Confidence*, June 1910, 142-143.

[471] Barratt, *In the Days of the Latter Rain*, 41, 65-66.

[472] "The Place of Tongues in the Pentecostal Movement," *Confidence*, August 1911, 177.

[473] Davies, *Worship and Theology in England*, vol. 4, *From Newman to Martineau*, 139.

[474] Wacker, *Early Pentecostals and American Culture*, 12.

[475] Faupel, *The Everlasting Gospel*, 37. Perhaps as an instance of the America-centric approach that has characterised much of Pentecostal studies, Faupel appropriates Barratt for the purposes of his argument without acknowledgement of his European status.

marginal groups such as the Montanists and the Carmisards.[476] The methods adopted call to mind an approach criticized by Knox as "the old discredited Frazer technique of piling up parallels which are not parallels at all."[477]

Furthermore Pentecostal pioneers would have constituted realistic contenders for categorisation as "incomplete and mutilated men" in the terms employed by Matthew Arnold in his signally influential work *Culture and Anarchy*, first published in 1869. Arnold memorably, and to the chagrin of many within the Nonconformist constituency, coined the term *Philistinism* to describe aspects of the Nonconformist attitude toward life and literature.[478] Certainly early English Pentecostalism exhibited scant aptitude for the scholastic and artistic tendencies that had been a notable feature of sectors of later nineteenth-century Nonconformity.[479] It might therefore be surmised that this first generation accorded more readily with the evangelical orientation toward usefulness that sought to encourage activity in the temporal realm.[480] Yet their activism was of an esoteric variety which eschewed the politicisation that characterised much of British Nonconformity.[481] In so doing, they remained faithful to the ethos captured in the utterance of Reader Harris: "Look at the political Nonconformists. May God deliver us from political sermons! Just think of it!"[482] Nor did they distinguish themselves in the much-vaunted cause of philanthropy,[483] and could scarcely have been described as "noisily

---

[476] Barratt, *In the Days of the Latter Rain*, 56-65. A similar chapter titled "Pentecostal Ourpourings in History" was presented by Stanley Frodsham in *The Story of the Pentecostal Revival*, 253-262. An article "The Glossolalia in the Early Church," based on the writings of Dean Farrar of Canterbury, sought to portray "the manifestation of the Spirit" which attended the worship of "a primitive Christian assembly." *Confidence*, May 1914, 85-89.

[477] Knox, *Enthusiasm*, 550-551.

[478] Matthew Arnold, *Culture and Anarchy: An Essay in Political and Social Criticism* Popular Edition (London: Smith, Elder & Co., 1901), 11. On this see also Clyde Binfield, *So Down to Prayers: Studies in English Nonconformity, 1780-1920* (London: J. M. Dent & Co., 1977), 162. McLeod has commented on what he terms a "revolt against the puritanism and aesthetic poverty of a Protestant upbringing" which attracted such "notable converts" as Gerard Manley Hopkins and Oscar Wilde. See *Religion and Society in England*, 39-40.

[479] They would certainly have had little in common with contemporaries such as Congregationalists and Unitarians who, according to Young, had been "nurtured in a strenuous intellectual tradition." See *Chapel*, 217-218. On this see also Bebbington, *Evangelicalism in Modern Britain*, 138.

[480] Helmstadter, "The Nonconformist Conscience," in Parsons, ed., *Religion in Victorian Britain*, vol. 4, *Interpretations*, 70.

[481] On the preponderance of politicisation among Nonconformists see Helmstadter, "Orthodox Nonconformity," in Paz, ed., *Nineteenth-Century English Religious Traditions*, 65-75.

[482] "Prayer Power," *Tongues of Fire*, January 1908, 2.

[483] On this see Donald M. Lewis, *Lighten Their Darkness: The Evangelical Mission to Working-Class London, 1828-1860* (Carlisle: Paternoster Press, 2001); K. S. Inglis,

interventionist in society."[484] Indeed the first generation of English Pentecostals may well be more properly numbered among the successors of those nineteenth-century evangelicals who engaged in a "repudiation of Christian social obligation."[485] They certainly ranked among those who emphasised affairs of the spirit above all else[486], and at times, to the exclusion of all else. They may not have welcomed the designation, but in terms employed by Arnold, they engaged enthusiastically and quite emphatically in *Hebraise*, or the development of one dimension of humanity (the spiritual dimension) at the expense of all others.[487]

Baser Enemies Yet

For Arnold, the dual tendencies which he designated *Hellenism* and *Hebraism* related to conceptions of reality typified in the respective approaches of Plato and St. Paul. The latter tendency he described as "severely preoccupied with an awful sense of the impossibility of being at ease in Zion." Its Christian manifestations strove for "self-conquest and rescue from the thrall of vile affections."[488] Other instances of, and variations on, the impetus toward self-conquest are routinely encountered in the literature of both pioneering Pentecostals and the conservative evangelical constituency within which they had been nurtured. Boddy, for instance, published a posthumous quotation from John Alexander Dowie on the occasion of his visit to Zion City, Illinois, in 1913. "Tobacco smokers" had been vituperatively addressed: "You dirty stinkpots! You may call yourselves Christians, but you smell like devils."[489] David Thomas, the missioner who had directly instigated the Bowland Street

---

Churches and the Working Classes in Victorian England (London: Routledge and Kegan Paul, 1963), 287-308; Murdoch, *Origins of the Salvation Army*, 113-167.

[484] This observation was made of the Salvation Army by Lauer in her study "Women in British Nonconformity," 36.

[485] Bebbington, *Evangelicalism in Modern Britain*, 120.

[486] Bebbington, *Evangelicalism in Modern Britain*, 120.

[487] Arnold, *Culture and* Anarchy, 6. This categorisation compares with that of Niebuhr who described the religious *dualist* as living "in conflict and in the presence of one great issue." See *Christ and Culture*, 155. On the wider occurrence of this tendency see Munson, *The Nonconformists*, 67-69.

[488] Arnold, *Culture and Anarchy*, 95-96. *Fetishism*, religious, moral and otherwise, as identified by Arnold has been explored in Peter Melville Logan, "Fetishism and Freedom in Matthew Arnold's Cultural Thinking," *Victorian Literature and Culture* 31.2 (2003): 555-574. For an overview of his theological outlook see John Caperon, "Between Two Worlds: The Theology of Matthew Arnold," *Theology* 104:821 (September-October 2001): 352-357.

[489] Boddy stated that this had appeared in Dowie's *Leaves of Healing* of 30 October 1895. See "Transatlantic Experiences: A Visit to Zion City (Ill.)," *Confidence*, February 1913, 36. Dowie's seminal influence on some who would become significant Pentecostal figureheads has been noted on pages 37-8 and 60 above.

Mission's formal association with the Pentecostal League of Prayer in 1904, later advocated that to whistle was preferable to smoking as "it is better to keep clear of vile, base, beastly and unnatural appetites and live clean, healthful, happy lives. If we do this we shall have music in our hearts, and life will go gladly whether we whistle or sing..."[490] While attending a convention in Morecambe, clergymen were witnessed "smoking their cigarettes and pipes," a spectacle which it was bemoaned, caused "the worldling" to "point the finger of scorn." Of such the editor of the *Holiness Mission Journal* stated:

> We have heard of smoking-rooms at certain Conferences and Conventions, which is painful to think of, but we praise God that there will be no smoking-rooms in Heaven, 'nothing that defileth shall enter therein.' We praise God that we in the Holiness Mission have in our conditions for membership that everyone must be a total abstainer from all intoxicants, and also a non-smoker. Praise the Lord. May God keep the work clean and under the control of the Holy Ghost until Jesus comes. Amen.[491]

The publication *Redemption Tidings* ventured even further, deriding smoking as not merely a "terrible vice," but "one of the most appalling evils" which constituted nothing less than an eschatological sign of the imminent end of all things.[492] It was proclaimed in the first issue of the periodical that members of the English Pentecostal fraternity were, in contrast, enjoying a condition of separation "from all carnal pleasures and influences" and were to be found striving to "worship the Lord in simplicity and apostolic primitiveness."[493]

A related ethical concern harboured by emerging Pentecostals was what was already widely promoted as the temperance cause. This has been described as perhaps the most characteristic Nonconformist effort at social reform in the early and mid-Victorian periods. According to Helmstadter it is not surprising that a religious constituency which promoted "sturdy independence, thrift, self-motivated effort and success," came to regard alcohol as a "device of the devil."[494] Members of Manchester's Star Hall routinely engaged in "personal dealing" with "poor drink victims" outside public houses. Those who had themselves been "the slaves of drink and gambling" gave testimony to how they had been "saved and sanctified."[495] Convictions regarding the self-

---

[490] "Whistling and Smoking," *The Holiness Mission Journal*, May 1920, 50.

[491] "Editor's Notes: The Smoking Parson," *The Holiness Mission Journal*, July 1920, 79.

[492] "The Last Days: Smoking," *Redemption Tidings*, April 1925, 8.

[493] "Editorial," *Redemption Tidings*, July 1924, 8.

[494] Helmstadter, "The Nonconformist Conscience," in Parsons, ed., *Religion in Victorian Britain*, vol. 4, *Interpretations*, 81. A broader perspective on this phenomenon is provided by L. Lewis Shiman, *The Crusade Against Drink in Victorian Britain* (New York: St. Martin's Press, 1988), and A. E. Dingle, *The Campaign for Prohibition in Victorian England* (London: Croom Helm, 1980).

[495] James Young, "Home News: Star Hall, Manchester," *The Way of Holiness*, February 1912, 8.

denigrations imposed by drunkenness were as pungent among English Pentecostals as among Americans who warned of divine imprecations against the conditions which could not only render the mind "imbecile," but cause the body to degenerate into "a dirty sot."[496] Yet beyond mere denunciation, Pentecostals ventured to present their message as a corrective and means of release and transformation for "dope, cigarette and whiskey gutter fiends."[497]

In this vein Smith Wigglesworth related to those who gathered for the last Bradford Convention how he had been summoned to visit a man confined in an asylum, an individual who he described as a "slave to intemperance and nicotine." This characteristically pointed diagnosis furnished the way for a similarly straightforward solution; he reported how "God gave authority over the power of evil" and "in the Name of Jesus we dealt with the two evil powers."[498] A member of All Saints' congregation, who acted as door-keeper during the Sunderland Conventions, related how he had been saved from a life of "drink, gambling and mischief." A labourer in the ironworks adjacent to the vicarage, at sixteen he had thought himself a man when he "could go into a public-house and call for beer." After a conversion experience he went to his bedroom and "asked the Lord to take...the desire for drink and everything bad," and he claimed that this had thereafter been his experience. Boddy regarded him to be so "wonderfully changed" that, had there been no other proof, "this would be sufficient to show how the Lord owns the Pentecostal Movement as His very own."[499] The palpable esteem in which such dramatic and seemingly efficacious conversion experiences were held was, if anything, surpassed by an even higher regard for the state of unsullied purity and moral rectitude evident in personal details such as those provided by Alfred Lewer to the Executive Council of the Pentecostal Missionary Union. In response to the question: "How long have you been a total abstainer and non-smoker?" he confidently asserted himself to have been "a life abstainer of both."[500]

Alexander Boddy's concern in the matter of temperance very definitely predated his involvement in the movement over which he was to exercise such a formative influence. His daughter stated that there had always been "a lot of drunkenness" in the neighbourhood of All Saints', and related how her father

---

[496] Copley, "The Seven Dispensational Parables," *The Pentecost*, December 1908, 9.

[497] Lou Wallick Dickerson, "A Dope Fiend Saved and Baptized," *The Pentecost*, January-February 1909, 11.

[498] Vipan, "Bradford Convention," *Confidence*, April-June 1920, 22.

[499] D. Laws, "The Story of a Sunderland Rivet-maker's Blessing," *Confidence*, February 1910, 34-35. It has been pointed out that evangelical conversion was "not an easy passage" for the late-Victorian or Edwardian male, not least because men were required to deny themselves attributes and activities that were integral to their secular domain. While the role of submissive believer often afforded women a new sense of power and moral authority, the language of penitence and surrender was the antithesis of a nineteenth-century masculinity characterised by boldness and self-mastery. See Bendroth, *Fundamentalism and Gender*, 22.

[500] Lewer, "Candidates' Schedule."

was particularly exercised regarding the depredations of this ill in his parish. She recalled how on Saturday nights he would "go round the public houses and take drunken men home." It had also been a particular habit of his to hold open-air services outside The Cambridge, the most prominent and notorious public house in the vicinity.[501] Some of the revelries conducted over the New Year period of 1913, elicited the remark that the "rowdy, drunken element" had been "shockingly in evidence."[502] Temperance appears to have been a cause of some note in Sunderland generally as it was the case that in furnishing prospective delegates to the first Whitsuntide Convention with details of suitable accommodation in the vicinity, a list of eight temperance hotels was provided.[503]

Betraying a similar concern to that of English counterparts, if adopting a decidedly different tone, a correspondent from Conneaut, Ohio, addressed himself to the subject of "Drink in Great Britain." This man, who had met Boddy at a Camp Meeting in Alliance, Ohio, before the war, expressed forthright views on the matter. He related a conviction that the international turmoil represented "God's hand upon these nations in judgement for their national sins," and that "very prominent among the national sins of the Allies" was the besmirching stain of "intemperance." He further confessed himself "profoundly impressed that God will not give us the victory until this sin is put away from us." In the light of this he stated how he had noted "with pain" that His Majesty's Government had granted an increase of twenty per cent in the allowance of grains for "the use of your brewing interests."[504]

In a manner out of keeping with the general tone of correspondence published in *Confidence*, this individual conveyed some querulousness in the assessment that his nation was being forced to eat "war bread" in order "that you people may have more grain to rot in brewing vats, with all the train of evils that follow in the consumption of its output." He was pleased to inform Boddy that what he termed the "temperance and Christian people of the States" were conducting a "nationwide agitation upon this outrage." This took the form of a "steady bombardment of the President for his action." His letter concluded abruptly and without ceremony with the interrogative: "What are you doing on your side?"[505] This blunt challenge, and the thinly veiled goading toward activism, was a rarity in English Pentecostal literature. That the letter appeared without editorial comment or disclaimer probably reflects a judgement on the part of Boddy that, while his readership would generally support the cause

---

[501] J. V. Boddy, *Memoir*, 3.

[502] "Scottish Conventions," *Confidence*, January 1913, 19.

[503] "The Whitsuntide Conference at Sunderland," *Confidence*, May 1908, 5.

[504] C. W. Pelton, "Drink in Great Britain: What U.S.A. Thinks," *Confidence*, April-June 1918, 32.

[505] Pelton, "Drink in Great Britain," *Confidence*, April-June 1918, 32-33. Similar views were being expressed by British activists such as Arthur Mee and J. Stuart Holden, *Defeat?: The Truth About the Betrayal of Britain* (London: Morgan & Scott, 1917).

espoused, the tone and manner in which it was conveyed required little clarification. Such a strident espousal of militant engagement would not resonate with the dominant thinking or ethos of England's Pentecostals. Temperance, along with other ideals of ethical primitivism, would not be attained by means of "steady bombardment" or "nationwide agitation," but by the ministrations of the Holy Spirit operating according to considerably more quietist or noetic means.[506]

In summary many of those first associated with Pentecostalism in England adopted otherworldly and counter-cultural stances very deliberately, at times even against their own natural propensities and inclinations. The option for primitivism was ideological in nature and while its ramifications did not always appear to result in the most sophisticated approach or outcome, the choice was frequently made by literate, intelligent, and informed participants. The intention was, as it had been for much of later Victorian Nonconformity, to provide a "spectacle of inspired self-sacrifice" to "a world stricken with moral enervation."[507] England's first Pentecostals would also have found themselves in sympathy with the fideistic observation that "when worldly wisdom cannot see a hand's-breadth before it...Faith can see God. For Faith sees best in the dark."[508] Boddy vaunted the fact that among the signatories of the London Declaration of 1909, there was "no array of learned names" but only "humble servants of the Lord Jesus." It was a source of comfort to him that according to Luke 10:21, true insight had been hidden from the "wise" and "the learned" and instead revealed to mere "babes."[509]

Conclusion

Historico-Thematic Summary

This thematic exploration of early English Pentecostal piety has adopted a broadly chronological approach to the emergence and development of recurrent

---

[506] The term *noetic* has been used to denote "states of insight into depths of truth unplumbed by discursive intellect," by Andrew M. Greeley and William C. McCready, in "Some Notes on the Sociological Study of Mysticism," in Edward A. Tirgakian, ed., *On the Margin of the Visible: Sociology, the Esoteric and the Occult* (London: John Wiley & Sons, 1974), 306. See also its usage in James, *Varieties of Religious Experience*, 292-293. It is interesting to note that the depth of feeling on this issue was such within the Pentecostal League of Prayer that it caused them to transcend their avowed disinclination toward political or social activism. At their annual gathering held during 1917 a petition was drafted to the effect that H.M. Government commandeer "for the manufacture of explosives the present immense stock of bonded spirits." This was immediately dispatched to the Rt. Hon. David Lloyd George. See "Prohibition," *Spiritual Life*, June 1917, 5. *Tongues of Fire*, the offical organ of the League, had been renamed and published as *Spiritual Life* from January 1916.

[507] Arnold, *Culture and Anarchy*, 96.

[508] Kierkegaard, *Gospel of Sufferings*, 36.

[509] "What We Teach," *Confidence*, December 1909, 286.

and pervasive emphases. *Initiation* is, by definition, of primary significance not only as the process whereby the individual crossed the threshold into the Pentecostal dimension, but also in terms of collective considerations as a fundamental building block of an identifiable movement. The emergent religious grouping rapidly developed norms and parameters for such encounters and was unwittingly aided in this by former Holiness collaborators. Criticisms expressed hastened the formation of an ideological framework which not only underscored the imperative of this spiritual rite of passage, but advanced a rationale for such physical manifestations, "concomitants" or "convincements," as typically accompanied it.

Progressing beyond patterns of individual identification with the Pentecostal cause, the tenor of collective expression and engagement, such as was to be found in the convention or mass-gathering has been subjected to scrutiny. Pentecostal worship as practised in England prior to the First World War was not unique in its claim to exuberant and, at times, ecstatic modes of expression. Neither was it, contrary to expectation or superficial observation, prey to unbridled emotional indulgence. While the tone of early meetings confirms the observation that from its onset this movement was "oral, musical, and experimental,"[510] excesses such as contributed to the "extraordinary scenes" witnessed during Barratt's 1907 mission, did not become normative. In a manner which intimated not merely an awareness of, but notable sympathy with contemporary thinking in the field of psychology of religion, the first generation of Pentecostal leaders were alive to both the emotional susceptibilities of certain dispositions, and the erratic and unpredictable interjection of the "unconscious mind." Eminently pragmatic, its custodians operated from the conviction that "nothing is to be gained by a foolish ignoring of obvious difficulties."[511] The disposition of the most influential pioneering leaders could be said to have been characterised by a sobriety which expressed full cognisance of the fact that "the rankest fanaticism runs closely along the line of the deepest spirituality."[512] The designation *reasonable enthusiast*, originally applied to a founding father of the English evangelical tradition,[513] could similarly be attributed to those who embodied the abiding plea: "Oh, for a baptism of revival wisdom as well as revival fire."[514] That this approach was not only successfully inculcated, but its legacy bequeathed to subsequent denominational Pentecostals is evinced by the proclamation that Elim had developed "along evangelical and yet deeply

---

[510] Mursell, *English Spirituality*, 405.

[511] "Prophetic Messages," *Confidence*, June 1908, 15; "Leaders' Meetings," *Confidence*, June 1909, 130.

[512] J. M. Pike, "The Coming Revival," *Flames of Fire*, August 1915, 2.

[513] Henry D. Rack, *Reasonable Enthusiast: John Wesley and the Rise of Methodism* 3rd ed. (London: Epworth Press, 2002). Challenges associated with this, at times precarious disposition, as well as its positive outworkings have been discussed in David Hempton, *Methodism: Empire of the Spirit* (New Haven and London: Yale University Press, 2005), 33-41.

[514] Pike, "The Coming Revival," *Flames of Fire*, August 1915, 2.

spiritual lines" while its leaders deliberately eschewed "extremism in any shape or form whatever."[515]

Having considered the manner of inauguration into what was perceived to constitute Pentecostal reality from 1907 onwards, as well as pertinent aspects of its collective expression, attention was turned to the movement's perspective on the wider world and its sense of place and purpose in it. Eschatological concerns were undeniably at the forefront of the spiritual cosmology of England's emerging Pentecostals. As was the case in North America, participants were already in possession of a veritable "cornucopia of symbols"[516] having inhabited an evangelical *milieu* characterised by the premillennial paradigm. Such views were, if anything, reinforced by virtue of Pentecostal emphases. From the earliest days of Barratt's seminal visit to Sunderland it was advocated that the reinstatement of the gifts of the Spirit "foreboded the end of the present order - the dawn of the Second Coming."[517] The seemingly unlikely fusion of extreme pessimism characteristic of the premillennial *eschatology of disaster* with the exuberant and expectant Pentecostal disposition, was enabled by the introduction of a concept known as the Latter Rain. Pentecostalism's unique addition to the dispensationalist schema fulfilled not only a mitigating function, but facilitated the development of an outward orientation which came to counteract potentially stultifying tendencies associated with this all-encompassing worldview.

This development can be interpreted as representing a notable shift in emphasis in the aims and understanding of revival. It has been demonstrated that, in broad terms, the pre-war pursuit of personal quickening and mutual edification within an existing *collegia pietatis*, gave way to more concerted and deliberate propagation and proclamation to the surrounding society in an attempt to realize "the speedy ripening of the harvest."[518] The Pentecostal movement came to increasingly exhibit a shared consciousness whereby it felt predestined to "shout out the midnight cry throughout the whole world."[519] Evangelists who came to prominence offered a singular fusion of the methods of planned revivalism with supernatural spontaneity and inspirationalism. This dimension, which saw figureheads function as direct agents of "transcendental intervention in human affairs,"[520] embodied a significant break with a cessationist perspective characteristic of much of the history of Protestant Christianity, not least as it had been represented in the British Isles. It also prevented Pentecostal spirituality from tending towards what Underhill has termed "an exclusive mysticism," and rendered it more amenable to the "generous realities of an incarnational faith."[521] It has been demonstrated that England was indeed witnessing the development of a tradition which, in the memorable words of sociologist David Martin, saw

---

[515] Boulton, *George Jeffreys*, 339.

[516] Wacker, "The Almost Chosen People," 155.

[517] "An Israelite's Passion," *Daily Chronicle*, 7 October 1907.

[518] "The Bridegroom Cometh," *Confidence*, April 1908, 19.

[519] Edel, "Behold, the Bridegroom Cometh!" *Confidence*, January 1914, 9.

[520] Wallis, "Introduction," in Wallis, ed., *Millennialism and Charisma*, 1.

[521] Underhill, *Worship*, 238.

"the saints vacate their plinths in Baroque space and walk the street as fellow artisans."[522]

Yet it would be inaccurate to conclude that the spiritual *pleroma* propounded by revivalists which had from the start suffused this strain of practical religion, was without qualification or limitation. On the contrary much evidence has been presented which supports the contention that "there has been no spiritual revival within Christianity" which has not involved a "return to St. Paul," and in particular, to his "disciplinarian" aspect.[523] The "resolute otherworldliness"[524] highlighted demonstrates that pre-denominational Pentecostal spirituality was permeated by what Niebuhr has termed an "emphatic negation" which saw the "counterpoint of loyalty to Christ and the brothers" as necessitating a "rejection of cultural society." Their developing teaching, practice, and general ethos provide eloquent testimony of the fact that a "clear line of separation" was cast "between the brotherhood of the children of God and the world." Pentecostal *Hebraism* directed loyalty "entirely toward the new order, the new society, and its Lord."[525] It has also been made apparent that, in this respect, those who attached themselves to the Pentecostal cause in Edwardian England demonstrated considerable continuity with the ideals and mores of the conservative evangelical constituencies where they had undergone their spiritual formation, and within which they had functioned. Rosman's observation that "evangelicals' linear scale of values and overwhelming sense of religious need mitigated against academic study, as against any activity which did not obviously contribute to the salvation of the world,"[526] finds ample resonance in the writings and utterances of the first generation of English Pentecostals. They remained resolutely in sympathy with the orientation which condemned and strove to elude the "deadening embrace of worldliness"[527] and, to this end, actively promoted the suppression of all forms of "irresponsible *Ersatz* for primary religious experience."[528]

Churchmanship

What has been presented within the framework of these five categories certainly offers much that enables an analysis and categorisation of early Pentecostal lived religion in terms of churchmanship or ecclesiastical tradition.

---

[522] This "brilliantly evocative image" has been cited by Graham Howes in "The Sociologist as Stylist: David Martin and Pentecostalism," in Andrew Walker and Martyn Percy, *Restoring the Image: Essays on Religion and Society in Honour of David Martin* (Sheffield: Sheffield Academic Press, 2001), 104.

[523] Inge, *Mysticism in Religion*, (London: Rider & Company, 1969), 40.

[524] Wacker, "The Almost Chosen People," 148.

[525] Niebuhr, *Christ and Culture*, 60-61.

[526] Rosman, *Evangelicals and Culture*, 208.

[527] "Editorials: Grand-motherly Ecclesiasticism," *Tongues of Fire*, May 1908, 6.

[528] Gerth and Wright Mills, eds., *From Max Weber: Essays in Sociology*, Part III, *Religion*, 342-343.

Those who underwent a Pentecostal experience, as it had come to be promulgated from 1907, were drawn from a variety of backgrounds but were united by the common denominator of their unimpeachable conservative evangelical credentials. Prominent figures such as Boddy and Polhill were, it must be acknowledged, reasonably exceptional in their Anglican allegiance, while the majority of congregations who aligned themselves with the movement appear to have been independent, unaffiliated, and largely under lay-leadership. A predisposing factor toward interest in the message that had emanated from North America had been an inclination toward, and commonly participation in, the British Holiness movement and its teaching. Reader Harris, an influential proponent of Wesleyan-Holiness views, took particular exception to the deliberate and overt adoption of an empirical sign, or signs, as evidence of spiritual baptism and empowerment. It is interesting to note that while this precipitated an abrupt conclusion to involvement in Harris' devotional network - ironically titled the Pentecostal League of Prayer - it placed emerging Pentecostals in continuity with other aspects of the Wesleyan tradition. Alongside a shared appreciation of visible "convincements," the *reasonable enthusiasm* inculcated and even enforced at moments of collective worship demonstrates further affinity with this strand of religious expression. While Salvationist exuberance and extemporaneousness as well as such displays of fervour and ecstasy as were commonplace during the Welsh Revival had formed part of the religious hinterland of many participants, leaders and convenors of Pentecostal gatherings sought to discourage, even suppress "pretended inspiration" and what were deemed to be spurious forms of enthusiasm. It is undeniably the case that "strong, determined, clear-eyed leaders"[529] exercised an authority which appears to have combined psychological insight into the nature of the religious impulse with a conservative evangelical disposition characterised by sobriety, moderation, and the ubiquitous recourse to Scripture. It would appear that under their tutelage the movement, in a manner similar to earlier Methodism, "thrived on the raw edge of religious excitement without capitulating, in the main, to some of the more extreme manifestations of populist religion."[530] What has been examined corroborates and substantiates the suggestion that the mainstream of English Pentecostalism "moved closer to broader evangelicalism" by virtue of an ingrained concern to distance itself from "prophetic excess."[531]

Further evidence of continuity with this tradition is to be found in the pervasiveness of pre-millennial expectation and dispensational thinking among those who comprised the Pentecostal movement in England. While subscribing to all the central tenets of this potent and engaging worldview, Pentecostals came to promulgate the Latter Rain, a nuanced development which accorded them a unique place in the spiritual cosmology. It has been contested that it was this that ultimately enabled adherents to face the aftermath of the First World

---

[529] Wacker, *Early Pentecostals and American Culture*, 141.

[530] Hempton, *Empire of the Spirit*, 41.

[531] Randall, "Pentecostalism and Evangelical Spirituality in England," 78.

War in a positive vein, and to engage the attentions of their surrounding society more effectively during the 1920s than was the case for many contemporary evangelicals. It has also been pointed out that a deep-seated sense of fidelity to Scripture empowered the developing mainstream of the movement to dissuade from excessively speculative tendencies during wartime, while a propensity for the miraculous enabled them to advance a Christian apologetic amid widespread fascination with strange providences and supernatural visitations.

The brand of revivalism that evolved and developed in the hands of emblematic figures such as George and Stephen Jeffreys and Smith Wigglesworth, not only entailed continuity with, but in vital respects, represented an extension of what has been termed the "last popular religious culture of British Nonconformity."[532] George Jeffreys, in particular, as his methods and effectiveness in this direction were refined and enhanced, attained an evangelical proclamation such as had not been witnessed in Britain since the halcyon days of this tradition exemplified by the campaigns of Moody and Sankey during the 1870s. The inclusion of an unapologetically miraculous dimension constituted a singular departure, not only from the heritage and paradigms of planned revivalism, but also from the "immense shrinkage in the scope of the sacred"[533] that had become the settled position of the Anglo-Saxon Protestant sphere. This development, the implications of which are difficult to overstate, retrospectively illuminates the severity of the opposition that had been expressed by Harris and other teachers in the Holiness fraternity.

While this divergence of perspectives may have in a very real sense created rival spiritual hemispheres, English Pentecostals continued to not only exhibit, but to stridently espouse, the moral ethos that permeated the conservative evangelical perspective. Suspicions harboured with respect of "weak" and nominal Christianity, the role of theology and academic endeavour in the pursuit of vital religion, and the perils of, among other baleful pursuits, novel-reading, intemperance, and nicotine consumption, all serve to categorise them with those designated Nonconformist *Hebraists*. What has been uncovered suggests that Pentecostal commitment did not dilute or displace these concerns; on the contrary a credible case could be made for its having brought about their intensification.

Theological World-View

This elemental *otherworldly* disposition, which has been shown to have pervaded the Pentecostal outlook throughout the years under consideration, is fundamental to another means of assessing the practical spirituality which united disparate congregations and groupings from the Edwardian period onwards. Wainwright has in broad terms, and without elaboration, categorised

---

[532] Kent, *Studies in Victorian Revivalism*, 153. This historical indebtedness has been confirmed by sociologist David Martin in his observation that "the Pentecostalists" are "the legatees of the revival spasm." See his *Sociology of English Religion*, 61-62.

[533] Berger, *The Social Reality of Religion*, 117.

Pentecostals among those groupings that have exhibited a *Christ Against Culture* disposition throughout the history of the Christian Church. What has been discussed in connection with the disposition of early Pentecostals – an orientation which saw them renounce all that did not overtly foster spiritual development or further the cause of the kingdom of God - certainly locates them among those who emphasised the affairs of the spirit above all else, frequently to the exclusion of all else. In continuity with the conservative evangelical orientation, Pentecostals were practitioners of a *this-worldly* asceticism, which instead of sheltering itself in monastery or cloister, "strode into the market-place of life" and thereafter sought to pursue an existence "in the world" but resolutely neither "of nor for this world."[534]

Yet while the "world" or *Culture* could be described by the primary architect of English Pentecostalism as "literally steeped in sin and wickedness from one end to the other,"[535] it is also the case that vast tableaus of transformation and redemption of cosmic proportions were also placed before the Pentecostal public. Promoting a distinctly incarnational spirituality, the existence of these contrary dispositions, frequently in paradoxical coalescence, was central to the ideological parameters within which England's first Pentecostals operated. Niebuhr himself highlighted the limitations of the typological schema he originally propounded, acknowledging that "when one returns from the hypothetical scheme to the rich complexity of individual events, it is evident at once that no person or group ever conforms completely to a type."[536] The exploration of original sources undertaken for this study demonstrates that convenient or superficial categorisation is not adequate with respect of Pentecostal lived religion as it emerged and developed in England. If typology is, however provisionally, to be employed, its complexity and fusion of contrary tendencies rendered English Pentecostal spirituality, if not a "world-accommodating religion," then at least a "variant of world-rejecting religion."[537]

Historiography

This section has offered much that challenges existing Pentecostal historiographies, three aspects being particularly highlighted. Firstly *sacred meteor* theories which imply that this "sweeping phenomenon"[538] was "forged outside of the ordinary processes of history,"[539] find little support in what has been presented. While widely and severely criticised and opposed in the

---

[534] Weber, *The Protestant Ethic*, 154.

[535] "Seven Signs of His Coming," *Confidence*, December 1910, 287.

[536] Niebuhr, *Christ and Culture*, 56-57.

[537] Christopher Partridge, *The Re-Enchantment of the West*, vol. 1, *Alternative Spiritualities, Sacralization, Popular Culture and Occulture* (London and New York: T. & T. Clark, 2004), 28-29.

[538] Robinson, *Early Pentecostalism in Ireland*, xxiv.

[539] Wacker, "Reflections on History Writing among Early Pentecostals," 81.

aftermath of T. B. Barratt's 1907 mission, Pentecostal leaders and protagonists, among whom the missioner was himself prominent, managed to draw upon reserves of conviction and fortitude and establish an ideological foundation on which they could build. Parameters and boundaries of theory and practice were forged within a relatively short timeframe, and frequently in pragmatic response to problems and difficulties encountered along the way. On the whole the years 1907-1925 represent an epoch of progression and controlled development, at times swift and dramatic, at other times gradual and incremental, for the brand of lived religion that has been under scrutiny. It has been shown that the Pentecostal movement was in England the beneficiary of sober, determined, and resourceful leaders, themselves schooled in the evangelical tradition, who carefully and deliberately managed and nurtured their charge from birth and infancy, through spiritual adolescence, and on toward maturation. The perspective advanced by Donald Gee - a variant of the *sacred meteor* theme which contended that a "most significant feature" of Pentecostal beginnings was that in contrast to "preceding religious movements" it had "sprung up...without any particular leader with whose name it could be connected"[540] - can no longer be perpetuated.

If the first generation of leaders succeeded in effecting the development of a movement which, while it may have descended "from heaven," did so anything but fully-formed, what has been presented also challenges the perspective that its pre-denominational custodians were ineffectual, irresolute, or at the very least, limited and wanting in their capacities. Aspects of the criticisms advanced in the writings of Gee relate to structural issues for the movement, and will be examined in the next section. It is the case, however, that suggestions of both lack of appreciation for, and mismanagement of, the inspirationalism and spiritual vitality integral to the Pentecostal impulse, are to be found in abundance. Having stated unambiguously that misguided leaders had "marred and clogged the Pentecostal Revival," he concluded an exposition on the demerits of Boddy and Polhill with the declaration: "There can be no doubt that for many precious years the Movement floundered for lack of strong, inspiring, distinctive leadership such as might have welded it into a mighty spiritual force in the land."[541] Gee was specific (and personal) in offering his posthumous assessment on Polhill, averring that "only his money secured his position" which "could never last in a growing Pentecostal Revival" as this "spiritual

---

[540] Gee, "The Pentecostal Movement," *Redemption Tidings*, August 1932, 3. These statements were not merely printed in this denominational magazine, but were reiterated in his *History* which enjoyed a considerably wider readership and more enduring appeal. There he spoke of "a spontaneous revival appearing almost simultaneously in various parts of the world" while propounding the notion that "one of the most beautiful things about the movement" had been that it had its genesis "peculiarly of the Spirit of God." See *The Pentecostal Movement*, 3.

[541] Gee, *The Pentecostal Movement*, 82-83, 98. The theme of spiritual "declension" was also pursued by another prominent figure, A. E. Saxby, in "Heart Searchings," *Things New and Old*, June 1923, 4-5.

movement...contained dynamic qualities" which the old Etonian "only dimly understood."[542] It is pertinent that these invectives contributed to the construction of a monolithic and enduring edifice, a perspective which failed or refused to recognise or acknowledge the energies exerted and qualities invested which would benefit all of British Pentecostalism during subsequent decades. What has been presented confirms that in the pursuit of a *reasonable enthusiasm*, pioneering leaders, despite personal foibles and shortcomings, succeeded in forging and establishing an inner ideological and organisational discipline that saved their movement from the ephemeral fate of other manifestations of popular religiosity.

Finally while it is obviously the case that the Pentecostal message owed much of its original impetus to influences emanating from North America, the foregoing exploration has demonstrated that the Pentecostalism that succeeded in establishing itself before the First World War was no mere foreign import transplanted to the 'old country,' but was distinct and identifiable in its own right. A salient factor in this is that early protagonists continued to betray the motivations and pre-occupations of the late-Victorian evangelical constituencies with which they had been integrally identified. Inherited and ingrained dispositions fused with a pneumatic dynamism to forge a characteristically English manifestation of Pentecostal religion. Foreign visitors, both American and European, recognised and commended aspects of the tenor and character of the Pentecostalism they encountered in England, as well as elsewhere in the British Isles. The examination of spirituality and ideology undertaken in this section significantly advances the understanding of the distinctives that suffused the English manifestation of an international phenomenon in its pre-denominational era.

---

[542] Gee, *Personal Memoirs of Pentecostal Pioneers*, 75-76.

SECTION THREE

Structural Developments

Introduction

The aim of this present section is to outline and examine the structural developments and status of the movement in its early years, while highlighting some of the principal factors which contributed to what has been described as the "almost unintentional" formation of separatist Pentecostal bodies.[1] The original ecumenical ideals of early leaders will be outlined, while tensions involved in their implementation will be considered. Factors such as the emergence and functioning of leadership elites, questions of orthodoxy and the maintenance of discipline, difficulties arising from the First World War, and the implications of a post-war expansionary phase, will be highlighted and explored as catalytic forces in the evolution of the movement. This section will conclude by returning to the four Centres of Pentecostal emergence with a view to assessing the impact of developments and outcomes for these specific localities.

While this study does not aim to provide a comprehensive history of the Pentecostal denominations that came to be formed in Britain,[2] developments that occurred in this direction while still in "its early uncrystallised form,"[3] also

---

[1] Wilson, "The Pentecostalist Minister," in Wilson, ed., *Patterns of Sectarianism*, 140.

[2] Overarching denominational histories of the Assemblies of God are to be found in William Kay's, *Inside Story: A History of the British Assemblies of God*, and Allen's unpublished thesis "Signs and Wonders" which traces the growth of the Assemblies of God in Britain and Ireland up to 1980. A more concentrated analysis of the formation of this body is to be found in Richard Dan Massey, "'A Sound and Scriptural Union': An Examination of the Origins of the Assemblies of God in Great Britain and Ireland During the Years 1920-1925" (Unpublished Ph.D. Dissertation: University of Birmingham, 1988). The history of the Elim Pentecostal Church has attracted little scholarly attention, a modest exception to this being Malcolm R. Hathaway's, "The Elim Pentecostal Church: Origins, Development and Distinctives," in Warrington, ed., *Pentecostal Perspectives*, 1-39. Hudson has offered a more substantial and focused exploration of a highly problematic episode for the denomination in his "A Schism and its Aftermath: An Historical Analysis of Denominational Discerption in the Elim Church, 1939-1940" (Unpublished Ph. D. Dissertation, King's College London, 1999).

[3] Wilson, "The Pentecostalist Minister," in Wilson, ed., *Patterns of Sectarianism*, 140.

described as the era of "the inchoate days of early Pentecostalism,"[4] will receive significant illumination. The few denominational studies undertaken have come to acknowledge the existence of a prelude or precursor to their formalised institutions, yet treatment of this phase has at best been limited in scope. It is therefore the intention in this context to explore pertinent structural aspects of this denominational pre-history in its own right and in more detail than has hitherto been achieved. Structural configuration and re-configurations between the years 1907-1925 will be seen to encompass the passage of the English Pentecostal movement from its *incipient phase*, via a phase of *enthusiastic mobilisation*, toward its *period of organisation*.[5]

The original *collegia pietatis* vision will be further explored in this section, and a chronological consideration will demonstrate its increasing unworkability and ultimate demise. Later denominational perspectives will be outlined and assessed and the shortcomings of received historical orthodoxies will become apparent in the light of the primary source evidence consulted. Similarities to, and influences from, denominational developments in North America will be acknowledged, but what occurred in England will be seen to further challenge the made-in-the-USA perspective. Finally, what is explored will serve to conclusively undermine the persistent notion that Pentecostalism emerged Melchizedek-like, without spiritual or structural lineage. It will rather be shown to have benefitted from the stewardship of prescient and determined leaders who wrestled with challenges and exigencies encountered, and sought in very definite ways to achieve the implementation of their organizational conceptions and deeply-held ideals.

Section 3.1: Early Conceptions and an Ecumenical Vision

While, as has been highlighted, there existed from 1908 a recognisably "distinct centripetal tendency of responsibility,"[6] it is also the case that Alexander Boddy consistently conceived of this as informal and associational in nature. There is no indication, and much to the contrary, that he ever intended denominational identities or allegiances to be subsumed within or diminished by virtue of participation in the Pentecostal movement. This approach significantly mirrors that of Reader Harris whose League was intended to function as "an Inter-denominational Prayer Union which any one may join,"[7] as well as the guiding

---

[4] Taylor, "Publish and Be Blessed," 345.

[5] These developmental categories have been employed by Robertson in his analysis of the Salvation Army. See Roland Robertson, "The Salvation Army: The Persistence of Sectarianism," in Wilson, ed., *Patterns of Sectarianism*, 50.

[6] Wilson, "An Analysis of Sect Development," in Wilson, ed., *Patterns of Sectarianism*, 35.

[7] This description was offered by Harris in an epilogue to his book *Is Sin a Necessity?: A Résumé of a Recent Controversy* (London: S. W. Partridge & Co., 1896), 95.

principles of "the Holiness Movement's most vigorous offspring,"[8] whose ethos is intimated in its self-designation, the Keswick Convention Movement for the Deepening of the Spiritual Life. It has been observed that while this movement functioned primarily as a "spearhead of 'conservative' Protestantism" within a largely Anglican constituency, it also served to "join hands across denominational frontiers."[9] It would appear to be the case that according to the conception of its evangelical Anglican custodian, the Pentecostal movement that began to emerge in Edwardian England would fulfil something approximating to the same function. In an explanation of the character and nature of the movement to a gathering of men at St. Gabriel's, Bishopwearmouth, in 1910, it was stated:

> We are all one in the Pentecostal Family, and there is a beautiful fellowship indeed. While Church people predominate, there are also Methodists, Salvationists, Presbyterians, Baptists, Primitives and Congregationalists.[10]

The assertion of Church predominance is curious as, in strictly numerical terms, this was never actually the case. Boddy could be deemed to have resorted to hyperbole in the course of an apologetic presentation which sought to advance a positive portrayal of the Pentecostal phenomenon to an Anglican audience in a neighbouring parish. It could otherwise be attributed to the perception that "buildings connected with the Church of England" had been providentially chosen "as the scene of blessing,"[11] or to the incontrovertible fact that for a decade both he and a noteworthy Anglican layman, were the most prominent and influential figures in the Pentecostal movement. However this is interpreted, it is pertinent to point out that Boddy did not, as a general rule, seek to advance some form of Church or Anglican hegemony, but rather that he repeatedly averred that the genius of Pentecostal Christianity lay in its propensity to unite individuals of varied backgrounds and persuasions.

---

[8] James D. G. Dunn, "Spirit-Baptism and Pentecostalism," *Scottish Journal of Theology* 23:4 (Nov. 1970), 398. It is interesting to note that while Holiness/Pentecostal indebtedness to the Wesleyan tradition with respect of the notion of a doctrine of subsequence has become something of a truism (Land, *Pentecostal Spirituality*, 47-53, 207), exploration of structural heritage is all but non-existent. It is suggested that investigation of the legacy of Wesleyan conceptions of "connectionalism" could significantly illuminate the associational nature of Holiness and early Pentecostal groupings such as consolidated around Sunderland between 1908-1914. Helpful preliminary reflections are to be found in H. O. Thomas, "John Wesley: Concept of 'Connection' and Theological Pluralism," *Wesleyan Theological Journal* 36.2 (Fall 2001): 88-92. It is pertinent to point out that the implications of Baptist influence has been given some consideration in Randall, "Baptists and the Shaping of Pentecostalism," in Bebbington, ed., *The Gospel in the World*, 80-104.

[9] Martin, *Sociology of English Religion*, 86.

[10] "Speaking in Tongues: What is it?" *Confidence*, May 1910, 103.

[11] "Unity not Uniformity," *Confidence*, March 1911, 60.

Pentecostal experience was held up as uniquely capable of providing an elusive solution to a seemingly intractable problem which had beset the Christian world throughout its history. Certainly Boddy and others were attuned to a *zeitgeist* which saw many deplore the scandal of Christian rivalry and disunity. Contributors to the *Daily Telegraph* survey of religious belief in 1904 had written disparagingly of "Christians of a hundred sects,"[12] and deplored the thought that allegiance to this faith had caused even those with the best intentions to "treat their fellows with such atrocity as might be displayed by Red Indians on the war-path."[13] While Dean of St. Paul's, W. R. Inge observed in 1912 that the "chaotic and fissiparous Churches of Northern Europe and America" represented an unfortunate "caricature of what the Church of Christ ought to be and may be."[14] Such matters had been the subject of widespread Christian concern during this period, a salient instance of which had been the World Missionary Conference held in Edinburgh in 1910 which heightened the impetus toward inter-church sympathy and co-operation. Europe's prominent Pentecostal leaders, including Boddy and Polhill, cited the Conference as significant in the promotion of aspirations, missionary and co-operative, which they shared.[15] The ethos which suffused this gathering and its deliberations had hailed the need for, and practical advantages of, "larger comprehension...larger community" and the "deeper realization" of such fellowship and co-operation as had been witnessed among delegates. Terms such as "revolution" and "transformation" were employed, and sanguine hopes were expressed for a future which would witness "a larger body of experience now happily placed at the disposal of all Christendom."[16] Boddy's influential ecclesiastical superior, the Right Rev. H. C. G. Moule, Bishop of Durham, had been integrally involved in the formulation of *English Church Teaching on Faith, Life and Order*, published in 1914, which acknowledged the divisions of Christendom to be "a most grievous stumbling block to the claims of Christ." This "standing obstacle" could be overcome if the sentiments of the Encyclical of the Lambeth Conference of 1888 which recognised "the real religious work which is carried on by Christian bodies not of our communion," were adhered to. Moule and his co-authors expressed a "real yearning for unity" and urged clergy to foster conditions where "the spirit of love" could "move on the troubled water of

---

[12] From "Josiah Oldfield, Harley Street, W.," in *Do We Believe?*, 137.

[13] From "Monte Cristo, Liverpool," in *Do We Believe?*, 278.

[14] Inge, *The Church and the Age* (London: Longmans, Green and Co., 1912), 59.

[15] See "Declaration: International Pentecostal Consultative Council," *Confidence*, December 1912, 277, and "The Next Great Revival," *Flames of Fire*, January 1913, 1-2. On the significance of this Conference for ecumenical advancement see Norman Goodall, *The Ecumenical Movement: What it is and What it does* (London: Oxford University Press, 1964), 8-16.

[16] John R. Mott, "Closing Address at the World Missionary Conference, Edinburgh 1910," in Michael Kinnamon and Brian E. Cope, eds., *The Ecumenical Movement: An Anthology of Key Texts and Voices* (Grand Rapids, MI.: Eerdmans, 1997), 10-11.

religious difference."[17]

Gilbert has observed that during the period from the repeal of the Test and Corporation Acts in 1828 to the era of ecumenical fraternity that occurred after the First World War, tension and conflict between Anglicanism and Dissent, Church and chapel, "became and remained the primary determinant of the role and significance of religion in public life." While instances of co-operation, shared enterprises, and overlapping allegiances must certainly be acknowledged "conflict, however, was the norm."[18] It was in such a context that a man of Boddy's sensibilities was pleased to announce that "the Lord in His great tenderness has sent a real Baptism of the Holy Ghost alike upon Quakers and Anglicans, and Plymouth Brethren and Baptists. He did more than some expected, and who dare criticise Him! Can not we too have His Spirit of Love? Yes, surely."[19] Such utterances confirm Jane Vazeille's opinion that her father "had always been very ecumenically minded, and indeed was much in advance of his day in his ideas of unity."[20] One of the foremost observers of the global Pentecostal phenomenon has retrospectively listed Boddy among the "ecumenical pioneers of Pentecostalism," a designation which he confers on only three other individuals.[21]

Boddy was eager to point out that the series of meetings which marked the advent of the Pentecostal message in England had been "presided over by an Anglican Clergyman," while "a Methodist Missioner" had been the "channel of blessing in these surroundings." The ethos which this Anglican clergyman sought to inculcate was that "a welcome was given to all, and no attempt was made to proselytize." Christians "of many kinds" came and went, returning to their own churches or places of meeting. While "differences existed as before, they were never emphasized." In his estimation it was a sign of "a slightly lower spiritual level" when attentions were turned toward disparity or difference.[22] It is indeed the case that Boddy, and by virtue of his status and influence, the movement over which he effectively presided until the Great War, displayed a "transdenominational and international ecclesial consciousness" which was characterised by a "subordination of church order to

---

[17] H. C. G. Moule, T. W. Drury and R. B. Girldlestone, *English Church Teaching on Faith, Life and Order* (London: Longmans, Green and Co., 1914), 196, 200-201.

[18] Alan A. Gilbert, *The Making of Post-Christian Britain: A History of the Secularization of Modern Society* (London and New York: Longman, 1980), 73. This assessment if borne out by observations and instances cited by Booth in his exploration of attitudes encountered among religious bodies in the metropolis. See *Life and Labour*, 3rd Series, *Religious Influences*, vol. 7, 418-421.

[19] "Unity, not Uniformity," *Confidence*, March 1911, 60.

[20] J. V. Boddy, *Memoir*, 6.

[21] Hollenweger, *Pentecostalism: Origins and Developments Worldwide* (Peabody, Mass.: Hendrickson Publishers, 1997), 343.

[22] "Unity, not Uniformity," *Confidence*, March 1911, 60.

evangelical piety."[23] This consciousness was abundantly in evidence in the following highly significant statement:

> The Editor of Confidence does not feel that the Lord's leading in these days is to set up a new Church, but to bless individuals where they are. There is just as much danger, sooner or later, for a 'Pentecostal Church' (so-called), as for any of the churches that have risen and fallen. Let each soul sink more deeply into God, and seek to do His will, and help others in His strength, and He will pour out such a blessing as can scarcely be contained.[24]

An indication of the seriousness, even solemnity, with which Boddy regarded such matters is to be found in his exposition on the subject of "Discerning the Lord's Body" (1 Cor. 11:29). He evidently regarded participation in the mystical Body of Christ to be "a subject for reverent congratulation, for awesome thankfulness." It was in the light of the profound nature of this condition that there should no "no schism in the body." Fellowship should be retained "so long as vital truths are not opposed or despised." He held that it was because of "sad divisions and separations," such as those which caused some to claim to be "of Paul" and others to be "of Apollos" (1 Cor. 1:12), that Paul had stated "for this cause many among you are weak and sickly, and not a few sleep" (1 Cor. 11:30). While Christian fellowship was seen to foster health for soul and body, it was ventured that "the opposite may bring sickness and death."[25] It was Boddy's conviction that while involvement in the movement had resulted in some being "spoken against, written against, shut out and banned,"[26] it was incumbent upon advocates of Pentecost that they "be quite willing to learn something even from the criticisms of opponents," as well as from "the warnings of those who say they are our friends."[27] Far from advocating what was colloquially termed "come-out-ism,"[28] separatism was

---

[23] Bruce Hindmarsh, "Is Evangelical Ecclesiology an Oxymoron? A Historical Perspective," in John Stackhouse, ed., *Evangelical Ecclesiology: Reality or Illusion?* (Grand Rapids, MI.: Baker Academic, 2003), 15.

[24] "Unity, not Uniformity," *Confidence*, March 1911, 60.

[25] "Not Discerning the Lord's Body," *Confidence*, November 1909, 252-253.

[26] "Speaking in Tongues: What is it?" *Confidence*, May 1910, 104.

[27] "Not Discerning the Lord's Body," *Confidence*, November 1909, 253.

[28] "The Pentecostal Revival," *Confidence*, March 1912, 62. "Come-out-ism" had also been criticised as transgressing the ethos of the Pentecostal League of Prayer. Harris stated that "Holiness people, with rare exceptions, love the Church and are its most faithful supporters." The notion of forming "little separate conventicles for the worship of God" was a "common temptation" deemed to originate with the "enemy of souls." See "Editorials: Come-out-ism or Put-out-ism," *Tongues of Fire*, June 1908, 6. These expressions serve to locate both Boddy and Harris on a definite side of a contentious issue that had exercised Holiness advocates for the previous three decades. Writing principally of the North American situation, although with obvious parallels for transatlantic co-religionists, Ware has observed that "from the early 1880s through the end of the nineteenth century a lengthy argument raged between those who believed that

only to be countenanced as a last and drastic resort:

> We desire true fellowship with all who honour His atoning Blood, and only when
> we are driven forth by condemnation and criticism will we be willing to separate
> from Brethren we honour in the Lord.[29]

In further continuity with previous Holiness associates, the ethos conveyed in
such utterances bares remarkable similarity to the position advanced by David
Thomas, the individual who had enlisted Smith Wigglesworth and the Bowland
Street Mission into the Pentecostal League before himself dissociating from
that body. In the official organ of the International Holiness Mission which he
went on to found, Thomas extolled the virtues of the trans-denominational
approach which eschewed what he decried as the "carnal proselytizing element
that endeavours to win those of other churches or denominations." He stated:

> There is nothing that has been more convincing to the outside world and to the
> churches that the Holiness movement is of God than the fact that it has been non-
> sectarian and has enabled men of all creeds and denominations to labour in perfect
> love and harmony with each other...All hands off this sacred ark, and let it be as
> free and untrammelled as the sun that shines, and the welcome rain that falls on all
> alike.[30]

T. M. Jeffreys was another prominent figure keen to celebrate the ecumenical
character of the early Whitsuntide Conventions in Sunderland of which he
stated: "No racial antipathies here!...No denominationalism!" On the contrary,
"Anglicans, Lutherans, and every kind of Nonconformist, all assented in a
common 'Yea and Amen' to the Bible faith which has been once for all
delivered unto the saints."[31] Ernest Moser, a leader of a small congregation in
Essex, boasted that prominent amongst the distinctive features of what he
termed the Pentecostal "New Testament Revival" was that "in this work we
have no man like Wesley, or Moody, or Finney, and certainly we have not got a
General Booth or a Dowie." During an address to the London Whitsuntide
Convention of 1916, he expressed some satisfaction that there was nobody
"trying to make a new organisation, or to get people to follow him."[32] Yet such
idylls proved difficult to sustain in the light of exigencies encountered by this
growing movement. Prominent among these, it will become apparent, was the

---

separate holiness denominations were necessary and those who relied on associations to
carry on the work." See Steven L. Ware, "Restoring the New Testament Church:
Varieties of Restorationism in the Radical Holiness Movement of the Late Nineteenth
and Early Twentieth Centuries," *Pneuma: The Journal of the Society for Pentecostal
Studies* 21.2 (Fall 1999): 243.

[29] "Not Discerning the Lord's Body," *Confidence*, November 1909, 253.

[30] "Sectarianism and Holiness," *The Holiness Mission Journal*, January 1916, 9-10.

[31] T. M. Jeffreys, "Sunderland International Pentecostal Congress: General
Impressions," *Confidence*, June 1909, 128.

[32] E. Moser, "Praying in the Holy Ghost," *Flames of Fire*, July 1916, 3.

fact that, as Gilbert has pointed out, clergy or professional ministers have frequently "diverged sharply" from their lay supporters in their motivations toward ecumenism.[33] The very diversity celebrated by Boddy and others introduced organisational and ideological dynamics which would come to challenge the ethos integral to original *ecclesiolae in ecclesia* aspirations.

Section 3.2: Organisation Disdained but Leadership Required

In 1910 Boddy heralded as evidence of Pentecostalism's "international and inter-denominational" nature the fact that a "Scottish Brother" had appraised him of a profound prejudice that had been overcome by virtue of his involvement. This Scot admitted: "To think that I should ever get good through the Established Church of England which we have always condemned, and yet we are glad to listen to Brother Boddy and join in his meetings."[34] Yet it would transpire that while some, indeed many, may have found that previous antipathies were subsumed in the euphoria of early experiences in Sunderland, ecclesiological fault-lines would resurface as time progressed and challenges were encountered. In a manner which parallels what Wacker has observed to be the case among North American contemporaries, emerging Pentecostals exhibited a "general suspicion of elites."[35] As will become apparent, this was to an extent due to an inclination toward voluntarism in the religious sphere which made for an uneasy co-habitation with what some perceived as Anglicanism's "monopolistic and prescriptive" orientation. A consolidating Pentecostalism did not prove immune to what has been described as a "deep, anti-Establishment animus" which has characterised much of the history of dissent.[36]

This movement found itself requiring direction and leadership, not least on account of what were designated "extremists"[37] within its own ranks, and yet felt its commitment to inspiration, charisma, and a strict associational ethos to have been compromised in the exercise of such leadership. Allied to the perceived need to maintain acceptable norms of belief and practice was the recognition that competent and reliable leadership was pre-requisite to the movement establishing itself on a credible footing which could guarantee its continuance beyond the short-term. In commenting on the years prior to the onset of the First World War, Gee ventured that what he termed "the local Pentecostal testimony" was "often hindered by crude and ungifted ministry."[38] In contemplating these issues, T. M. Jeffreys glanced retrospectively at the experience of the Welsh Revival which, he suggested less than five years after the event, held salutary lessons for the custodians of the Pentecostal message.

---

[33] Gilbert, *The Making of Post-Christian Britain*, 127. This tendency has also been noted by Cox in *The English Churches in a Secular Society*, 260.

[34] "Speaking in Tongues: What is it?" *Confidence*, May 1910, 103-104.

[35] Wacker, "The Almost Chosen People," 146.

[36] Gilbert, *The Making of Post-Christian Britain*, 73.

[37] "The Pentecostal Revival," *Confidence*, March 1912, 62.

[38] Gee, *The Pentecostal Movement*, 99.

In the intervening period "hundreds of new-born babes" had been "going on in the divine life," but this was observed to have taken place largely outside established church boundaries. There had been formed throughout the principality "dozens of little assemblies of these *Plant y Diwyyiad*, 'The Children of the Revival,'" but the "sad part" was that they had no "shepherds." "True," he allowed, "God can keep them, and He has - gloriously. But in many centres deluding spirits have crept in...strange doctrines and self-opinionated notions have possessed many, and sad havoc has 'the wolf' wrought among the little bands."[39]

Jeffreys' perspective has been borne out even in the works of apologists for the Revival, characterised by a recent commentator as "wistful evangelicals" and "latter-day chroniclers of the supernatural."[40] In this vein a contemporary minister had vaunted the fact that the Revival had taken the form of "one immense prayer-meeting from north to south, from east to west...without leaders, or organisation, or direction."[41] A more recent and less effusive analysis has highlighted the deleterious effect of the leaderless ethos which suffused much of the phenomenon in spirit as well as in reality. This was responsible for "the major failing of the revival" which went beyond its propensity for emotional excess, to a more incriminating inability to "pass on the gospel message of salvation to the next generation." Failure to translate significant religious awakening into meaningful and enduring structural expression has elicited the assessment of an unwittingly collusion in the decline of chapel life in twentieth-century Wales.[42] Jeffreys, therefore, demonstrated considerable prescience in his willingness and ability to venture beyond prevalent romantic notions in issuing a forthright expression of grave concern regarding the problematic ecclesiological legacy of the Welsh Revival.

No less a personage that T. B. Barratt, the iconic figure who as "Methodist Missioner" had functioned as the "channel of blessing"[43] for Pentecostal Christianity in England, was at the forefront of the advocacy of what he termed "fellowship between the Pentecostal Centres on practical lines." He, too, was cognizant of the situation that pertained in the aftermath of the Welsh Revival, where "the older Christian communities" had largely "shut out the fresh glorious flow of Revival, grace and power." He detected an exact parallel, stating that "mainly due to the opposition the (Pentecostal) Revival has met from the churches generally," separatism was taking root as Centres were

---

[39] T. M. Jeffreys, "The Cardiff Conference," Special Supplement to *Confidence*, April 1909, 1.

[40] Hayward, "The Transformation of Prophecy," in Taithe and Thornton, eds., *The Power of Inspired Language in History*, 161.

[41] Lewis, *Incidents and Impressions of the Welsh Revival*, 95.

[42] Robert Pope "'The Welsh Religious Revival, 1904-5," *Christianity and History Bulletin* 2 (Summer 2005): 35-37. Other aspects of the ambiguity that surrounded the 'leadership' of the Revival have been highlighted in Geraint Tudor, "Evan Roberts and the 1904-5 Revival," *The Journal of Welsh Religious History* 4 (2004): 80-101.

[43] "Unity, not Uniformity," *Confidence*, March 1911, 60.

"springing up in every country outside the churches."[44] Barratt stated that he had broached this subject with both Boddy and Pastor Paul while at conferences in Hamburg and Sunderland, but added that he had "found that the time was not ripe" for him to formally present his ideas to a wider audience. While not explicitly stated, the evidence suggests that support from "Brother Boddy" was somewhat less forthcoming than from others with whom he shared his ideas. What he went on to propose, albeit ambiguously, was a "spiritual union between all Pentecostal friends" - a suggestion which envisaged the movement progressing beyond what he called the "Evangelical Alliance system," an approach acknowledged to have "worked well"[45] during the incipient phase. Reflective of *reticulate* and *acephalous*[46] structural aspirations, Barratt, like Moser, expressed reluctance to employ "the old cumbersome word 'organisation,'" and instead advocated "a real and brotherly co-operation within and between the various Pentecostal Centres."[47]

It was remarked that the "misuse of titles and Church authority in the past and present history of Christendom" had engendered a "feeling of resentment in most Pentecostal circles to ecclesiastical terms and methods." Yet a pronounced primitivist impulse inspired the interpretation that, in contrast, the "apostolic churches" succeeded in "very easily" divorcing what was termed "perfect freedom from any arbitrary spirit." Barratt, apparently suffused by ecclesiological idealism, if not well-intentioned but outright naivety, ventured that this pattern could be repeated more easily than might be supposed. He held that biblical passages such as 1 Peter 5:2-11, and Hebrews 13:12-21, indicated that Christian leaders were always to "act and speak as standing in their Master's presence, in the spirit of perfect love. If such injunctions were followed, those who possessed a "stern, criticising, harsh spirit" would be readily detected. While "lording it over the brethren" was to be "severely condemned," "due respect and love" would be naturally forthcoming to "acknowledged leaders." Yet the practicality or attainability of such a system was rendered the more questionable by his assertion that in its "pure, simple, and unadulterated" form, the Pentecostal movement was "unlike anything on earth" and, as such, could "not be swallowed up by, or be adjusted to, or merely

---

[44] Barratt, "An Urgent Plea for Charity and Unity," *Confidence*, February 1911, 30.

[45] Barratt, "An Urgent Plea for Charity and Unity," *Confidence*, March 1911, 63. For insights into the means whereby this body sought to exercise a "pan-evangelicalism" function see John Wolffe, "The Evangelical Alliance in the 1840s: An Attempt to Institutionalise Christian Unity," in W. J. Sheils and Diana Wood, eds, in *Studies in Church History*, vol. 23, *Voluntary Religion* (Oxford: Basil Blackwell, 1986), 333-346.

[46] These terms denote seemingly contradictory tendencies whereby religious collectives are composed of "units or affiliated groups of units" which are "linked in various ways" while remaining "essentially 'headless.'" Such contrary aspirations seem to have been widespread among pioneering figures in England. Gerlach and Hine, "Growth and Spread of a Modern Religious Movement," 30, 39.

[47] Barratt, "An Urgent Plea," *Confidence*, February 1911, 30.

tacked on to any human, man-made organisation."[48] A figure who came to prominence in the post-war period wrote of the "danger of organisation by which assemblies are grouped under self-constituted central authority." In an allusion to Colossians 2:19 it was averred that the acceptance or appointment of a "visible representative" amounted to a transgression no less than the adoption of a head "other than Christ."[49]

Arthur Booth-Clibborn, who prior to his association with the Pentecostal movement had imbibed both Quaker, and more significantly, Salvationist ideas and methods,[50] pronounced: "It has been the unanimous testimony of many Christians of long experience and of tried faith, men and women well versed in the Scriptures, that these gatherings have been amongst the most remarkable, the most hallowed, and the most truly Christian that they had ever attended." Clearly impressed by what he encountered in Sunderland and elsewhere, he questioned why any should be derided as "fanatics, fools, or faddists" who merely yearned "to have Christianity exactly as Christ made it." In his estimation, "whoever wishes to have it different - either less or more than that Divine original - sets himself above God."[51] Yet in terms of structural considerations, the quest for the "Divine original" proved frustratingly elusive for the movement as it progressed from its *incipient phase* toward and through *enthusiastic mobilisation*. The suggestions offered by this Pentecostal patriarch for the oversight and functioning of the movement with which he had allied himself proved as quixotic as those ventured by others during this period. He commended the conferences as illustrating "one of the best features of this revival," which was that "it is a world-wide Movement, but not a world-wide organisation."[52] The concept of *organism* was preferred to that of *organisation*,

---

[48] Barratt, "An Urgent Plea," *Confidence*, February 1911, 30.

[49] A. E. Saxby, "Organization, or Organism?" *Things New and Old*, April 1922, 5-7. On Saxby's role and influence see pages 215-216 below.

[50] For details of his early life and influences see James Robinson, "Arthur Booth-Clibborn: Pentecostal Patriarch," *Journal of the European Pentecostal Theological Association*, XXI (2001): 68-79, and *Early Pentecostalism in Ireland*, 49-67. Polhill recorded that the conference he had hosted in London's Holborn Hall at the beginning of 1912 had welcomed Mrs. Booth-Clibborn, *La Marechale* (the Field-Marshall), esteemed daughter of William and Catherine Booth, on the platform. He qualified this by stating that she was there with other "honoured friends" who were "in no sense pledged in all points to the views of the Pentecostal movement," but he welcomed such a "closer drawing together" with others "who believe the vital facts of the Christian religion." See "Editorial," *Flames of Fire*, March 1912, 1. Kate Booth-Clibborn never associated with the Pentecostal cause as explicitly as did her husband. Robinson comments on this in the above article p. 81-82.

[51] Booth-Clibborn, "The Why and How of this Revival," *Confidence*, June 1910, 142-143.

[52] Booth-Clibborn, "The Why and How of this Revival," *Confidence*, June 1910, 144.

as many of the latter were deemed to be conspicuously bereft of "life."[53] It was held that within the ideal *organism*, "every assembly is independent," their "mutual bond" consisting solely of "esteem and confidence." According to Booth-Clibborn such a "bond" could function by means of a "rapid means of transit" or "flow of teaching, admonition and experience...in the person of men and women who are felt to have been sent by Him." Exchanges according to this pattern would allow for "full and free development" whereby a "bouquet of flowers" was formed instead of a "flaring" of merely one variety. A notably sanguine assessment of the prospects for this organic structure was set before *Confidence* readers:

> Each group profits by the experiences which others have made through full and free development. Excesses or abuses are thus more easily detected and corrected. The unity of the Spirit can be kept in the bond of peace. Man-made bonds have hitherto failed. Were this revival to be organised or centralised, it would quickly go wrong, because carnal unity soon becomes a dead uniformity.[54]

It is interesting that this envisaged scenario was related by one who had already participated at the highest levels in, yet become disaffected from, one of the most dynamic religious movements of late Victorian Britain. His relations with the Salvation Army, both familial and organisational, had unravelled largely on account of perceived authoritarian encroachments.[55] In common with others embraced by the Holiness-Pentecostal milieu, he had come to subscribe to the perspective that the Christian Church had "been depending too much upon a cultivated ministry, upon church organisation," and that this was to be replaced by a "full, candid, manifest recognition of the Holy Spirit, and a glad surrender to His control." The outcome would be that the Holy Spirit could then "work within us all the good pleasure of His will."[56] Booth-Clibborn stated that "the hand of God" was already "manifest in the instruments he has chosen to be in the forefront of in this revival." He ventured: "Nothing was more evident than the disappearance (if an Irishman may coin an Irishism) of the two Presidents of the Conferences, so far as they were personally concerned."[57] These references to Boddy, Polhill, and the gatherings they oversaw, concur with

---

[53] "Session of the International Council at Amsterdam," *Confidence*, December 1912, 284.

[54] Booth-Clibborn, "The Why and How of this Revival," *Confidence*, June 1910, 145.

[55] On this disjuncture with the Salvation Army which occurred in 1902 see Pamela J. Walker, *Pulling the Devil's Kingdom Down: The Salvation Army in Victorian Britain* (Berkeley and Los Angeles: University of California Press, 2001), 236. For a more partial version of these events which displays little sympathy with Booth-Clibborn or his wife, *La Marechale*, see Arch R. Wiggins, *The History of the Salvation Army*, vol. 4, *1886-1904* (London: Thomas Nelson & Sons Ltd., 1964), 367.

[56] "The Executive of the Godhead," *Flames of Fire*, May 1914, 3.

[57] Booth-Clibborn, "The Why and How of this Revival," *Confidence*, June 1910, 145.

Wacker's summation of the North American outlook:

> The Holy Ghost ran everything. Of course certain men and women seemed to
> manage things. But appearances were deceiving. In reality the figures who stood
> behind the pulpits, or edited the periodicals, or planned the meetings were only
> yielded instruments - vessels, they liked to call themselves - awaiting the Lord's
> bidding. In saints' eyes autocrats and bureaucrats filled the ranks of other
> traditions, but not theirs. The revival had come into existence without human
> direction and, thankfully, operated that way ever since. Here, as elsewhere, we
> dare not take Pentecostals solely at their word...[58]

The juxtaposition of a leadership which disappears with optimal orchestration
and organisation indicates the paradoxical nature, not just of what Booth-
Clibborn termed an "Irishism," but the inner convolutions inherent in this
aspect of the fledgling Pentecostal outlook. These contradictions were in no
sense merely incongruous or beyond logic as "the revival's torchbearers"
succeeded in harnessing them to notable effect. Wacker has remarked on the
transformation of coercive power into a moral authority which allowed "Holy
Ghost officials" to persuade and inspire others to act, ostensibly at least, of their
own accord.[59] Yet it would transpire that such sublimation of power was not
always achievable, nor could the tensions and contradictions inherent in this
Pentecostal logic be sustained indefinitely. The suggestion that "all must be
allowed to act in accordance with their own personal view" without being
"criticized, judged, or condemned by others," while at the same time "persons
chosen by God...to strengthen the faith of Christians and build up the Church of
God" be accorded due recognition,[60] was fraught with potential for conflict.
And this potential would be realised in various ways as English Pentecostalism
moved beyond its *incipient phase*.

Section 3.3: Exertions of Censure and Power

William Oliver Hutchinson and the Apostolic Faith Connection

It has already been pointed out, that despite having been recognised as a trans-
local leader within the emerging network, William Oliver Hutchinson
summarily vanished from the pages of *Confidence* magazine after it was
reported that he had addressed a conference in Kilsyth alongside Smith
Wigglesworth at the beginning of 1911.[61] Hutchinson's effective disappearance,
although never explained or made explicit to the wider Pentecostal
constituency, certainly not to the readers of Boddy or Polhill's periodicals, was
the outcome of a definitive exercise of leadership in the face of perceived
heterodox tendencies. It is only in Kent White's deeply partisan account of the

---

[58] Wacker, *Early Pentecostals and American Culture*, 141.

[59] Wacker, *Early Pentecostals and American Culture*, 141.

[60] Barratt, "An Urgent Plea," *Confidence*, March 1911, 63-64.

[61] "The Kilsyth Conference," *Confidence*, January 1911, 17.

emergence of the Apostolic Faith Church that his leader's separation from what might be deemed the Boddy/Polhill axis of the movement was directly addressed. While *The Word of God Coming Again*, written in 1919, could neither be considered a work of scholarship nor a classic of the biographical genre, in common with a body of writing undertaken by former associates and admirers of ministers and leaders,[62] it conveys not just useful information but a sense of the character and vitality of a religious culture not available elsewhere. It makes apparent that, as befitted the position he had attained in the wider movement, Hutchinson had been invited to address the London Conference which was hosted by Polhill at Holborn Hall toward the end of May 1911. It transpired that the content of the message he sought to deliver was deemed so unacceptable that within a short space of time he was requested to vacate the platform. According to White the bemused would-be preacher was only later informed that exception had been taken to his contention that "the word coming through the gifts of the Holy Ghost was the word of God." Despite the fact that "good men" had been in charge and that the movement had been the channel of "great blessing in the beginning," spiritual "bondage" had been encountered as those in charge had, according to the Hutchinson perspective, "failed to break from the old dead forms."[63]

The advance notification of this conference issued by Polhill had stated that while it was "earnestly desired" that the meetings be "in the freedom of the Holy Spirit," those who attended were expected to "yield to the ruling of the chair, should it at any time be deemed necessary."[64] In the case of Hutchinson this had indeed been deemed necessary but the construction advanced by Kent was that such intervention involved a retention of "dead forms," a hindering of "the Spirit's operations," and a lack of "faith for the operation of the gifts, beyond the mere sign of tongues." While White acknowledged that "disturbing persons in meetings…had to be controlled," to his mind a less commendable exercise of authority was at the root of this ostensible spiritual stultification. It was retrospectively recorded that an ecstatic utterance in Hutchinson's circle some time prior to the Holborn Conference had conveyed the intelligence that "there would be a blood line of division drawn, but it was not then known what

---

[62] On the utility of such writings see Helmstadter, "Orthodox Nonconformity," in Paz, ed., *Nineteenth-Century English Religious Traditions*, 77-78.

[63] White, *The Word of God*, 54. It is of interest to note on that, according to their official web-site, the Apostolic Faith Church retains a single building in Britain, the original Emmanuel Mission Hall which is now known to members as "the Root." They do claim, however, that others in unspecified parts of England, Scotland and Wales remain "faithful to the vision of the Word come again." Reiterating the verdict delivered on the Boddy/Polhill axis of the movement in the aftermath of the disjuncture of 1911, it is stated that this "Word" continues to lead them "onward in a depth of vision that is unparalleled in any of the known Pentecostal and mainstream churches." See http://www.afc-bmth.supanet.com/AbouttheAFC.htm.

[64] "The London Conference," *Confidence*, May 1911, 108.

meaning God had in it, and many wondered."[65] It could be surmised that portents of this ideological rupture had been foreseen by both sides and that this was the manner in which what was perceived to be inevitable had been broached in Bournemouth. This development also illuminates concerns expressed by leaders at the 1909 Sunderland Convention that the "workings of the sub-conscious mind" were too often apparent in prophetic messages, and that the exercise of vigilant "scriptural discrimination" was becoming increasingly necessary.[66]

The exclusion and resultant sense of isolation was initially keenly felt by Hutchinson, but toward the end of 1911 he appears to have reached something of a personal resolution. His readership was not to be denied a rationale for the unprecedented situation in which they found themselves, and while no specific individuals were identified - to do so would surely have been superfluous - the areas of contention were highlighted in broad or perhaps more accurately spiritual terms. In a report of the gathering which was held on Sunday 5th, November 1911, to mark the third anniversary of the official opening of the Emmanuel Mission Hall, Hutchinson stated:

> The remembrance of the opening meeting is still with us...The formal ways, as are usual on such occasions were left behind, and bless the Lord. The Spirit has led us in this free way ever since...We have passed through great testings on believing the Spoken Word. A training which shall never be forgotten. God wrought something in us then that will stand the fire.[67]

He continued by means of *captivity narrative*[68] to advance his perspective on this rupture within the hitherto cohesive Pentecostal constituency:

> From the beginning we have stood for 'tongues' being the sign of the baptism and had sweet fellowship with many who now, sad to say, have receded from the 'word' on this important point because of man's experience and circumstances. In our first year opposition to this truth came from brethren outside the Pentecostal blessing; but, lo! today we see a change, and strong contention has come in amongst those who were at one time in unity with us on this.[69]

Hutchinson, who found himself both advantageously buoyed by strong

---

[65] White, *The Word of God*, 53-55.

[66] "Sunderland International Pentecostal Congress," *Confidence*, June 1909, 130.

[67] "Into Our Fourth Year," *Showers of Blessing*, no. 8, n.d., 6.

[68] Stuart A. Wright, "Exploring the Factors that Shape the Apostate Role," in David G. Bromley, ed., *The Politics of Religious Apostasy: The Role of Apostates in the Transformation of Religious Movements* (Westport, CT, and London: Praeger, 1998), 97-98. Gerlach and Hine have commented on the cohesive potential of a *persecution psychology* as well as the observable recurrence of *positive fatalism* among religious idealists. See "Growth and Spread of a Modern Religious Movement," 35-37. For further evidences of this see also pages 204-206 and 225-226.

[69] "Into Our Fourth Year," *Showers of Blessing*, no. 8, n.d., 6.

convictions and freed from former constraints, set about the construction of what in sociological terms would be described as an alternative "religious constellation."[70] This *Lebenswelt* professed its own "supernatural legitimation" and thereby claimed the "transcendent allegiance" of adherents, in the process establishing itself as a separate entity or sub-grouping within British Pentecostalism.[71] The assembly in Bournemouth had been newly designated as the Apostolic Faith Church in May 1911 and before the end of the year there were six assemblies in Scotland, eleven in England, and thirteen in Wales in what Weeks describes as "active fellowship" with their Bournemouth mentor.[72] From the Apostolic Faith perspective these assemblies "joined together in brotherly fellowship in a way that God recognised…on the order and plan of His Church for the last days."[73] The links and relationships that had been forged, primarily within the various forums established by Alexander Boddy, formed the basis for the cooperation and development of common methods and practices for those of similar inclination. It was, for instance, at the Whitsuntide Convention of 1909 that Hutchinson first met future collaborator Andrew Murdoch, an elder of the independent evangelical congregation which met at Kilsyth's Westport Hall.[74] It could be stated that the network which functioned under Boddy's auspices had not only fulfilled its intended purpose but had also unwittingly come to subvert itself by facilitating the generation of what would prove to be an additional, and indeed rival, strand of Pentecostal expression.

It is certainly the case that within a short space of time an alternative London Conference was established. This was held for the first time in Arthur Street Chapel between 28-31st of May 1912, and it seems apposite that according to the account provided in *Showers of Blessing*, the event was opened by the delivery of an ecstatic message in tongues which was accompanied by an interpretation.[75] Addressing what can only have appeared a depleted body of delegates in comparison with previous Pentecostal conferences, Pastor Hill of Swansea spoke of "two religious ways" and extolled the benefits of the narrow path which was inhabited by "very few." He likened their situation to that of Gideon, whose army became truly effective only when it had been drastically whittled down.[76] It was at this gathering in 1914 that D. P. Williams and

---

[70] Berger, *The Social Reality of Religion*, 117.

[71] Wilson, *The Social Dimension of Sectarianism: Sects and New Religious Movements in Contemporary Society* (Oxford: Clarendon Press, 1992), 179. For a flavour of the rationale offered in support of a separatist position see Hutchinson, "Concerning This Sect," *Showers of Blessing*, June 1915, 2-3, and Pastor Williams article "Out and Out Separation," in the same issue, 5-6.

[72] Weeks, "A History of the Apostolic Church," 42.

[73] White, *The Word of God*, 63.

[74] On this see "Kilsyth Pentecostal Conference," *Confidence*, December 1910, 292; "The Whitsuntide Conference at Kilsyth," *Showers of Blessing*, June 1915, 7-8; Worsfold, *The Origins*, 114-115.

[75] "London Conference," *Showers of Blessing*, no. 9, n.d., 1.

[76] Pastor Hill, "Our God is a Consuming Fire," *Showers of Blessing*, no. 9, n.d., 2.

Andrew Murdoch were "called" and instated as apostles to lead and oversee the congregations in Wales and Scotland respectively. These exalted positions would only be presided over by Hutchinson himself who functioned as the "Chief Apostle,"[77] the entire process attesting to a harnessing of the pneumatic for the purpose of establishing an apostolic ecclesiology. According to White, "Pastor H. in no sense pressed himself forward into the office" but was instead "chosen and set in office through the operation of the gifts of the Holy Ghost moving and speaking through a period of 18 months or more."[78] Reflecting an unmollified perspective on this methodology which became characteristic of mainstream or middle-ground Pentecostal thinking, George Jeffreys later denounced both Winton, Bournemouth, and Penygroes, South Wales, as proponents of a "pernicious system."[79]

Cases such as the censure and exclusion of Hutchinson underscore the veracity of the observation that, despite protestations to the contrary, "strong, determined, clear-eyed leaders orchestrated the revival from first to last."[80] From this juncture onwards pre-denominational bodies such as the Pentecostal Missionary Union and the International Consultative Council, accorded themselves executive powers while remaining largely unaccountable to the wider Pentecostal public. The latter, whose English members were predictably Boddy and Polhill, declared that "as an Advisory Council, it must be self-elected, and not subject to the control of votes of Assemblies."[81] While the operations of this body would not survive the First World War, the similarly constituted P.M.U.[82] would exert a more durable influence in the English context, albeit one which came to prove problematic for some. Although unseemly machinations were again largely withheld from the readerships of Pentecostal periodicals, tensions and resentments were undeniably aroused with respect of its *migratory elite*.[83]

Misses Elkington and Jones

The manner in which a controversy which surrounded the Misses Elkington and

---

[77] Weeks, "A History of the Apostolic Church," 49.

[78] White, *The Word of God*, 64

[79] G. Jeffreys, *Pentecostal Rays: The Baptism and Gifts of the Holy Spirit* (London: Elim Publishing Company, 1933), 172-173. Similar views were expressed by an erstwhile devotee of Hutchinson who defected and went on to become a teacher of some prominence in the Elim Pentecostal Church. See William G. Hathaway, *The Gifts of the Holy Spirit in the Church* (1933; repr. London: Benhill Church Press, 1963), 64-72, and *A Sound from Heaven* (London: Victory Press, 1947), 76-77, 82-86.

[80] Wacker, *Early Pentecostals and American Culture*, 141.

[81] "Declaration of the International Pentecostal Consultative Council - Paragraph II," *Confidence*, December 1912, 277.

[82] See "Principles of the Pentecostal Missionary Union for Great Britain and Ireland - Paragraph 3: Constitution" (Unpublished manuscript, DGC).

[83] Martin, *Sociology of English Religion*, 109.

Jones was dealt with is instructive not only with regard to the inner workings of the machinery of pre-denominational Pentecostal bureaucracy, but also for its encapsulation of a disavowal of perceived extremism in favour of an option for moderation respectability. When these ladies, two of the P.M.U.'s five missionaries in India, returned home during 1919, it was announced that after a time of rest they would "be very glad to speak for India and the work of the Lord there." The Pentecostal network was informed that Centres wishing to arrange for a visit from them should contact T. H. Mundell.[84] Their reports and correspondences had been regularly published by both Boddy and Polhill[85] and it would appear that these two young women had been among the most prized, certainly the most visible, candidates working for the P.M.U. Yet early the following year they found themselves summoned "by special arrangement" to a meeting of the Union's Executive Council whose members were greatly perturbed about a strain of quasi-mystical teaching which these missionaries had come to espouse.[86]

Mundell issued a communication to both ladies then residing at 157 Darnly Road, Gravesend, on 26 February 1920. In this he requested them to be at the Women's Training Home at 7 Eton Road, Haverstock Hill, at 4 p.m. on Saturday 28th of that month. It was recorded that they had become "influenced by so-called 'Bride teaching.'" When questioned Miss Elkington and Miss Jones "expressed belief in seeking and experiencing physical manifestations from, and asking Christ Jesus our Lord to kiss them, which they said He had done." The Council promptly condemned "this wrong and unscriptural doctrine and practice" which it was feared, if persisted in, would lead to "disastrous results."[87] These missionaries were evidently gravitating toward a form of *affective mysticism* which explicitly or implicitly describes the union of Christ and the soul in terms of the marriage, or even the sexual encounter, between bride and bridegroom. Such nuptial imagery has typically found its principal inspiration in the interpretation of the Song of Songs as an allegory of the Christian message and has been identified as a constant category of women's, or more generally, feminine mystical experience.[88] Misses Elkington and Jones were to discover that this was not a category which would be countenanced by the ideolects of the movement to which they had given devoted service.

A resolution which was proposed by Polhill, and seconded by Mundell, resulted in the declaration that unless these sisters were prepared to "renounce"

---

[84] "The Pentecostal Missionary Union," *Confidence*, July-September 1919, 50.

[85] A selection of their letters and reports are to be found in "The Pentecostal Missionary Union," *Confidence*, February 1911, 45; August 1911, 190; February 1915, 38; "Tidings from Tibet and Other Lands," *Flames of Fire*, December 1916, 4-5. Polhill spent "a few pleasant days" with them "in the heart of the United Provinces" during 1914 as reported in "Tidings from Mr. Cecil Polhill," *Flames of Fire*, March 1914, 2-3.

[86] P.M.U. Council Minutes of 28 February 1920, Book II, 152.

[87] P.M.U. Council Minutes of 28 February 1920, Book II, 153.

[88] Christina Mazzoni, *Saint Hysteria: Neurosis, Mysticism, and Gender in European Culture* (New York and London: Cornell University Press, 1996), 6.

this *Bride-teaching* as "error," the Council would be compelled to ask them to resign their positions. Faced with this prospect, Elkington and Jones demonstrated a single-minded resilience in their express determination "not to renounce or give up...truths which God had shown them, nor would they consent to resign." It was recorded that "thereupon the Council notified them that they would from today cease to be connected with, or represent, the P.M.U." The fact that they were to receive three months allowance and £2 toward their travel expenses from Eastbourne was the only concession that would be forthcoming.[89] The swift and seemingly draconian measures taken by Polhill and the other Council members against two of their hitherto most approbated missionary candidates, undoubtedly owed much to a fear of a particular manifestation of hysteria which has latterly been described as "the most 'popular' neurosis of the European *fin-de-siecle*."[90] In the eventuality that this be construed as a demonstration of misogyny on the part of Pentecostal patriarchs, it will become apparent that the incidence of *affective mysticism* was by no means limited to Pentecostal women, nor did it meet with more sympathy where it found male advocates. The perceived heterodox tendencies of those to whom considerable autonomy had been granted - and not gender considerations - formed the primary basis of this act of censure and exclusion.

It is the case that in the aftermath of the sundering of relations, Mundell responded to Boddy's request that he revise the list of acting P.M.U. missionaries. The Secretary informed Boddy that he had "struck out the names of Misses Elkington and Jones and added the name of our Honorary Auditor." The latter was described as "an earnest Christian" who had five or six brothers then serving as missionaries with the C.M.S. This pedigree, while not explicitly Pentecostal in orientation, denoted an individual of sympathetic and equable disposition. As this man, Herbert Cox, was to only receive "an Honorary fee of £2:2:0" by way of non-remunerative recompense, Mundell had "arranged with him that his name should appear in *Confidence*." That Cox embodied a preferential contrast to the undesirable tendency that had been so swiftly cauterised was rendered more apparent by Mundell's utterance: "It is difficult to make any special reference to the Misses Elkington and Jones, and it may be well to say nothing about them in *Confidence*. I have written to Mr. Boyce giving him particulars of why they have left the Mission."[91] While the next issue of *Confidence* proclaimed an esteemed "Honorary Auditor" in the form of a chartered accountant of the London firm Woodman, Cox & Co.,[92] the dismissal of two female missionaries went unannounced and, it would appear to have been hoped by the leadership, unnoticed by the wider Pentecostal constituency.

---

[89] P.M.U. Council Minutes of 28 February 1920, Book II, 153-154.

[90] Mazzoni, *Neurosis, Mysticism and Gender*, 5.

[91] P.M.U. Correspondence, Letter from Mundell to Mr. Boddy, 19 April 1920, 964.

[92] "The Pentecostal Missionary Union," *Confidence*, April-June 1920, 28.

The Suppression of Bracknell Teaching

It must be pointed out that the error to which these lady missionaries had developed a fatal attraction had been previously espoused in Pentecostal circles, and their summary dismissal owed much to the previous discomfiture it had generated. It had been announced during mid-1915 that Smith Wigglesworth along with John Leech, K.C., of Dublin and Ernest Moser of Southsea, had been appointed to the P.M.U. Council. This development had occurred in the wake of the resignation of "Messrs. J. S. Breeze, T. Myerscough and W. H. Sandwith."[93] It is probable that few who were not already aware of the circumstances that had precipitated these resignations would have ventured to put a negative construction on this change of personnel, but it had certainly not come about without considerable acrimony attendant upon a serious divergence of opinion. The nature of this protracted process, fascinating not merely because of the ideological issues involved, but also for the insights it affords into the structural functioning at this stage of the movements evolution, is worthy of consideration.

Mundell was informed in a missive dated 2 September, 1914, that "after waiting upon the Lord for guidance," a group of local leaders had felt prompted to "personally" invite him and others to "a gathering of saints" that would take place at Oswaldkirk, Bracknell, Berkshire shortly thereafter. This seemingly select gathering[94] would, it was hoped, "search the Word together, under the guidance of the Holy Spirit, touching the near coming of the Lord Jesus Christ, in view of the War now in progress in Europe, to the end that we may hear His voice concerning the preparation necessary for translation." This final oblique comment was somewhat compounded by the inclusion of a verse attributed to Canticles 2:13: "Arise, my love, my fair one, and come away,"[95] the significance of which would only subsequently become apparent. Ensuing developments would eloquently testify to the veracity of the asseveration that "the concept of individual access to the spiritual source of authority, when taken seriously, tends to prevent organizational solidarity and centralized control."[96]

It would transpire that less than a fortnight after the conference in Bracknell, concerns were being voiced with regard to the doctrinal rectitude of some of what was propagated during the event. There followed a series of communications and exchanges between some of the organisers who had been implicated in, or tainted by, perceived infringements of orthodoxy, and members of the P.M.U. Executive Council. James Breeze, who appears to have acted as principal interlocutor for the offending party, was at this time listed

---

[93] "The Pentecostal Missionary Union," *Confidence*, June 1915, 116.

[94] Significantly this event was never announced in advance, or subsequently reported on in *Confidence* magazine or *Flames of Fire*.

[95] Letter of James S. Breeze, W. H. Sandwith, Rowland Sandwith and Max Wood Moorhead, to T. H. Mundel, 2 September 1914.

[96] Gerlach and Hine, "Growth and Spread of a Modern Religious Movement," 26.

among "other acting members" of the Council. It is also the case that W. H. Sandwith functioned as "Hon. Treasurer," while his wife fulfilled the role of "Missionary Box Secretary."[97] Having been requested by Polhill to meet to discuss the, as yet unspecified, but evidently problematic issue, Breeze stated that they "had the feeling to decline to meet the Council in the way suggested." He instead proposed that those concerned convene "as Brethren in an unofficial way" in a manner which would enable them to "confer together on the subject."[98] The request that both parties meet at Mrs. Cantell's, a neutral venue which it was hoped might facilitate the discussion of "matters in a friendly spirit,"[99] was made merely days in advance of a questioning of the validity and desirability of the Executive Council's casting itself in the role of arbiter of matters doctrinal. Breeze went on to express deeply-felt concerns which culminated in a stark warning:

> I have felt that if the Council allows itself to become a body or board to which reference concerning theological doctrines may be made, that its character as a purely missionary union is destroyed, and that if doctrine is to be adjudged by it and its decisions are to be accepted by the general Pentecostal public of this country, it even becomes possible for it to fall into the same condition, and produce the same result, as did the 'General' Oversight amongst the earlier Brethren. This body ultimately exercised a dangerous form of popery...which led to numerous divisions.[100]

In conjunction with the others on whose behalf he engaged in this series of exchanges, Breeze had come to form the opinion that Polhill had arrogated to himself a role and function akin to Grand Inquisitor,[101] pitting himself against both their perceived transgression and their personal autonomy. He stated that this body was originally construed as "interdenominational" and suggested that other contentious matters such as the practice of "infant sprinkling" would, if canvassed, not find unanimity among Council members. In the light of this he appealed for latitude, and conveyed the willingness of his party to meet Mundell in the company of Polhill and Small in such a manner that matters

---

[97] "The Pentecostal Missionary Union," *Confidence*, September 1914, 176.

[98] Letter of James S. Breeze to T. H. Mundell, 29 October 1914.

[99] Letter of James S. Breeze to T. H. Mundell, 2 November 1914.

[100] Letter of James S. Breeze to Cecil Polhill, 7 November 1914. Breeze elsewhere stated that he "came into fellowship" with the Open Brethren "about 1883-1884" and that he spent "about twenty-five years ministering the Word among them." He exhibits a fascinating spiritual eclecticism in his ready acknowledgement of Baptist and Keswick influences prior to a "struggle" in the quest for Pentecostal experience. See "The Testimony of James S. Breeze," *Confidence*, December 1912, 272-275. An overview of the difficulties that arose within the early Brethren movement with the advent of centralising tendencies is to be found in Peter L. Embley, "The Early Development of the Plymouth Brethren," in Wilson, ed., *Patterns of Sectarianism*, 213-243.

[101] For more see for instance "The Legend of the Grand Inquisitor," in *The Gospel in Dostoyevsky* (Farmington, PA: Plough Publishing House, 1996), 21-37.

could be "talked over in a friendly spirit, but not under the aegis of the P.M.U. Council."[102] Beyond these "structural strains,"[103] Breeze also expressed a degree of chagrin that those involved in the Bracknell conference had been condemned and portrayed as offenders for "innocently using an expression which is common amongst deeply taught children of God throughout the Church's history." Employing the precedence of received Christian spirituality he stated:

> You will find this personal reception of the Lord Jesus Christ as Bridegroom constantly referred to in the writings of John Tauler, Madame Guyon, Nicholas of Basle, Henry Suso (some of whose hymns I have no doubt have appealed to your spiritual sense in a wonderful way) and other writers, so that it is by no means a modern expression...Mrs. Frances Bevan in her translation of the works of Tauler, Suso and Nicholas of Basle, etc. does not hesitate to refer to it in this way, and yet her writings and hymns are accepted and delighted in by multitudes of spiritually minded people.[104]

It is worthy of mention that this seemingly unusual appreciation of mystical writers, while never commonplace, was far from unique in early Pentecostal literature. Both Alexander Boddy and A. E. Saxby reprinted extracts from the writings of Madam Guyon,[105] and in the first issue of the *Elim Evangel* the benefits of "the Power of Stillness" were extolled while being attributed to "an old medieval message." The writer described his encounter with this emphasis as "one of the turning points of my life," and the second issue of the periodical also sought to inspire meditative reflection, prominently featuring a spiritual aphorism derived from "the words of a medieval saint."[106] These elements are suggestive of further indebtedness to the Wesleyan tradition whose founder's formation "so largely involved absorption in spiritual writers, rather than traditional theologians." John Wesley had been unquestionably "drawn to an

---

[102] Letter from James S. Breeze to T. H. Mundell, 11 November 1914. Harry Small of East Wemyss had been among the seven original members of the P.M.U. Executive Council which convened for the first time in All Saints' vicarage early in 1909. See "The Pentecostal Missionary Union," *Confidence*, January 1909, 13.

[103] John Wilson, "The Sociology of Schism," in Michael Hill, ed., *A Sociological Yearbook of Religion in Britain*, vol. 4 (London: SCM Press, 1971), 5.

[104] Letter from James S. Breeze to T. H. Mundell, 16 November 1914. Breeze is here referring to Francis Bevan, *Three Friends of God: Records from the Lives of John Tauler, Nicholas of Basle, Henry Suso*, 2nd ed. (London: James Nisbet & Co. 1889). For more on Bevan see http://www.stempublishing.com/hymns/biographies/bevan.html.

[105] "The Divine Movements: An Extract from 'The Book of Jeremiah' by Madame Guyon," *Confidence*, August 1912, 186-187; "Living by the Moment," *Things New and Old*, January 1922, 3.

[106] A. B. Simpson, "The Power of Stillness," *Elim Evangel*, December 1919, 7; *Elim Evangel*, March 1920, 21.

affective, emotional spirituality,"[107] and his extensive devotional reading had taken him into "remote territories" and rendered him "intimately acquainted with writers such as Tauler, Madame Guyon, and Brother Lawrence.[108] It has been observed of Wesley's *Christian Library*, which popularised an array of spiritual writings for preachers as well as members of the early Methodist societies, that "all the strands of the religion of the heart movements were represented."[109] Those who sought to propagate what was commonly termed "Biblical Holiness," Methodism's "grand *depositum* of spiritual truth"[110] in the latter half of the nineteenth century, had also transmitted this tendency in devotional writings such as Hannah Whitall Smith's *The Christian's Secret of a Happy Life* and Andrew Murray's *With Christ in the School of Prayer*.[111] Breeze certainly felt a degree of security in claiming a lineage and affinity with this strand of devotional writing. So confident was he in the correctness of what had been espoused at Bracknell that he went on to suggest the possibility that in relation to ongoing contentions, "the enemy" was seeking to thwart "a deeper line of truth."[112] As another aspect of this *whistleblower narrative*,[113] the logic which had previously been advanced on behalf of the Pentecostal cause generally was redeployed in this fraternal controversy:

> Just as Satan attacked the Pentecostal movement on ethical lines and in fact has done to almost every other movement for the deepening of the spiritual life, so he is attacking this in the same way and seeking to besmirch and dishonour what God the Holy Spirit has been and is doing...As the truth of the baptism in the Holy Spirit did not begin with the leaders of Christian thought but with humble, and to others, the most unlikely of believers, so now God is taking one here and another there and bringing them into a realisation of union with Christ...and it would be

---

[107] David Lyle Jeffrey, "Introduction: The Age of Wesley," in Lyle Jeffrey, ed., *English Spirituality in the Age of Wesley* (Grand Rapids, MI.: Eerdmans, 1994), 30. See also Gordon S. Wakefield, *Methodist Devotion:The Spiritual Life in the Methodist Tradition, 1791-1945* (London: Epworth Press, 1966), 25-32.

[108] Davies, *Worship and Theology in England*, vol. III, *From Watts and Wesley to Maurice, 1690-1850*, 185.

[109] Ted A. Campbell, *The Religion of the Heart: A Study of European Religious Life in the Seventeenth and Eighteenth Centuries* (Columbia, S.C.: University of South Carolina Press, 1991), 124.

[110] Dieter, "Wesleyan-Holiness Aspects of Pentecostal Origins," in Synan ed., *Aspects of Pentecostal-Charismatic Origins*, 60-61.

[111] Hannah Whitall Smith, *The Christian's Secret of a Happy Life* (London: Morgan and Scott, 1875), and Andrew Murray, *With Christ in the School of Prayer: Thoughts on the Training for the Ministry of Intercession* (London: James Nisbet & Co., 1888).

[112] Letter from James S. Breeze to T. H. Mundell, 9 December 1914.

[113] David G. Bromley, "The Social Construction of Contested Exit Roles: Defectors, Whistleblowers and Apostates," in Bromley, ed., *The Politics of Religious Apostasy*, 32-33.

very serious indeed to in any way interfere with it.[114]

The inclination observed to beset spiritual purists which has been termed "the quest for a smaller and purer communion,"[115] appears to have here been accentuated in the face of perceived bureaucratic encroachment. Not only was an uncritical and unanalytical attitude characterised by "implicit faith and trust" among the "simple," the "childlike" and "the willing," held as the ideal, but the potential incursion of divine wrath for those who would withstand or "fight against God," was invoked as a deterrent against further opposition or investigation.[116] It is interesting to note that from a movement of renewal which had itself been, and continued to be, critical of the spiritual condition of the wider Christian world, tendencies began to emerge which sought to assert the need for further revelation and renovation. For some the innovators had, by the onset of the First World War, become institutionalized, and an increasingly sterile and critical authority-circle were held to be in danger of threatening further progress. Wacker's observations regarding the disjuncture with Pentecostalism's Holiness antecedents are applicable in this context. Early Pentecostals were among those who "refused to countenance any finite level of spiritual achievement as sufficient," and instead urged believers to satiate their spiritual appetites by striving for "an ever-deeper walk with Christ." It is perhaps not surprising, therefore, that the inculcation of spiritual rapacity would redound to the vexation of the leaders of the movement as they sought to negotiate the "complex process of self-definition and legitimation."[117]

Nothing of the disagreement that surrounded *Bracknell teaching* was mentioned or even intimated in the pages of *Confidence* magazine. An uneasy resolution arrived in the form of a letter dated 20 May, 1915, which conveyed the simultaneous resignations of those who had been implicated, along with that of Thomas Myerscough of Preston. Two specific reasons were identified for the fact that the correspondents were "not in accord," nor could they see a way to agree with decisions that had been taken by the Council. They were evidently unhappy that students at the Training Homes were attending a Church of England. It was alleged that for some this "went against their conscience," and it was held that it betrayed a "growing denominational bias" which could not "but have far-reaching effects." A further point of disagreement related to an executive insistence that two missionaries, "Messrs. Corry and Clelland,"

---

[114] Letter from James S. Breeze to T. H. Mundell, 9 December 1914.

[115] Stunt, *Radical Evangelicals*, 312.

[116] Letter from James S. Breeze to T. H. Mundell, 9 December 1914.

[117] Wacker, "Evangelical Responses to Pentecostalism," 505, 527, 507. This interpretation is corroborated by Ware's observations regarding "spiritual" and "ecclesiastical" forms of restorationism, and tensions that arise from their pursuit. See "Varieties of Restorationism," 243. For some of the structural tensions associated with religious voluntarism see Roger E. Olson, "Free Church Ecclesiology and Evangelical Spirituality: A Unique Compatibility," in Stackhouse, ed., *Evangelical Ecclesiology*, 167-173.

return to Abbottabad in India where they had encountered significant difficulties. It is perhaps not surprising that the correspondents, having begun by offering particular incidences for dissatisfaction, proceeded to announce a more abiding cause for disquiet. These developments were deemed at variance "with the original purpose for which the Union was called into existence," and it was held that this structural entity was becoming an "organization under which private judgement is not permissible."[118]

Smith Wigglesworth and Pentecostal Officialdom

These heartfelt protestations are reminiscent of sentiments expressed by Smith Wigglesworth after his tenure in Pentecostal officialdom came to an abrupt and evidently premature end. It was announced in the June 1915 issue of *Confidence* that Wigglesworth, along with Leech and Moser, had been appointed to the P.M.U. Council "on the resignation of Messrs. J. S. Breeze, T. Myerscough, and W. H. Sandwith."[119] In the light of what had ensued, Wigglesworth appears to have been considered a stalwart and reliable proponent, while it could not be claimed from a perusal of minutes of meetings and deliberations that he was one of the more vociferous, prolific, or industrious members of the Council. Percy has written of exertions of charismatic leadership which deliberately seek to avoid a tendency toward routinization and mere bureaucratic power. In such situations there is a concerted effort to eschew the perception that leadership is static, while the religious community is dynamic. It could be surmised that considerations of this nature were operative in the appointment of Wigglesworth in the light of the role he had increasingly come to fulfil across the movement. While others, such as Polhill, might be regarded as leaders "*around* which power revolved" instead of "*through* which it flowed"[120] there was little danger of any such perception where Smith Wigglesworth was concerned. Yet this dynamic, however advantageous for the collective functioning of the components of the movement, would itself prove difficult to sustain. On the afternoon of Tuesday 16th of November 1920, Cecil Polhill presided over the Council meeting that convened at the Women's Training Home at 7 Eton Road, Haverstock Hill, Hampstead, London. When the Treasurer's report had been approved, Polhill proceeded to regretfully inform the Council of the resignation of a member of more than five years. He read the following terse statement: "I wish to resign from the Council of the P. M. U., Smith Wigglesworth." Polhill went on to appraise them of the fact that this step had been taken in the light of circumstances "which he thought it would be well not to go into." Both he and the Hon. Secretary had given grave consideration to the circumstances alluded

---

[118] Letter of James S. Breeze, W. H. Sandwith and Thomas Myerscough to T. H. Mundell, 20 May 1915.

[119] "The Pentecostal Missionary Union," *Confidence*, June 1915, 116.

[120] Percy, *Power and the Church: Ecclesiology in an Age of Transition* (London: Cassell, 1998), 11.

to, and were of like opinion that this was the appropriate outcome. No objection was raised by any of the other Council members present.[121]

It is suggested that the laconic nature of this communication owed less to Wigglesworth's literary capacities, than to the manner in which it has been elicited. No further deliberation or discussion appears to have taken place on this matter in the P.M.U. forum, much less in *Confidence* or the other periodicals, and it is only personal correspondence between the individuals immediately concerned that reveals the nature of the circumstances that had been decorously avoided. Wigglesworth had travelled with a Mr. Sam Broom of Leeds,[122] and it was believed to have been from him that notions of *spiritual affinity* were imbibed.[123] This notion espoused the possibility of a special relationship between members of the opposite sex, and while these were held to be noetic and essentially Platonic in nature, the mere potential for immoral behaviour prompted apprehension and the vehement disapproval of Pentecostal leaders.[124] Polhill initially received a letter accusing Wigglesworth of entertaining spiritual designs on two women, one of whom was identified as a Miss Amphlett. The matter was treated with the utmost discretion and few ever came to know of it. Polhill consulted John Leech for the benefit of his legal expertise and subsequently enjoined Wigglesworth to "abstain for a prolonged season from participation in the Lord's public work; and seek to retrieve your position before God and man, by a fairly long period of godly quiet living, so showing works meet for repentance."[125] The initial letter of accusation does not survive,[126] but Wigglesworth wrote to Mundell on several occasions both during and after this episode, and considerable light is thereby shed on not only this issue, but the disintegration of relations with the President of the P.M.U. Executive Council.

Wigglesworth expressed the forthright opinion that "Mr. Polhill has stepped over the Boundary this time." He was affronted by the insinuation that what had transpired was as grave as "fornication or adultery." There was indeed a clear admission on his part of having "acted folishley (sic)," but also a stated assurance that "this thing was settled in the Scriptural way" and that "God has

---

[121] P.M.U. Council Minutes of 16 November 1920, Book II, 248-249.

[122] See "Pentecostal Items," *Confidence*, November-December 1917, 91. Broom may be the companion described by Wigglesworth as a "dear English brother" while travelling in America during the autumn of 1914. See "Bro. Smith Wigglesworth," *Confidence*, December 1914, 228.

[123] Letter from Polhill to Wigglesworth, 20 October 1920.

[124] This notion had previously been decried by Boddy as "one of the awful onslaughts of the enemy." See "Spiritual Affinity: A Dangerous Error," *Confidence*, November 1911, 256.

[125] Letter from Polhill to Wigglesworth, 21 October 1920.

[126] Desmond Cartwright, who has acted as custodian of Wigglesworth's extant correspondence which was made available for this study, made this observation in his *The Real Smith Wigglesworth*, 94.

forgiven me."[127] Many of his subsequent letters refer back to this painful episode which evidently had a lingering effect. Twelve months later he wrote that it had been an unfortunate "mistake" to involve Polhill who was "not the man of mind to settle this."[128] He informed Mundell that Boddy had expressed relief to have been absent from the Council meeting when the resignation had been presented.[129] A further letter not only confirms in the starkest terms the final fate of what had been a constructive relationship between prominent figures in early English Pentecostalism, but provides a unique and startling insight into the mind of the one who had emerged as its talisman. Wigglesworth wrote to Mundell:

> Do not worry about my fellowship with Polhill. I paid the Price and now am free and I have no desire to again Unite. He has Destroyed my love through his Baby mind. Poor silly thing. I have no Room for him in my Prayers or thoughts. He is to me as one Dead.[130]

This episode has scarcely been alluded to, much less explored in works relating to the *Apostle of Faith*. In an effort to provide a portrait more attuned to the historical reality, Cartwright brought this matter to light in his article "The Real Wigglesworth" published in the *Journal of the European Pentecostal Theological Association*.[131] The biography which he subsequently produced introduces what he terms this "unfortunate incident"[132] with evident reticence and reluctance. He was doubtless aware of the veracity of Hollenweger's assessment that few among contemporary Pentecostalism's leadership, much less its "rank and file," are conversant with the output of their scholarly "critical tradition."[133] Venturing beyond the pages of academic theological journals, the more general biographical popularizing of this aspect of Wigglesworth's history involved heightened transgressive potential in view of the sensibilities of a readership for which hagiographical balm has become normative (pages 11-15 above). In the final outcome, Cartwright succeeds in introducing this foible while employing ample qualification and delicacy to assuage all but the most intractable devotee.

The present study has introduced the termination of Wigglesworth's tenure in Pentecostal officialdom, not merely as a neglected aspect of the historical record, but as a development which encapsulates and embodies deepening structural tensions and incompatibilities. While spiritual propensities and inclinations sought untrammelled freedom, expression, even indulgence,

---

[127] Letter from Wigglesworth to Mundell, 21 October 1920.

[128] Letter from Wigglesworth to Mundell, 7 November 1921.

[129] Letter from Wigglesworth to Mundell, 17 January 1921.

[130] Letter from Wigglesworth to Mundell, c. October/November 1921. Cartwright has suggested this approximate date for an otherwise undated letter.

[131] Cartwright, "The Real Wigglesworth," 90-96.

[132] Cartwright, *The Real Smith Wigglesworth*, 89.

[133] Hollenweger, "The Critical Tradition of Pentecostalism," 7-8.

centralising tendencies necessitated the imposition of strictures and constraints in the pursuit of acceptable mores. The exertions of censure examined in this section convey unprecedented glimpses of increasingly fraught relations and power dynamics and, in so doing, serve to significantly illuminate the impetus toward another form of polity within English Pentecostalism.

Section 3.4: The Impetus Toward Another Form of Polity

Decline of the Boddy/Polhill Axis

The Pentecostal movement, a phenomenon which has been described as "constantly in need of the refreshing waters of religious experience,"[134] provided particular challenges both to British leaders who sought to effect *mobilisation* and later *organisation*, as well as to those who sought to resist these developments in the name of freedom, spontaneity, and inspiration. While Polhill may have gained the ascendancy with respect of the situations that have been outlined, it is by no means the case that this represented the ultimate vindication or triumph for him as an individual, or institutionally for his strain of leadership or mode of power. He would not be permitted to exercise a form of "benevolent despotism" such as had been exemplified in John Wesley's "highly autocratic and centralized" leadership of early Methodism by means of Conference.[135] Although the *résumé* Gee includes in his *Personal Memoirs of Pentecostal Pioneers* is demonstrably partisan and a notable departure from his characteristic tact and even-handedness, even his ungenerous remarks remain of the utmost significance. As much about the author as the object of his effusions, these observations reveal the depth of antipathy that came to be felt by those who deplored a perceived betrayal of the *charisma* or genius of the movement. Beyond the unpublicised functioning of organisational polity such as was exercised within the confines of the Executive Council of the P.M.U., it is evident that many came to resent the importation of "reverends" for the purpose of "respectability." While Gee refers to such figures in relation to the London Conventions of which he states, "the latter became positively dreary,"[136] it the case that Polhill was keen to utilise men of ministerial and educational stature in other strategic departments of the movement.

Another such interposition, albeit one which has to this point remained unexplored, occurred when the President recommended to the Council that a Rev. Dr. Middleton of Rugby be invited to become a member. It was recorded that letters from "several" other members were read, and that these were "generally approving" of this proposed course of action. Ernest Moser, a notable exception, expressed "grave doubts as to the wisdom of Dr. Middleton

---

[134] Poloma, "The Millenarianism of the Pentecostal Movement," in Hunt, ed., *Christian Millenarianism*, 186.

[135] Wilson, "The Sociology of Schism," in Hill, ed., *Sociological Yearbook of Religion in Britain*, vol. 4, 13.

[136] Gee, *Personal Memoirs of Pentecostal Pioneers*, 74-75.

becoming a Member of the Council owing to the doctrine of Baptismal Regeneration expressly taught in the Prayer Book and practised by its Ministers including Dr. Middleton." It was asserted that this was "quite contrary to the sound teaching which all Pentecostal people strive to maintain."[137] Some months later Boddy announced to the general readership of *Confidence* that this Vicar of St. Matthew's, Rugby, had been appointed to "act as Vice-President of the P.M.U." for the duration of the absence of "our honoured leader" in China.[138] This represented a dexterous handling of a sensitive appointment, certainly one which precipitated the resignation of Moser from the P.M.U. Council.[139] In this manner another of the stalwarts who had been brought in to fill the positions vacated by Myerscough, Breeze and Sandwith, found themselves in turn disenfranchised from this significant arm of the movement's polity.

Boddy had sought to reassure readers of *Confidence* that the Whitsuntide Convention of 1922, held in London's Kingsway Hall, had seen attendances that were "as good as ever." The singing had been led by Donald Gee, then a pastor in Leith and was deemed to have been nothing less than "wonderful." It was stated that Dr. Robert Middleton had given "many excellent Bible readings and addresses," as well as conducting a daily "interim Missionary Meeting" before the usual afternoon gatherings in the large hall.[140] What amounted to an exercise in positive public relations was evidently insufficient to mollify the sensibilities of Moser, and it would appear that he was far from alone in these convictions. Neither was it the case that such views were confined to malcontents on the fringes of the movement, as no less a figure than the young pastor who had been commissioned by Polhill to direct music at these London gatherings, later revealingly hailed Moser as having taken "an uncompromising stand for the distinctive truths of the Pentecostal Movement."[141]

Coinciding with the publicising of Middleton's meteoric rise to the unprecedented position of Vice President, Boddy announced further developments in a casual a fashion which similarly belied their significance for the wider movement. It was stated that the Council of the P.M.U. regretted that "owing to a serious deficit in their income" they were compelled to close the Women's Training Home, a facility which had been available in London since 1909. It was also the case that "for the same cause," they were similarly unable to continue the maintenance of the Men's Training Home. There followed the somewhat curious announcement:

> The Council are pleased, however, to record that they have arranged with Pastor A. H. Carter (whose valued services as Superintendent at the Home since

---

[137] P.M.U. Council Minutes of 7 November 1921, Book II, 422.

[138] "The Pentecostal Missionary Union," *Confidence*, July-September 1922, 44.

[139] P.M.U. Council Minutes of 18 August 1922, Book III, 22.

[140] "The Whitsuntide Convention at Kingsway," *Confidence*, July-September 1922, 34.

[141] Gee, *The Pentecostal Movement*, 58.

> February 1922, have been much appreciated) to be responsible for the Men's
> Home on and after the 29th September next...Pastor Carter will carry on the Home
> as an 'Undenominational Bible Training School'...[142]

It is suggested that the "serious deficit" in income cannot but have had something to do with a change in the disposition of the "honoured leader." When the Men's Home had opened in London in 1913 it has been undertaken "entirely at Mr. Polhill's expense."[143] Ingratitude which in notable instances inclined toward scarcely concealed resentment, even on the part of beneficiaries of this liberality, is likely to have communicated itself to Polhill at some level, and it would appear that his former munificence was being curtailed. Perhaps an even more pertinent factor was that it was also becoming unavoidably apparent that the reforms and methods of the "honoured leader" had not met with universal approval, and that he was finding himself increasingly forced to acknowledge that the momentum of English Pentecostalism, while undeniably indebted to his influence, was gravitating in a different direction.

The establishment of an Undenominational Bible Training School under Howard Carter marked, despite its nomenclature, a gravitation toward a denominational form of polity. Carter had been approached by Mundell as the Men's Training Home had undergone uncertain fortunes since its official designation in 1915 as "*the* training home of the society."[144] The solicitor had managed to persuade the young pastor from Duddeston, Birmingham, to take on the position, and both Mundell and Carter would negotiate the transition from pre-denominational to denominational Pentecostalism. The former continued as Secretary to the P.M.U. after it "merged" (Gee's term) or became subsumed into the Assemblies of God. He relinquished this position in 1929, but retained his place on the Council until his death in 1934.[145]

Carter, who had undergone a Pentecostal initiation in 1915, was among

---

[142] "The Pentecostal Missionary Union," *Confidence*, July-September 1922, 44-45.

[143] "Pentecostal Items," *Confidence*, August 1913, 165.

[144] Titterington, "P.M.U. Men's Training Home, London," *Flames of Fire*, April 1915, 6. This effectively ended Thomas Myerscough's Training Centre for Men in Preston. It is not fanciful to suggest that something approaching an unfavourable contrast had already been drawn between attending evening Bible classes offered by an estate agent in Lancashire and the prospect of enrolling in a residential training home which was being overseen by one of the Cambridge Seven, and offered the tutorial abilities of Rev. H. E. Wallis, M.A., an alumnus of Queen's College, Cambridge. See the article "The London Missionary Training Home," *Confidence*, November 1913, 216. The last mention of Myerscough's training facility occurred in the February 1915 issue of *Confidence* magazine. Wallis was succeeded by Titterington, and it was announced in 1917 that the Men's Home was to be "suspended for this war-time." See "The Pentecostal Missionary Union," *Confidence*, May-June 1917, 42. More than two years later it was announced that it would be re-established under the jurisdiction of a former missionary couple, Mr. J. Hollis acting as Principle, and Mrs. Hollis as Superintendent. See "The Pentecostal Missionary Union," *Confidence*, July-September 1919, 50.

[145] Gee, *The Pentecostal Movement*, 55.

those who "went to prison for conscience sake" during the Great War. These considerations along with his leadership of a "little assembly," categorise him among what was in effect a second generation of Pentecostal leaders who felt increasingly alienated from the Boddy/Polhill axis, not least in the light of their sympathies for the war effort. Boddy's enthusiasm for this cause has merited comment in historical analyses of the Church of England's attitude toward the war, an inclusion which is the more notable in the light of the fact that his Pentecostal activities are conspicuously absent from religious histories of the period. While consideration of Bishop Handley Moule's convictions and campaigning in such studies could be presumed in the light of his ecclesiastical prominence,[146] the views and activities of a vicar from an unprepossessing urban parish in the industrial North East of England would scarcely merit comment unless exceptional. Yet contrary to expectation, Boddy achieved a degree of notoriety in this direction on account of his fervid and "emotional telling of the tale" of the Real Angels of Mons which was published with the permission of the official censor on account of its potential as an aid to recruitment.[147] In similar fashion Polhill's practice of the closing of meetings in Sion College with the National Anthem[148] proved too Erastian for many Pentecostal sensibilities.

In the context of what was probably the most extensive and forthright of Boddy's many apologias for Christian involvement in the war effort, he had informed readers of *Confidence* toward the end of 1914 that he had cancelled the All Saints' Annual Tea and in its place delivered a lecture on Belgium. This declamation, illustrated by recent photographs, was reminiscent of the lantern lectures of his early years in Sunderland. A dozen wounded soldiers had been brought by motor car from the hospital where his daughter had been assisting, and they were reported to have been welcomed with "loving rounds of cheers often repeated."[149] Bernard Shaw castigated what he perceived to be an unjustifiable tribalism exhibited by clergymen during this period. He stated:

> They have turned their churches into recruiting stations and their vestries into munition workshops...They have stuck to their livings and served Mars in the name of Christ, to the scandal of all religious mankind...as far as I have observed, the only people who gasped were the Freethinkers.[150]

This indictment could not be wholly attributed to Boddy, although it was the

---

[146] See Alan Wilkinson, *The Church of England and the First World War* (London: SPCK, 1978), 33, 54. Boddy had presented Moule's strident advocacy of involvement in the war effort to his Pentecostal readership in "The Bishop of Durham Writes," *Confidence*, January 1915, 5-6.

[147] Martin, *The Last Crusade*, 137.

[148] Gee, *The Pentecostal Movement*, 114.

[149] "The War," *Confidence*, November 1914, 203-204.

[150] Bernard Shaw, "Appendix to the Play," *Androcles and the Lion* (1916; repr. London: Penguin Books, 1946), 155-156.

case that All Saints' Parish Hall had been converted for usage as a military Detention Hospital. The cessation of the Sunderland Convention had occurred, it was implausibly publicised, on account of the fact that Caxton Hall in Westminster represented a safer environment for a gathering of that nature.[151] More abstruse primary sources, however, reveal that missionaries then abroad were somewhat more realistically informed that the upheaval was the result of the utilisation of parish buildings for military purposes.[152] Certainly some within the Pentecostal family would come to feel increasingly less fraternal towards Boddy as the war progressed. Had the output of the Anglo-Irish playwright formed part of their reading matter, they may have felt something akin to a shudder of recognition and thereby found themselves in unwonted and unprecedented sympathy with those of the free-thinking persuasion.

Gee has described the years of the Sunderland Conventions, 1908-1914, as "the initial period of the revival." This was followed, in his estimation, by a "new stage" which "though unrecognised as a crisis, was steadily gathering momentum, and possessed irresistible tendencies." Polhill's continuation of the Whitsuntide Conventions and his co-ordination of the P.M.U. may have mitigated against any fatalistic sense of crisis, but as his leadership came to be less regarded, there followed "a difficult and discouraging time" for the movement in England. The years 1920 to 1924 have been characterised by Gee as "the proverbial darkest hour before the dawn."[153] While such perspectives were not expressed in either *Confidence* magazine or *Flames of Fire*, indirect indications of Pentecostals having collectively entered into a problematic phase are not difficult to detect, even in these publications. For instance, in a manner calculated to boost or maintain morale, Boddy stated of the London Convention of 1917:

> The attendances were good, very good. On the whole it was, as Pastor Saxby said, one of the best (for him, he said, the very best) of the London Pentecostal Conferences. There was no signs in the meetings of the Pentecostal Movement slackening or dying down.[154]

Boddy advanced a similarly positive construction of the event in the post-war period when he reported that "the meetings were excellent...and the attendances were as good as ever." He stated that Polhill himself "considered this one of the best conventions he has summoned." Boddy particularly mentioned the "ministers from Wales" whom he described as having been "full of fire and enthusiasm,"[155] but his sanguine assessment did not represent the universal

---

[151] Gee, *The Pentecostal Movement*, 104.

[152] P.M.U. Correspondence, Letter from Mundell to Frank Trevitt, 29 January 1915, 47; Letter from Mundell to Misses Jenner, Defries, Cook and Millie, 23 April 1915, 68-69.

[153] Gee, *The Pentecostal Movement*, 121, 123.

[154] "The Whitsuntide Convention," *Confidence*, July-August 1917, 56.

[155] "The Whitsuntide Convention at Kingsway," *Confidence*, July-Sept. 1922, 34.

position. Gee disparaged what he deemed Polhill's tendency to fill the platform with "obscure Welsh" ministers who allegedly "accepted the wealthy chairman's hospitality in a London Hotel, but scorned the little Pentecostal Assemblies in Wales." What was perhaps, from a Pentecostal perspective, one of the severest indictments that could have been delivered was arraigned against them to devastating effect: "Their ministry was dry, to say the least."[156]

From 1917 onwards it also began to become apparent that the future of *Confidence* magazine was itself far from assured. During this year it appeared bi-monthly, but thereafter it was only issued on a quarterly basis until the end of 1924. It had also fallen to 16 pages per issue from April 1916, and this fell to 10 pages from July 1923.[157] It would appear that the publication, which according to Blumhofer had generated a sense of community and cohesiveness within British Pentecostalism which its North American counterpart had lacked,[158] was approaching the end of its evolutionary cycle. This was the assessment offered by Boddy himself at the beginning of 1923 when he stated: "It may be that the time is approaching when *Confidence* shall have completed the special work which it was raised up to fulfil."[159] Its editor had resisted "considerable pressure" which had been exerted in the direction of the establishment of a separate religious body, and had remained "firm in his allegiance to the Church of England."[160] The original vision for an associational Pentecostalism leavening throughout the wider Church came to be regarded, quite possibly even by its originator (although never directly articulated), as inadequate to the requirements of the evolving movement. According to Gee, the period 1920-1924 was one which saw leadership waver and disappoint, enthusiasm become more sentimental than actual, and "old fellowships" undergo "painful strain." Evidently mindful of the Boddy/Polhill axis, he stated:

> In remaining within their own Church, and encouraging others in other Churches to do the same, the leaders of the Pentecostal Movement acted from the best of motives, but strangely failed to recognise the unalterable principle uttered by our Lord that new wine cannot be put into old bottles.[161]

---

[156] Gee, *Personal Memoirs of Pentecostal Pioneers*, 75.

[157] "The Future of *Confidence*," *Confidence*, March-April 1917, 22. The final two issues, one of which was published in May 1925, and the last of which appeared undated during 1926, were a mere eight pages each. See Taylor, "Publish and Be Blessed," 128-129.

[158] Blumhofer, "Alexander Boddy," 34-35.

[159] "Personal Jottings," *Confidence*, January-March 1923, 62. Wakefield appropriately describes the magazine as acquiring a "slightly nostalgic feel" while pointing out that it increasingly contained "retrospective" articles, now of significant value to the historian interested in Boddy and/or early Pentecostalism. See *Pentecostal Anglican Pioneer*, 201.

[160] J. V. Boddy, *Memoir*, 8.

[161] Gee, *The Pentecostal Movement*, 123, 82.

A. E. Saxby

Something of a false dawn occurred in the rise to prominence of an individual who had addressed the London Conference of 1917. Boddy had then described Pastor Saxby as a "very earnest brother" who "reminds one of Brother Wigglesworth in his joyful sincerity." He also observed that Saxby had "suffered for his convictions." This suffering was twofold as he had been forced to leave the pastorate of a Baptist church in Harringay on account of his Pentecostal convictions,[162] while his pacifism later caused considerable difficulties for both himself and members of the Derby Hall congregation which he had established. His message to the London Convention of 1917 had addressed the issue of "Progress in Pentecost" and saw him describe the phenomenon as "not a Monument, but a Movement."[163] Gee wrote in admiring tones of the "great step of faith" undertaken by the "leader of a little assembly in North London" when Polhill could not host the Whitsuntide Convention on account of an extended visit to China. A significant watershed, 1919 was the first year since its inception in 1908 that neither Boddy nor Polhill would be at the helm of the most prominent event of the English Pentecostal calendar. Saxby's convening of the gathering that year was deemed his "finest hour," and this departure from precedent "proved a milestone in the history of the British Movement."[164]

In the aftermath of the success of this event, Saxby was in constant demand on Pentecostal platforms, and among these was what had come to be an annual gathering at the Holiness Mission Hall in Croydon where he was the main speaker in 1920.[165] The first Pentecostal Conference to be held in Swanwick which also took place that year represented a further departure from what had been the Boddy/Polhill hegemony. Saxby's ministry was so well received at this event that, according to Gee, it seemed that he was destined to be the leader for which the movement had been waiting.[166] Conforming to the established leadership paradigm Saxby founded his own periodical, *Things Old and New*, whose title, wittingly or otherwise, reflected the Janus-faced aspect of the movement when it appeared in April of 1921. Boddy referred his own readership to this new publication, as well as that of the Elim evangelists initially consolidating their activity in Northern Ireland, when *Confidence* looked likely to be discontinued in 1923.[167] Yet any impetus toward a trans-local leadership role for Saxby was to prove abortive on his apparent adoption

---

[162] Randall has pointed out that Albert Saxby was the most prominent of "a few Baptist ministers" who left Baptist life on account of Pentecostal involvement. He remarks that while pastor of Duckett Road Baptist Church, a church defence league had been formed to withstand unwelcome Pentecostal encroachments. See his "Days of Pentecostal Overflowing," in Bebbington, ed., *The Gospel in the World*, 93.

[163] "The Whitsuntide Convention," *Confidence*, July-August 1917, 56.

[164] Gee, *Personal Memoirs of Pentecostal Pioneers*, 80-82.

[165] "Home News," *Things New and Old*, June 1922, 9.

[166] Gee, *Personal Memoirs of Pentecostal Pioneers*, 82.

[167] "Personal Jottings," *Confidence*, January-March 1923, 62.

and espousal of a form of universalism known as *Ultimate Reconciliation*.[168] As Massey has observed in his concentrated study of the years 1920-1925, many among the still disparate Pentecostal leadership were unnerved by this teaching and as a consequence "the urgent need for some kind of structural, protective organisation for the Pentecostal assemblies became even more obvious."[169]

Parallel Trajectory to Structural Developments in North America

It is interesting to note that the process which took place in England during this phase mirrored, in vital respects, what had occurred in North America prior to the onset of the First World War. In 1913 it was mooted that a permanent Bible Training School with a capacity for between 300 and 500 students be established, while questions of church-government and leadership were the subject of considered attention.[170] During the same year M. M. Pinson and E. N. Bell merged their respective periodicals, *Word and Witness* and *The Apostolic Faith*, to form one publication for which Bell would function as principal editor. It was in the pages of the newly constituted *Word and Witness*, which went on to become the official organ of the Assemblies of God, that a "General Council" of all "Pentecostal saints" was summoned to meet in Hot Springs, Arkansas, for the discussion of mutual concerns and problems.[171] Synan notes that while the more than 300 ministers and laymen that gathered in the Grand Opera House in April 1914 may have vigorously disclaimed any intention to inaugurate a new sect or denomination, they succeeded in doing just that.[172]

One of the express reasons for collaboration, as revealed in December 1913, was "that we may do away with so many divisions, both in doctrine and in the various names under which our Pentecostal people are working...unity our chief aim." It was stated: "Many of the saints have felt the need of chartering the churches of God in Christ, putting them on a legal basis and thus obeying the laws of the land...We confess we have been 'slothful in business' on this point."[173] Yet in spite of this it was fulsomely asserted that those involved were "determined not to organise a man-made church and charter it as a new sect in the land." The tendency toward cohesion did not preclude an antipathy toward organisational bureaucracy which, it was feared, could precipitate a descent

---

[168] Probably allowing for the esteem in which Saxby had been held, Gee presented a measured but definite refutation of such ideas in "Human Destiny: An Open Letter by Pastor Donald Gee," *Elim Evangel*, February 1924, 35-38.

[169] Massey, "Origins of the Assemblies of God," 20.

[170] "Permanent Home for Holy Ghost Bible Training School Now in Prospect," *Word and Witness*, January 1913, 1; "God's Own Church and His Churches," *Word and Witness*, June 1913, 2.

[171] "General Convention of Pentecostal Saints and Churches of God in Christ," *Word and Witness*, December 1913, 1.

[172] Synan, *The Holiness-Pentecostal Tradition*, 154-155, 158.

[173] "General Convention of Pentecostal Saints," *Word and Witness*, Dec. 1913, 1.

into "unscriptural lines of fellowship."[174] This notwithstanding, it was somewhat triumphantly reported that "all approved and unanimously adopted" a series of resolutions described as "a sort of *Magna Charta*." With an evident determination to deflect suspicion or opposition, the Pentecostal readership were informed that this represented a "declaration of religious freedom," a "pledge against sectarianism and 'bossism,'" and an "owning of Christ as our Lord and Head." The General Council did not propose to "usurp authority" over local assemblies or "deprive them of their scriptural and local rights and privileges." Rather it would assist leaders in the suppression of "unscriptural methods and conduct" as the task of the "Presbytery or body of Elders" was "simply to be stewards for God." That resolutions were adopted "amid great joy and shouting,"[175] confirms Blumhofer's observation that "four days of rousing Pentecostal meetings helped allay the reservations of some who feared organization."[176]

William F. P. Burton, who returned from the Congo for his first missionary furlough in 1921, had encountered the outworking of these developments in the U.S.A. His extensive itinerancy among Centres and assemblies across England convinced him that there was a "widespread need of a co-ordinated fellowship."[177] Himself an *alumnus* of Thomas Myerscough's Training School in Preston,[178] Burton was, according to Massey, "finding the support infra-structures of the British assemblies clumsy, uncoordinated, and unable to adequately finance the expanding overseas work." The result was that he, along with other English leaders,[179] drafted and issued a "manifesto"[180] or *Circular Letter* to "all the Saints in the British Isles who stand for the latter rain outpouring with signs following." It stated:

---

[174] "Hot Springs Assembly: God's Glory Present," *Word and Witness*, April 1914, 1.

[175] This was presented as a token of the fact that, according to the published report, "nothing was ever more manifestly approved of God." See "Hot Springs Assembly," *Word and Witness*, April 1914, 1.

[176] Edith L. Blumhofer, *The Assemblies of God: A Chapter in the Story of American Pentecostalism, Volume 1 - To 1914* (Springfield, MO.: Gospel Publishing House, 1989), 201. In this context Blumhofer makes some interesting observations with regard to this seemingly endemic aversion to/suspicion of organisation and denominational structures.

[177] Massey, "Origins of the Assemblies of God," 23.

[178] Gee, *Personal Memoirs of Pentecostal Pioneers*, 68. This early association has been highlighted in David John Garrard, "The History of the Congo Evangelistic Mission From 1915 to 1982" (Unpublished Ph.D. dissertation: University of Aberdeen, December 1983), 6-13.

[179] Massey has observed that by this time the Apostolic Church was "well entrenched" in Wales, while the Elim Pentecostal Alliance was "already controlling Ireland." In the broader context of the British Isles it was therefore the case that "the English assemblies were at the centre of events involving the formation of the British Assemblies of God." See "Origins of the Assemblies of God," 23-24, 10.

[180] Gee, *The Pentecostal Movement*, 141.

Many are, at this time, expressing a desire for more concerted action among the assemblies of Spirit-filled saints. Misunderstandings could be cleared away, the work solidified, and protection offered against errors which are spreading in the movement, by leaders coming together mutually to discuss our common interests. Without necessarily creating executive authority, or otherwise curtailing the liberty and independence of the local assemblies, it would surely be wholesome to have some meetings...[181]

This *Letter*, undated but probably circulated early in 1922, was followed by a second which bore the signatures of thirteen local leaders, one of whom was Ernest Moser of Southsea. Massey has highlighted the delicate position which would have pertained on account of his being the first signatory of such a document while maintaining the position of "Hon. Treasurer" of the P.M.U.[182] Conflicting allegiances between the trans-denominational ethos of the P.M.U. and prominent involvement in the search for an agreeable form of Pentecostal union was therefore conveniently, and tellingly, resolved by his afore-mentioned resignation from the Council on the grounds of an encroaching Anglican bias. Kay's observation regarding J. Nelson Parr that, in contradistinction to Boddy, he "had no vision of renewed national church,"[183] could be extrapolated to Moser and many others among the emerging coterie of leaders.

Gee's summary of these developments through which he and others negotiated their path, betrays a classic dialectical exchange between charismatic domination and the encroachments of routinization,[184] while demonstrating aspects of the anti-Establishment animus already noted.[185] Within five years of the foundation of the denomination in which he would play a singularly influential role, he stated:

In the early days of this Pentecostal Outpouring there were those who emphatically taught believers to receive the Baptism in the Holy Spirit, but to 'stay in their churches'...The futile endeavour to force the New Wine of 'Pentecost' into the Old Bottles of existing Denominations produced the double disaster predicted by our Lord. Many, alas, lost the Wine and are today utterly dried-up compared to those glorious months of Divine Intoxication which they

---

[181] *1ˢᵗ Sheffield Circular Letter*, in Massey, "Origins of the Assemblies of God," 25-26. Gee recounted a decade later that disparate Pentecostal Assemblies had "determined to come together into a closer fellowship for the safeguarding of the testimony from error, and for its better furtherance at home and abroad." See "The Pentecostal Movement," *Redemption Tidings*, November 1932, 6.

[182] "Appendix 2: Pastors and Leaders Involved in the Formation of the A.O.G.," in Massey, "Origins of the Assemblies of God," 332-337.

[183] Kay, "Assemblies of God," in Warrington, ed., *Pentecostal Perspectives*, 46.

[184] On this tendency see Ken Morrison, *Marx, Durkheim and Weber: Formations of Modern Social Thought* (London: Sage Publications, 2002), 286-288.

[185] See p. 189 above.

experienced when the Spirit first fell upon them in Pentecostal fullness.[186]

According to this ecclesiological perspective, "New Wine" could only be preserved in "New Bottles" and it was contested that "every fresh Revival - Protestant, Quaker, Methodist, Salvationist, etc.," had found itself compelled "sooner or later, however reluctantly, to face this inevitable step." This logic prompted the conclusion that "the Pentecost Experience sooner or later inevitably demands the Pentecostal Assembly."[187] According to a prime-mover of denominational Pentecostalism in England, the fact that earlier Conventions had been held "more or less under the auspices of the Church of England" had resulted in a protracted "futile attempt" to resist unavoidable, even essential structural developments. An irretrievable indictment was retrospectively pronounced on the Boddy/Polhill custodianship of the emerging movement: "The spread of the Revival in the British Isles was undoubtedly hindered in this way for several years."[188]

It is interesting to note that while the original reticulous or networked structure that had been espoused owed its essentials to previous Holiness associations - most notably the Pentecostal League of Prayer - the British Holiness world would also become "the focus of more specifically denominational expression."[189] For Pentecostals themselves this progression and the final relinquishing of the ecumenical vision which it necessarily entailed, would have negative as well as positive implications for the structures under development. David Allen has, for instance, offered the assessment that in matters of involvement in social and political issues, the Assemblies of God adopted "a supposedly biblical but impossibly other-worldly attitude." He states with some bewilderment that in the context of the General Strike of 1926 "Parr's eyes were fixed firmly on the *Parousia*," while Gee's concern was that nothing should spoil arrangements for the Kingsway Hall Convention!" This commentator, himself a denominational spokesperson, has frankly observed that it would be more than three decades before Gee came to recognise the fallacy of "the ostrich-like isolationism and other-worldliness that had characterised the Assemblies from the outset."[190] Furthermore in spite of

---

[186] Gee, *Concerning Shepherds and Sheepfolds: A Series of Studies Dealing with Pastors and Assemblies* (1930; repr. London: Elim Publishing Co., 1952), 15.

[187] Gee, *Studies Dealing with Pastors and Assemblies*, 15-16. The same rationale had been advanced for developments within the Apostolic Faith Church. It was claimed by his propagandist that Hutchinson had been "led out of the old denominational lines of work" as "new wine could not be put into old wineskins (Matt. ix. 17)." See White, *The Word of God*, 48-49.

[188] Gee, "The Pentecostal Movement," *Redemption Tidings*, October 1932, 2.

[189] While noting this general tendency Warburton proceeds to examine a particular instance, the establishment of the Emmanuel Holiness Church. See his "Organization and Change in a British Holiness Movement," in Wilson, *Patterns of Sectarianism*, 109, 111-137.

[190] Allen, "The Glossolalic Ostrich: Isolationism and Other-worldliness in the British

protestations regarding "New Wine," "Old Wineskins," and spiritual desiccation, a more recent denominational analyst has likewise acknowledged that the body which was founded transpired to be both "rather insular" and characterised by a "parochial stolidity." It is his estimation that "imagination and visionary flair" would have prevented it "from becoming what it eventually became - somewhat mundane."[191] It seems that for those who pronounced negatively (and ungenerously) upon Boddy and Polhill, the delicate balance between *charisma* and the encroachments of routinization would transpire to prove as challenging to their second generation of as it had for the first.

Section 3.5: Outcomes for Pentecostal Localities

Sunderland

The more immediate outcomes for the specific Pentecostal localities examined in this study also reflect this seemingly ineluctable interplay between charismatic and routinizing tendencies. On 25th January 1921, a letter from the Rev. A. A. Boddy was read to the Executive Council of the P.M.U. He requested that they accept his resignation from the Council, citing a deterioration in health and an inability to regularly attend its meetings. The Minutes record that, after a general and sincere expression of "regret and sympathy," it was unanimously held that they could not see their way to the acceptance of this resignation. It was decided that he be asked to continue in the work "with which he had been for so long associated" and where his "presence and counsel" were "so much appreciated." The non-attendance of this singularly iconic figure was held to be preferable to his outright withdrawal which, it was felt, would be "a serious blow" and one which "might prejudicially affect the work."[192] At their next meeting a further letter was read, in which Boddy thanked the Council for their goodwill, and offered to withdraw his resignation "for the time being." He then disclosed that beyond his stated grounds there was a further "doctrinal reason" which he would bring before them at a future date.[193]

This reason never came before the Council and Boddy's participation, which had been minimal for some time, was effectively at an end. The first overtures made toward the P.M.U. by those forming the Assemblies of God in 1922,[194]

Assemblies of God," *EPTA Bulletin*, XIII (1994): 54-55. For a commentary on this tendency in the North American context see Wacker, "The Almost Chosen People," 141-151.

[191] Massey, "Origins of the Assemblies of God," 307. Two other denominational commentators have confirmed this analysis: while Hudson has described British Pentecostalism generally as entering a period of "stagnation," Kay acknowledges that the Assemblies of God "slowed almost to a halt." See Hudson, "Worship," and Kay, "Assemblies of God," in Warrington, ed., *Pentecostal Perspectives*, 181-182, 58.

[192] P.M.U. Council Minutes of 25 January 1921, Book II, 284-285.

[193] P.M.U. Council Minutes of 8 February 1921, Book II, 290-291.

[194] This took the form of a letter from Pastor Boulton of Hull who requested that the

ultimately bore fruit in their amalgamation under that denominational umbrella in 1925.[195] Wakefield aptly summarises the situation when he points out that the "shoots of separate organisations" were becoming increasingly visible, "a trend which Boddy had sought to resist but was now powerless to prevent." The Pentecostal message had not infiltrated the wider churches and so "pressure was growing for a new direction."[196] Neither Boddy nor Polhill would play any role in the newly-formed Pentecostal bodies.[197] In the penultimate issue of *Confidence* which appeared in May 1925, Boddy commended their fledgling publications. The *Elim Evangel*, whose early issues contained accounts of Jeffreys' revivalist campaigns, was described by the movement's patriarch as "very thrilling," while those seeking news of missionary work were directed toward *Redemption Tidings*.[198] The former made no mention of his death in 1930, while the latter contained a very brief entry which managed to misspell his name.[199] Robinson has described this heedlessness as "a suitable obituary from a movement that had forgotten him."[200]

P.M.U. "unite with them in fellowship." P.M.U. Council Minutes of 19 September 1922, Book III, 40.

[195] The readers of *Redemption Tidings* were assured, for the prospect of securing ongoing financial support, of the continuity of the overseas work of the Missionary Union. See "Missionary Notes: Assemblies of God and P.M.U.," *Redemption Tidings*, June 1925, 16.

[196] Wakefield, *Pentecostal Anglican Pioneer*, 199.

[197] It was stated in the spring of 1925 that there had been "great surprise" when it was announced by T. H. Mundell that the "well known Friday night services at Sion College, Blackfriars," were to be terminated. It was diplomatically put that Polhill had come to this decision "after much consideration" and "in view of his many engagements." The extent of Polhill's patronage is hinted at but not directly acknowledged in Mundell's expression of "great trepidation" at the prospect of the Bible School being financially responsible for the continuation of these gatherings. In this manner one of the early focal points of English Pentecostalism passed from pioneering to denominational hands. See "Reports from Far and Near: Showers of Blessing at Sion College," *Redemption Tidings*, April 1925, 18. Peter Hocken, one of the few researchers to explore the role of Cecil Polhill, is to be commended for disclosing that in later life he did not attend the Pentecostal church in his native Bedford, nor - significantly - did he direct any of his substantial bequests toward Pentecostal agencies. See "Cecil H. Polhill - Pentecostal Layman," 137.

[198] "Items of Interest," *Confidence*, May 1925, 162.

[199] "Travelogue," *Redemption Tidings*, November 1930, 18. Ross has observed that reaction to Gee's series of articles surveying the rise of English Pentecostalism in *Redemption Tidings* in 1932 caused him to acknowledge "a shocking lack of knowledge and appreciation of the movement's past on the part of its own membership." This proved the impetus for his widely-read volume *The Pentecostal Movement* which appeared almost a decade later. See Ross, "Donald Gee," 48.

[200] Robinson, "The Charismatic Anglican," 107. This was in pointed contrast to the manner in which the death of Smith Wigglesworth was announced in the same publication. E. C. W. Boulton, then President of the Elim Churches, paid fulsome tribute

When Bishop Hensley Henson, Moule's successor, sent Boddy to Hallgarth Church in Pittington in 1922, he was approaching seventy years of age, and his role as Pentecostal protagonist had effectively ceased. It is certainly of significance that in an extensive farewell address to his Monkwearmouth parishioners in which he recounted the notable events and occurrences of his 38-year tenure, Boddy made no direct reference to his years of Pentecostal involvement and activity. He offered only a vague intimation in the statement that he owed "many spiritual blessings to my fellowship with earnest Nonconformists at different periods in my life." For the readers of *Confidence* he did, however, append to this a letter from George H. Birney, described as a "building worker," who appears to have been part of the Sunderland Centre from its inception. This man gratefully recounted his participation in the early waiting meetings, and evidently relished how "our little Church" had been the focus of many who were drawn there in search of the "Baptism of the Holy Ghost and Fire."[201] Revisiting All Saints' Church in 1954, more than thirty years after her father's departure, Jane Vazeille was informed by the then incumbent that the senior members of the congregation still spoke of the "old Vicar" with great affection, and that those who had been involved in the Pentecostal Conventions were still regarded as the most faithful members of the Church.[202]

Bradford

It would appear that 1920 must have been something of an *annus horribilis* for Bradford's preaching plumber. In addition to his inauspicious departure from the P.M.U., it transpired that 1919 was the last year in which he was to convene his annual Easter event at Bowland Street. Cartwright is vague on this point, stating merely that "at some time, while away preaching, Wigglesworth lost control of the leadership of Bowland Street Mission."[203] It could reasonably be surmised that control had been effectively lost or forgone some time before the final disintegration. Wigglesworth's first exposure on America's Pentecostal platforms had occurred during the latter half of 1914, and during six months of peripatetic ministry, he claimed to have witnessed "not less than 1,500 people healed" and "great numbers baptised in the Holy Spirit."[204] This was but the first of numerous overseas excursions which saw the Bradford preacher

---

to the departed pioneer, while an extensive editorial pronounced him "Promoted to glory!" See Boulton, "A Christian Soldier Lays Down His Sword: Home-call of Mr. Smith Wigglesworth," *Elim Evangel*, 24 March 1947, 149, and H. W. Greenway, "Editorial," *Elim Evangel*, 24 March 1947, 150. The following issue of the *Evangel* prominently reproduced one of Wigglesworth's sermons. See "The Active Life of the Spirit-Filled Believer," *Elim Evangel*, 31 March 1947, 1-3.

[201] "From Sunderland to Pittington," *Confidence*, January-March 1923, 66-67, 70.

[202] J. V. Boddy, *Memoir*, 9.

[203] Cartwright, *The Real Smith Wigglesworth*, 87.

[204] "Bro. Smith Wigglesworth," *Confidence*, December 1914, 228.

bestride the burgeoning international Pentecostal network "like a victorious warrior,"[205] and while the demise of his local leadership of Bowland Street Mission may not have been a necessary or inevitable consequence of repeated and prolonged absences, the alteration of his priorities appears to have precipitated this outcome. The almost uniform lack of detail relating to this departure owes less to a deliberate suppression of unflattering and unedifying information, than to an established pattern of a wholesale neglect of such documentation in the face of all eventualities. If the inception and development of the Bowland Street Mission were recorded merely in terms of generalities, its disintegration and associated machinations were similarly surrounded with vagaries and spiritual platitudes.

It is interesting to note that although the Mission may have been disbanded, Wigglesworth's attachment to his annual Convention was by no means so easily relinquished. It was announced during the spring of 1920 in a manner which would have been very familiar to regular readers of *Confidence* during the previous decade that "Bro. Smith Wigglesworth will convene this gathering as before. He is expecting much blessing and a great awakening of Missionary interest." The nearest thing to a reference to the recent disjuncture was the matter-of-fact statement that "the place of meeting will be the Presbyterian Church, Infirmary Street."[206] A commonplace notification - likely to have been interpreted as the acquisition of a larger venue for a popular event - represented the only obsequies which the Bowland Street Mission would receive in the pages of the foremost disseminator of news for the English Pentecostal movement. The notes of this last Bradford Convention taken by "Miss Vipan,"[207] record a telling utterance by Wigglesworth: In the immediate aftermath of the demise of his formerly beloved Bowland Street Mission he stated: "It is more important our unity with Jesus than anything else."[208]

Peter Hocken, who has documented Wigglesworth's subsequent role and influence in the spread of charismatic Christianity, makes little more than an allusion to his tenure as leader of a modest Mission Hall in Bradford. Any sense of dissidence or animosity is absent from his innocuous observation that "a number of the Bowland Street believers then joined the Apostolic church, a recently-formed Pentecostal denomination just beginning its work in

---

[205] "Westward Ho!" *Confidence*, December 1914, 223.

[206] "Bradford Convention," *Confidence*, January-March 1920, 6. Arthur Booth-Clibborn offered a report of this Convention in "'Spring' Pentecostal Conventions," *Elim Evangel*, June 1920, 48-49.

[207] This lady had served as Box Secretary to the P.M.U. although it was feared in 1921 that "owing to the continuance of the Miners' Strike," and an expected reduction in donations, her services might no longer be required. See P.M.U. Council Minutes of 6 June 1921, Book II, 351-352. Florence Vipan's already noted associations with the Elim Evangelistic Band in Ulster and the Bradford Convention exemplify the fluid and organic nature of the movement at this stage of its development.

[208] Vipan, "Bradford Convention," *Confidence*, April-June 1920, 22.

Bradford."[209] Gordon Weeks, who in advancing a determinedly Apostolic perspective is less reticent in this respect, identifies not only some of the key individuals involved, but also what he regards as the ideological fault-line on which relations foundered. In his presentation of the convoluted, often tortuous, origins of the Apostolic Church in Britain, he is less inclined than other Pentecostal writers to perpetuate idealistic representations of the man who embodied the "rugged earnestness" of the "genuine old Bradford oddities" of the pulpit.[210]

He points out that Wigglesworth, in sympathy with the position arrived at and promulgated by Boddy, Polhill, and others, declared a definite suspicion of, and antipathy toward, directive prophecy.[211] He records the reminiscence of D. P. Williams, a prominent figure in the emerging Apostolic Church, that when two young men, H. V. Chanter and A. W. Rhodes, began to engage in this form of prophecy in Bowland Street, Wigglesworth declared: "I will have nothing to do with the prophetical word here. I cannot trust or believe it, and therefore it is not going to be here." This firm and forthright pronouncement did not meet with universal acceptance and, according to the account presented, a "simple young sister" retaliated with the prognostication: "Being that you have finished with Me and My Voice, I finish with you, and there is a day coming when you will see the door of this assembly shut, but I will have another place, and I have faith in the heart of some of the young in this congregation."[212]

This version of events may appear to have been gratifyingly fulfilled, yet it must be recognised, not least in the manner of its presentation, as an *apologia* for this conception of prophecy in general and the perspective of the Apostolic Church in particular.[213] The weight of available evidence points toward more

---

[209] Hocken, *Streams of Renewal: The Origins and Early Development of the Charismatic Movement in Great Britain* (Exeter: Paternoster Press, 1986), 25.

[210] Wigglesworth seems to have exhibited many of the characteristics of Bradford's typical "old style of local preacher." Fascinating, colourful, and frequently entertaining examples of such figures were presented by Scruton in *Pictures of Old Bradford*, 244-249. It is interesting to reflect that the Pentecostal network opened a unique opportunity by securing a broader platform where Wigglesworth's idiosyncrasies and eccentricities came to be welcomed and indeed celebrated as evidence of *charisma* and inspiration.

[211] Weeks, "A History of the Apostolic Church," 68-69. The exercise of prophecy and the problematic issues that surrounded it had been repeatedly explored in articles such as "Prophetic Messages and their Trustworthiness," *Confidence*, February 1909, 42-44; "Prophecy," *Flames of Fire*, November 1914, 1-2; "Prophecy in the Church: Part I," *Flames of Fire*, February 1915, 1-2; and "Prophecy in the Church: Part II," *Flames of Fire*, March 1915, 1-3.

[212] Weeks, *Chapter Thirty Two*, 50-51.

[213] Weeks claims that Wigglesworth subsequently engaged in this form of prophecy himself in his much-publicised message to David du Plessis. See "A History of the Apostolic Church," 68-69. For the official position of the Apostolic Church see *The Apostolic Church: Its Principles and Practices* (1937; repr. Bradford: Apostolic Publications, 1961), 95-96.

prosaic reasons for the closure of the Bowland Street Mission: the inspirationalism which Wigglesworth came to embody, and of which he became something of an exemplar across the emerging movement, proved unconducive to the establishment and maintenance of a settled ministry. What Wilson termed the realm of "pronounced revival,"[214] a dimension which Wigglesworth came to singularly inhabit, precluded his fulfilling a meaningful role as religious functionary in a localised and routinized context.

Bournemouth

Hutchinson and those loyal to his Apostolic Faith project had managed to regroup and consolidate around their central emphases in the aftermath of the "painful sunderings" of 1911.[215] The Bournemouth leader proved adept at subjecting a difficult and potentially traumatic situation to spectacular spiritual reinterpretation, employing the pejorative designation that had been given to the early believers in Rome as similarly appropriate to, and a vindication of, the Apostolic Faith experience almost nineteen centuries later: "Concerning this sect, we know that everywhere it is spoken against" (Acts 28:22). The principal offenders were not the "unsaved World" but, as Christ was rejected by "His own" who "received Him not," Hutchinson's loyalists were enjoined to "bless the Lord for the persecution" from others within the Pentecostal fold. It was presented as natural and appropriate that they "might expect to be branded something like our Master was."[216] The sense of embattled cohesiveness generated appears to have afforded adherents an opportunity for a more *emphatic belonging*, and thereby reduced the potentially debilitating effects of a collective sense of *anomie*.[217] McLeod has commented that one of the attractions of what he deems "ultra-Evangelicalism" in the late nineteenth century was the fact that it could explain and dismiss persecution in terms of factors such as original sin, wilful unbelief, and/or the adverse effects of alcohol. In his estimation "such means of automatic rejection of criticism made an important contribution to the survival of eccentric minorities."[218] It would transpire that while Hutchinson as moral entrepreneur had valiantly engaged in plausibility generation of this nature,[219] the maintenance of this cognitive minority would, over time, prove problematic.

The conflation of several issues which included resentment of authoritarian tendencies, tensions with regard to Welsh, Scottish, and English representations, and concerns regarding financial stewardship, constituted the preamble to an acrimonious general meeting at the Apostolic Faith Church in

---

[214] Wilson, "The Pentecostalist Minister," in Wilson, ed., *Patterns of Sectarianism*, 147.

[215] White, *The Word of God*, 53-54.

[216] "Concerning This Sect," *Showers of Blessing*, June 1915, 3.

[217] McGuire, *Religion: The Social Context*, 38, 35.

[218] McLeod, *Class and Religion in the Late Victorian City*, 71.

[219] Berger, *The Social Reality of Religion*, 188.

Ammanford, South Wales, during January 1916. What was later deemed "the most unkindest cut of all" inflicted by those who evoked an *"Et tu, Brute,"* saw the defection of all but three of the Welsh congregations from Hutchinson's control. This development, particularly in the aftermath of what had occurred in 1911, would prove "a bitter portion indeed to drink" and was attributed by Hutchinson's biographer and devotee to a "Judas spirit still abroad on the earth." Yet with a seemingly indefatigable, perhaps even megalomaniac sense of destiny, it was averred that "God was refining the ore, testing and proving the steel for the framework in the building He was putting up...a new construction work of His kingdom."[220]

Hutchinson came to adopt and then promulgate the teachings of British Israelism during the 1920s, and thereby compounded an already strange concatenation of doctrines and ideas which ultimately saw him heralded as "a greater leader than Moses."[221] D. P. Williams, the erstwhile apostle for Wales, went on to establish the Apostolic Church from his base in Pen-y-groes, Carmarthenshire. While never attaining to anything approaching the scale of the Elim Pentecostal or Assemblies of God denominations, the Apostolic Church succeeded in consolidating a sustainable footing,[222] and it was to them that disaffected members of Bradford's Bowland Street Mission would turn. Hutchinson's original enterprise, in contrast, "shrunk to a tiny remnant" as his theological views became "increasingly divergent from those of the majority of Pentecostals and evangelicals."[223] It is therefore not surprising that, as Worsfold has pointed out, the Apostolic Church maintained a seventy-five year silence about its inauspicious beginnings.[224]

---

[220] White, *The Word of God*, 72-75

[221] "Wanted - A Great Leader with a New Vision," *Showers of Blessing*, January-February 1924, 99. By the mid-1920s claims were being issued which asserted that previous dispensations and epochs had been surpassed and supplanted and that the era known as "the Hutchinson covenant" had been inaugurated. See David Thomas, "Steps in the Apostleship," *Showers of Blessing*, March-April 1925, 157. A typical indication of the extremity of the collective conscious that was being generated across a network of no more than several hundred people is to be found in the concluding remarks of the official stenographer for a conference held at the beginning of 1924: "Thus finished the season of the most remarkable meetings that have ever been held in Scotland." See Gordon Dennis, "Apostolic Faith Church: Annual New Year Scottish Conference, 1924," 22.

[222] By the turn of the century the Apostolic Church in Britain had a reasonably stable membership of 5,302 individuals spread across 110 congregations. This was a fraction of the 61,599 members and 630 congregations of the Assemblies of God, as well as of the Elim Pentecostal Church's 51,020 members across 490 congregations. See Brierly, ed., *United Kingdom Christian Handbook Religious Trends No. 4 2003/2004*, 9.12.

[223] Kay, *Pentecostals in Britain*, 19.

[224] Worsfold has described the policy adopted by the Apostolic Church with regard to its Bournemouth progenitor as "total blackout." See *The Origins*, 313.

Croydon

It might reasonably be surmised that Croydon's Holiness Mission Hall would have chosen to formally associate itself with either the Elim or Assemblies of God as they became officially constituted. It is certainly the case that those instrumental in the emergence of the Elim branch of Pentecostalism had previously employed their evangelistic endeavours on behalf of Pastor Inchcombe. The founder and overseer of the Holiness Hall had sent a report to Boddy toward the end of 1914 which referred to a fourteen-day mission that had been conducted by "Bro. Geo. Jeffreys" at Coulsdon, a "Mission Station" which they had established. He wrote of days of "great power and blessing" during which "souls were saved, back-sliders reclaimed, and many baptised in the Holy Ghost with Bible signs," and this had been taken to amount to a "splendid index" which brought considerable inspiration to those involved in the work of the fledgling Mission.[225]

When the P.M.U. was first approached by those working towards establishing the Assemblies of God, Polhill as President, recognised that such a development could ensure a viable future for Pentecostal missions. In spite of this acknowledgement he himself chose to terminate his personal involvement not only with this, but with all recognisable forms of Pentecostal Christianity from 1925.[226] On the other hand, the P.M.U.'s Honorary Secretary of longstanding, T. H. Mundell, negotiated the merging of the missionary body with the fledgling denomination and himself embarked upon active and wholehearted participation in the Assemblies.[227] As a prominent figure associated with Croydon's Holiness Mission it could be expected that this hitherto independent Mission would follow his example in establishing a formalised connection. Yet it does not appear under the official listings of congregations "recognised as Assemblies in fellowship with the Assemblies of God."[228] Any reference to the Mission is likewise absent from those who identified themselves with what had become known as the Elim Pentecostal Alliance.[229] Despite its nomenclature it also remained aloof from the Holiness Mission network.[230] The Mission at 95 Sydenham Road, therefore, appears to have been numbered among the Pentecostal Centres which Massey describes as

---

[225] "Croydon: Mission at Coulsdon by Bro. G. Jeffreys," *Confidence*, December 1914, 233. This account appears to have been used verbatim, though unattributed, in Boulton's *George Jeffreys*, 20.

[226] See note 195 above.

[227] He contributed an article, "He was Moved with Compassion," to the missionary section of their official organ which replicated the format of *Confidence*. See "Missionary Supplement" to *Redemption Tidings*, April 1928, 1.

[228] It is absent from, for instance, "London Assemblies," *Redemption Tidings*, April 1927, 15; "Assemblies of God in Great Britain and Ireland," *Redemption Tidings*, July 1927, 15, and from under the same designation in *Redemption Tidings*, July 1928, 15.

[229] E. B. Pinch, "The Foursquare Gospel Churches of the British Isles," *Elim Evangel*, 1 July 1926, 151.

[230] "International Holiness Missions," *The Holiness Mission Journal*, Dec. 1923, iv.

"fringe assemblies" by virtue of the fact that they had had "general or direct links with the emerging movement, but for unknown reasons failed to pursue membership."[231]

The branch that had been established at Coulsdon came to embrace a different status amid the structural developments then occurring across the movement. It was announced in the *Elim Evangel* that a convention would be held at the Smitham Hall in Coulsdon between 26th - 28th July 1924, and that this was being hosted by its leaders, Pastor and Mrs. E. B. Pinch of Peniel, Vincent Road, Coulsdon, Surrey.[232] Two years later this assembly undertook the construction of a new place of worship, Salem Tabernacle in Chipstead Road,[233] and a series of "Special Opening Services" held between 21-25th July 1926 marked its official inauguration as a "Church of the Foursquare Gospel."[234] Its pastor was not only a prominent conference speaker,[235] but was also integrally involved in the establishment of a Provisional Executive Presbytery of the Foursquare Gospel Churches. He functioned as one of only two ministerial representatives on this body and it was from him that details or "full particulars" of this advance in Elim church polity were to be obtained.[236]

The last reference to the annual Easter meetings held at the Holiness Mission Hall that has been detected in Pentecostal periodicals, occurred in a report by A. E. Saxby who regretted that he could only be present for the final two days of the event in 1922. His observations are suggestive of the final outcome of the Mission. He described its members as consisting of a "spiritually healthy people, trained to look alone to Jesus." In his estimation they were "a satisfied yet hungry congregation to whom it was delightful to minister." He identified both Pastor Inchcome and his wife as particularly worthy of admiration and concluded: "God has been good to Croydon to give such leaders there for so many years."[237] He subsequently announced that the Inchcombes had marked the fortieth anniversary of their Holiness Mission and lauded as something of a rarity in English Pentecostalism the stability, equanimity, and wholesomeness they had managed to foster and engender.[238] It appears, therefore, that Inchcombe ended his ministry in much the same manner as Saxby did himself, not occupying a dominant place in the movement, but "in quiet

---

[231] The extent of this occurrence is clarified by the observation that of 53 assemblies that had been involved to varying degrees in preparatory negotiations, 15 chose not to join the A.O.G. at its inception in 1925. While some of these joined the Elim Pentecostal Alliance, others "remained entirely independent." See Massey, "Origins of the Assemblies of God," 162, 158.

[232] "Items of Interest," *Elim Evangel*, July 1924, 162.

[233] "Items of Interest," *Elim Evangel*, February 15, 1926, 43.

[234] "Salem Tabernacle, Coulsdon: Special Opening Services," *Elim Evangel*, 1 July 1926, 144.

[235] "August Elim Conventions," *Elim Evangel*, 1 September 1925, 196-197.

[236] G. Jeffreys, "The Foursquare Gospel Church," *Elim Evangel*, 15 Feb. 1926, 41.

[237] "Home News," *Things New and Old*, June 1922, 9.

[238] "Croydon," *Things New and Old*, October 1922, 10.

retirement...lovingly revered by those to whom he had been a beloved pastor in some of life's most trying hours."[239]

This "small cause" or "local initiative"[240] had evidently proven successful for no less than four decades. It had been in existence for a quarter of a century prior to any Pentecostal involvement and by then its stability and independent status had been amply established. It had benefited considerably from inclusion in the *collegia pietatis* or reticulate conglomeration of distinctive and autonomous congregations as originally envisaged by Alexander Boddy. The most extensive survey of religious life of London in the early years of the twentieth century enumerated a total of 422 unaffiliated evangelical Missions, a figure which exceeded the 345 Congregational chapels or 254 Methodist places of worship, and collectively attracted in the region of 21,000 attendances.[241] The meaningful participation of Croydon's Holiness Mission in this religious culture which has been described as a "fantastically diversified would-be evangelization,"[242] was only enhanced by its involvement in the early years of the English Pentecostal experience. In keeping with the faith mission ethos, it affiliated itself with this movement, not for the purpose of acquiring or adhering to an amenable organisational structure, but rather towards a supra-denominational end, the aim of which was to "galvanise the Christian community into action and to lift it to a higher spiritual plane."[243] While the Pentecostal denominations may not have been in a position to claim it as a congregation or assembly, the Holiness Mission Hall represents a primary (if unexplored) example of the Pentecostal phenomenon feeding into, and enhancing, a notable aspect of England's evangelical constituency.

Conclusion

This examination of structural aspects of pre-denominational Pentecostalism in England began by exploring the early conception and organisational ideals shared by pioneering leaders. Hollenweger has described the emergent Pentecostal phenomenon as an "ecumenical revival movement whose leaders remained in their churches." While what has been outlined with respect of the English context substantiates the observation that this movement regarded "the experience of the Holy Spirit as the one important force" that could supplant "all denominational, racial, educational and social divides,"[244] the designation

---

[239] Gee, *Personal Memoirs of Pentecostal Pioneers*, 83.

[240] Morris, *Religion and Urban Change*, 72-73.

[241] "Table showing Denominational Totals for Greater London," and "Table showing Total Number of Places of Worship in the Metropolis," in Mudie-Smith, ed., *The Religious Life of London*, 446-447.

[242] Kent, *Studies in Victorian Revivalism*, 301.

[243] Warburton, "The Faith Mission," 76

[244] Hollenweger, "Crucial Issues for Pentecostals," in Allan H. Anderson and W. J. Hollenweger, eds., *Pentecostals after a Century: Global Perspectives on a Movement in Transition* (Sheffield: Sheffield Academic Press, 1999), 187.

ecumenical requires qualification. It is not unreasonable to suggest that later commentators have, at least partially, been motivated by subsequent ecumenical stances and aspirations and that this has resulted in retrospective interpretations being, at times, foisted on an idealised golden era. Geoffrey Wainwright, for example, in a recent paper, seeks to advance the cause of Pentecostal involvement in contemporary ecumenical dialogue and exchange. While engaging in scriptural exegesis and interacting with the writings of Lesslie Newbigin, his foray into the historical records is brief and clearly ideologically driven. He merely states, without documentation, that central to the agenda of North American Pentecostal pioneers was their perception of themselves as "apostles of unity" who were "standing for 'Christian unity everywhere.'"[245] It would be both anachronistic and mistaken to suggest that early English Pentecostals functioned according to the guiding principles of a later ecumenism which promoted an ethos summarized in the dictum: "I need your faith to make mine whole."[246]

The present historically-based analysis has certainly demonstrated the encouragement of an ecumenical or inclusive outlook by leaders such as Boddy, Barratt, T. M. Jeffreys, and others. This was in vital respects a continuation of the "spiritual oecumenicity" espoused by the Keswick Convention's "All One in Christ Jesus" ethos,[247] and the Pentecostal League's "inter-denominational union."[248] The variety of churches and backgrounds that involved themselves in the Pentecostal *collegia pietatis* was celebrated and extolled by leading figures and it was anticipated that individuals would remain active within, and thereby invigorate, their original congregations. Concern about the perceived scandal of inter-church disharmony was a potent motivating factor and Pentecostal advocates were pleased to portray themselves as effectively counteracting, indeed offering something which to their minds approached a panacea, to this persistent tendency. Ultimately, however, Pentecostal "oecumenicity" consisted in a readiness to welcome and engage with all who were open to, curious about, or in search of an encounter with the Holy Spirit according to their understanding. Other traditions were not embraced on their own merits or for what Pentecostals could derive or learn from them. In this respect the early Pentecostal outlook is not dissimilar to Britain's later "charismatic phalange" of whom it has been observed that they have frequently been content to engage with the larger body of the Christian

---

[245] Wainwright, "The One Hope of Your Calling?: The Ecumenical and Pentecostal Movements after a Century," *Pnuema: The Journal of the Society for Pentecostal Studies* 25.1 (Spring 2003): 8.

[246] David Butler, *Dying to be One: English Ecumenism – History, Theology, and the Future* (London: SCM Press, 1996), 205.

[247] Orr, *The Second Evangelical Awakening*, 220.

[248] "The Outlook," *Tongues of Fire*, January 1905, 7.

Church "as long as they can lead that body by the nose."[249]

Another outworking of emphatic commitment to the Pentecostal experience which had transdenominational implications was that as a religious grouping the movement fostered *Gesellschaft* more than *Gemeinschaft* relations among devotees. Official structures and mechanisms were, therefore, regarded as secondary to the shared commitment to central ideologies and insights. Emerging English Pentecostals, particularly in the years 1907-1914, were firmly among those for whom "the *gnosis*, 'the principle,'"[250] and not structural accoutrements, was paramount. This categorisation is appropriate to the extent that Pentecostals conceived of themselves as a "separated and voluntary religious minority religious movement" motivated by the imperative of issuing "a religious challenge based on a new apprehension of the divine." Yet it is also the case that while during the first phase of its existence, involvement may have implied a degree of "distance from"[251] other religious bodies, outright hostility toward other forms of Christian expression was seldom in evidence and rarely encouraged by the ideolects of the Pentecostal mainstream. A secessionist outlook, which on the basis of a perceived apostasy of Christendom, rejected both Establishment and dissenting identities, was never a feature of early Pentecostal ecclesial piety as it had been for the Brethren movement.[252] On the contrary, a spreading influence was envisaged by those who insisted that "a welcome was given to all"[253] to participate in "the overpowering, overwhelming, empowering, enveloping, mysterious, divine, unquestionable, enduement of the Baptism of the Holy Ghost."[254] The English Pentecostal movement was therefore in its early years open, inclusive, and ecumenical to the extent that it subordinated church order to the promotion of a deeply-held evangelical piety.

It has been pointed out that developments that led up to and occurred in the aftermath of a general gathering of interested parties at Montgomery Hall,

---

[249] Walker, "Sectarian Reactions: Pluralism and the Privatization of Religion," in Haddon Wilmer, ed., *20/20 Visions: The Futures of Christianity in Britain* (London: SPCK, 1992), 61.

[250] Wilson, "An Analysis of Sect Development," in Wilson, ed., *Patterns of Sectarianism*, 43-44.

[251] Wilson, *Religious Sects*, 27.

[252] This perspective has been extensively explored by James Patrick Callahan in *Primitivist Piety: The Ecclesiology of the Early Plymouth Brethren* (Unpublished Ph.D. Dissertation: Marquette University, 1994), 97-102, 119-124. Seminal influences in this direction are to be found in the writings of J. N. Darby in treatises such as "Separation from Evil God's Principle of Unity," in *The Collected Works: Ecclesiastical*, vol. 1, ed. William Kelly (London: George Morrish, n.d.), 538-557, and "What the Christian Has Amid the Ruin of the Church," in *The Collected Works: Ecclesiastical*, vol. 3, ed. William Kelly (London: George Morrish, n.d.), 413-456.

[253] "Unity, not Uniformity," *Confidence*, March 1911, 60.

[254] "What is the Baptism of the Holy Ghost and Fire?" *Flames of Fire*, October 1911, 1.

Sheffield, in 1922, bore notable similarity to the impetus which surrounded the General Council of Pentecostal Saints which had met at the General Opera House in Hot Springs, Arkansas, during 1913. The form of polity which emerged from these earlier deliberations allowed for an essentially congregational form of church government within an overall denominational structure. It has been made apparent that issues which included a perceived lack of overarching inspirational leadership, the "two-fold menace"[255] of doctrines and practices deemed unacceptable to what were essentially conservative evangelical sensibilities, and a perceived diffusion of the Pentecostal witness on British soil, contributed to a widely felt need for more cohesive structural integrity. Such exigencies precipitated the impetus away from *Gesellschaft* forms of association toward what has been termed a more "all in" form of organisational *Gemeinschaft*.[256] It has also been shown that there were further parallels evident in the expression of reluctance and recalcitrance with regard to the adoption of formalised bureaucratic machinery. Remarkably similar apprehensions were voiced on both sides of the Atlantic, while pragmatic arguments were put forward which portrayed this development as a practical expedient which, if carefully managed, need not curtail spiritual vitality. Indeed what was deemed the relative success of the Assemblies of God formed after the convocation in Hot Springs was cited as evidence that such a system could be reproduced in the English context. The structure, as indeed the terminology (*assemblies* as opposed to Boddy's *centres*) appealed to the Brethren-derived sensibilities shown to have been pervasive among those who associated themselves with the Pentecostal cause. While the Pentecostalism that emerged and developed in England between 1907 and 1925 should not be regarded as a made-in-the-USA phenomenon merely transplanted onto British soil, such structural developments as occurred, particularly with respect of the Assemblies of God denomination, derived both influence and inspiration from what had been adopted there several years earlier.

It is interesting that in an encyclopaedic treatment of global Pentecostalism, Hollenweger has highlighted what he deems to be the failure of the "ecumenical vision" which, to his mind, can be attributed to the demise of the leadership of Alexander Boddy and Cecil Polhill. He avers that this development did not come about "because of theological differences, but because of cultural and class differences which were then rationalised with half-baked arguments."[257] The more extensive and focused examination of primary historical data that has been undertaken in the present study permits the conclusion that this assessment, while valuable, does not convey the more complex realities then being encountered. While a potent anti-Establishment animus has been detected, and impassioned expressions of fear of a perceived Anglican hegemony have been disclosed - particularly when the goodwill engendered by the Sunderland Conventions had begun to wane - divergences of

---

[255] Gee, *The Pentecostal Movement*, 140.

[256] Martin, *Sociology of English Religion*, 105-106.

[257] Hollenweger, *Pentecostalism*, 344-345.

theology and conviction have also been shown to have been operative. While the present writer would not venture so far as to describe the rationale advanced in support of the search for a "distinctly Pentecostal organisation"[258] as "half-baked," the short-sightedness of prominent arguments as well as their subsequent ambiguous outcomes, have been considered in more detail than Hollenweger could deploy.

The notion of an unqualified demise of the original pioneering vision could also be challenged by closer historical scrutiny. The body which grew organically from the revivalist apparatus of George Jeffreys itself exhibited a notable and protracted ambiguity toward denominationalism. The variously titled Elim Evangelistic Band, Elim Pentecostal Alliance, and Foursquare Gospel Alliance, proclaimed an inclusivist agenda in its stated desire to propagate "the onward march of the Revival spirit."[259] This was to be undertaken in a manner which did not overtly encourage proselytism from other churches.[260] Rather the intention was to forge an alliance that was "undenominational in character" and it was being claimed by Jeffreys' chronicler in 1928 that some from "those of every fellowship who stand staunchly for all the inspired revelation of God" had been attracted to the cause.[261] Jeffreys' subsequent difficulties in dealing with the bureaucratic dimension of the structure that had evolved in the wake of his evangelistic campaigning, caused him to embark on what Cartwright has euphemistically termed "a time in the wilderness."[262] Lingering intimations of an original trans-denominational orientation are also to be seen in other individuals such as Jeffreys' brother and fellow revivalist Stephen, and the man who would become something of an international Pentecostal icon, Smith Wigglesworth. Although associated with both Elim and then the Assemblies of God for periods of time, it was recorded of Stephen Jeffreys' abiding outlook that "he was a spiritual tramp, and wander-lust ran strongly through his veins." According to his son and biographer, "God never intended him to settle down

---

[258] Gee, *The Pentecostal Movement*, 121.

[259] Boulton, *George Jeffreys*, 172.

[260] Interestingly Boddy had made precisely this claim in 1911 in his statement that at the Sunderland Conventions "a welcome was given to all" and "no attempt was made to proselytize." See "Unity, not Uniformity," *Confidence*, March 1911, 60.

[261] Boulton, *George Jeffreys*, 341.

[262] Cartwright, *The Great Evangelists: The Remarkable Lives of George and Stephen Jeffreys* (Basingstoke: Marshall, Morgan and Scott, 1986), 158. The internal struggles between Jeffreys as "charismatic apostle" and E. J. Phillips as "executive leader" have been highlighted by Walker and Hudson in "George Jeffreys, Revivalist and Reformer," in Walker and Aune, eds., *On Revival*, 147, and by the latter in "A Schism and its Aftermath," 135-153, 329-332. Roy Wallis has highlighted the case of Jeffreys as exemplifying the "precariousness of charisma" in *The Elementary Forms of the New Religious Life* (London: Routledge & Kegan Paul, 1984), 111.

in a regular pastorate – well he knew it!"[263] A former Head of Religious Broadcasting at the BBC observed of another English Pentecostal virtuoso: "The truth is that any denomination would have had a problem comprehending a man like Wigglesworth."[264] Others such as Pastor Inchcombe, the Croydon solicitor and lay-leader of the Holiness Mission Hall, oversaw the incorporation of the Pentecostal dimension into their local contexts and having enjoyed the benefits that accrued from association with the *collegia pietatis*, chose to remain aloof from subsequent denominational structures and developments. It is, therefore, the case that vestiges of the concept of a Pentecostal umbrella functioning in an extra- or supra-denominational capacity and capable of sheltering and accommodating a wide range of religious affiliations, survived in a number of guises beyond the decline of the first generation of originators in England.

Finally some consideration has been given to the extent to which the four Centres that received specific attention in this study came to embrace, incorporate, or react against the developments that had occurred by 1925. All Saints', Monkwearmouth, had not only witnessed the advent of Pentecostalism on British soil but also functioned as the nucleus of the movement until the First World War, and its Vicar attained the status of Pentecostal grandee by virtue of the singular influence he came to exert. The principle of *ecclesiolae in ecclesia* has been shown to have been operative at a local level as Pentecostal activities were conducted in a manner that was separate from, and supplementary to, the ongoing work and activities of the parish. Boddy appears to have avoided significant controversy or disruption but of more significance for this scrupulous and conscientious pastor, involvement in this wider devotional network successfully augmented, enhanced, and revivified the spiritual climate of All Saints'. When others sought to move toward more definite forms of organisational polity, Boddy was content to commend their publications and evangelistic activities while entertaining no notion of involving himself in their structural ventures. His retrospective acknowledgement of the "many spiritual blessings" which accrued from "fellowship with earnest Nonconformists"[265] reflected not only characteristically broad sympathies and an inclusive disposition, but his conception of the Pentecostal movement as having been a vehicle for spiritual-deepening and mutual edification across the church spectrum.

Of the four localities considered, Bradford's Bowland Street Mission most readily exemplified the collision of inspirational and charismatic tendencies with the mundane requirements of bureaucratic organisation and stability. Evidence has been presented which suggests that its leader's propensity for the

---

[263] E. Jeffreys, *Stephen Jeffreys*, 18. Of his relations with Pentecostal officialdom Cartwright has stated: "Stephen's ministry in Elim was of brief duration. His stay with the Assemblies of God was not much longer..." See *The Great Evangelists*, 73.

[264] David Winter, "Foreword" to Jack Hywel-Davies, *Baptised by Fire: The Story of Smith Wigglesworth* (London: Hodder & Stoughton, 1982), 12.

[265] "From Sunderland to Pittington," *Confidence*, January-March 1923, 66.

Pentecostal dimension was not initially matched by a similar aptitude among his congregation. The allure of an increasingly trans-local ministry which saw Wigglesworth first traverse the British Isles and then venture further afield, came to preclude his fulfilling a meaningful role in a localised and routinized context. The charismatic or prophetic religious identity has been described as typically rejecting formal learning as a means of attaining spiritual truth and power; emotionally expressive and often eccentric in behaviour; displaying an inner certitude which can be intolerant and iconoclastic in its methods; exhibiting a pre-occupation with "rites of transformation and crisis;" and having few if any territorial ties.[266] What has been presented certainly demonstrates the founder of this Mission to have exhibited all of these tendencies. Furthermore there is an undeniable conjunction between what was described by A. E. Saxby as "the forceful style of which Brother Wigglesworth is a past master,"[267] and a colourful feature of Northern England's religious heritage epitomised by the "genuine local preacher" known for his "rugged earnestness." Had circumstances been otherwise Wigglesworth could have functioned and earned local notoriety extending the lineage of the "genuine old Bradford oddity,"[268] but the network that arose among those bound together in Pentecostal affiliation secured him a broader platform. While the preaching plumber's contribution to the structural development of the movement may have been slight, his emblematic role as prophetic exemplar saw him fulfil a much wider function across the movement, albeit to the detriment of the Mission he had founded. Yet the fact that some who had been members at Bowland Street went on to associate themselves with the consolidating Apostolic cause represents evidence of expansion and development to the point that in England the Pentecostal movement had, even by 1920, become a phenomenon which was "multifaceted, diverse, and expansive, capable even of being at odds with itself."[269]

What occurred in Winton, Bournemouth, under the leadership of William Oliver Hutchinson represented a singular amalgamation of the charismatic dimension with a distinctive form of bureaucratic engagement. The construction of the first place of worship for explicitly Pentecostal use proved a harbinger of dissent from the *ecclesiolae in ecclesia* conception of the movement. Perceived heterodox tendencies precipitated an act of censure and exclusion, and the structural identities of both the mainstream and the nascent sub-tradition were advanced by this disjuncture. While the main body of the movement continued to function in a trans-denominational and associational

---

[266] Hiebert, Shaw, and Tienon, *Understanding Folk Religioin*, 327-328.

[267] "Home News," *Things New and Old*, January 1922, 7.

[268] Scruton, *Pictures of Old Bradford*, 249.

[269] I have borrowed an observation made regarding the charismatic movement of some seven decades later. This can be found in Percy, "The City on the Beach: Future Prospects for Charismatic Movements at the End of the Twentieth Century," in Stephen Hunt, Malcolm Hamilton and Tony Walter, eds., *Charismatic Christianity: Sociological Perspectives* (New York: St. Martin's Press, 1997), 207.

manner, Hutchinson with Bournemouth as his epicentre, embarked on the construction of a system which sought to promote apostolic and prophetic pronouncement as integral to its overall functioning. Further schismatic extension within this sector exacerbated disquiet among other Pentecostals after the First World War and what was perceived by some as a "two-fold menace" hastened the impetus toward the development of "distinctive agencies."[270] It is perhaps ironic that the most ideologically heterodox segment of English Pentecostalism was for a time also the most structurally developed and, in this respect, it held an appeal among those who felt themselves adrift and unaffiliated within a religious minority. Hutchinson may indeed have functioned within "the fuzzy penumbra of the movement,"[271] but the influences, direct and indirect, that emanated from his Bournemouth Centre were considerable across the more readily recognisable mainstream of English Pentecostalism.

Croydon's Holiness Mission Hall may have most closely represented a typical and successful Pentecostal Centre of the pre-denominational era. Its structural make-up and progression owed much to the pattern of the "small cause" or local initiative which had been prevalent during the last decades of the nineteenth-century, a period of unprecedented buoyancy and expansion for the Free Church and evangelical constituency. Under the lay leadership of a London solicitor it had incorporated the Pentecostal dimension in a manner which eschewed extremism. Pastor Inchcombe never departed from the espousal of what was recognised as "his special theme of Holiness,"[272] and the fact that this had only been augmented by Pentecostal participation is evident from his claim, advanced in 1912, that "the Lord is manifesting His power in saving, sanctifying, and baptising in the Holy Ghost."[273] The Mission Station which had been started at Coulsdon, Surrey, had benefitted from a developing branch of Pentecostal activity in the form of the early evangelical endeavours of George Jeffreys. By the mid-1920s this local enterprise became officially connected with the Foursquare Gospel Churches, its pastor playing the role of a prominent functionary in the emerging organisational structure. The parent congregation, however, remained independent of denominational developments. The Holiness Mission Hall in Croydon, therefore, provides fascinating insights into an early English Pentecostal persuasion which sought to unite on faith mission principles for the purposes of spiritual advancement and co-operation. The history of the mission affords an unprecedented glimpse into the successful working of this original conception which envisaged a loosely-aligned *collegia pietatis* within which affiliating congregations retained their autonomy and identity, while benefitting from an association with others similarly seeking to actualise the Pentecostal dimension in their varied local contexts.

---

[270] Gee, *The Pentecostal Movement*, 140, 122.

[271] Jacobsen, *Theologies of the Early Pentecostal Movement*, 286, 290.

[272] "The Whitsuntide Convention," *Confidence*, July-August 1917, 57.

[273] "Croydon: Times of Blessing," *Confidence*, March 1912, 67.

CONCLUSION

This dissertation has sought to redress a deficit in the growing and internationalising field of Pentecostal studies. While what has become a diffuse movement of global proportions has in recent decades witnessed the scholarly investigation and assertion of ethnic and national characteristics and identities, British contributions to this body of work have, as yet, been few in number. This historical examination of the roots and early development of a Pentecostal movement in England has not only gone some way toward the lessening of this relative sparseness, its very undertaking represents a further depreciation of the made-in-the-USA perspective which has been a lingering feature of early Pentecostal historiography.

It is perhaps understandable that the emergent and formative phase of English Pentecostalism has been neglected on account of later denominational pre-occupations and sensitivities. Operating outside of these constraints, the present study has, where appropriate, challenged unsympathetic and frequently simplistic assessments that have been advanced by denominational commentators and opinion leaders. Strongly worded pronouncements regarding the calibre of the first generation of leaders, principally revolving around a supposed lack of ability to foster the inspirational dimension, were frequently, if somewhat ironically, issued by those engaged in a protracted struggle to retain spontaneity and *charisma* within their own organisational edifices. What has been examined here with respect of the handling of features such as external criticism and opposition; the unusual *concomitants* of initiation into the Pentecostal experience; emotional indulgence and excessive exuberance in early collective worship; and the management of extremist tendencies - doctrinal and otherwise - amid an overarching pursuit and propagation of a form of *reasonable enthusiasm*, all argue for a strong and effectual leadership who bequeathed much to their denominational legatees.

A prominent basis for such, at times, ungenerous retrospective assessments as have been highlighted has undoubtedly been the fact that the organisational ethos espoused by pioneering leaders was ideologically opposed to the establishment of separatist Pentecostal structures. In the context of religious diversification and fragmentation which had occurred during the last quarter of the nineteenth-century, most noticeably within England's "pluralised" Protestant constituency,[1] the notion of a spiritual association or *collegia pietatis* held appeal not only for the vitality it could confer, but also for its potential to counteract the scandalous indictment of "chaotic and fissiparous churches" and "Christians of a hundred sects." Yet many of the rank and file members who

---

[1] McLeod, *Religion and Society in England*, 1, and Snell and Ell, *Geography of Victorian Religion*, 265-266.

involved themselves in the Pentecostal cause post-1907 were more attuned to what's been described as the "free, spontaneous, lay revivalist style" which had been fostered in Britain since the Moody and Sankey campaigns of the 1870s. They were constituents of a "fantastically diversified would-be evangelisation"[2] and as such their sympathies lay with the "new temper" and "new ethos" which according to Bebbington combined the "Methodist spirit" with that of the "Brethren sect."[3] This outlook did not celebrate the coming together of churches and denominations under the aegis of the Pentecostal cause with the evident relish of leaders such as the Rev. Alexander Boddy or Cecil Polhill. In fact, on the contrary, something of an anti-Establishment animus has been detected from an early stage. Exigencies encountered, not least the upheavals associated with the First World War and the manner in which power and censure came to be exercised, served to deepen a sense of disenfranchisement for some from Boddy's form of spiritual association or *ecclesiolae in ecclesia* model. Yet one of the significant achievements of this study has been the exploration of this original conception on its own terms, free from the constraints of later denominational interpolations and perspectives. While an impracticality that became increasingly evident has been acknowledged and explored, the commendable features of the associational network, itself indebted to Reader Harris' League of Prayer, has received more serious consideration than has hitherto been the case. Charismatic and neo-Pentecostal readers will, in particular, find much that resonates with and elucidates their own outlook.

In the course of what has been presented, much has been uncovered which confirms and expands upon the observation that the lived religion of English Pentecostalism should be understood as "part of the wider story of the evangelical search for spiritual experience."[4] We have encountered striking similarities with an early Wesleyan penchant for primary religious encounter, as well as by the reasonable tenor in which this was to be conducted. Expressions of collective worship, it seems, owed much to received patterns and did not exceed the exuberance that had previously occurred in Welsh Revival or Salvation Army contexts, both of which proved formative for emerging Pentecostal practice. Not merely an interest in, but a very definite practice of, divine healing predated Pentecostal involvement for key individuals such as Smith Wigglesworth and Alexander and Mary Boddy who had engaged with movements of faith healing already operative among late-Victorian evangelicals. The revivalist impulse which intensified in the aftermath of the Great War betrayed further continuity with a popular religious culture of British Nonconformity, and a pre-occupation with pre-millennial and dispensationalist perspectives showed them to have been in accord with the dominant form of advent hope among evangelicals, yet Pentecostal pioneers were not averse to venturing beyond received parameters.

---

[2] Kent, *Studies in Victorian Revivalism*, 114, 301.

[3] Bebbington, *Evangelicalism in Modern Britain*, 117.

[4] Randall, "Pentecostalism and English Spirituality in England," 80.

A pervasive restorationist impulse was responsible for the *Latter Rain*, a novel dispensationalist category, as well as for an unapologetic advocacy of the miraculous dimension. This has been particularly highlighted with respect of post-war revivalist practice but has been shown to have suffused their lived religion. Pointedly aware of the significance of this departure from the settled position of the Anglo-Saxon Protestant sphere, English Pentecostals rapidly came to perceive it to be their duty to embody and convey quintessential aspects of an apostolic Christianity which had atrophied or otherwise been lost to the detriment of the Church. While this disposition opens up fascinating and, as yet, largely unexplored continuities with other aspects of Christian tradition, England's first Pentecostals displayed a persistent affinity with compatriots and contemporaries who, while being challenged to "abandon all things for the sake of God," found themselves also "being sent back into the world to teach and practice all the things" that had been commanded them.[5] Analysis of the *otherworldliness* which consistently characterised the Pentecostal outlook has demonstrated that, with respect of an ethical primitivism, they remained wedded to the dominant conservative evangelical orientation. While they may have departed from previous Holiness views in their advocacy of tongues as evidence of spiritual baptism, they continued to denounce and shrink from modes of behaviour and indulgence held to detract from or hinder the attainment of primary religious experience.

A feature of this study has been an endeavour to distinguish between fact and fiction, certainly between hagiographical writings or episodic chronicles penned for personal edification and the bolstering of collective morale, and such primary source materials as can form the basis of recognisable historical investigation. While appreciating the relative values of both *genres* of writing, the pronounced reliance on the latter has furthered the case for the scholarly approach among British Pentecostals and others seeking to analyse or understand this religious phenomenon. The historical method employed has been characterised by an imaginative sympathy with the inner logic of Pentecostalism's lived religion, but has not succumbed to such uncritical infatuation as has frequently been evident in previous writing. A pertinent manifestation of this has been the persistence of the self-serving *sacred meteor* theory. This study has achieved more than heretofore in its investigation of the very real and concrete historical contexts in which Pentecostal religion emerged in England, particularly with respect of previous and pre-disposing Holiness involvement.

It is appropriate that influences from, and interaction with, North American Pentecostalism have been acknowledged and documented, yet this study constitutes a further departure from Americo-centric perspectives in Pentecostal historiography. While other international representations have already mitigated against such views, British contributions in this direction have been curiously slow to appear. In this respect, as it is hoped in others, this volume should prove foundational. Not only has the understanding of a distinctly

---

[5] Niebuhr, *Christ and Culture*, 43.

English Pentecostal identity been significantly advanced, but it developments across the regions of Britain should be rendered more comprehensible in the light of this examination of the emergent movement in England. Although much remains to be undertaken, what has been uncovered will not only preclude the further propounding of one-dimensional notions of Pentecostal origins, but should prove seminal to further investigation of continuity with, and indebtedness to, other strands of England's religious tapestry. What has been apparent throughout is that those involved found themselves impelled by a spiritual hunger, forged in their various evangelical contexts, which the Pentecostal movement emerged "to meet and satisfy."[6] It is hoped that present and future custodians of what has now become a feature of the wider religious landscape will derive benefit and enlightenment from this exploration of the origins and fortunes of the formative years of the Pentecostal phenomenon.

---

[6] "The Pentecostal Movement," *Confidence* August 1910, 192.

Bibliography

Primary Sources

Periodicals Consulted

Confidence (Sunderland, England).
Flames of Fire (London, England).
Tongues of Fire (London, England).
Showers of Blessing (Bournemouth, England).
The Holiness Mission Journal (London, England).
The Way of Holiness (Manchester, England).
The Christian (London, England).
Spiritual Life (London, England).
Things New and Old (London, England).
The Apostolic Faith (Los Angeles, California).
Word and Witness (Malvern, Arkansas).
The Pentecost (Indianapolis, Indiana, and Kansas City, Missouri).
Redemption Tidings (Stockport, England).
The Elim Evangel (Belfast, Ireland and London, England).

Newspaper Articles

"The Welsh Revival," *The Times*, 3 January 1905.
"Speaking in Tongues: Rival Pentecostals," *Sunderland Echo*, 2 October 1907, 4.
"Revival Scenes: The Converts Speak in Strange Tongues," *Morning Leader*, 2 October 1907, 1.
"Revival Scenes: Weird Services in Sunderland Mission Hall," *Daily Chronicle*, 2 October 1907.
"Northern Revival Fervour: Extraordinary Scenes at the Meetings," *Morning Leader*, 3 October 1907.
"Alleged Healing: North Country Stirred by Strange Signs," *Daily Chronicle*, 5 October 1907.
"Amazing Statement by Vicar of Monkwearmouth Church: Mr. Boddy Ostracised," *Lloyd's Weekly* News, 6 October 1907.
"Revival Scenes: Weird Chants and Frenzied Appeals," *Daily Chronicle*, 7 October 1907, 6.
"An Israelite's Passion," *Daily Chronicle*, 7 October 1907.
"Revival Scenes: Incoherent Ravings Interpreted as Heavenly Messages," *Lloyd's Weekly*, 8 October 1907, 6.
"Revivals: More Strange Experiences in London," *Daily Chronicle*, 11

October 1907.

"Claims Gift of Tongues: Woman Translates a Man's Strange Message at
    Pentecostal Meeting," *The Daily Mirror*, 15 May 1913, 13.

Minutes of the Pentecostal Missionary Union Council

"Students Visiting Centres," Book I, 21 February 1910, 42.
"Pastor Niblock's Withdrawal from Charge of Students," Book I, 21
    March 1910, 52-53.
"The Bride Teaching," Book I, 10 December 1914, 381-383.
"The Baptism in the Holy Spirit and the Scriptural Sign of Tongues,"
    Book I, 23 May 1916, 464.
"The Baptism of the Holy Spirit and Mr. Moser's Paper," Book I, 24 July
    1916, 471-472.
"The Baptism of the Holy Spirit," Book I, 7 November 1916, 493-494.
"The Baptism with the Holy Ghost and Tongues," Book I, 5 December
    1916, 501-502.
"Military Service in China: Missionary Volunteering will Sever their
    Connection with the P. M. U.," Book II, 11 July 1918, 30-31.
"Miss Elkington and Miss Jones," Book II, 12 June 1919, 93-94.
"Misses Elkington and Jones: Mr. Polhill's Donation," Book II, 22 July
    1919, 98.
"Misses Elkington and Jones Retirement Owing to 'Brideteaching,'"
    Book II, 28 February 1920, 152-154.
"Mr. Wigglesworth's Resignation," Book II, 16 November 1920, 248-249.
"Rev. A. A. Boddy's Offers to Resign," Book II, 25 January 1921, 284-285.
"Rev. A. A. Boddy," Book II, 8 February 1921, 290-291.
"Pastor Carter," Book II, 19 May 1921, 337.
"Miss Vipan," Book II, 6 June 1921, 351-352.
"Revd. Dr. Middleton's Invitation to Join the Council," Book II, 7
    November 1921, 422.
"Mr. Moser's Resignation as Treasurer," Book III, 18 August 1922, 22.
"The Assemblies of God in Britain and Ireland," Book III, 19 September
    1922, 40.
"Mr. John Leech (Resignation)," Book III, 4 May 1923, 133-134.
"Men's Training Home," Book III, 4 May 1923, 135-136.

Letters and Personal Correspondence

Jessie Penn-Lewis to Alexander A. Boddy, 28 October 1907.
Jessie Penn-Lewis to Alexander A. Boddy, 9 November 1907.
James S. Breeze, W. H. Sandwith, Rowland Sandwith, and Max Wood
    Moorhead to T. H. Mundell, 2 September 1914.
James S. Breeze to T. H. Mundell, 29 October 1914.
James S. Breeze to T. H. Mundell, 2 November 1914.
James S. Breeze to Cecil Polhill, 7 November 1914.
James S. Breeze to T. H. Mundell, 11 November 1914.
James S. Breeze to T. H. Mundell, 16 November 1914.

James S. Breeze to T. H. Mundell, 9 December 1914.

T. H. Mundell to Frank Trevitt, 29 January 1915, P. M. U.
Correspondence, 47.

T. H. Mundell to Thomas Myerscough, 27 February 1915, P. M. U.
Correspondence, 63.

T. H. Mundell to Misses Jenner, Defries, Cook, and Millie, 23 April 1915,
P. M. U. Correspondence, 68-69.

James S. Breeze, W. H. Sandwith, and Thomas Myerscough to T. H.
Mundell, 20 May 1915.

T. H. Mundell to Mr. Swift, 18 July 1918, P. M. U. Correspondence, 555.

T. H. Mundell to Mr. Boddy, 19 April 1920, P. M. U. Correspondence,
964.

Cecil Polhill to Smith Wigglesworth, 20 October 1920.

Cecil Polhill to Smith Wigglesworth, 21 October 1920.

Smith Wigglesworth to T. H. Mundell, 21 October 1920.

Smith Wigglesworth to T. H. Mundell, 17 January 1921.

Smith Wigglesworth to T. H. Mundell, undated (October/November
1921).

Smith Wigglesworth to T. H. Mundell, 7 November 1921.

Unpublished Pamphlets and Manuscripts

Barratt, T. B. "The Truth about the Pentecostal Revival: Lecture given
by Pastor T. B. Barratt in Zurich, London and elsewhere." Unpublished pamphlet.
Pentecostal Archive, Regents Theological College, Nantwich, Cheshire.

Boddy, Alexander Alfred. "Speaking in Tongues: Is this of God?" Leaflets on
Tongues No. 1. Unpublished pamphlet. Donald Gee Centre for Pentecostal
and Charismatic Research, Mattersey Hall.

— "These Signs Shall Follow: They shall speak with Tongues,
etc." Leaflets on Tongues No. 3. Unpublished pamphlet. Donald Gee Centre for
Pentecostal and Charismatic Research, Mattersey Hall.

— "Tongues in Norway: A Pentecostal Experience." Leaflets on
Tongues No. 6. Unpublished pamphlet. Donald Gee Centre for Pentecostal and
Charismatic Research, Mattersey Hall.

— "Tongues in Sunderland: The Beginnings of a Pentecost for England."
Leaflets on Tongues No. 9. Unpublished pamphlet. Donald Gee Centre for
Pentecostal and Charismatic Research, Mattersey Hall.

— "Young People at Sunderland: Their Pentecost with Tongues." Leaflets on
Tongues No. 10. Unpublished pamphlet. Donald Gee Centre for
Pentecostal and Charismatic Research, Mattersey Hall.

— "A Pentecost at Home (Tongues as a Sign): Testimony by a Busy Mother."
Unpublished pamphlet. Donald Gee Centre for Pentecostal and Charismatic
Research, Mattersey Hall.

— "The 'Pentecostal Baptism': Counsel to Leaders and Others."
Unpublished pamphlet. Donald Gee Centre for Pentecostal and Charismatic
Research, Mattersey Hall.

Boddy, Jane Vazeille. "Alexander Alfred Boddy, 1854-1930."
Unpublished manuscript (photocopy). Pentecostal Archive, Regents Theological
College, Nantwich, Cheshire.

Boddy, Mary. "Pentecost at Sunderland: Testimony of a Vicar's Wife."
    Unpublished pamphlet. Donald Gee Centre for Pentecostal and Charismatic
    Research, Mattersey Hall.
Dennis, G. Gordon. "Apostolic Faith Church: Annual New Year
    Scottish Conference 1924." Unpublished manuscript (photocopy). Donald Gee
    Centre for Pentecostal and Charismatic Research, Mattersey Hall.
Gee, Donald. "Alfred G. Lewer: A Pioneer Missionary." Unpublished
    pamphlet. Donald Gee Centre for Pentecostal and Charismatic Research, Mattersey
    Hall.
Lewer, Alfred George. "'Candidates' Schedule' for the Pentecostal
    Missionary Union of Great Britain and Ireland." Donald Gee Centre for Pentecostal
    and Charismatic Research, Mattersey Hall.
Wigglesworth, Smith. "An Evangelist's Testimony: His Pentecost with
    Tongues." Leaflets on Tongues No. 12. Unpublished pamphlet. Donald Gee Centre
    for Pentecostal and Charismatic Research, Mattersey Hall.

Published Materials

Bartleman, Frank. *Azusa Street: The Roots of Modern-day Pentecost*. 1925;
    reprint, Plainfield, N. J.: Logos International, 1980.
Barratt, T. B. *In the Days of the Latter Rain*. 1909; reprint, London: Elim
    Publishing Company, 1928).
— *When the Fire Fell and An Outline of My Life*. Oslo: Alonso etc.,
    1927.
Boddy, Alexander A. *To Kairwan the Holy: Scenes in Muhammedan Africa*.
    London: Kegan Paul, Trench & Co., 1885.
Booth, Charles. *Life and Labour of the People of London*. 3rd series,
    Religious Influences, vol. 3. London: Macmillan and Co., 1902.
— *Life and Labour of the People of London*. 3rd series, *Religious
    Influences*, vol. 5. London: Macmillan and Co., 1902.
— *Life and Labour of the People of London*. 3rd series, *Religious
    Influences*, vol. 7. London: Macmillan and Co., 1902.
Boulton, E. C. W. *George Jeffreys: A Ministry in the Miraculous*. London:
    Elim Publishing Company, 1928.
Corum, Fred T. *Like As of Fire: A Reprint of the Old Azusa Street Papers*.
    Willington, MS.: n. p., 1981.
Courtney, W. L. Introduction to *Do We Believe?: A Record of a Great
    Correspondence in 'The Daily Telegraph,' October, November, December
    1904*. London: Hodder and Stoughton, 1904.
Crockford's Clerical Directory for the Year 1930. London: Oxford
    University Press, 1930.
Frodsham, Stanley Howard. *With Signs Following: The Story of the
    Pentecostal Revival in the Twentieth Century*. Springfield, MS.: Gospel
    Publishing House, 1941.
— *Smith Wigglesworth: Apostle of Faith*. London: Elim Publishing
    Company, 1949.
Gee, Donald. *The Pentecostal Movement: A Short History and an
    Interpretation for British Readers*. London: Victory Press, 1941.
— *Concerning Shepherds and Sheepfolds: A Series of Studies Dealing*

with Pastors and Assemblies. 1930; reprint, London: Elim Publishing
  Company, 1952.
— *These Men I Knew: Personal Memoirs of Pentecostal Pioneers*
  (London: Evangel Press, 1980).
Harris, Richard Reader. *Is Sin a Necessity?: A Résumé of a Recent
  Controversy.* London: S. W. Partridge & Co., 1896.
— *Power for Service: The Personality and Work of the Holy Spirit.* 6th
  ed. London: Christian Literature Crusade, 1953.
— *The Lost Tribes of Israel.* 6th ed. London: Covenant Publishing
  Company, 1921.
— *Daniel the Prophet.* London: Partridge & Co., 1909.
Howard Hooker, Mary. *Adventures of an Agnostic: Life and Letters of
  Richard Reader Harris.* London: Marshall, Morgan & Scott, 1959.
Jeffreys, George. *Healing Rays.* London: Elim Publishing Company,
  1932.
— *Pentecostal Rays: The Baptism and Gifts of the Holy Spirit.*
  London: Elim Publishing Company, 1933.
Mann, Horace. *Census of Great Britain, 1851: Religious Worship - Report
  and Tables.* London: Her Majesty's Stationary Office, 1853.
Masterman, Charles F. G. "The Problem of South London." In *The
  Religious Life of London*, ed. Richard Mudie-Smith, 187-218. London:
  Hodder and Stoughton, 1904.
Mudie-Smith, Richard. "The Methods and Lessons of the Census." In
  The Religious Life of London, Richard Mudie-Smith, 1-14. London:
  Hodder and Stoughton, 1904.
Myland, D. Wesley. *The Revelation of Jesus Christ: A Comprehensive
  Harmonic Outline and Perspective View of the Book.* Chicago, Ill.:
  Evangel Publishing House, 1911.
The Apostolic Church: Its Principles and Practices. 1937, reprint, Bradford:
  Apostolic Publications, 1961.
White, Kent. *The Word of God Coming Again: Return of Apostolic Faith and
  Works Now Due on Earth. With a Sketch of the Life of Pastor W. Oliver
  Hutchinson.* Bournemouth: Apostolic Faith Church, 1919.

Secondary Sources

Books and Essays

Albrecht, Daniel E. *Rites in the Spirit: A Ritual Approach to
  Pentecostal/Charismatic Spirituality.* Journal of Pentecostal Theology
  Supplement Series, no. 17. Sheffield: Sheffield Academic Press, 1999.
Alexander, William Lindsay. *Memoirs of the Life and Writings of Ralph
  Wardlaw, D.D.* Edinburgh: A. & C. Black, 1856.
Anderson, Allan. *An Introduction to Pentecostalism: Global Charismatic
  Christianity.* Cambridge: Cambridge University Press, 2004.
Anderson, Gerald H., ed. *Biographical Dictionary of Christian Missions.*
  Grand Rapids, MI., and Cambridge: Eerdmans Publishing Company,
  1998. S. v. "Cecil Polhill (1860-1938)," by Gary B. McGee.

Anderson, Robert Mapes. *Vision of the Disinherited: The Making of American Pentecostalism*. Oxford: Oxford University Press, 1979.

Arnold, Matthew. *Culture and Anarchy: An Essay in Political and Social Criticism*. London: Smith, Elder & Co. 1901.

Arthur, William. *The Tongue of Fire; or the True Power of Christianity*. Peoples' Edition. London: Charles H. Kelly, 1856.

Balleine, G. R. *A History of the Evangelical Party in the Church of England*. London: Longmans, Green and Co., 1933.

Battersby Harford, John, and Frederick Charles Macdonald. *Handley Carr Glyn Moule, Bishop of Durham: A Biography*. 2nd ed. London: Hodder and Stoughton, 1923.

Bebbington, David. *Evangelicalism in Modern Britain: A History from the 1730s to the 1980s*. Grand Rapids: Baker Book House, 1992.

— *Victorian Nonconformity*. Bangor: Headstart History, 1992.

— *Holiness in Nineteenth-Century England*. The 1998 Didsbury Lectures. Carlisle: Paternoster Press, 2000.

— "Revival and Enlightenment in Eighteenth-Century England." In *On Revival: A Critical Examination*, ed. Andrew Walker and Kristin Aune, 71-86. Carlisle: Paternoster Press, 2003.

— "Holiness in the Evangelical Tradition." In *Holiness Past and Present*, ed. Stephen C. Barton, 298-315. London and New York: T. & T. Clark, 2003.

Bendroth, Margaret Lamberts. *Fundamentalism and Gender, 1875 to the Present*. New Haven and London: Yale University Press, 1993.

Berger, Peter L. *The Social Reality of Religion*. London: Penguin University Books, 1973.

Bevan, Francis. *Three Friends of God: Records from the Lives of John Tauler, Nicholas of Basle, Henry Suso*. 2nd ed. London: James Nisbet & Co., 1889.

Binfield, Clyde. *So Down to Prayers: Studies in English Nonconformity, 1780-1920*. London: J. M. Dent & Co., 1977.

Bloch-Hoell, Nils. *The Pentecostal Movement: Its Origins, Development and Distinctive Character*. Oslo and London: Universitatsforlaget, 1964.

Blumhofer, Edith L. *The Assemblies of God: A Chapter in the Story of American Pentecostalism*. Vol. 1, *To 1914*. Springfield, MO.: Gospel Publishing House, 1989.

Borella, Jean. *The Sense of the Supernatural*. Translated by G. John Champoux. Edinburgh: T. & T. Clark, 1998.

Boulton, E. C. W. *George Jeffreys: A Ministry in the Miraculous*. London: Elim Publishing Company, 1928.

Bradley, Ian. *The Call to Seriousness: The Evangelical Impact on the Victorians*. London: Jonathan Cape, 1976.

Bradstock, Andrew. "'A Man of God is a Manly Man': Spurgeon, Luther and 'Holy Boldness.'" In *Masculinity and Spirituality in Victorian Culture*, eds. Andrew Bradstock, Sean Gill, Anne Hogan, and Sue Morgan, 209-221. London: Macmillan, 2000.

Bridges Johns, Cheryl. *Pentecostal Formation: A Pedagogy Among the Oppressed*. Sheffield: Sheffield Academic Press, 1993.

Brierley, Peter, ed. *United Kingdom Christian Handbook Religious Trends No. 4 2003/2004*. London: n. p., 2003.

Bromley, David G. "The Social Construction of Contested Exit Roles:

Defectors, Whistleblowers and Apostates." In *The Politics of Religious Apostasy:The Role of Apostates in the Transformation of Religious Movements*, ed. David G. Bromley, 19-48. Westport, CT., and London, Praeger, 1998.

Brown, Malcolm. *The Imperial War Museum Book of 1918: Year of Victory*. London: Sidgwick & Jackson, 1998.

Brown, Nicola, Carolyn Burdett, and Pamela Thurschwell, eds. *The Victorian Supernatural*. Cambridge: Cambridge University Press, 2004.

Bucknall, Alison M. "Martha's Work and Mary's Contemplation? The Women of the Mildmay Conference and the Keswick Convention 1856-1900." In *Studies in Church History*, vol. 34, *Gender and Religion*, ed. R. N. Swanson, 405-420. Woodbridge: Boydell Press, 1998.

Bueno, Ronald N. "Listening to the Margins: Re-historicizing Pentecostal Experiences and Identities." In *The Globalization of Pentecostalism: A Religion Made to Travel*, eds. Murray W. Dempster, Byron D. Klaus and Douglas Petersen, 268-288. Oxford: Regnum, 1999.

Burgess, Stanley M., ed. *The New International Dictionary of Pentecostal and Charismatic Movements*. Grand Rapids, MI.: Zondervan, 2002. S. v. "Stanley Howard Frodsham," by W. E. Warner.

Butler, David. *Dying to be One: English Ecumenism – History, Theology, and the Future*. London: SCM Press, 1996.

Butterfield, Herbert. *The Whig Interpretation of History*. 1931; reprint, London: Pelican, 1973.

Campbell, Ted A. *The Religion of the Heart: A Study of European Religions Life in the Seventeenth and Eighteenth Centuries*. Columbia, S. C.: University of South Carolina Press, 1991.

Carr, Edward H. *What is History?* New York: Vintage Books, 1961.

Carter, John. *Howard Carter: Man of the Spirit*. Nottingham: Assemblies of God Publishing House, 1971.

— *Donald Gee: Pentecostal Statesman*. Nottingham: Assemblies of God Publishing House, 1975.

Cartwright, Chris. Introduction to *The Real Smith Wigglesworth: The Man, the Myth, the Message*, by Desmond Cartwright. Tonbridge: Sovereign World, 2000.

Cartwright, Desmond. *The Great Evangelists: The Remarkable Lives of George and Stephen Jeffreys*. Basingstoke: Marshall, Morgan and Scott, 1986.

— *The Real Smith Wigglesworth: The Man, the Myth, the Message*. Tonbridge: Sovereign World, 2000.

Case, Shirley Jackson. *The Millennial Hope: A Phase of Wartime Thinking*. Chicago: University of Chicago Press, 1918.

Chadwick, Owen. *Victorian Miniature*. 2nd ed. Cambridge: Cambridge University Press, 1991.

Chan, Simon. *Pentecostal Theology and the Christian Spiritual Tradition*. Journal of Pentecostal Theology Supplement Series, no. 21. Sheffield: Sheffield Academic Press, 2000.

Christie-Murray, David. *Voices from the Gods: Speaking with Tongues*. London and Henley: Routledge and Kegan Paul, 1978.

Clarke, Basil F. L. *Church Builders of the Nineteenth Century: A Study of the Gothic Revival in England*. 1938; reprint, Trowbridge: Redwood Press, 1969.

Clarke, David. *The Angel of Mons: Phantom Soldiers and Ghostly Guardians*. Chichester: Wiley, 2004.

Cohn, Norman. *The Pursuit of the Millennialism: Revolutionary Millenarians and Mystical Anarchists of the Middle Ages*. London: Paladin Books, 1978.

Corrigan, John. *Business of the Heart: Religion and Emotion in the Nineteenth Century*. Berkeley: University of California Press, 2002.

Cox, Harvey. *Fire From Heaven: The Rise of Pentecostal Spirituality and the Reshaping of Religion in the Twenty-first Century*. London: Cassell, 1996.

Cox, Jeffrey. *The English Churches in a Secular Society: Lambeth, 1870-1930*. Oxford: Oxford University Press, 1982.

Currie, Robert, Alan Gilbert, and Lee Horsley. *Churches and Churchgoers: Patterns of Church Growth in the British Isles since 1700*. Oxford: Oxford University Press, 1977.

Daniels, W. H. *D. L. Moody and His Work*. London: Hodder and Stoughton, 1875.

Davenport, Frederick Morgan. *Primitive Traits in Religious Revivals: A Study in Mental and Social Evolution*. London: Macmillan & Co., 1906.

Davies, C. Maurice. *Unorthodox London: Phases of Religious Life in the Metropolis*. 2nd ed. London: Tinsley Brothers, 1876.

Davies, Horton. *Christian Deviations: Essays in Defence of the Christian Faith*. London: SCM Press, 1957.

— *Worship and Theology in England*. Vol. 2, *From Andrewes to Baxter and Fox, 1603-1690*. Princeton: Princeton University Press, 1975.

— *Worship and Theology in England*. Vol. 3, *From Watts and Wesley to Maurice, 1690-1850*. Grand Rapids, MI.: Eerdmans, 1996.

— *Worship and Theology in England*. Vol. 4, *From Newman to Martineau, 1850-1900*. Grand Rapids, MI.: Eerdmans, 1996.

Davies, Lynne. *Theology Out of Place: A Theological Biography of Walter J. Hollenweger*. Journal of Pentecostal Theology Supplement Series, no. 23. Sheffield: Sheffield Academic Press, 2002.

Davies, Rupert. "The Spirituality of Ecumenism." In *Christian Spirituality: Essays in Honour of Gordon Rupp*, ed. Peter Brooks, 307-328. London: SCM Press, 1975.

Dayton, Donald. "From 'Christian Perfection' to the 'Baptism of the Holy Spirit.'" In *Aspects of Pentecostal-Charismatic Origins*, ed. Vinson Synan, 39-54. Plainfield, N.J.: Logos International, 1975.

Desroche, Henri. *The Sociology of Hope*. Translated by Carol Martin-Sperry. London: Routledge & Kegan Paul, 1979.

Dieter, Melvin E. "Wesleyan-Holiness Aspects of Pentecostal Origins." In *Aspects of Pentecostal-Charismatic Origins*, ed. Vinson Synan, 55-80. Plainfield, N.J.: Logos International, 1975.

— *The Holiness Revival of the Nineteenth Century* 2nd ed. Lanham. Md. and London: Scarecrow Press, 1996.

Dingle, A. E. *The Campaign for Prohibition in Victorian England*. London: Croom Helm, 1980.

Douglas, David. "Pit Life in Co. Durham: Rank and File Movements and Workers' Control." History Workshop Pamphlets No. 6 (1972).

Drummond, Lewis A. *Charles Grandison Finney and the Birth of Modern Evangelism*. London: Hodder and Stoughton, 1983.

Edwards, David L. *Christian England*. Vol. 3, *From the Eighteenth Century to the First World War*. London: Collins, 1984.

Eliade, Mircea. *Birth and Rebirth: The Religious Meanings of Initiation in Human Culture*. Translated by William R. Trask. London: Harvill Press, 1958.

Embley, Peter L. "The Early Development of the Plymouth Brethren." In *Patterns of Sectarianism: Organisation and Ideology in Social and Religious Movements*, ed. Bryan R. Wilson, 213-243. London: Heinemann, 1967.

Ervine, John. *God's Soldier: General William Booth*. Vol. 1. London: Heinemann, 1934.

Faupel, D. William. *The Everlasting Gospel: The Significance of Eschatology in the Development of Pentecostal Theology*. Journal of Pentecostal Theology Supplement Series, no. 10. Sheffield: Sheffield Academic Press, 1996.

Fausset, A. R. *The Signs of the Times in Relation to the Speedy Return of Our Lord Jesus in Person to Reign*. 2nd ed. London: J. Nisbet & Co., 1896.

Finney, Charles G. *Lectures on Revivals of Religion*. 12th ed. Halifax: Milner and Sowerey, 1860.

— *Charles G. Finney: An Autobiography*. London: Salvationist Publishing, n. d.

Ford, Jack. *What the Holiness People Believe: A Mid-Century Review of Holiness Teaching among the Holiness Groups of Britain*. J. D. Drysdale Memorial Lecture 1954. Birkenhead: Emmanuel Bible College, 1954.

— *In the Steps of John Wesley*. Kansas: Nazarene Publishing House, 1968.

Fox, Charles A. "Keswick's Twenty-Fifth Feast of Tabernacles." In *Keswick's Triumphant Voice: Forty-Eight Outstanding Addresses Delivered at the Keswick Convention 1882-1962*, ed. Herbert F. Stevenson, 26-32. London: Marshall, Morgan & Scott, 1963.

Gaebelein, Frank E. *The Story of the Scofield Reference Bible, 1909-1959*. New York: Oxford University Press, 1959.

Garrard, Mary N. *Mrs. Penn-Lewis: A Memoir*. 1930; reprint, Bournemouth: The Overcomer Book Room, 1947.

Garrett, Clarke. *Spirit Possession and Popular Religion: From the Camisards to the Shakers*. Baltimore and London: John Hopkins University Press, 1987.

Gascoyne-Cecil, William. "The Upper Classes: The Old Squire and the New." In *Facing the Facts, or An Englishman's Religion*, ed. W. K. Lowther Clarke, 29-54. London: Nisbet, 1911.

Gilbert, Alan A. *The Making of Post-Christian Britain: A History of the Secularization of Modern Society*. London and New York: Longman, 1980.

Gilbert, A. D. *Religion and Society in Industrial England: Church, Chapel and Social Change, 1740-1914*. London: Longman, 1976.

Gill, Robin. *The Myth of the Empty Church*. London: SPCK, 1993.

Gillett, David K. *Trust and Obey: Explorations in Evangelical Spirituality*. London: Darton, Longman and Todd, 1993.

Goodall, Norman. *The Ecumenical Movement: What it is and What it does.* London: Oxford University Press, 1964.

Gottschalk, Stephen. *The Emergence of Christian Science in American Religious Life.* Berkeley and Los Angeles: University of California Press, 1973.

Green, S. J. D. *Religion in an Age of Decline: Organisation and Experience in Industrial Yorkshire, 1870-1920.* Cambridge: Cambridge University Press.

Gresford Jones, H. "In a Day of Departure from God." In *Keswick's Triumphant Voice: Forty-Eight Outstanding Addresses Delivered at the Keswick Convention 1882-1962*, ed. Herbert F. Stevenson, 39-45. London: Marshall, Morgan & Scott, 1963.

Hacking, W. *Reminiscences of Smith Wigglesworth.* London: Peniel Press, 1973.

Hall, Basil. "The Welsh Revival of 1904-5: A Critique." In *Studies in Church History.* Vol. 8, *Popular Belief and Practice*, ed. G. J. Cuming and Derek Baker, 291-301. Cambridge: Cambridge University Press, 1972.

Hardesty, Nancy A. *Faith Cure: Divine Healing in the Holiness and Pentecostal Movements.* Peabody, MS.: Hendrickson, 2003.

Harrison, J. F. C. *The Second Coming: Popular Millenarianism, 1780-1850.* London and Henley: Routledge and Kegan Paul, 1979.

Hathaway, Malcolm R. "The Elim Pentecostal Church: Origins, Development and Distinctives." In *Pentecostal Perspectives*, ed. Keith Warrington, 1-39. Carlisle: Paternoster Press, 1998.

Hathaway, W. G. *The Gifts of the Holy Spirit in the Church.* 1933; reprint, London: Benhill Church Press, 1963.

— *A Sound from Heaven.* London: Victory Press, 1947.

Hayward, R. "From the Millennial Future to the Unconscious Past: The Transformation of Prophecy in Early Twentieth-Century Britain." In *Prophecy: The Power of Inspired Language in History 1300-2000*, ed. Bertrand Taithe and Tim Thornton, 161-180. Stroud: Sutton Publishing, 1997.

Heffernan, Thomas J. *Sacred Biography: Saints and their Biographers in the Middle Ages.* Oxford: Oxford University Press, 1992.

Helmstadter, Richard J. "Orthodox Nonconformity." In *Nineteenth-Century English Religious Traditions: Retrospect and Prospect*, ed. D. G. Paz, 57-84. Westport, Connecticut, and London: Greenwood Press, 1995.

— "The Nonconformist Conscience." In *Religion in Victorian Britain.* Vol. 4, *Interpretations*, ed. Gerald Parsons, 61-95. Manchester and New York: Manchester University Press, 1988.

Hempton, David. *The Religion of the People: Methodism and Popular Religion c. 1750-1900.* London and New York: Routledge, 1996.

— *Methodism: Empire of the Spirit.* New Haven and London: Yale University Press, 2005.

Henry, G. W. *Shouting: Genuine and Spurious.* Chicago: Metropolitan Church Association, 1903.

Her Majesty's Stationary Office. *Papers of British Churchmen, 1780-1940.* Guides to Sources for British History, 6. London: Her Majesty's Stationary Office, 1987.

Hibbert, Albert. *Smith Wigglesworth: The Secret of His Power*. Tulsa:
  Harrison House, 1982.
Hiebert, Paul, E., R. Daniel Shaw and Tite Tiernon. *Understanding Folk
  Religion: A Christian Response to Popular Beliefs and Practices*. Grand
  Rapids, MI.: Baker Books, 1999.
Hill, Christopher. *Antichrist in Seventeenth-Century England*. London:
  Oxford University Press, 1971.
Hindmarsh, Bruce. "Is Evangelical Ecclesiology an Oxymoron? A
  Historical Perspective." In *Evangelical Ecclesiology: Reality or Illusion?*,
  ed. John G. Stackhouse, 15-37. Grand Rapids, MI.: Baker Academic,
  2003.
Hocken, Peter. *Streams of Renewal: The Origins and Early Development of
  the Charismatic Movement in Great Britain*. Exeter: Paternoster Press,
  1986.
Holmes, Janice. *Religious Revivals in Britain and Ireland, 1859-1905*.
  Dublin: Irish Academic Press, 2000.
Hollenweger, Walter J. *The Pentecostals*. London: SCM Press, 1972.
— *Pentecostalism: Origins and Developments Worldwide*. Peabody,
  Mass.: Hendrickson Publishers, 1997.
— "Pentecostals and the Charismatic Movement." In *The Study
  of Spirituality*, ed. Cheslyn Jones, Geoffrey Wainwright, and Edward
  Yarnold, 549-554. London: SPCK, 1996.
Holt, Bradley P. *A Brief History of Christian Spirituality*. Oxford: Lion
  Publishing, 1997.
Houtepen, Anton. *God: An Open Question*. Translated by John Bowden.
  London: Continuum, 2002.
Howes, Graham. "The Sociologist as Stylist: David Martin and
  Pentecostalism." In *Restoring the Image: Essays on Religion and Society
  in Honour of David Martin*, ed. Andrew Walker and Martyn Percy, 98-
  108. Sheffield: Sheffield Academic Press, 2001.
Hudson, D. Neil. "Worship: Singing a New Song in a Strange Land." In
  Pentecostal Perspectives, ed. Keith Warrington, 177-203. Carlisle:
  Paternoster Press, 1998.
— "Strange Words and Their Impact on Early Pentecostals – A
  Historical Perspective." In *Speaking in Tongues: Multi-Disciplinary
  Perspectives*, ed. Mark J. Cartledge, 52-80. Carlisle: Paternoster Press,
  2006.
Hynes, Samuel. *The Edwardian Turn of Mind*. London: Oxford
  University Press, 1968.
Inge, William Ralph. *The Church and the Age*. London: Longmans,
  Green and Co., 1912.
— *Lay Thoughts of a Dean*. New York and London: Putnam's
  Sons, 1926.
— *Protestantism*. London: Ernest Benn, 1927.
— *Mysticism in Religion*. London: Rider & Company, 1969.
Jacobsen, Douglas. *Thinking in the Spirit: Theologies of the Early
  Pentecostal Movement*. Bloomington, IN.: Indiana University Press,
  2003.
James, William. *The Varieties of Religious Experience: A Study in Human
  Nature*. London: Longmans, Green and Co., 1922.
Jeffrey, David Lyle, ed. *English Spirituality in the Age of Wesley*. Grand

Rapids, MI.: Eerdmans, 1994.

Jeffreys, Edward. *Stephen Jeffreys: The Beloved Evangelist*. London: Elim
   Publishing Company, 1946.

Jowitt, Tony. "The Pattern of Religion in Victorian Bradford." In
   Victorian Bradford: Essays in Honour of Jack Reynolds, ed. D. G. Wright
   and J. A. Jowitt, 37-61. Bradford: Bradford Metropolitan Council,
   1982.

Kay, William K. *Inside Story: A History of the British Assemblies of God*.
   Nottingham: AOG Publishing House, 1990.

— "Assemblies of God: Distinctive Continuity and Distinctive
   Carlisle: Paternoster Press, 1998.

— *Pentecostals in Britain*. Carlisle: Paternoster Press, 2000.

Kent, John. *Holding the Fort: Studies in Victorian Revivalism*. (London:
   Epworth Press, 1978.

Kieckhefer, Richard. "Major Currents in Late Medieval Devotion." In
   Christian Spirituality: High Middle Ages and Reformation, ed. Jill Raitt,
   75-108. London: SCM Press, 1989.

— "Imitators of Christ: Sainthood in the Christian Tradition." In
   Sainthood: Its Manifestations in World Religions, ed. Richard Kieckhefer
   and George D. Bond, 1-42. Berkeley: University of California Press,
   1990.

Kierkegaard, S. *Gospel of Sufferings: Christian Discourses*. Translated by
   A. S. Aldworth and W. S. Ferrie. London: James Clarke & Co., 1955.

Knox, R. A. *Enthusiasm: A Chapter in the History of Religion*. Oxford:
   Clarendon Press, 1950.

Land, Steven J. "Pentecostal Spirituality: Living in the Spirit." In
   Christian Spirituality: Post-Reformation and Modern, ed. Louis Dupre
   and Dan E. Saliers, 479-499. London: SCM Press, 1990.

— *Pentecostal Spirituality: A Passion for the Kingdom*. Journal of
   Pentecostal Theology Supplement Series, no. 1. 1993; reprint,
   Sheffield: Sheffield Academic Press, 2001.

Larson, Timothy, D. W. Bebbington, and Mark A. Noll, eds. *Biographical
   Dictionary of Evangelicals*. Leicester: Inter-Varsity Press, 2003. S. v.
   "Alexander Boddy (1854-1930)," by Nigel A. D. Scotland.

Lash, John. *The Hero: Manhood and Power*. London: Thames and
   Hudson, 1995.

Lauer, Laura. "Soul-Saving Partnerships and Pacifist Soldiers: The Ideal
   of Masculinity in the Salvation Army." In *Masculinity and Spirituality
   in Victorian Culture*, ed. Andrew Bradstock, Sean Gill, Anne Hogan
   and Sue Morgan, 194-208. London: Macmillan, 2000.

Lavin, Peter. *Alexander Boddy: Pastor and Prophet*. Sunderland: Wearside
   Historic Churches Group, 1986.

Lewis, H. Elvert. *With Christ Among the Miners: Incidents and Impressions
   of the Welsh Revival*. London: Hodder and Stoughton, 1906.

Lewis, I. M. *Ecstatic Religion: An Anthropological Study of Spirit Possession
   and Shamanism*. London: Penguin Books, 1971.

Liardon, Roberts. *Smith Wigglesworth: The Complete Collection of His Life
   Teachings*. Edited by Roberts Liardon. Tulsa: Albury Publishing,
   1996.

— "Smith Wigglesworth: Apostle of Faith." In *God's Generals:
   Why They Succeeded and Why Some Failed*, 195-226. Tulsa: Albury

Publishing, 1998.

Lineham, Peter J. "The Protestant 'Sects.'" In *Nineteenth-Century English Religious Traditions: Retrospect and Prospect*, ed. D. G. Paz, 143-170. Westport, Connecticut, and London: Greenwood Press, 1995.

Macquarrie, John. *Paths in Spirituality*. 2nd ed. London: SCM Press, 1992.

Madden, P. J. *The Wigglesworth Standard: The Standard for God's End-time Army*. Springdale, PA.: Whitaker House, 1993.

Martin, Albert. *The Last Crusade: The Church of England in the First World War*. Durham, N.C.: Duke University Press, 1974.

Martin, Bernice. "The Spiritualist Meeting." In *Sociological Yearbook of Religion in Britain*, vol. 3, eds. David Martin and Michael Hill, 146-161. London: SCM Press, 1970.

— "The Pentecostal Gender Paradox: A Cautionary Tale for the Sociology of Religion." In *The Blackwell Companion to Sociology of Religion*, ed. Richard K. Fenn, 52-66. Oxford: Blackwell, 2003.

Martin, David. *A Sociology of English Religion*. London: SCM Press, 1967.

— *Pentecostalism: The World Their Parish*. Oxford: Blackwell, 2002.

Massey, Richard. *Another Springtime: The Life of Donald Gee, Pentecostal Leader and Teacher*. Guildford, Surrey: Highland Books, 1992.

Mazzoni, Christina. *Saint Hysteria: Neurosis, Mysticism, and Gender in European Culture*. New York and London: Cornell University Press, 1996.

Maclean, J. Kennedy. *Torrey and Alexander: The Story of Their Lives*. London: S. W. Partridge & Co., 1905.

McCready, William C. "Some Notes on the Sociological Study of Mysticism." In *On the Margin of the Visible: Sociology, the Esoteric and the Occult*, ed. Edward A. Tirgakian, 303-322. London: John Wiley & Sons, 1974.

McGuire, Meredith B. *Religion: The Social Context*. 3rd ed. Belmont, CA.: Wadsworth Publishing, 1992.

McLeod, Hugh. *Class and Religion in the Late Victorian City*. London: Croom Helm, 1974.

— *Religion and Society in England, 1850-1914*. New York: St. Martin's Press, 1996.

McLoughlin, William G. *Modern Revivalism: Charles Grandison Finney to Billy Graham*. New York: Ronald Press Company, 1959.

Mee, Arthur and J. Stuart Holden. *Defeat? The Truth About the Betrayal of Britain*. London: Morgan & Scott Ltd., 1917.

Moody, W. R. *The Life of Dwight L. Moody*. London: Morgan and Scott, 1900.

Morgan, D. Densil, *The Span of the Cross: Christian Religion and Society in Wales 1914-2000*. Cardiff: University of Wales Press, 1999.

Morgan, J. Vyrnwy. *The Welsh Religious Revival 1904-5: A Retrospect and a Criticism*. London: Chapman & Hall Ltd., 1909.

Morris, Jeremy. *Religion and Urban Change: Croydon 1840-1914*. Woodbridge: Boydell Press, 1992.

Morrison, Ken. *Marx, Durkheim and Weber: Formations of Modern Social Thought*. London: Sage Publications, 2002.

Mott, John R. "Closing Address at the World Missionary Conference, Edinburgh 1910." In *The Ecumenical Movement: An Anthology of Key Texts and Voices*, eds. Michael Kinnamon and Brian E. Cope, 10-11. Grand Rapids, MI.: Eerdmans, 1997.

Moule, H. C. G. *Thoughts on Sanctity*. London: Seeley & Co., 1885.

— *Veni Creator: Thoughts on the Person and Work of the Holy Spirit of Promise*. London: Pickering & Inglis, 1890.

Moule, H. C. G., T. W. Drury, and R. B. Girldlestone. *English Church Teaching on Faith, Life and Order*. London: Longmans, Green and Co., 1914.

Mouw, Richard. "Evangelical Ethics." In *Where Shall My Wond'ring Soul Begin?: The Landscape of Evangelical Piety and Thought*, eds. Mark A. Noll and Ronald F. Theimann, 71-86. Grand Rapids, MI.: Eerdmans, 2000.

Munson, James. *The Nonconformists: In Search of a Lost Culture*. London: SPCK, 1991.

Murdoch, Norman H. *Origins of the Salvation Army*. Knoxville: University of Tennessee Press, 1994.

Murray, Andrew. *The Spirit of Christ: Thoughts on the Indwelling of the Holy Spirit in the Believer and the Church*. London: Nisbet & Co., 1888.

— *The Coming Revival*. Evangelical Heritage Series. London: Marshall Pickering, 1989.

Mursell, Gordon. *English Spirituality: From 1700 to the Present*. London: SPCK, 2001.

Niebuhr, H. Richard. *Christ and Culture*. London: Faber and Faber Limited, 1952.

Noel, Conrad. "Organized Labour: The Working Classes." In *Facing the Facts, or An Englishman's Religion*, ed. W. K. Lowther Clarke, 89-119. London: Nisbet, 1911.

Noll, Mark A. *Turning Points: Decisive Moments in the History of Christianity*. Leicester, IVP, 1997.

Oliver, W. H. *Prophets and Millennialists: The Uses of Biblical Prophecy in England from the 1790s to the 1840s*. Auckland: Auckland University Press, 1978.

Olson, Roger E. "Free Church Ecclesiology and Evangelical Spirituality: A Unique Compatibility." In *Evangelical Ecclesiology: Reality or Illusion?*, ed. John G. Stackhouse, 161-178. Grand Rapids, MI.: Baker Academic, 2003.

Orr, J. Edwin. *The Second Evangelical Awakening in Britain*. London: Marshall, Morgan & Scott, 1949.

— *The Flaming Tongue: Evangelical Awakenings, 1900-*. Chicago: Moody Press, 1975.

Palmer, Charles Follen. *Inebriety: Its Source, Prevention, and Cure*. New York: Fleming H. Revell Company, 1896.

Parsons, Gerald. "Introduction: Victorian Religion, Paradox and Variety." In *Religion in Victorian Britain*. Vol. 1, *Traditions*, ed. Gerald Parsons, 1-13. Manchester and New York: Manchester University Press, 1988.

— "Emotion and Piety: Revivalism and Ritualism in Victorian Christianity." In *Religion in Victorian Britain*. Vol. 1, *Traditions*, ed. Gerald Parsons, 213-234. Manchester and New York: Manchester

University Press, 1988.

Partridge, Christopher. "Alternative Spiritualities, New Religions, and the Re-enchantment of the West." In *The Oxford Handbook of New Religious Movements*, ed. James R. Lewis, 39-67. Oxford: Oxford University Press, 2004.

Pascoe, Charles Eyre. *London of Today: An Illustrated Handbook.* London: Sampson Low, Marston, Searle, and Rivington Ltd., 1888.

Patterson, Mark. "Creating a Last Days Revival: The Premillennial Worldview and the Albury Circle." In *On Revival: A Critical Examination*, ed. Andrew Walker and Kristin Aune, 87-104. Carlisle: Paternoster Press, 2003.

Pember, G. H. *The Great Prophecies of the Centuries.* 1881; reprint, London and Edinburgh: Oliphants Ltd., 1941.

Penn-Lewis, Jessie, and Evan Roberts. *War on the Saints: A Text Book on the Work of Deceiving Spirits among the Children of God, and the Way of Deliverance.* 3rd ed. Leicester: The Overcomer Book Room, 1922.

Percy, Martyn. "The City on the Beach: Future Prospects for Charismatic Movements at the End of the Twentieth Century." In *Charismatic Christianity: Sociological Perspectives*, ed. Stephen Hunt, Malcolm Hamilton and Tony Walter, 205-228. New York: St. Martin's Press, 1997.

— *Power and the Church: Ecclesiology in an Age of Transition.* London: Cassell, 1998.

Pollock, J. C. *The Cambridge Seven.* London: Inter-Varsity Press, 1955.

— *The Keswick Story: The Authorized History of the Keswick Convention.* London: Hodder and Stoughton, 1964.

Poloma, Margaret. "The Millenarianism of the Pentecostal Movement." In *Christian Millenarianism: From the Early Church to Waco*, ed. Stephen Hunt, 166-186. Bloomington and Indianapolis: Indiana University Press, 2001.

Prosser, Peter E. *Dispensationalist Eschatology and Its Influence on American and British Religious Movements.* Lampeter: Edwin Mellen Press, 1999.

Rack, Henry D. "Doctors, Demons and Early Methodist Healing." In *Studies in Church History.* Vol. 19, *The Church and Healing*, ed. W. J. Sheils, 137-152. Oxford: Blackwell, 1982.

— *Reasonable Enthusiast: John Wesley and the Rise of Methodism.* 3rd ed. London: Epworth Press, 2002.

Randall, Ian M. *Evangelical Experiences: A Study in the Spirituality of English Evangelicalism, 1918-1939.* Carlisle: Paternoster Press, 1999.

— "'Days of Pentecostal Overflowing': Baptists and the Shaping of Pentecostalism." In *The Gospel in the World: International Baptist Studies*, ed. D. W. Bebbington, 80-104. Carlisle: Paternoster Press, 2002.

Reardon, Bernard M. G. *Religious Thought in the Victorian Age: A Survey from Coleridge to Gore.* 2nd ed. London: Longman, 1995.

Reed, John Shelton. *Glorious Battle: The Church Politics of Victorian Anglo-Catholicism.* Nashville and London: Vanderbilt University Press, 1996.

Richardson, John. *The Local Historian's Encyclopaedia.* New Barnet, Herts.: Historical Publications, 1993.

Robertson, Roland. "The Salvation Army: The Persistence of
    Sectarianism." In *Patterns of Sectarianism: Organisation and Ideology in
    Social and Religious Movements*, ed. Bryan R. Wilson, 49-105. London:
    Heinemann, 1967.
Robinson, James. *Pentecostal Origins: Early Pentecostalism in Ireland in the
    Context of the British Isles*. Carlisle: Paternoster Press, 2005.
Roebeck, Jr. Cecil M. *The Azusa Street Mission and Revival: The Growth of
    the Global Pentecostal Movement*. Nashville: Thomas Nelson, 2006.
Rosman, Doreen M. "'What Has Christ to do with Apollo?':
    Evangelicalism and the Novel, 1800-1830." In *Studies in Church
    History*. Vol. 14, *Renaissance and Renewal in Christian History*, ed.
    Derek Baker, 301-311. Oxford: Basil Blackwell, 1977.
— *Evangelicals and Culture*. London and Canberra: Croom
    Helm, 1984.
Ross, Willian. *D. L. Moody: The Prince of Evangelists*. London: Pickering
    & Inglis, 1900.
Rowdon, Harold H. *The Origins of the Brethren, 1825-1850*. London:
    Pickering & Inglis Ltd., 1967.
Rupp, Gordon. "The Victorian Churchman as Historian: A
    Reconstruction of R. W. Dixon's 'History of the Church of England.'"
    In *Essays in Modern English Church History*, ed. G. V. Bennett and J. D.
    Walsh, 206-216. London: Adams & Charles Black, 1966.
Russell, Bertrand. *History of Western Philosophy*. 1946; reprint, London:
    Routledge, 1995.
Sandeen, Ernest R. *The Roots of Fundamentalism: British and American
    Millenarianism, 1800-1930*. Chicago and London: University of
    Chicago Press, 1970.
Sanders, Cheryl. "Disciplined Spirituality." In *Where Shall My
    Wond'ring Soul Begin?: The Landscape of Evangelical Piety and Thought*,
    eds. Mark A. Noll and Ronald F. Theimann, 61-70. Grand Rapids,
    MI.: Eerdmans, 2000.
Sanders, Rufus G. W. *William Joseph Seymour: Black Father of the 20th
    Century Pentecostal/Charismatic Movement*. Sandusky, OH.: Xulon
    Press, 2003.
Scott, Patrick. "Victorian Religious Periodicals: Fragments That
    Remain." In *Studies in Church History*. Vol. 11, *The Materials, Sources
    and Methods of Ecclesiastical History*, ed. Derek Baker, 325-339. Oxford:
    Basil Blackwell, 1975.
Scroggie, W. Graham. *The Baptism of the Spirit: What is it?, and Speaking
    with Tongues: What Saith the Scriptures?* London: Pickering & Inglis,
    1956.
Scruton, William. *Pen and Pencil Pictures of Old Bradford*. 1891; reprint,
    Otley: Amethyst Press, 1985.
Shaw, Bernard. Appendix to the Play. *Androcles and the Lion*. 1916;
    reprint, London: Penguin Books, 1946.
Sheldrake, Philip. *Spirituality and History: Questions of Interpretation and
    Method*. London: SPCK, 1995.
— *Spirituality and Theology: Christian Living and the Doctrine of
    God*. London: Darton, Longman and Todd, 1998.
Shiman, L. Lewis. *The Crusade Against Drink in Victorian Britain*. New
    York: St. Martin's Press, 1988.

Shirley, Ralph. *Prophecies and Omens of the Great War*. London: William Rider, 1914.

— *Occultists and Mystics of All Ages*. London: William Rider & Son, 1920.

Simon, Edith. *The Saints*. London: Pelican Books, 1972.

Society for the Liberation of Religion from State-Patronage and Control. *Voluntaryism in England and Wales; or, The Census of 1851*. London: Simpkin Marshall and Co., 1854.

Snell, K. D. M., and Paul S. Ell. *Rival Jerusalems: The Geography of Victorian Religion*. Cambridge: Cambridge University Press, 2000.

Spurgeon, C. H. *An All-Round Ministry: Addresses to Ministers and Students*. 1900; reprint, London: Banner of Truth Trust, 1972.

Stackhouse, John G. *Evangelical Ecclesiology: Reality or Illusion?* Grand Rapids, MI.: Baker Academic, 2003.

Stackhouse, Reginald. *The End of the World? A New Look at an Old Belief*. New York: Paulist Press, 1997.

Stevenson, Herbert F. "Keswick and its Message." In *Keswick's Triumphant Voice: Forty-Eight Outstanding Addresses Delivered at the Keswick Convention 1882-1962*, ed. Herbert F. Stevenson, 13-16. London: Marshall, Morgan & Scott, 1963.

Stunt, Timothy C. F. *From Awakening to Secession: Radical Evangelicals in Switzerland and Britain, 1815-1835*. Edinburgh: T. & T. Clark, 2000.

— "Influences in the Early Development of J. N. Darby." In *Prisoners of Hope? Aspects of Evangelical Millennialism in Britain and Ireland, 1800-1880*, eds. Crawford Gribben and Timothy C. F. Stunt, 44-68. Carlisle: Paternoster Press, 2004.

Synan, Vinson. *The Holiness-Pentecostal Tradition: Charismatic Movements in the Twentieth Century*. 2nd ed. Grand Rapids, MI.: Eerdmans, 1997.

Taggart, Norman W. *William Arthur: First Among Methodists*. London: Epworth Press, 1993.

Thomas, Keith. *Religion and the Decline of Magic: Studies in Popular Beliefs in Sixteenth- and Seventeenth-Century England*. London: Penguin Books, 1973.

Torrey, R. A. *How to Work for Christ: A Compendium of Effective Methods*. London: Nisbet & Co. Ltd., 1901.

— *Revival Addresses*. New York: Fleming H. Revell Company, 1903.

Underhill, Evelyn. *Worship*. 1936; reprint, Guildford: Eagle, 1991.

Vidler, Alec R. *The Church in an Age of Revolution*. London: Penguin Books, 1990.

Vitebsky, Piers. *The Shaman: Voyages of the Soul, Trance, Ecstasy and Healing from Siberia to the Amazon*. London: Duncan Baird Publishers, 1995.

Wach, Joachim. *Sociology of Religion*. London: Kegan Paul, 1947.

Wacker, Grant. *Heaven Below: Early Pentecostals and American Culture*. Cambridge, Mass.: Harvard University Press, 2001.

Wacker, Grant, Chris R. Armstrong, and Jay S. F. Blossom. "John Alexander Dowie: Harbinger of Pentecostal Power." In *Portraits of a Generation: Early Pentecostal Leaders*, eds. James R. Goff and Grant Wacker, 3-19. Fayetteville: University of Arkansas Press, 2002.

Wainwright, Geoffrey. "Types of Spirituality." In *The Study of*

Spirituality, ed. Cheslyn Jones, Geoffrey Wainwright, and Edward
    Yarnold, 549-554. London: SPCK, 1996.
Wakefield, Gavin. *The First Pentecostal Anglican: The Life and Legacy of
    Alexander Boddy*. Cambridge: Grove Books, 2001.
— *Alexander Boddy: Pentecostal Anglican Pioneer*. Milton Keynes:
    Authentic Media, 2007.
Wakefield, Gordon S. *Methodist Devotion: The Spiritual Life in the
    Methodist Tradition, 1791-1945*. London: Epworth Press, 1966.
— *Methodist Spirituality*. Peterborough: Epworth Press, 1999.
Walker, Andrew. "Sectarian Reactions: Pluralism and the Privatization
    of Religion." In *20/20 Visions: The Futures of Christianity in Britain*, ed.
    Haddon Wilmer, 46-64. London: SPCK, 1992.
— *Restoring the Kingdom: The Radical Christianity of the House
    Church Movement*. 2nd ed. Guildford, Surrey: Eagle, 1998.
Walker, Andrew, and Neil Hudson. "George Jeffreys, Revivalist and
    Reformer: A Revaluation." In *On Revival: A Critical Examination*, eds.
    Andrew Walker and Kristin Aune, 137-156. Carlisle: Paternoster
    Press, 2003.
Walker, Pamela J. *Pulling the Devil's Kingdom Down: The Salvation Army
    in Victorian Britain*. Berkeley and Los Angeles: University of
    California Press, 2001.
Wallis, Roy. "Introduction: Millennialism and Charisma." In
    Millennialism and Charisma, ed. Roy Wallis, 1-11. Belfast: Queens
    University Press, 1982.
— *The Elementary Forms of the New Religious Life*. London:
    Routledge & Kegan Paul, 1984.
Walsh, Timothy. "'Signs and Wonders that Lie': Unlikely Polemical
    Outbursts Against the Early Pentecostal Movement in Britain." In
    Studies in Church History. Vol. 41, *Signs, Wonders, Miracles:
    Representations of Divine Power in the Life of the Church*, ed. Kate
    Cooper and Jeremy Gregory, 410-422. Woodbridge, Suffolk: Boydell
    Press, 2005.
Walsham, Alexandra. "Miracles in Post-Reformation England." In
    Studies in Church History. Vol. 41, *Signs, Wonders, Miracles:
    Representations of Divine Power in the Life of the Church*, ed. Kate
    Cooper and Jeremy Gregory, 273-306. Woodbridge, Suffolk: Boydell
    Press, 2005.
— *Providence in Early Modern England*. Oxford: Oxford
    University Press, 2001.
Warburton, T. Rennie. "Organisation and Change in a British Holiness
    Movement." In *Patterns of Sectarianism: Organisation and Ideology in
    Social and Religious Movements*, ed. Bryan R. Wilson, 106-137. London:
    Heinemann, 1967.
— "The Faith Mission: A Study in Interdenominationalism." In
    Sociological Yearbook of Religion in Britain, vol. 2, ed. David Martin, 75-
    102. London: SCM Press, 1969.
Wardlaw, Ralph. *On Miracles*. 2nd ed. Edinburgh: Fullarton and Co.,
    1853.
Warfield, Benjamin B. *Counterfeit Miracles*. 1918; reprint, London:
    Banner of Truth Trust, 1972.
Weber, Max. *The Sociology of Religion*. Translated by Ephraim Fischoff.

Boston: Beacon Press, 1964.

— *From Max Weber: Essays in Sociology*. Part III, *Religion*.
Translated and edited by H. H. Gerth and C. Wright Mills. London:
Routledge & Kegan Paul, 1964.

— *The Protestant Ethic and the Spirit of Capitalism*. Translated by
Talcott Parsons. 1930; reprint, London and New York: Routledge,
1992.

Weber, Timothy P. *Living in the Shadow of the Second Coming: American
Premillennialism, 1875-1925*. New York and Oxford: Oxford
University Press, 1979.

Webster, Robert. "Seeing Salvation: The Place of Dreams and Visions in
John Wesley's *Arminian Magazine*." In *Studies in Church History*. Vol.
41, *Signs, Wonders, Miracles: Representations of Divine Power in the Life
of the Church*, ed. Kate Cooper and Jeremy Gregory, 376-388.
Woodbridge, Suffolk: Boydell Press, 2005.

Wells, David F. "Living Tradition." In *Where Shall My Wond'ring Soul
Begin?: The Landscape of Evangelical Piety and Thought*, eds. Mark A.
Noll and Ronald F. Theimann, 87-96. Grand Rapids, MI.: Eerdmans,
2000.

Weeks, Gordon. *Chapter Thirty Two - Part of: A History of the Apostolic
Church, 1900-2000*. Barnsley: By the author, 2003.

Whellan, William. *History, Topography and Directory of the County
Palatine of Durham*. London: Whittaker and Company, 1856.

Whittaker, Colin. *Seven Pentecostal Pioneers: The Inside Story of the
Pentecostal Movement and its Present-day Influence*. Basingstoke:
Marshall, Morgan & Scott, 1983.

Wiggins, Arch R. *The History of the Salvation Army*. Vol. 4, *1886-1904*.
London: Thomas Nelson & Sons Ltd., 1964.

Wilkinson, Wilfred R. *Religious Experience: The Methodist Fundamental*.
London: Holborn Publishing, 1928.

Williams, Rowan. *Why Study the Past? The Quest for the Historical
Church*. London: Darton, Longman and Todd, 2005.

Wilson, Bryan R. *Sects and Society: The Sociology of Three Religious Groups
in Britain*. London: William Heinemann Ltd., 1961.

— "An Analysis of Sect Development." In *Patterns of
Sectarianism: Organisation and Ideology in Social and Religious
Movements*, ed. Bryan R. Wilson, 22-45. London: Heinemann, 1967.

— "The Pentecostalist Minister." In *Patterns of Sectarianism:
Organisation and Ideology in Social and Religious Movements*, ed. Bryan
R. Wilson, 138-157. London: Heinemann, 1967.

— *Religious Sects: A Sociological Study*. London: Weidenfeld and
Nicolson, 1970.

— *The Noble Savages: The Primitive Origins of Charisma and Its
Contemporary Survival*. Berkeley: University of California Press, 1975.

— *The Social Dimensions of Sectarianism: Sects and New Religious
Movements in Contemporary Society*. Oxford: Clarendon Press, 1992.

Wilson, John. "British Israelism: The Ideological Restraints on Sect
Organisation." In *Patterns of Sectarianism: Organisation and Ideology in
Social and Religious Movements*, ed. Bryan R. Wilson, 345-376. London:
Heinemann, 1967.

— "The Sociology of Schism." In *A Sociological Yearbook of*

Religion in Britain, vol. 4, ed. Michael Hill, 1-20. London: SCM Press, 1971.

Wilson, Stephen. "Introduction." In *Saints and Their Cults: Studies in Religious Sociology, Folklore and History*, ed. Stephen Wilson, 1-53. Cambridge: Cambridge University Press, 1987.

Winston, Diane. *Red-Hot and Righteous: The Urban Religion of the Salvation Army*. Cambridge, MS. and London: Harvard University Press, 1999.

Wolffe, John. "The Evangelical Alliance in the 1840s: An Attempt to Institutionalise Christian Unity." In *Studies in Church History*. Vol. 23, *Voluntary Religion*, ed. W. J. Sheils and Diana Wood, 333-346. Oxford: Basil Blackwell, 1986.

— "Anglicanism." In *Nineteenth-Century English Religious Traditions: Retrospect and Prospect*, ed. D. G. Paz, 1-31. Westport, Connecticut, and London: Greenwood Press, 1995.

Worsfold: James E. *The Origins of the Apostolic Church in Great Britain*. Wellington, New Zealand: Julian Literature Trust, 1991.

Wright, Stuart A. "Exploring the Factors that Shape the Apostate Role." In *The Politics of Religious Apostasy: The Role of Apostates in the Transformation of Religious Movements*, ed. David G. Bromley, 95-114. Westport, CT., and London: Praeger, 1998.

Young, Kenneth. *Chapel: The Joyous Days and Prayerful Nights of the Nonconformists in their heyday, c. 1850-1950*. London: Eyre Methuen, 1972.

Scholarly Articles

Allen, David. "The Glossolalic Ostrich: Isolationism and Other-worldliness in the British Assemblies of God." *EPTA Bulletin*, XIII (1994): 50-62.

Blumhofer, Edith. "Alexander Boddy and the Rise of Pentecostalism in Great Britain." *Pnuema: The Journal of the Society for Pentecostal Studies* 8:1 (Spring 1986): 31-40.

Bridges Johns, Cheryl. "Partners in Scandal: Wesleyan and Pentecostal Scholarship." *Pnuema: The Journal of the Society for Pentecostal Studies* 21.2 (Fall 1999): 183-197.

Caperon, John. "Between Two Worlds: The Theology of Matthew Arnold." *Theology* CIV.821 (September-October 2001): 352-357.

Cartwright, Desmond W. "The Real Wigglesworth." *Journal of the European Pentecostal Theological Association* XVII (1997): 90-96.

Chapman, Diana. "The Rise and Demise of Women's Ministry in the Origins and Early Years of Pentecostalism in Britain." *Journal of Pentecostal Theology* 12.2 (2004): 217-246.

Coleman, Simon, and Peter Collins. "The 'Plain' and the 'Positive': Experience and Aesthetics in Quakerism and Charismatic Christianity." *Journal of Contemporary Religion* 15:3 (2000): 317-330.

Collins, Kenneth J. "What is Spirituality? Historical and Methodological Considerations." *Wesleyan Theological Journal* 31.1 (Spring 1996): 76-94.

Dunn, James D. G. "Spirit-Baptism and Pentecostalism." *Scottish Journal of Theology* 23.4 (Nov. 1970): 397-401.

Dye, Colin. "Are Pentecostals Pentecostal?: A Revisit to the Doctrine of Pentecost." *Journal of the European Pentecostal Theological Association* XIX (1999): 56-80.

Gerlach, Luther P., and Virginia H. Hine. "Five Factors Crucial to the Growth and Spread of a Modern Religious Movement." *Journal for the Scientific Study of Religion* 7.1 (1968): 23-40.

Hathaway, Malcolm R. "The Role of William Oliver Hutchinson and the Apostolic Faith Church in the formation of the British Pentecostal Churches." *Journal of the European Pentecostal Theological Association* XVI (1996): 40-57.

Hill, Christopher. "History and Denominational History." *Baptist Quarterly* 22 (1967-68): 65-71.

Hocken, Peter. "Cecil H. Polhill: Pentecostal Layman." *Pnuema: The Journal of the Society for Pentecostal Studies* 10:2 (Fall 1988): 116-140.

Hollenweger, Walter J. "The Critical Tradition of Pentecostalism." *Journal of Pentecostal Theology* 1 (1992): 7-17.

Hudson, Neil. "The Earliest Days of British Pentecostalism." *Journal of the European Pentecostal Theological Association* XXI (2001): 49-67.

Inglis, K. S. "Patterns of Religious Worship in 1851." *Journal of Ecclesiastical History* XI (1960): 74-86.

Logan, Peter Melville. "Fetishism and Freedom in Matthew Arnold's Cultural Thinking." *Victorian Literature and Culture* 31.2 (2003): 555-574.

Maddox, Randy L. "A Decade of Dissertations in Wesley Studies: 1991-2000." *Wesleyan Theological Journal* 37.2 (Fall, 2002): 103-113.

Marsden, George, and John Woodbridge. "Christian History Today." *Christian History* XX.4 (2001): 50-54.

Pope, Robert. "The Welsh Religious Revival, 1904-5." *Christianity and History Bulletin* 2 (Summer 2005): 27-41.

Randall, Ian M. "Cultural Change and Future Hope: Premillennialism in Britain Following the First World War." *Christianity and History Newsletter* 13 (June 1994): 19-27.

— "Old Time Power: Relationships between Pentecostalism and Evangelical Spirituality in England." *Pneuma: The Journal of the Society for Pentecostal Studies* 19.1 (Spring 1997): 53-80.

Robeck, Cecil M. "The Use of Biography in Pentecostal Historiography." *Pneuma: The Journal of the Society for Pentecostal Studies* 8.2 (Fall 1986): 77-80.

Rupp, E. G. "The Importance of Denominational History." *Baptist Quarterly* 17 (1957-58): 312-319.

Thomas, H. O. Tom. "John Wesley: Concept of 'Connection' and Theological Pluralism." *Wesleyan Theological Journal* 36.2 (Fall 2001): 88-104.

Tudur, Geraint. "Evan Roberts and the 1904-5 Revival." *The Journal of Welsh Religious History* 4 (2004): 80-101.

Vondey, Wolfgang. "The Symbolic Turning: A Symbolic Conception of the Liturgy of Pentecostalism." *Wesleyan Theological Journal* 36.2 (Fall 2001): 223-247.

Wacker, Grant. "Are the Golden Oldies Still Worth Playing? Reflections on History Writing among Early Pentecostals." *Pnuema: The Journal of the Society for Pentecostal Studies* 8.2 (Fall 1986): 81-100.

— "Travail of a Broken Family: Evangelical Responses to Pentecostalism in America, 1906-1916." *Journal of Ecclesiastical History* 47.3 (July 1996): 505-528.

— "Early Pentecostals and the Almost Chosen People." *Pneuma: The Journal of the Society for Pentecostal Studies.* 19.2 (Fall 1997): 141-166.

Wainwright, Geoffrey. "The One Hope of Your Calling?: The Ecumenical and Pentecostal Movements after a Century." *Pneuma: The Journal of the Society for Pentecostal Studies.* 25.1 (Spring 2003): 7-28.

Walsh, Timothy. "'A Sane People, Free From Fads, Fancies and Extravagances': Rhetoric and Reality of Collective Worship During the First Decade of the Pentecostal Movement in Britain." *Journal of the European Pentecostal Theological Association* XXIV (2004): 101-119.

— "Eschatology and the Fortunes of Early British Pentecostalism," *Theology* 113.871 (January-February 2010): 31-43.

Walsham, Alexandra. "Sermons in the Sky: Apparitions in Early Modern Europe." *History Today* 51.4 (2001): 56-63.

Ware, Steven L. "Restoring the New Testament Church: Varieties of Restorationism in the Radical Holiness Movement of the Late Nineteenth and Early Twentieth Centuries." *Pnuema: The Journal of the Society for Pentecostal Studies* 21.2 (Fall 1999): 233-250.

White, B. "The Task of a Baptist Historian." *Baptist Quarterly* 22 (1967-68): 398-408.

Yule, Robert M. "Recent Writing on Christian Spirituality: An Article Review." *Scottish Journal of Theology* 28.6 (1975): 588-598.

Unpublished Dissertations

Allen, David. "Signs and Wonders: The Origins, Growth, Development and Significance of the Assemblies of God in Britain and Ireland, 1900-1980." Ph. D. diss., University of London, 1990.

Callahan, James Patrick. "Primitivist Piety: The Ecclesiology of the Early Plymouth Brethren." Ph. D. diss., Marquette University, 1994.

Chadwick, Rosemary E. "Church and People in Bradford and District, 1880-1914: The Protestant Churches in an Urban Industrial Environment." Ph. D. diss., University of Oxford, 1986.

Fewkes, Geoffrey Norman. "Richard Reader Harris, 1847-1909: An Assessment of the Life and Influence of a Leader of the Holiness Movement." M. A. diss., Victoria University of Manchester, 1995.

Garrard, David John. "The History of the Congo Evangelistic Mission From 1915 to 1982." Ph. D. diss., University of Aberdeen, 1983.

Kay, Peter K. "The Four-fold Gospel in the Formation, Policy and Practice of the Pentecostal Missionary Union, 1909-1925." M. A. diss., Cheltenham and Gloucester College of Higher Education, 1995.

Lauer, L. F. "Women in British Nonconformity, circa 1880-1920, with special reference to the Society of Friends, Baptist Union and

Salvation Army." Ph. D. diss., University of Oxford, 1997.

Llewellyn, Henry Bryon. "A Study of the History and Thought of the Apostolic Church in Wales in the Context of Pentecostalism." M. Phil. diss., University of Wales, 1997.

Massey, Richard Dan. "'A Sound and Scriptural Union': An Examination of the Origins of the Assemblies of God in Great Britain and Ireland During the Years 1920-1925." Ph. D. diss., University of Birmingham, 1988.

Robinson, Martin. "The Charismatic Anglican - Historical and Contemporary. A Comparison of Alexander Boddy and Michael C. Harper." M. Litt. diss., University of Birmingham, 1976.

Ross, Brian Robert. "Donald Gee in Search of a Church: Sectarian in Transition." D. Th. diss., Knox College, Toronto, 1974.

Taylor, Malcolm John. "Publish and Be Blessed: A Case Study in Early Pentecostal Publishing History, 1908-1926." Ph. D. diss., University of Birmingham, 1994.

Turner, Christopher Ben. "Revivals of Popular Religion in Victorian and Edwardian Wales." Ph. D. diss., University of Wales, 1979.

Warburton, T. Rennie. "A Comparative Study of Minority Religious Groups: With Special Reference to Holiness and Related Movements in Britain in the last 50 Years." Ph. D. diss., University of London, 1966.

Wood, Colin Henry. "Personalities and Powers: Crises in the British Holiness Movement 1934-1976." M. A. diss., Victoria University of Manchester, 1996.

Unpublished Papers

Alexander, Philip S. "Dispensationalism, Christian Zionism and the State of Israel." Presidential Lecture for the Manson Society, University of Manchester, 2001.

Bebbington, David. "Evangelicalism and Cultural Diffusion." Paper presented to the 'Evangelical Identities: Past, Present, and Future Prospects' Conference, King's College London, 2004.

McGrath, Alister E. "Evangelical Spirituality: Past Glories, Present Hopes, Future Possibilities." St. Antholin's Lectureship Charity Lecture, London, 1993.

Milburn, Geoffrey E. "Religion in Sunderland in the Mid-Nineteenth Century." Occasional Paper No. 3: Department of Geography and History, Sunderland Polytechnic, 1983.

— "Church and Chapel in Sunderland, 1780-1914." Occasional Paper No. 4: Department of Geography and History, Sunderland Polytechnic, 1984.

Walsh, Timothy. "'Talking About the End of the World': The Rev. Alexander A. Boddy, Britain's First Pentecostals, and the Eschatology of Disaster." Paper presented to the Ecclesiastical History Society Postgraduate Conference on the History of Christianity, University of Manchester, 2004.

Internet Sites

http://www.afc-bmth.supanet.com/AbouttheAFC.htm

http://www.communigate.co.uk/brad/columbaclub/page5.phtml

http://www.communigate.co.uk/brad/columbaclub/page7.phtml

http://www.fordham.edu/halsall/mod/1910oathvmodernism.html

http://www.genuki.org.uk/big/eng/YKS/Misc/Transcriptions/WRY
/BradfordChurches1929.html

http://www.paulct.webspace.fish.co.uk/history.htm

http://www.stempublishing.com/hymns/biographies/bevan.html

General Index